The Legacy of *The X-Files*

The Legacy of *The X-Files*

James Fenwick and Diane A. Rodgers

BLOOMSBURY ACADEMIC
NEW YORK • LONDON • OXFORD • NEW DELHI • SYDNEY

BLOOMSBURY ACADEMIC
Bloomsbury Publishing Inc, 1385 Broadway, New York, NY 10018, USA
Bloomsbury Publishing Plc, 50 Bedford Square, London, WC1B 3DP, UK
Bloomsbury Publishing Ireland, 29 Earlsfort Terrace, Dublin 2, D02 AY28, Ireland

BLOOMSBURY, BLOOMSBURY ACADEMIC and the Diana logo are trademarks of
Bloomsbury Publishing Plc

First published in the United States of America 2024
Paperback edition published 2025

Copyright © James Fenwick and Diane A. Rodgers and contributors, 2024

Cover design: Eleanor Rose
Cover image: Gillian Anderson and David Duchovny in *The X-Files*,
USA, 1997 © colaimages / Alamy

All rights reserved. No part of this publication may be: i) reproduced or transmitted in any form, electronic or mechanical, including photocopying, recording or by means of any information storage or retrieval system without prior permission in writing from the publishers; or ii) used or reproduced in any way for the training, development or operation of artificial intelligence (AI) technologies, including generative AI technologies. The rights holders expressly reserve this publication from the text and data mining exception as per Article 4(3) of the Digital Single Market Directive (EU) 2019/790.

Bloomsbury Publishing Inc does not have any control over, or responsibility for, any third-party websites referred to or in this book. All internet addresses given in this book were correct at the time of going to press. The author and publisher regret any inconvenience caused if addresses have changed or sites have ceased to exist, but can accept no responsibility for any such changes.

A catalog record for this book is available from the Library of Congress.

ISBN: HB: 978-1-5013-8763-0
PB: 978-1-5013-8760-9
ePDF: 978-1-5013-8761-6
eBook: 978-1-5013-8762-3

Typeset by Newgen KnowledgeWorks Pvt. Ltd., Chennai, India
For product safety related questions contact productsafety@bloomsbury.com.

To find out more about our authors and books visit www.bloomsbury.com
and sign up for our newsletters.

CONTENTS

List of contributors viii

Introduction: A critical reflection on thirty years of *The X-Files* 1
James Fenwick and Diane A. Rodgers

Part One Cultural legacies: Landscape, environment, technology
James Fenwick

1 Space and location in *The X-Files* 23
   Matthew Melia

2 'Mulder, it's me': Intimacy, invasion and mobile phones 45
   Victoria Scrimer and Nicholas Stanton

3 Artificial intelligence, surveillance and the (post-)human in *The X-Files* 59
   Alex Goody and Antonia Mackay

4 Agentic oil and petrocultures: Black oil in *The X-Files* 75
   Chantelle Mitchell and Jaxon Waterhouse

5 Believe the lie: Digital visual effects in *The X-Files* 87
   Tom Livingstone

Part Two Contemporary legend: Conspiracy, belief and politics
Diane A. Rodgers

6 'I want to believe': How UFOs conquered *The X-Files* 105
David Clarke

7 (Cult)ural tensions: New religious movements and *The X-Files* 121
Racheal Harris

8 The end of history?: Contesting the legacy of the 1960s and 1970s in *The X-Files* 135
Gregory Frame

9 'You believe what you want to believe – that's what everybody does now': *The X-Files*, fake news and the rise of QAnon 149
Bethan Jones

Part Three The X-Philes: Fandom and paratextual narratives
Diane A. Rodgers

10 To escape a legacy: The influence of *Twin Peaks* on *The X-Files* 167
Briac Picart Hellec

11 A very scary X-Mas: An examination of the Christmas episodes of *The X-Files* and *Millennium* 181
William J. Lorenzo

12 'The Truth is …' inside the panels!: Comic adaptations of *The X-Files* 195
Iris Haist

13 'X Files till I DIE': Fan memory from the X-Philes 207
Natalie Le Clue and Janelle Vermaak-Griessel

14 Reading into the romance: Gender, genre and the rabid fangirls of *The X-Files* 219
Marissa Spada

15 'The real is out there': Digital games and cyberculture at the threshold of virtual reality in *The X-Files* 233
Ivan Girina and Andra Ivănescu

Part Four Intersectional legacies: Identity and representation
James Fenwick

16 A reparative reading of mad/disabled Black veterans in 'Sleepless' 255
Lzz Johnk and Gabrielle Miller

17 'I'm a medical doctor, and a scientist': Powerful women, angry men and representational violence in *The X-Files* 271
Erin Siodmak

18 Invasion of body snatchers: Fox Mulder's queerness, monstrosity and status quo 287
Klára Feikusová

19 'A collection of human curiosities': Disability in *The X-Files* 301
Andrew Sydlik

20 The Scully effect: *The X-Files* and women in STEM 315
Jolene Mendel

Appendix 1: List of series, episodes and films in chronological order 327
Appendix 2: The X-Files *main and recurring cast* 335
Index 337

CONTRIBUTORS

David Clarke is Associate Professor in the Department of Culture and Media at Sheffield Hallam University, UK.

Klára Feikusová is a PhD student in Television Studies at Palacký University, Czech Republic.

James Fenwick is Associate Professor in the Department of Culture and Media at Sheffield Hallam University, UK.

Gregory Frame is Teaching Associate in Film and Television Studies at the University of Nottingham, UK.

Ivan Girina is Lecturer in Game Studies at Brunel University London, UK.

Alex Goody is Professor of Twentieth-Century Literature and Culture at Oxford Brookes University, UK.

Iris Haist holds a PhD in art history and is an art historian, author and a comics researcher located in Germany.

Racheal Harris is a late-stage PhD candidate in sociology at Deakin University, Australia.

Andra Ivănescu is Lecturer in Game Studies and Ludomusicology at Brunel University London, UK.

Lzz Johnk is a writer, editor and independent scholar from Michigan, USA.

Bethan Jones is a post-doctoral research associate at the University of York's School of Arts and Creative Technologies, UK.

CONTRIBUTORS

Natalie Le Clue is a researcher and lecturer currently serving as a research associate in the department of Media and Communication at Nelson Mandela University in Port Elizabeth, South Africa.

Tom Livingstone is a research fellow at the University of the West of England, UK. He is currently working on myWorld, a creative research and development programme.

William J. Lorenzo is an independent film and television historian located in New York, USA.

Antonia Mackay is Senior Lecturer in Publishing at Oxford Brookes University, UK.

Matt Melia is Senior Lecturer in Film, Media and Television at Kingston University, UK.

Jolene Mendel is Assistant Professor of English at American Public University, USA.

Gabrielle Miller works in the libraries at Grand Valley State University, USA.

Chantelle Mitchell is an independent artist and researcher based in Australia.

Briac Picart Hellec is a PhD candidate at Le Havre Normandy University, France.

Diane A. Rodgers is Senior Lecturer in the Department of Culture and Media at Sheffield Hallam University, UK.

Victoria Scrimer holds a PhD in Theatre and Performance Studies and teaches dramatic literature and theatre history at the University of Mary Washington, USA.

Erin Siodmak is Professor of Gender Studies and Sociology at Tulane University, USA, and at the City University of New York, USA.

Marissa Spada is a PhD candidate in the Department of Film, Television, and Media at the University of Michigan, USA.

Nick Stanton studies creative writing at the University of Denver, USA.

Andrew Sydlik is an independent scholar with a PhD in English from the Ohio State University, USA.

Janelle Vermaak-Griessel is Senior Lecturer and Head of the Department of Media and Communication at the Nelson Mandela University, South Africa.

Jaxon Waterhouse is an independent artist and researcher based in Australia.

Introduction:
A critical reflection on thirty years of *The X-Files*

James Fenwick and Diane A. Rodgers

Where does one begin with the legacy of *The X-Files*? It is a television series that has been deemed a cultural phenomenon and, particularly during the peak of its popularity and success in the late 1990s, is amongst several programmes – including *Twin Peaks* (1990–1) and *Buffy the Vampire Slayer* (1997–2003) – attributed with changing the face of television in this period (Jowett and Abbott 2013: 9). Its lexicon of catchphrases – trust no one, the truth is out there, I want to believe – appeared to resonate with a mood of distrust, scandal, desperation and paranoia in the United States and the West more generally. FBI Agents Fox Mulder and Dana Scully, the main characters of the series, became icons of sex, conspiracy and science fiction whose frequent guest appearances and name-checks throughout popular media of the day (such as in the 1997 episode of *The Simpsons* (1989–) 'The Springfield Files' and the 1998 UK chart-topping song 'Mulder and Scully' by Catatonia) indicated the reach, acceptance and familiarity of the characters and the series far beyond its core audience. No longer merely a 'cult' television series as it was initially considered to be (Appelo 1994), *The X-Files* had become, by the end of the 1990s, a powerful brand; a merchandising commodity; an end-of-century cultural zeitgeist; Hollywood global entertainment; and, most of all, a resounding television success.

Into the 2020s, popular film and television continues to acknowledge the importance of *The X-Files* in terms of its dissection and mythologization of American history and politics, as well as a significant forerunner and inspiration for contemporary media texts. In sci-fi horror film *Something in the Dirt* (2022), characters discuss the legacy of political paranoia and conspiracy theories that seem to have invaded everyday life, noting that 'now, *everything* is *The X-Files*'. The New Zealand mockumentary series *Wellington Paranormal* (2018–22) is explicit about its indebtedness to *The X-Files* as police chief Maaka (Maaka Pohatu) sports 'The Truth Is in Here' underpants, displays an 'I Want to Believe' poster in his office and his subordinates compare themselves to 'Scully because she's logical' and 'Mulder because I'm a man with dark hair'. *Stan Against Evil* (2016–18), a comedy horror series, taking its cue in part from *The Evil Dead* film series (1981–) owes much of its investigative DNA to *The X-Files*, dedicating an entire episode 'The Hex Files' (S3: E02) to the arrival of agents who look uncannily like Mulder and Scully and state knowing dialogue like 'But I don't want to believe'. Thirty years after its initial broadcast, *The X-Files* can still be found prominently in examples of popular culture across all forms of media, whether central to the narrative, referenced in the mise en scène (such as in the 2021 Netflix series *Midnight Mass*) or discussed explicitly in both documentary and fiction podcasts (like *No Place Like Home* (2021) and *Video Palace* (2018–)).

But to understand the legacy of *The X-Files*, and to contextualize the chapters in this collection, we have to return to the beginning, before any of the above triumphs, accolades or fan worship came about (and, as some have suggested, problems, more on which is discussed later in the text). The television series was the idea and creation of former journalist turned screenwriter Chris Carter. Born in Bellflower, California, in 1956, Carter began working for *Surfing Magazine* in the 1970s, before progressing into a career as a screenwriter at Disney Studios (Hyman 1993: 15D). His career as a screenwriter came about through fortuitous connections and encounters, allowing him to move from one contract to another. Employed by Disney via a mutual contact of his future wife, Carter was later hired by NBC through a meeting with its executive at a baseball game. Finally, Carter moved to work for Fox after a new production executive at the company had been impressed with an unproduced script of his – most of Carter's screenwriting had largely been unproduced (Lowry 1995: 4). The limited screenwriting work that had been produced at the point that Fox hired Carter in 1992 had been youth-oriented comedy: two television films for the anthology series *The Disney Sunday Movie* (1986–8) ('The BRAT Patrol' (1986) and 'Meet the Munceys' (1988)) and two episodes of NBC's musical comedy *Rags to Riches* (1987–8). As such, Carter's turn to writing *The X-Files* was, in the context of his career at that stage, unusual. He later revealed in interviews that his intention had been to create a 'scary' television show that drew upon his formative childhood and teenage television experiences, specifically the original series of *The Twilight Zone* (1959–64) and *Kolchak: The Night Stalker* (1974–5). In an interview with the *Las Vegas Review* in 1993, Carter said 'I didn't have any agenda … I just wanted to create a wildly entertaining show that would scare the pants off you' (Hyman 1993: 15D).

Kolchak: The Night Stalker was a particularly significant influence upon Carter and *The X-Files*. Featuring an investigative journalist as the title character, *Kolchak* explored different supernatural phenomena within a continuous serialized format, but in self-contained weekly episodes with their own resolved narratives. Often cited as exemplary of 'monster-of-the-week' television, *Kolchak* 'repackaged' the formula of investigating and defeating a different supernatural creature by the episode's end each week: 'the narrative formula is fixed and weekly variation is provided by the monster and the methods Kolchak uses to stop it' (Jowett and Abbott 2013: 44). Adopting conventions from both horror and crime drama, the narrative of *Kolchak* is grounded in the real world despite uncovering crimes committed by 'a revivified Jack the Ripper', aliens, werewolves, zombies or even the devil, presenting such stories using realist location shooting and grainy, hand-held cinematography (Jowett and Abbott 2013: 45). It is easy to draw direct lines of comparison between this and *The X-Files*, particularly as Kolchak even frequently tried to expose institutional corruption, finding himself up against political cover-ups, 'Men in Black' and government officials in denial. Though two decades on in the 1990s, the decision by Fox to hire Carter to write a new television series in a similar vein (given that *Kolchak* was cancelled after one year due to mediocre ratings) was potentially a risky venture, particularly given the unusual combination of science fiction, horror and dramatic thriller genres. There had been precedents for such material at that time with *Twin Peaks*, but that series too ultimately suffered from low audience ratings: despite an initial success with audiences and being one of the most watched programmes of 1990, it was cancelled after just two seasons and thirty episodes. The wider television landscape of the time favoured crime dramas and sitcoms. Film, English and horror scholar Jan Delasara has argued that *The X-Files* was unusual at the time, even in the context of the initial success of *Twin Peaks*:

> It appeared in the midst of the usual cop shows and situation comedies just as *Star Trek: The Next Generation* was preparing to abandon regular production and move into a series of films. At that point, dramatic shows with a speculative flavor seemed to be disappearing from the screen, leaving only television's peculiar notion of Real Life ('Real TV') and hyperbolic fictional humor or violence. (Delasara 2000: 7)

The decision to allow the development of a programme like *The X-Files* can be seen in the wider context of the evolution of the Fox network. Fox was still a fledgling broadcast network when *The X-Files* was commissioned in 1992. The Fox Broadcasting Company, as it was originally known, commenced broadcasting in 1986, with a primetime launch several months later in early 1987. The network was owned by Rupert Murdoch and was part of a wider global expansion by his media conglomerate, News Corporation, into television in the mid-to-late 1980s (Holt 2011: 86–9). Fox aimed to challenge the 'Big Three' US television networks at the time: ABC, CBS and NBC. And it targeted a young demographic audience (Carter 1991: D1), particularly with edgier programming like *The Late Show* (1986–8), sitcoms such as *Married ... with Children* (1987–97), adult cartoons like *The Simpsons*, police dramas like *21 Jump Street* (1987–91) and crime reality television and documentary such as *Cops* (1989–) and *America's Most Wanted* (1988–2021). But despite some initial programming success, by the 1991–2 season Fox's ratings had dropped and it was still significantly outcompeted by the 'Big Three' networks. In 1992, the chairman of Fox, Barry Diller, resigned and his day-to-day activities were temporarily taken over by Murdoch directly (Coe 1992). Murdoch's strategy going forward was to significantly increase the network's programme budget by 40 per cent to 'accomplish its goal of a full 7-nights-a-week schedule' by 1993, and he initiated a national television news service that would become Fox News (Mermigas 1992: 26).

There were other significant changes too at Fox's television production unit, Twentieth Television, where Peter Roth had become president of production in June 1992 (Anon. 1992: 59). As a profile of Roth at the time noted, he became 'an integral part in the expansion of that division's network programming' (Anon. 1992: 59). Roth's previous role had been at Stephen J. Cannell Productions, where he had been involved in the production of crime and police dramas such as *21 Jump Street*, *The Commish* (1991–6) and *Wiseguys* (1987–90): all these programmes had been filmed in Vancouver, Canada, rather than Los Angeles, at the urging of Roth to reduce production costs. Roth would have a significant influence on the aesthetic of *The X-Files* when he pushed for that too to be filmed in Vancouver for its first five seasons. Roth reflected on the use of Vancouver in his television productions in an interview in 1997:

> 'I'm a real Vancouverphile', Roth says. 'When I was first exposed to the city, it struck me as such a refreshing and beautiful, perfect Hollywood North. It had all of the value, I thought, of what we could do in Hollywood, with magnificent weather, incredible scenery, never-before-seen locations and, frankly, a willingness on the part of the crews unlike anything we saw in Hollywood.' (Strachan 1997: C2)

Roth was the creative gatekeeper responsible for commissioning *The X-Files*. He had been the executive who had read an unmade pilot script by Chris Carter and, impressed, hired him to develop a script for Fox. Over lunch, Roth and Carter had discovered they had a shared enthusiasm for *Kolchak* and together they developed the initial idea for the series (Strachan 1997: C2): two FBI agents working in a marginalized investigation unit, the X-Files, that examined paranormal or unexplained events, crimes and mysteries. The idea was initially rejected by Fox, but Roth and Carter persisted, pitching the idea to the highest executives at Fox, including to Murdoch himself (Rhodes 1993: 8). Carter was insistent that the series was not science fiction, but rather a fast-moving, suspense and thriller series (Hyman 1993: 15D). Murdoch and Fox relented, and the series was allowed to go ahead.

Upon its debut in autumn 1993, *The X-Files* had low audience ratings overall, though they were high compared to the average for Fox on the Friday night slot to which it had been scheduled (Rhodes 1993: 8). Carter immediately ascribed this large Friday night audience to what he termed the 'thousands of X-Filophiles' in the United States: individuals who he said were believers in UFOs and, more importantly, believed they had seen or encountered extraterrestrials (Rhodes 1993: 8). In December 1993, halfway into the first season, Carter outlined to the *Los Angeles Times* how this audience of believers was leading to a cult audience from the get-go for *The X-Files*:

> 'They wholeheartedly believe they have had these experiences'. says Carter, who has gotten word of a growing 'X-File' cult not only from letters and phone calls but also from a flurry of activity on computer-modem bulletin boards. 'And who am I to say they haven't?' And, what's more, they're not alone. According to a 1992 Roper poll, more than 2% of all Americans believe they may have been abducted by aliens and at least 16% believe they've had some kind of contact with beings from another realm. 'That's an amazing amount of people,' says Carter, who knows a hot demographic when he sees one. 'That's millions of people who believe.' (Rhodes 1993: 8)

From the very beginning, the series producers were engaging with their audience and with fledgling internet forums to gain feedback. As Carter said in one 1993 interview, 'We get the most amazing mail ... We get letters from at least two electronic bulletin boards, so we get immediate feedback. It's valuable stuff. I'll say that 95 percent of it is wildly positive' (Hyman 1993: 15D). Carter also recognized the potential cynicism of a broader, more general television audience in the United States. As he noted,

> The comment I get a lot is, 'This isn't something I would normally be interested in, but I love your show.' ... That was the thing that was really surprising in my research and in the tests of the pilot (episode), was how pervasive the belief is that the government acts in secretive ways. (Hyman 1993: 15D)

Whatever the secret to the series' success, it was proving popular, at first with a 'cult' audience, who were quickly termed 'X-Philes' (Littlefield 1994: E11). By its second season in 1994–5, the audience share had grown to 17 per cent of the total Friday night network audience (Shrieves 1994: 31). In the UK, *The X-Files* – initially broadcast on the BBC – was drawing an audience of 6 million viewers. Its success was contributing to what Mark Simpson in the *Independent* called a growing belief in the 'weird' (Simpson 1994). Simpson singled out the 'Weird Night' of programming on BBC2, which featured as its centrepiece an episode of *The X-Files*. As Simpson described it:

> 'It's a whole evening devoted to the uncanny, the bizarre, the peculiar – and the downright freaky,' enthuses Michael Jackson, Controller of BBC2. … one of the featured programmes in 'Weird Night' is an episode of *The X-Files* … *The X-Files*' phenomenal popularity marks a watershed not just in how people watch TV but how they see the world. (Simpson 1994)

'Weird', spooky fare was not unknown to the BBC, whose commissioners had traditionally made space for ambitious, intellectually challenging fare such as the *Play for Today* (BBC1, 1970–84) series, which included many experimental offerings, including the folk horror 'Robin Redbreast' (1970), time-travelling science fiction 'The Flipside of Dominick Hyde' (1980) and post-apocalyptic 'Z for Zachariah' (1984). The 1970s were an especially rich period for 'wyrd' British television, an era in which folklore and contemporary legend were treated with some gravity in mainstream media (Rodgers 2019). Series like the BBC's *Ghost Story for Christmas* (1971–8) captured the popular imagination (and paved the way for later controversially spooky 'cult' fare like 1992's *Ghostwatch*) but particularly of note here is the lesser-known production *The Omega Factor* (1979). The short-lived series centred on journalist Tom Crane who, possessing psychic powers, joins a secret government department which investigates supernatural phenomena including telekinesis, brainwashing and poltergeist activity. Combining science fiction, horror and thriller elements with narrative focus on shadowy government activity and conspiracies, *The Omega Factor* has obvious links with its US counterpart *Kolchak*, both of which are echoed in *The X-Files*. It is interesting that *Doctor Who* (1963–), perhaps the most famous science fiction series stalwart of British television screens (combining science fiction and horror themes throughout its tenure) since 1963, faced its only major lull in the 1990s when, according to script editor Andrew Cartmel, the series was 'held universally in contempt by the powers-that-be' who cancelled it in 1989 (Jeffery 2019). Though it was cancelled due to several complex factors, including the BBC's fluctuating distaste for 'cult' science fiction (Johnston 2009), perhaps the timely space left by *Doctor Who* was in part what helped encourage 1990s audiences to find programmes like *The X-Files*.

As *The X-Files*' television audience grew, both in the United States and the UK, so too did its internet audience. By season two, 800 messages a day were being posted to the alt.tv.x-files newsgroup from users across the world, suggesting a growing global audience (Littlefield 1994: E11). Newspaper reports indicated that a fan base had begun circulating VHS tapes of *The X-Files* at science fiction and UFO conventions, while some had been attracted by the series' crossover appeal with *Twin Peaks* (Shrieves 1994: E1). But it was the growing success with a broader demographic, specifically eighteen- to forty-nine-year-olds, and a core audience of men aged eighteen to thirty-four that indicated the series had migrated rapidly from cult phenomenon to mainstream television success (Shrieves 1994: E1). In 1994, it won the Golden Globe for Best Drama Series and in 1995 it received Emmy Award nominations for Outstanding Drama Series, the first such nominations in the top award categories for any Fox series (Hopkins 1995: 2). But there was a tension between the cult origins of the series and its growing mainstream popularity, which had led to an increasing merchandising operation, including a tie-in comic book series published by Topp Comics between 1995 and 1998 and tie-in novels (including *Goblins* (1994), *Whirlwind* (1995) and *Ground Zero* (1995)). Chris Carter, interviewed about the growing popularity of the series in 1995, said he was cautious about the marketing and merchandising operation that had now grown around *The X-Files*:

> 'I said no to *The X-Files* boxer shorts last week,' he said with a laugh. 'I think this show has a subversive, anti-establishment quality that over-marketing can work against. The message should be that this show has its feet firmly planted in the cult world of television.' (Hopkins 1995: 2)

By the time of the series' third season premiere in September 1995, talk of a feature film was already circulating in the trade press. No longer confined to cult status, the desire to move into feature film territory suggested how, far from Carter and the series' producers wanting to keep *The X-Files* in the 'cult world of television', there was an ambition for Hollywood franchise success. The first *X-Files*' film – titled *The X-Files* though also known as *The X-Files: Fight the Future* – was released in 1998, between the fifth and sixth seasons. The film was a box office success, grossing over $80 million in the United States and nearly $190 million total worldwide (Scott 1998: 31).

Yet, the transition to blockbuster feature film seemed to impact on the overall popularity and momentum of *The X-Files*. Season six, which had transferred production from Vancouver to Los Angeles at the urging of David Duchovny, suffered from a drop in audience ratings. Television critic Bill Carter, writing in the *New York Times* at the time of season six's broadcast, argued that the series was inevitably going to suffer from its transition to the cinema screen:

> 'The X-Files' has reached an age at which many highly regarded television shows have been known to start losing their way. Plus it finds itself in a position no television show has ever been in before: following up a big-budget Hollywood movie packed with action scenes and the spectacular take-off of a giant spaceship in Antarctica, part of an elaborately constructed plot that was an extension of the story line of the television series. If the burden of serving as a 22-episode sequel to a movie were not enough of a challenge, 'The X-Files' is coming out of a summer in which ratings for its repeat episodes have drastically fallen off, most likely as a result of multiple exposure of the early episodes on cable and broadcast channels. (Carter 1998: B7)

A sense of exhaustion and a feeling that the series had reached the end of a particular phase in its life was reflected by the move from Vancouver to Los Angeles and, perhaps more significantly, to bring about the end to a major component of *The X-Files*: it's series-long myth-arc. *The X-Files* feature film had revealed many key answers to the government conspiracy – the 'truth' Mulder and Scully had doggedly been searching for since the pilot episode. The decision was taken to destroy the central cabal at the heart of the conspiracy, the so-called Syndicate, in the episodes 'Two Fathers' (S6: E11) and 'One Son' (S6: E12). As such, the series had entered a period of renewal, of a new beginning. But it never truly recovered the height of popularity it had achieved during the 1990s. There were attempts to engage audiences with spin-off series, such as *The Lone Gunmen* (2001) or with new Chris Carter-branded series like *Millennium* (1996–9), but neither of these ever achieved the ratings or cultural impact of *The X-Files* at its peak. Carter had talked of *The X-Files* going through regular reboots, with new main characters taking over from Mulder and Scully. This idea partially came to realization in seasons eight and nine, following the semi-departure of David Duchovny from the series and the introduction of two new main characters in place of Mulder and Scully: FBI Agents John Doggett and Monica Reyes. But such attempts at renewal overlooked how the success of *The X-Files* owed much to the central pairing of Mulder and Scully, and the casting of Duchovny and Anderson in the roles. Mulder and Scully personified *The X-Files* and had become cultural icons as a result. To forever continue the series without them would mean a television series that was just not the same.

The decline in audience ratings led to Fox cancelling any further seasons of *The X-Files*, with the ninth season to be its last. Following the conclusion of the original run of the series in 2002, there was repeated speculation in the media of a franchise film series that would focus on the alien myth-arc, supported by online fan communities (Williams 2015: 166). However, to date there has only been one further *The X-Files* film: *The X-Files: I Want to Believe* released in 2008, a stand-alone film that had nothing to do with extra-terrestrials but instead centred on a plot about organ harvesting, with wider themes of spirituality, family and faith. Merchandise such as comics and novels continued the series in a paratextual form; this included a comic series by IDW Publishing that was branded as 'season eleven' of the series. Then, in 2015, it was confirmed that both Duchovny and Anderson would return in a six-episode 'revival' series, to be overseen by Chris Carter. What became known as season ten also revived the myth-arc of the original series and included the return of the sinister Cigarette Smoking Man, only this time setting the conspiracy in the post 9/11 and 'post-truth' era.

Whilst the first episode of the new series, 'My Struggle' (S10: E01) attracted a sizeable audience, viewing figures sharply declined from episode two onwards. Despite this, a second revival series, season eleven, was commissioned by Fox, but the viewing figures were even lower. As of the writing of this introduction, there has been no confirmation of a twelfth series. And whilst Carter indicated he would like to develop another series, Gillian Anderson firmly ruled it out in an interview in 2022, stating that it 'just feels like such an old idea … there would need to be a whole new set of writers and the baton would need to be handed on for it to feel like it was new and progressive' (Boyle 2022). *The X-Files* had lost its popular appeal and its revival series, and the various paratexts, merchandise and other spin-off series, were targeted and consumed by the cult audience that had originally driven the series to mainstream success. *The X-Files* had become, as Anderson argued, a television series of the past (Boyle 2022).

The point of this introduction is not to recount the production history of *The X-Files*: others have done that in the many books, articles and chapters written about the programme. Rather, it is to indicate the early contexts of the programme's origins and initial broadcast and reception to begin to understand its legacy thirty years later. The seeds of the programme's legacy were planted from the very beginning and arguably led to it being part of, and even contributing to, a television revolution: the globalization of television and the expansion of new conglomerates into television ownership and production; the intersection and collision of the programme's creation with the rise of the internet and new fan forums; and the fusion of genre with wider public cynicism in politics (perhaps the latter is the programme's most consequential and inadvertently dangerous legacy). But given that the series' peak of popularity was over twenty-five years ago and was incredibly brief, lasting only a few years up to the release of the first feature film in 1998, the question of *The X-Files*' legacy and its place within broader television history is ripe for discussion. Does *The X-Files* have a legacy? And does it even matter?

Television legacies

Television historian Helen Wheatley, in the introduction to her edited collection *Re-viewing Television History: Critical Issues in Television*

Historiography (2007), argues that a key problem in the field of television history is a tendency towards nostalgia (Wheatley 2007: 10). The television programmes scholars choose to focus on, memorialize and ascribe cultural value to are incredibly subjective. After all, a series like *The X-Files* may well have been popular and influential, but without a detailed, measurable, even quantifiable study of that influence, why should it be taken more seriously and ascribed greater cultural value than any other television programme from the time? This is not to devalue the importance of a series like *The X-Files* nor to suggest scholars should not undertake research into the series, but rather to question *why* we do so. Television historian John Ellis, in his discussion of the possibility (or impossibility) of constructing a television 'canon', argues the following:

> Any canon, or 'list of greats', discriminates. That is its purpose. A canon tells us what is important, what we need to know, and what it regards as having enduring value. Any good canon will also expose its biases and its underlying rationales. Now that television has become an object of study, it too is subjected to the activity of canon building, if only because lecturers and students choose to study and write about one programme, series or genre rather than another. A canon is implicit in every such choice. (Ellis 2007: 15)

Ellis's argument focuses on the tension in the field of television history between what he terms textual historicism and immanent readings: the former places television programmes within their historical context, 'tying meaning to the period' (Ellis 2007: 15); the latter involves textually analysing and 'reinterpreting them through a modern optic' (Ellis 2007: 15–16). Television is a time-limited medium, which references its historical period, and this in turn leads to the nostalgia that Wheatley warns can impact on scholarly analysis.

But can a television programme break its temporal restrictions to become a media object that defies historical limitations and that resonates across time, cultures and generations? Granted, even a programme like *The X-Files* is confined to time-specific references (images of a particular US president adorning the walls of the FBI, for example, or the references to media technology now defunct such as fax machines). Nonetheless, *The X-Files* was also designed, as Carter admitted, to appeal to a broad audience through its use of genre (suspense, horror, thriller, science fiction) and stardom (the sex appeal of its main stars being used to appeal to a young audience). More importantly, the series appealed to a wider national and international belief in the paranormal and government conspiracies, something that defies a particular time period, even if there may be time-specific cultural, political and social contexts for such beliefs. The aesthetic and narrative of *The X-Files* was constructed to have a universal appeal and so the legacy of the programme could be, and probably should be, studied from both textual-historical and immanent perspectives in order to understand the time-specific and intergenerational nature of this universalism. Whilst *The X-Files* had greatest impact and popularity in the 1990s, its appeal does endure through the fact that it continues to reappear, recirculate and resonate in the 2020s, some three decades later. Of course, one must be careful in the claims made about its continuing popularity. The programme has not had anywhere near its success of the 1990s in the succeeding years. But it has been repeated on television, had new television and film releases, new merchandise and receives continuing critical and scholarly interest.

Scholarly output relating to *The X-Files* is also indicative that the programme has some kind of television legacy. Academics are typically attracted to studies of objects of the moment, as was very much the case with *The X-Files*. But ever since the media hype surrounding the series has diminished, television and cultural historians have remained interested in *The X-Files*, with a revived awareness coinciding with the 'post-truth' era and the rise of populist politics, most obviously the election of Donald Trump as US president in 2016. *The X-Files*' focus on 'the truth', cynical and revisionist interpretations of history and a belief that those in power are lying resonated with culture and society in the late 2010s and the post-2008 global financial crisis. The first scholarly outputs on *The X-Files* centred on themes of paranoia, distrust and conspiracy that pervade current political discourse in the West. In the edited collection, *Deny All Knowledge: Reading* The X-Files (1996), English scholars David Lavery, Angela Hague and Maria Cartwright argue that the series was a production of its 'cultural moment' and reflected the scandal-ridden presidency of Bill Clinton (Lavery, Hague and Cartwright 1996: 2). Similarly, television critic Charles Taylor, in an early review of the series in *Millennium Pop*, calls *The X-Files* 'subversive TV' and argued that it was imbued with a sense of overriding cynicism at contemporary politics (Taylor 1994: 9).

Public perception of political culture in the United States has been, at least since Watergate, cynical, and by the 1990s this cynicism had tainted the very way in which political discourse was conducted. It was a theme further picked up by English professor Robert Markley:

> At the beginning of every episode, viewers of *The X-Files* are confronted by the paradoxical mantras of post-Watergate consciousness: white capital letters appear against menacing backgrounds warning us to 'Trust No One' and declaring that 'The Truth Is Out There'. The episodes that follow these injunctions fascinate us not because we necessarily believe in government conspiracies, alien assassins, and bizarre invasions of the body politic by unearthly genetic material, but because we respond viscerally as well as intellectually to weekly suggestions that we are

trapped in a history that we have not made and no longer trust. (Markley 1997: 77)

Whereas Lavery, Hague and Cartwright, and Taylor suggest that *The X-Files* was of the moment and reflective of a very particular set of political circumstances – the comedown from the Reagan/Bush era and the intensity of the Clinton-era that was building towards the Monica Lewinsky scandal via the ever-more convoluted White Water scandal – Markley argues that the series represents a much deeper cultural phenomenon that goes beyond the moment, one that connects to the fears, paranoia and cynicism that people have that the world is not everything we see and that there are forces beyond comprehension that seek to subvert truth. *The X-Files* was, in Markley's assessment, tapping into a much darker force of conspiratorial belief and unleashing that on both a mainstream network television and global audience. In other words, the series was a precursor to the post-truth age. Joe Bellon, in an assessment of the series' appeal, argues that *The X-Files* allowed audiences to recognize and challenge those in authority: 'Against the monolith of authority, *The X-Files* presents a subversive, liberating vision. Its narrative does more than teach us to distrust authority; it teaches us to trust ourselves' (Bellon 1999: 152). Bellon's argument suggests that *The X-Files* was responsible for releasing a repression of mistrust and bringing to 'waking consciousness' public doubts, fears, paranoia and cynicism of government, politicians, the media and reality (Bellon 1999: 152).

The original run of the series ended just after the 9/11 attacks in 2002. The attacks were carried out by the terrorist group al-Qaeda and overseen by Osama Bin Laden. But conspiracies about the attacks soon began to proliferate, blaming a range of other nefarious, hidden, secret governmental forces. The 9/11 conspiracies began conflating alternative theories of US history with the terrorist atrocities, blurring the lines between fact and the 'paranoid structure of history' (Markley 1997). Yet, despite the proliferation of conspiracy theories about 9/11, some of which gained mainstream attention through social media channels and new sharing platforms like YouTube, belief in conspiracies had largely been stable since the 1960s and had even begun to decline by the 2010s (Uscinski and Parent 2014: 110–11). Joseph Uscinski and Joseph Parent, in their empirical study of conspiracy theories, conclude that 'we do not live in an age of conspiracy theories and have not for some time' (Uscinski and Parent 2014: 110–11). There have been peaks of conspiracy belief in the West, but generally belief has been a lot less pronounced than media and at times academic perception. Indeed, the scholarly output on *The X-Files* has typically assumed that the series has had an impact on conspiracy belief and led to its increase, but with no empirical evidence to indicate this has actually been the case. Enrica Picarelli and M. Carmen Gomez-Galisteo (2013) claim that in the wake of 9/11, *The X-Files* in fact became less relevant to television audiences. In depicting the government as the enemy, the series did not engage with a collective societal need for security in the face of ever-growing global disasters. The enemy was now an unseen enemy overseas, not from within a shadow government at home. As they argue, 'In the aftermath of 9/11, the "Trust No One" of *The X-Files* became too subversive and out of touch with the public need to trust the government to keep them safe from future attacks' (2013: 83).

The argument that *The X-Files* fell out of touch with audiences is extended by American Studies scholar Felix Brinker to the 2016 'revival' series. Brinker describes the revival series as being 'out of step with today's "Quality TV"' as a result of its short run (six episodes) and its focus on stand-alone, self-contained 'monster of the week' episodes. As Brinker suggests,

> Compared with contemporary shows that eschew episodically contained plots to tell sprawling stories about ever-shifting political alliances and lines of conflict among large casts of central and recurring characters – like HBO's *Game of Thrones* (2011–) and Netflix's *House of Cards* (2013–), for instance – or series that exploit their serial form to construct elaborate narrative puzzles – like HBO's *Westworld* (2016–) – the latest iteration of *The X-Files* offers a television experience that is far more conducive to casual or even distracted viewing. (Brinker 2018: 341)

In Brinker's assessment, *The X-Files* has not evolved or adapted to meet the aesthetic and narrative properties of contemporary television but rather remained firmly grounded in the spirit and even nostalgia of its original run. But Brinker does not deem this a failure; it is instead an antidote to the hyper-intense, binge-watching culture of 'Quality TV' (Brinker 2018: 341).

The revival series was arguably more of a nostalgic return for pre-established fans of the series. And so, if *The X-Files* is now out of time, out of place and out of influence, and if contemporary, 'Quality TV' has rapidly moved on, just what is the legacy of the series, if it even has one? In their assessment of the series' twentieth anniversary in 2013, television scholars Stacey Abbott and Simon Brown argued that *The X-Files* impacted on the seriousness of science fiction on television, bringing it – quite literally – back down to earth (2013: 1). *The X-Files* influenced the swathe of science fiction television that emerged in its wake in the 1990s. And while television narrative structures may have changed since its original broadcast, the genre legacy of *The X-Files* can still be detected in recent popular science fiction series such as *Stranger Things* (2016–) or the revived *The Twilight Zone* (2019–20) series developed by Jordan Peele's Monkeypaw Productions (for which Glen Morgan, a writer on *The X-Files*, was executive producer).

The X-Files' relationship to fan culture has also been significant. The early cultivation, and recognition, of internet fan forums influenced the series and, as film and American Studies scholar Adrienne McLean argues,

'[X-Philes] were among the first to use cyberspace to create their own virtual fan culture and specialized interest groups (there are now nearly 500 websites devoted to "The X-Files")' (McLean 1998: 3). Fan forums on the internet allowed for a global community to interact and share fan fiction in fan-grown forums, as well as to participate in official forums established by Fox. Bertha Chin summarizes the extensive fan activity as follows: 'X-Philes built their communities around newsgroups, mailing lists and forums, developing an active fandom and a celebrated centralized system whereby fan fiction can be posted and archived on one website, called The Gossamer Project, which is still active' (Chin 2013: 92). There is even evidence that the FBI was a fan of the show. The conclusion of a lengthy real-life investigation into a complex heist involving a valuable pair of ruby slippers worn by Judy Garland in *The Wizard of Oz* (1939) ended with a team of FBI agents delivering the shoes to Ryan Lintelman, entertainment curator at the Smithsonian (the world's largest museum complex, in the United States) in 2018. Lintelman offered to show the FBI agents some film memorabilia during their visit including 'Batman's cowl and Rocky's robe and boxing gloves' amongst other things. However, it was when Lintelman recalled that '"we've got Mulder and Scully's FBI badges from The X-Files" that the agents' eyes "lit up" and was the only thing "they really wanted to take photos with, take back and show the guys at the FBI!"' (*No Place Like Home*, 20 July 2021).

Measuring *The X-Files*' legacy, or legacies, is not an exact science, at least not in terms of quantifying it over the past three decades. Its immense popularity in the 1990s undoubtedly led to other television series that were directly or indirectly inspired by *The X-Files* such as those mentioned earlier as well as porn film parodies, such as *The Sex Files: A Dark XXX Parody* (2009), which television and fan studies scholar Bethan Jones (2013) argues can be interpreted as an adaptation of the series and fan fiction. Its impact on conspiracy belief is less certain, even if it did bring into the mainstream certain conspiratorial or paranormal ideas. *The X-Files* was a series of its time, but also a series that explored themes that resonate across time (faith, religion, spirituality, family). And the series turned its two main actors into television stars.

The aim of this collection is to revisit the series on its thirtieth anniversary to reconsider the series' legacy/ies and to contemplate its ongoing relevance to television, television history and television studies. It is not the intention for the collection to serve as a hagiography, but rather for it to scrutinize the series' themes and impact, to consider how it can be used and interpreted through current scholarly interests and perspectives, and to re-evaluate its underpinning representations and ideologies. The essays in the collection touch upon the key thematic legacies, or potential legacies, of the series: race, gender, politics, genre, technology, history, fandom and sexuality. It is hoped that these chapters, and the collection as a whole, will serve not only as a guide to understanding, reflecting and scrutinizing the place of *The X-Files* within television history, but also as a way to address broader thematic, philosophical, historical, methodological and political topics within television and cultural studies.

References

Abbott, S., and S. Brown (2013), 'Introduction: The Truth Is (still) Out There: *The X-Files* Twenty Years On', *Science Fiction Film and Television*, 6 (1): 1–6.

America's Most Wanted (1988–2021), [TV programme] Fox.

Anon. (1992), 'Fifth Estater: Peter Alan Roth', *Broadcasting*, 15 June: 59.

Appelo, T. (1994), 'X-Files' Appeal', *Entertainment Weekly*, 18 March: n.p.

Bellon, J. (1999), 'The Strange Discourse of *The X-Files*: What It Is, What It Does, and What Is at Stake', *Critical Studies in Media Communication*, 16 (2): 136–54.

Boyle, K. (2022), '"The X-Files": Gillian Anderson on Why a Season 12 Wouldn't Work', *TV Insider*, 1 April. Available online: https://www.tvinsider.com/1039056/the-x-files-season-12-gillian-anderson/ (accessed 13 October 2022).

Brinker, F. (2018), 'Conspiracy, Procedure, Continuity: Reopening *The X-Files*', *Television & New Media*, 19 (4): 328–44.

Buffy the Vampire Slayer (1997–2003), [TV programme] The WB, UPN.

Carter, B. (1991), 'Fox Slows but Stays Restless', *New York Times*, 20 May: D1.

Carter, B. (1998), 'X-Files Tries to Keep Its Murky Promise', *New York Times*, 7 November: B7.

Chin, B. (2013), 'The Fan–Media Producer Collaboration: How Fan Relationships Are Managed in a Post-Series *X-Files* Fandom', *Science Fiction Film and Television*, 6 (1): 87–99.

Coe, S. (1992), 'Diller's New Departure; Fox's New Order', *Broadcasting*, 2 March: 4.

The Commish (1991–6), [TV programme] ABC.

Cops (1989–), [TV programme] Fox.

Delasara, J. (2000), *PopLit, PopCult and The X-Files: A Critical Exploration*, Jefferson, NC: McFarland.

The Disney Sunday Movie (1986–8), [TV programme] ABC.

Doctor Who (1963–), [TV programme] BBC1.

Ellis, J. (2007), 'Is It Possible to Construct a Canon of Television Programmes? Immanent Reading versus Textual-Historicism', in H. Wheatley (ed.), *Re-viewing Television History: Critical Issues in Television Historiography*, 15–26, London: I.B. Tauris.

Ghost Story for Christmas (1971–8), [TV programme] BBC.

Ghostwatch (1992), [TV programme] BBC1.

Holt, J. (2011), *Empires of Entertainment: Media Industries and the Politics of Deregulation, 1980–1996*, New Brunswick, NJ: Rutgers University Press.

Hopkins, T. (1995), 'X Marks the Spot', *Dayton Daily News*, 15 September: 2.

Hyman, J. (1993), 'X-Files' Creator Promises Fans a "Wildly Entertaining" and Scary Show', *Las Vegas Review*, 24 December: 15D.

Jeffery, M. (2019), 'Doctor Who's Ex-script Editor Says the BBC "Ghosted the Show in 1989"', *Radio Times*, 3 December. Available online: https://www.radiotimes.com/tv/sci-fi/doctor-who-cancellation/ (accessed 1 November 2022).

Johnston, D. (2009), 'Genre, Taste and the BBC: The Origins of British Television Science Fiction', PhD thesis, University of East Anglia.

Jones, B. (2013), 'Slow Evolution: "First Time Fics" and *The X-Files* Porn Parody', *Journal of Adaptation in Film & Performance*, 6 (3): 369–85.

Jowett, L., and S. Abbott (2013), *TV Horror*, New York: I. B. Tauris.

Kolchak: The Night Stalker (1974–5), [TV programme] ABC.

The Late Show (1986–8), [TV programme] Fox.

Lavery, D., A. Hague and M. Cartwright (1996), 'Introduction: Generation X – *The X-Files* and the Cultural Moment', in D. Lavery, A. Hague and M. Cartwright (eds), *Deny All Knowledge: Reading The X-Files*, 1–21, Syracuse, NY: Syracuse University Press.

Littlefield, K. (1994), 'X-citement Grows for Hot TV Show', *Toronto Star*, 12 May: E11.

The Lone Gunmen (2001), [TV programme] Fox.

Lowry, B. (1995), *The Truth Is Out There: The Official Guide to The X-Files*, New York: Harper.

Markley, R. (1997), 'Alien Assassinations: *The X-Files* and the Paranoid Structure of History', *Camera Obscura*, 14 (1&2): 75–102.

Married … with Children (1987–97), [TV programme] Fox.

McLean, A. (1998), 'Media Effects: Marshall McLuhan, Television Culture, and *The X-Files*', *Film Quarterly*, 51 (4): 2–11.

Mermigas, D. (1992), 'Murdoch Outlines the Future of Fox', *Advertising Age*, 30 March: 26.

Midnight Mass (2021), [TV programme] Netflix.

Millennium (1996–9), [TV programme] Fox.

No Place Like Home (2021), [Podcast] Apple.

The Omega Factor (1979), [TV programme] BBC1.

Picarelli, E., and M. Carmen Gomez-Galisteo (2013), 'Be Fearful: *The X-Files*' Post-9/11 Legacy', *Science Fiction Film and Television*, 6 (1): 71–85.

Play for Today (1970–84), [TV programme] BBC1.

Rags to Riches (1987–8), [TV programme] NBC.

Rhodes, Joe. 1993. 'Fox's "X-Files" Makes Contact with a Friday-Night Audience', *Los Angeles Times*, 12 December: 8.

Rodgers, D. A. (2019), 'Something "Wyrd" This Way Comes: Folklore and British Television', *Folklore*, 130 (2): 133–52.

Scott, M. (1998), 'X-Files – The Truth Is International', *Screen International*, 6 December: 31.

Shrieves, L. (1994), '*The X-Files*' Followers', *The Record*, 30 October: 31.

Simpson, M. (1994), 'The Generation X Files', *The Independent*, 17 December: n.p.

The Simpsons (1989–), [TV programme] FOX.

Stan Against Evil (2016–18), [TV programme] IFC.

Strachan, A. (1997), 'Fox Entertainment Chief Forged His TV Career in Vancouver', *The Vancouver Sun*, 16 August: C2.

Stranger Things (2016–) [TV programme] Netflix.

Taylor, C. (1994), 'Truth Decay: Sleuths after Reagan', *Millennium Pop*, 1 (1): 9–10.
21 Jump Street (1987–91), [TV programme] Fox.
The Twilight Zone (1959–64), [TV programme] CBS.
The Twilight Zone (2019–20), [TV programme] CBS.
Twin Peaks (1990–1), [TV programme] ABC.
Uscinski, J. E., and J. M. Parent (2014), *American Conspiracy Theories*, Oxford: Oxford University Press.
Video Palace (2018–), [Podcast] Shudder.
Wellington Paranormal (2018–22), [TV programme] TVNZ2.
Wheatley, H. (2007), 'Introduction: Re-viewing Television Histories', in H. Wheatley (ed.) *Re-viewing Television History: Critical Issues in Television Historiography*, 1–12, London: I.B. Tauris.
Williams, R. (2015), *Post-Object Fandom: Television, Identity and Self-Narrative*, London: Bloomsbury.
Wiseguys (1987–90), [TV programme] CBS.
The Wizard of Oz (1939), [Film] Dir. Victor Fleming, USA: Metro-Goldwyn-Mayer.

PART ONE

Cultural legacies: Landscape, environment, technology

James Fenwick

Key to the legacy of *The X-Files* is the series' aesthetic style: its 1990s-era fashion trends, its use of the wild, brooding landscape of British Columbia and the brutalist, urban exteriors of downtown Washington DC. The series – particularly the first five seasons – utilizes a distinct visual palette: grey, washed-out hues; beige and grey interiors; dark underground corridors; secret passageways and hidden rooms. The environments that Mulder and Scully inhabit include woods, forests, urban back alleys, bureaucratic office spaces, mortuaries, scientific laboratories, military bases and more. In these spaces, a range of technology often aids (or impedes) their quest for the truth: mobile phones; surveillance equipment; cars; aeroplanes; military vehicles; UFOs; torches; guns and extra-terrestrial weapons.

In Part One of this edited collection, contributors analyze the legacy of the depiction of landscape, environment and technology. In Chapter 1, Matthew Melia considers the ways in which the built environment and architecture are depicted in the series, analysing space and location to understand the ways in which *The X-Files* provides a cultural history into the landscapes and environments of the contemporary United States. Melia focuses on the 'monster-of-the-week' episodes in order to present a taxonomy of built environments, architectures, terrains and landscapes, which he argues are organized thematically and are key to understanding the series' organization as a whole.

In Chapter 2, Victoria Scrimer and Nicholas Stanton focus on the use of the mobile phone (or cell phone in the United States) in the series and the way in which it is a vital communicative tool not only in the context of the relationship between Mulder and Scully, but also as a plot device to move the story forward in any given episode. Scrimer and Stanton have compiled a publicly available dataset (bit.ly/x_files_telecomm) that documents every instance of telephone and radio communication across the entire series. In doing so, they present a clear argument as to how communication technology was vital to the series, to the plot, but more broadly to the cultural contexts of the era. As such, Scrimer and Stanton – like Melia's history of the built environment – are presenting a cultural history of communication technology.

In Chapter 3, Alex Goody and Antonia Mackay focus on surveillance technology and artificial intelligence in the series, analysing the cultural anxieties that existed in the 1990s about such technologies. Their analysis discusses the ways in which *The X-Files* was consistently looking towards the future and a 'post-human technological world'. Goody and Mackay place *The X-Files* within the broader cultural and research landscape of surveillance technology and artificial intelligence to demonstrate how it has contributed to the wider discourse of a post-human technological world, and continues to do so.

In Chapter 4, Chantelle Mitchell and Jaxon Waterhouse focus on the ecological legacy of *The X-Files*, centring their analysis on the presence of the 'Black Oil' in the series – the alien substance first used in season three and which becomes central to the series' myth-arc. Mitchell and Waterhouse provide an analysis of the black oil through a new materialist framework and contemporary petrocultures to argue that *The X-Files* has, and continues to contribute to, discourse on fossil fuel extraction, oil disasters and the climate crisis. As such, just like Goody and Mackay, Mitchell and Waterhouse demonstrate how the series has become a cultural historical object that now directly comments on contemporary politics, society and the environment.

In Chapter 5, Tom Livingstone provides a detailed analysis of the special effects technology employed (or, rather, not) in *The X-Files*. Livingstone argues that the series played a vital role in the history and evolution of special effects technology, but more importantly subverted the increasing dominance of special effects in the television and film, preferring practical effects over the 'illusory affordances of digital effects'. In doing so, Livingstone positions the series as an important cultural object in wider histories of digital technology in contemporary storytelling.

Taken together, these chapters provide illuminating arguments as to how *The X-Files*' primary legacy is now as a cultural and historical object, either for its representations and depictions of landscape and technology, or for the way in which it has contributed, and continues to do so, to debates about technology, the environment and broader histories and theories of film and television.

1

Space and location in *The X-Files*

Matthew Melia

In the first UK trailer for *The X-Files*, which aired on BBC 2 on 9 September 1994 (ahead of the first episode ten days later on 19 September), a shot was included from the final episode of season one ('The Erlenmeyer Flask' (S1: E01)) of the sinister Cigarette Smoking Man walking between rows of shelves in a cavernous clandestine warehouse (not unlike the final shot of Steven Spielberg's *Raiders of the Lost Arc* (1981)). *The X-Files* was established from the outset as a show that was preoccupied with built and designed spaces, secret spaces, disturbing landscapes and uncanny architectures of all kinds: from the bureaucratic spaces of the FBI to the verdant forests of Vancouver (where the series was filmed between seasons one and five, if not set – such as in 'Darkness Falls' (S1; E20)), the queasy and uneasy spaces of suburban America ('Arcadia' (S6: E15); 'Theef' (S7: E14)) to post-industrial farmlands ('Home' (S4: E02); 'Our Town' (S2: E24)) and urban space ('Squeeze' (S1: E3)).

In the existing critical literature on *The X-Files*, there has been surprisingly little devoted to the role and presentation of such locales, much less on the *The X-Files* as a space-aware (and spatially aware) series. Film and television scholars Simon Brown and Stacey Abbot, however, have observed that one of the pioneering aspects of the series was the way in which it grounded science fiction television, bringing the genre (mostly) back down to earth. They state that it 'relocated the SF narrative away from outer space and placed it firmly on contemporary Earth' (Abbot and Brown 2013: 1–6). While *The X-Files* was a series that looked outward to the cosmos in its alien abduction conspiracy narrative arc (the myth-arc), its sinister appeal lay as well in the uncanny rendering of all too familiar terrestrial (and very American) spaces.

Across its eleven-season run and two feature films, *The X-Files* offered a typology of spaces to which it would repeatedly return – noticeably so in the 'monster-of-the-week' episodes, which strayed from and were set apart from the overarching myth-arc, and which will form the focus of the analysis in this chapter. These spaces formed a canvas upon which to project a selection of (often self-aware and postmodern) story types that existed outside of the series' myth-arc (even though, at times, they overlapped). They were also spaces where the relationship between Mulder and Scully could be established, framed and developed.

With this chapter, I am interested in looking at how the series uses space and location, with a focus on the 'monster-of-the-week' episodes. These stand-alone episodes provide a lens through which we may examine *The X-Files'* depiction of space, place and architecture away from the influence of the ongoing myth-arc. It is therefore the aim of the chapter to provide a critical overview of the series' use of space and its spatial awareness to consider how such spaces are portrayed and how the series draws, and frequently subverts, cultural understandings of such spaces, architectures and locales.

Contextualizing space in *The X-Files*

Before considering the breakdown of space and location within *The X-Files*, I want to first consider the era out of which the series emerged – an era of crises in national and political space – as context. *The X-Files* was first broadcast in the United States on 10 September 1993 (it would be just over a year later when it was first broadcast in the UK), eight months into the presidency of Bill Clinton. The series' narrative(s) chimed with an era of major political change and conflict – post-Bush, post-Gulf War/Operation Desert Storm (a conflict which has a distinct presence in the early series) and only three years after the fall of the Berlin wall, with communism giving way to emergent globalization and late-twentieth-century global capitalism. In an area where there was no longer an identifiable ideological Bogeyman, American politics and militarism were also looking to reassert their global dominance – the United States appointing itself as world police against a variety of lesser despots such as Manuel Noriega in Panama and Saddam Hussein in Iraq, wars in which the United States could continue to perpetuate its imperialist frontier myth. Furthermore, on 29 January 1991, President George Bush Snr, in his State of the Union address, had proposed a 'New World Order' and that 'only the US has both the moral standing and means to back it up'.

If, as I shall argue, *The X-Files* is a series that is preoccupied by spaces, architectures and locales of all kinds, might we understand this preoccupation as a response to the shifting position of the United States in the post-Cold War global space? Katherine Kinney (2001) has already noted and discussed the position of *The X-Files* in relation to the space of post-Cold War America, while Picarelli and Gomez-Galisteo (2013) have considered the position of the series in relation to the space of the post-9/11 world. Kinney observes that the political and international boundaries and borders that had become entrenched during the Cold War, creating power blocks formed along geographical as well as ideological fault lines and spatial demarcations (and which had clearly delineated marked-out territory, space and power), had begun to collapse; borders, space and ideological identity were becoming more uncertain and unstable. In other words, the Cold War had consolidated fixed certainties over borders, national spaces and American identity. Kinney notes that when the 'Soviet Union collapsed, it carried with it the totalizing narrative of otherness on which this expanded notion of American nationalism depended. The U.S., in effect, returned to its own borders and found them suddenly vulnerable and in crisis' (Kinney 2001: 54).

The argument may be made that it is precisely these 'narratives of otherness' that the United States depended on in the reassertion of its own global identity. Across its series run, *The X-Files* is nothing if not preoccupied also with otherness, with the strange, aberrant and invasive, reasserting as well as ironizing this political narrative – frequently within the series it is the conversative and conforming that are presented as aberrant and monstrous (see this chapter's later discussion of the series' suburban episodes). Picarelli and Gomez-Galisteo contribute to a wider discussion of the series' reaction to unstable geopolitical space by arguing its irrelevance in the post-9/11 world (the series' original run concluded with season nine, which coincided with the 9/11 attacks); that its preoccupation with a conspiratorial government in possible collusion with invasive alien beings and its paranoid outlook of 'Trust No One' (which had its roots in the paranoid conspiracy culture of the post-Watergate 1970s; see Gregory Frame's chapter in this collection) was no longer appropriate nor resonated with a viewing audience in an era in which people were looking to trust the government in fighting the 'War on Terror' (Picarelli and Gomez-Galisteo 2013: 71–85).

However, *The X-Files* offers a cabinet of curiosities and monsters who are set in contrast to the (often sinister) conservatism of white America – fluke men occupying city sewers ('The Host' (S2: E02)); postmodern Frankensteins in reality-TV-obsessed, picket-fenced America ('The Post Modern Prometheus' (S5: E05)); carnival freaks and 'Conundrums' ('Humbug' (S2: E20)), with carnivals and fairgrounds being recurring spaces throughout the series and, of course, extraterrestrial interlopers and invaders. Across its run, *The X-Files* would also return to, for example, the gated communities of white middle America ('Arcadia' (S6: E15)), where conformity is the order of the day and where 'otherness' is deemed disruptive and aberrant. Such ordered and built 'domestic space' is contrasted with 'other'/indigenous spaces – forests and Navajo lands, for instance (represented by the character Albert Hostein (Floyd 'Red Crow' Westerman)) with Mulder a traveller between these two spaces.

Kinney further notes that 'at the heart of the new meanings being ascribed to the "border" in a post-Cold War world is the need to address a basic uncertainty in the relation of foreign and domestic, public and private' (Kinney 2001: 55). It is this uncertainty that, she observes, 'animates the shadows of "The X-Files"' (Kinney 2001: 55). Spaces, locales and architectures in *The X-Files* are in part defined through their self-contained-ness and separation from each other. Hence, we may argue that the series' preoccupations with uncertain spaces of all different kinds become a metonym for the United States' own uncertain position and occupancy of post-Cold War space during which time it was unclear what its new role would be.

Star Trek and *The X-Files*

Perhaps in illustrating (and returning to Abbot and Brown's assessment of *The X-Files*' grounding of science fiction within terrestrial space) the breakdown and erosion of these certainties, we may draw an initial comparison with that other space-obsessed and era-defining American science fiction series, *Star Trek* (1965–9). During the Cold War (and as the Vietnam War was at its height), *Star Trek* celebrated American global supremacy and leadership; its expansionism, democratic values and diplomacy – all embodied through the character of Captain James T. Kirk – with its mantra of 'boldly going where no man has gone before', of 'seeking out strange new worlds and new civilizations' – reasserted the romantic and colonialist frontier myth of 'manifest destiny'. *Star Trek* and *The X-Files* present two polarities in American science fiction television, with *The X-Files* presenting a diametrically opposite perspective. With its ongoing alien conspiracy myth-arc, the hopefulness of *Star Trek*'s propulsive journey across 'Space – the final frontier' is inverted and *The X-Files* instead presents a set of anxieties about the testing of terrestrial (domestic) space and alien intrusions into our 'space'. A returning character across the series, the Alien Bounty Hunter (Brian Thompson), can shape-shift and adapt his appearance in order to walk amongst us, a deliberate reminder of Cold War anxieties over 'reds under the bed' and perhaps that those anxieties over space and insidious invasion which defined the Cold War era had not completely disappeared.

Furthermore, the 'bodysnatching' narratives of pre-*Star Trek* paranoid Cold War B-movies are recycled and reinvented in *The X-Files*' ongoing myth-arc, which reveals a government conspiracy to hybridize alien and human DNA and to hide 'the Truth' (which is, of course, 'out there' as opposed to 'in here'). As I have noted elsewhere, the technicolour 'heroic' persona of Captain Kirk re-negotiates the construction of the television hero, reconstructing it for the cultural climate and progressive of the mid-'60s: he is a figure who personifies stability, steadfastness and moral righteousness ... but whose character also works to establish and stabilise a new type of male [television] hero apposite to the changing climate of the '60s. Significantly, *Star Trek* was first broadcast two years, ten months and five days after the assassination of John F. Kennedy. It is difficult not to see Kirk, the youngest Captain in Starfleet, as an embodiment of the romantic, youthful, charisma and liberal values of the late president. (Melia 2016)

If *Star Trek* had presented in Captain James T. Kirk a central hero so clearly modelled on President John F. Kennedy, then it is worth noting that *The X-Files* presents, in Fox Mulder, a central hero and protagonist who is (potentially) modelled on President Bill Clinton (who – for a time at least – occupied a similar cultural position of democratic, liberal hope) and who, in the early stages of the series at least, had not yet been mired in sex scandals and allegations of corruption. If *Star Trek* is clearly a product of the Kennedy era, then as Kinney notes,

> *The X-Files* is unmistakably a product of the Clinton era, in which government was consistently divided in power, practice, and vision. Clinton's troubled relationships with the military and with 'family values' were the focus of repeated attacks directed by conservatives against Clinton personally and against the liberal agenda he claimed to uphold. National and domestic borders were hysterically claimed in danger; endangered, many of the most vocal insist, by the very man charged with defending them. Fox Mulder emerges as a perfect hero in such a time, endlessly engaged in a struggle to defend home and country from threats that are never quite as alien as they might seem. (Kinney 2001: 55)

A full critical comparison of both *Star Trek* and *The X-Files*, however, will form the basis of another study. If *Star Trek* looks outward to the cosmos presenting a television narrative that championed the United States as *the* leading democratic nation, *The X-Files* turned its gaze inward upon a conspiratorial American government working *against* the people; across the series we see evidence of characters who look not outward, but inward (notably so in 'Home'). Mulder, then, stands out as a character who, rather than seeking an interior truth or looking inward, is convinced that 'the truth is out there'. As Lincoln Geraghty has noted of series creator Chris Carter, 'The inspiration for the show was his fascination with the conspiracy culture surrounding the Watergate scandal, and this was identified most of all in how he did not hesitate "to register its reverberations in 1990s America on the psyche of his alter ego Fox Mulder, a man similarly haunted by the debacle of 1973"' (Geraghty 2009).

'FBI's Most Unwanted'

I will turn now to a discussion of some of the spaces within and presented by *The X-Files*. As I have noted, there is little discussion in existing critical literature on *The X-Files*' 'typology of spaces'. From a survey of the series made in preparation for this chapter, a selected sample overview of some of the repeated spatial types might look like this:

Repeated Spaces in *The X-Files*: Sample Selection
Official spaces (FBI locations/buildings)
Post-industrial spaces
Forests/natural spaces
Suburbs/suburban spaces/gated communities
Fairgrounds and carnivals

Before embarking on more expansive study of the series and these locales, let's first begin in the basement of the J. Edgar Hoover Building – the FBI's headquarters – in downtown Washington, DC. The basement is, by tradition, a gothic space, and it has a distinct presence across horror culture. The basement or cellar is somewhere secret where the aberrant and monstrous lurk or are sequestered away. It is in the cellar of the Bates motel, in *Psycho* (1960), where Norman keeps the corpse of his mother and it is here, in a cluttered antechamber of the basement (or dungeon) of the FBI's headquarters that, along with the young and newly minted FBI Agent Dana Scully, *we* are first introduced to Fox Mulder, the 'FBI's most unwanted'.

If, throughout its run, *The X-Files* experiments with the palette and aesthetic language of the gothic, the first 'monster' we are introduced to is none other than Mulder himself. In the immediately preceding sequence, Scully is tasked, in the environs of the office of Section Chief Blevins (Charles Cioffi) (predecessor to Assistant Director Walter Skinner whose office we and the agents will return to in almost each episode from season two), to monitor and report back on pariah agent Fox 'Spooky' Mulder. The scene, of course, deliberately recalls a similar sequence towards the start of *The Silence of the Lambs* (1991), in which trainee agent Clarice

Starling (Jodie Foster) is sent by Agent-In-Charge of Behavioural science Jack Crawford (Scott Glenn), to extract information from refined cannibal psychiatrist Hannibal Lecter. In *The X-Files* 'Pilot' episode (S1: E01), we are presented with a similar transition between adjacent and contrasting spaces as we are led from bureaucratic, 'official' space to the cloistered and gothic basement space containing an aberrant 'monstrous' outsider (something 'created' by the FBI, now an embarrassing secret). Blevins describes Mulder's preoccupation with the X-Files to Scully as 'consuming' – further recalling 'Hannibal the Cannibal' intertextually connecting these two sequences. His warnings to Scully also recall Crawford's warning to Starling: 'Do you scare easily?'

The Silence of the Lambs was released two years prior to the broadcast of the 'Pilot' episode of *The X-Files* in the United States and both were instrumental in establishing a new framework for the FBI procedural drama. *The X-Files* series producer Glen Morgan even claimed that the pilot episode was a 'merging of *Silence of the Lambs* and *Close Encounters of the Third Kind*' (this was the episode that established the show's myth-arc) (Edwards 1996). The clanking metal doors and dank corridors of the dungeon in the Chesapeake asylum into which FBI ingenue Clarice Starling (Jodie Foster) descends for her first confrontation with Lecter in *The Silence of the Lambs*, are recalled in this early *X-Files* sequence by the lift door that signifies Scully's transition from above ground 'Official' space to a buried subterranean gothic space. Mulder's office is a cluttered cave of ephemera that Scully approaches through a dimly lit claustrophobic corridor – we follow her via a tracking shot. Once inside the office, we view the covered walls through Scully's eyes: a panning shot which begins on the iconic 'I Want to Believe' poster and ends on the figure of Mulder hunched over a set of slides (Figure 1).

FIGURE 1 *Fox Mulder.*

Mulder is presented as a combination of both Lecter *and* Sherlock Holmes. In Dr Watson's first encounter with Holmes in the novel *A Study in Scarlet* (1887), the detective is similarly engaged in a scientific experiment. While it is not the purpose of this chapter to engage in a prolonged critical comparison between Conan Doyle's stories and *The X-Files*, the parallel is worth bearing out here – and we might suggest that there are elements of the famous detective in both Mulder *and* Scully. Although Scully is a medical doctor, clearly aligning her with Watson to Mulder's dogged Holmes, her commitment to rationality in the face of the incredible and unbelievable also aligns *her* with the great detective.

This cluttered oubliette (Figure 2) stands in stark contrast to the comparatively featureless (bar some fish) space of Mulder's apartment – another point of repeated return in the series. In traversing both of these Mulder-oriented sites across the series, we may note that by comparison Scully has a much less well-defined set of locales; we occasionally visit her home, but it is with much less frequency and with much less familiarity. In terms of a 'space' Scully is, perhaps, apportioned the dissecting mortuary chamber, a site of rational, methodical deconstruction which is in stark contrast to the cluttered space of Mulder's office.

'Above ground', the offices of Mulder and Scully's FBI superiors at the J. Edgar Hoover building appear to epitomize the order and superiority of American power – offices graced with presidential pictures, grand desks, uncluttered open space. The office of Assistant Director Walter Skinner, Blevins's replacement from season two onwards and Mulder and Scully's above-ground ally (increasingly so across the series), is an example of just

FIGURE 2 *Mulder's office.*

such a space. Nevertheless, these are spaces which, although appearing to embody the incorruptible superiority of American power, are nonetheless inherently corrupted spaces. This is established from the start. In the first instance of meeting Scully in Blevins's office, standing in the background of the shots is the Cigarette Smoking Man or, as also known, 'Cancer Man', himself a cancer corrupting these romantic notions of incorruptible American power and a returning background presence across the series' office scenes (Figures 3 and 4).

Furthermore, Bill Clinton's presence and image is pervasive presence within the (earlier) series, with Skinner behind his 'Resolute Desk' becoming a cipher for fallible presidential power and authority (Figure 5).

Post-industrial spaces

I would like to now turn to another recurrent spatial 'type' in *The X-Files* – the post-industrial space. Kirk Boyle has already made some critical inroads here. His article 'The Truth Is Outsourcing: Notes on the Post-Industrial Spaces of *The X-Files*' provides discussion of the series' use of the post-industrial spaces – warehouses, factories, abandoned spaces and locations around Vancouver where seasons one to five were filmed (Boyle 2017). Boyle refers to Emily Davis's argument that, through its generic hybridity, '*The X-Files* makes the perfect vehicle for representing ways in which anxieties about the dangerous intimacies of the ever-smaller global village – along with more general anxieties about social change, sexual taboo, and technological development – come together' (Boyle 2017). For Boyle, *The X-Files* presents a sociopolitical study of an America coping with the loss of its industrial identity, an America of empty and abandoned spaces where the monstrous find refuge. Of course, given *The X-Files* was predominantly filmed in Canada, this further adds to the ambiguity of spatial identity in the series – Vancouver's Pacific Northwest identity standing in for the United States. In focusing on the series' use of Vancouver, Boyle observes:

> I … am interested in *The X-Files* as an allegory, the resonance of its dark and mysterious spaces, and how the show expresses general anxieties about the social changes wrought by the millennial forces of globalization. But my curiosity lies with an 'allegory file' yet to be opened, one that delves into the meaning of the post-industrial spaces that make up the backdrops of many of *The X-Files*' episodes, specifically those of the first five seasons filmed in Vancouver, British Columbia. Why do so many episodes contain climatic scenes set in dark abandoned warehouses and factories? Are these settings merely a convention of the sci-fi/neo-noir/horror genre, or do they register latent anxieties about life in a post-industrial society? … what is difficult to accept, cope with,

FIGURES 3 AND 4 *The Smoking Man.*

and understand is not a U.S. governmental conspiracy to conceal the existence of extra-terrestrials, but the country's rocky transition away from a manufacturing-based economy. (Boyle 2017)

While I earlier attempted to contextualize *The X-Files* against the backdrop of the changing and unstable spaces of the post-Cold War world, the

FIGURE 5 *Skinner's office*.

ensuing emergence of globalized markets, increased consumption and the conditions of a post-industrial society provide a further backdrop. Boyle notes (citing Douglas Kellner) that in the last decade of the twentieth century, *The X-Files* 'shows a society in transition', which 'involves turn-of-the-century capitalism's systematic dismantling of industrial society' (2017). This is illustrated perhaps in the first classic 'monster-of-the-week' episode, 'Squeeze' (S1: E03). In this episode we (and the agents) are introduced to Eugene Tooms (Doug Hutchison), an exterminator (and therefore a member of the increasingly disenfranchised industrial working class) who (Mulder later deduces) is a mutant human being able to hibernate for decades and who emerges every twenty years to feed on the bile from his victim's liver to prolong his existence. Tooms has a unique ability to squeeze his body through the smallest of spaces in order to secure his prey, and he is able to challenge and compromise the borders which demarcate space. However, his adaptability is a skill which finally ends up costing him his life. In the second episode of this two-part story, 'Tooms' (S1: E21), the agents finally confront Tooms in that most of American spaces, the shopping mall, a temple to capitalism and consumption (and recalling George Romero's similar use of just such a location in *Dawn of the Dead* [1978]). 'Squeeze' and 'Tooms' provide an extended narrative about consumption and survival – Tooms consumes his victims' livers to prolong his existence and, in the episode's finale, he is *himself* consumed, ground up by the gears and mechanism of the mall elevator. If Tooms has been able to prolong himself throughout the course of twentieth-century American history with all its economic and cultural transitions, he is unable to weather this 'great transition' to a post-industrial society – chewed up in the grinding mechanism of late-twentieth-century global consumer capitalism. Furthermore, Tooms, as Boyle notes, lives in abandoned downtown apartment block as do many of the 'monsters-of-the-week' across the series. They 'live and die' in similar post-industrial spaces:

> In the episode 'Beyond the Sea', Lucas Henry falls to his death in a deserted brewery. Mulder shoots and kills John Lee Roche in the Translink bus graveyard in Surrey, B. C. Samuel Aboah is killed in a demolition site and Augustus Cole in an abandoned part of a rail yard. The Pusher escapes two cops in an empty factory, and his twin sister Linda Bowman almost convinces Mulder to shoot Scully in the same dark and empty factory. Even the Jersey Devil is pursued through a dilapidated building before being hunted down in the woods. The gloomy spaces in which Mulder and Scully confront these monsters are post-industrial. They represent the return of the repressed of the post-industrial order. (2017)

It is interesting also to note (and further aligning Mulder with the monstrous, aberrant and Gothic) Mulder's own apartment space, which (as I have discussed) is comparatively featureless and spartan, as if he too has taken up residence in some abandoned space – not unlike the creatures he and Scully hunt. In fact, further comparison may be made between Mulder and these 'monsters-of the-week', as Boyle asks:

> What happens to the atomized individuals who lose faith in authority, and for whom all belief systems bow down before the so-called 'free market'? They become fetishistic believers like Scully (who believes in her religion although she knows better), paranoiacs like Mulder (who finds conspiracy everywhere, especially when wrapped in another conspiracy), or Monsters of the Week, those genetic mutants who do all they can to survive in a hostile world. Might not the Eugene Toomses, Donnie Pfasters, and Robert Modells of the 'creature feature' episodes be surrogates for the displaced workers of post-industrial society? These monstrous metaphors represent the 'paranoid sense that individuals have lost control of their institutions and even the ability to map and understand the machinations of a complex global society and culture.' (2017)

These are the displaced of the post-industrial society. But Mulder too has been displaced, a relic of the 'crackpot' conspiracy culture of the 1970s, seeing little (grey) men around every corner. There is no place for him in the new FBI.

Perhaps one of the series' most notorious episodes is 'Home' (S4: E02), a (folk/rural) horror and 'American Gothic' that takes clear inspiration from *The Texas Chainsaw Massacre* (1974) in its grisly depiction of its central 'redneck' family. In this episode, we again see the series depict the spaces and the results of post-industrialization. Just as the family in Hooper's nightmarish horror film are ex-abattoir workers put out of business by mechanization and outsourcing, so the inbred Peacock family in 'Home' are (or appear to be) farmers or victims of an agrarian industry in decline. The series is pre-occupied with the domestic interior, especially given the number of episodes given over to white middle-class homes in residential, suburban communities. Here the Peacocks' own abode stands in direct contrast – or does it? While their home is a booby-trapped charnel house of horrors, horror and aberration are as equally present in the series' suburban spaces – just hidden better.

The field around the Peacock home is a barren wasteland fit only for amateur baseball (what more nostalgic all-American pastime?) and burying the increasingly wasted and deformed seed of their family line – the abortive product of the monstrous brother's liaisons with their mother. The incestuous and inbred Peacocks, a family of brothers, continue the family line through the impregnation of their own mother (a limbless torso kept under a bed) and pay the price for looking inward (domestically) rather than outward (for which read globally). Like other 'monsters-of-the-week', the Peacocks attempt to prolong their existence in the face of a declining domestic economy.

This theme also provides the narrative for 'Our Town' (S2: E24), in which a chicken processing plant at the centre of a rural community becomes the focus of the investigation into a breakout of Creutzfeldt-Jakob Disease (CHD), which at the time of the episode's broadcast in 1995 had just been identified as the human form of Bovine Spongiform Encephalitis or 'Mad Cow Disease'. The townspeople, it is revealed, are practising cannibalism to extend their lives with the human remains being both fed to the chickens about to be processed and, it is suggested, becoming part of the runoff from the plant – poisoning the local streams. Scenes in the episode depict the grisly industrial workings of the plant. The industrial cycle of consumption is a running theme: its catastrophic environmental (spatial) knock-on impact on the natural world and environment.

Natural spaces

Forests, woodlands and other natural spaces (such as the fictional 'Lake Okobogee' Sioux City, Iowa, in the alien abduction story 'Conduit' (S1: E04)) are among the more commonly recurring spaces and locales (either as part of or as the main episode locale) in the series – especially across the early seasons. The verdant greenery of British Colombia denotes another 'episode' type that stands in contrast to the built and designed spaces of the 'suburban' episodes or the urban decay of the 'post-industrial' episodes. Over twenty episodes across seasons one to five alone use forests as a key location and, as Eric Grundhauser and Emma Morton have noted, Vancouver's Lower Seymore Conservation Reserve became the go-to location for most of them, including 'Pilot', 'The Jersey Devil' (S1: E5), 'Darkness Falls' (S1: E20), 'Die Hand Die Verletz' (S2: E14) and 'Jose Chung's From Outer Space' (S3: E20) (Grundhauser and Morton, 2015). Each season consists an average of twenty episodes, meaning that one entire season's worth of episodes are 'forest' episodes. There are of course practical and budgetary reasons for the reuse and recycling of a single locale as well as allowing episodes which are 'variations on a theme'.

But these natural spaces also allowed the series to engage with contemporary environmental and industrial questions and debates, combining them with the series' narrative interests in the arcane, folkloric and occult. They also provide a backdrop for an episode 'type' in which the forest-scape itself becomes a (super) natural aggressor. The episode 'Darkness Falls', for instance, deals with the logging industry, eco-terrorism and the release of a dormant organism from a felled tree (manifested in a swarm of deadly luminous green insects). As Jean M. Daniels points out, since the 1960s, the US logging industry had been driven by demand from Japan for quality timber for their construction industry, much of which came from the Pacific Northwest (PNW), filming location for *The X-Files* (Daniels 2005). These forest spaces within the series, like the Indian lands of British Colombia. are contested spaces, invaded and colonized. We might even consider them 'post-industrial spaces' as, according to Daniels, by the 1990s Japanese demand for PNW timber was drying up (Daniels 2005). In 'Darkness Falls', the forest space is (again) prey to the forces of global capitalism.

Similar variations on the theme of natural-space-as-aggressor may also be observed in both the episodes 'Field Trip' (S6: E21) and 'Detour' (S5: E04). In the latter, Mulder is diverted en-route through Appalachia to a team building conference by an investigation into the disappearance of people deep within the forest. The pre-title sequence features two surveyors who are mapping out an area for deforestation. After planting their equipment (and joking that this would be where the Blockbuster video was going to be built), the forest earth appears to bleed. One of the surveyors then suddenly vanishes as if devoured by the forest itself while the other witnesses two red eyes staring from the wood (Figure 6). The 'monsters-of-the-week' are creatures who have adapted to blend in with the forest environment, and who, Mulder later deduces, are primal humans descended from Spanish Conquistadors and who over time have learned to adapt to their natural environment (Figure 6).

The colonization and invasion of natural space is a theme in this episode – invaders into the forest space become their/its prey: the surveyors and a father out hunting with his son, for instance. As with Eugene Tooms,

FIGURE 6 *A pair of red eyes ('Detour' S5E04).*

these primitive creatures can physically adapt to the space and environment around them, they are part of it – inextricably linked to their surrounding environment. As Zack Handlen notes in his review of the episode, 'Cities and towns and neighbourhoods, those were designed by humans to fit humans. When it comes to nature, it's the other way around: We should be designed to fit *it*. And we aren't anymore, not really. Being in a forest now, for most of us, is like being an alien in our own backyard' (Handlen 2011).

'Detour' both foregrounds the theme of survival of the fittest, adaptability (or the inability to adapt), and enforces the idea that such spaces are *living* spaces which will defend themselves against invasion with aggression. Opening point of view shots of the forest present a disorienting and sinister space, and later in the episode the agents and their guides are hunted by these seemingly invisible creatures – characters are depicted being literally swallowed by the environment around them. According to Hurwitz and Knowles in *The Complete X-Files* (2008), shooting the episode with the space of the forest environment also posed a series of challenges including the weather conditions, with nonstop rain holding up and delaying production (58). There is also a degree of intertextuality in the episode with thematic and visual references to *The Invisible Man* (1933) and *Predator* (1987).

The later episode 'Field Trip' that, like 'Detour', was written by executive producer Frank Spotnitz, again sees Mulder and Scully venturing out into the wilderness (this time the mountains of North Carolina) after the discovery of a pair of embracing skeletons – remains of which belong to a married pair of hikers found in a bog. The episode takes the viewer into a set of narratively disorienting and concentric hallucinations (experienced by the characters) caused by the spores of a carnivorous subterranean fungus. This continues the theme of a living and aggressive natural space. The episode, a mycological horror story, is spatially organized between the above-ground landscape and the subterranean stygian caverns where victims are digested. While these caverns were constructed on the studio lot at Fox, the cave entrance itself was the same one used in the opening titles of the *Batman* (1966–8) television series, in Bronson Canyon, Los Angeles.

Suburban spaces

In a 1994 article for the *New Yorker*, James Wolcott draws a comparison between *The X-Files* and *The Twilight Zone* (1959–64). He observes,

> Like 'The Twilight Zone', 'The X-Files' expresses a national unease, which helps explain its hold on our nerves. 'The Twilight Zone', first broadcast in 1959, was the dark negative of the sunny snapshots of suburbia shown on sitcoms like 'Ozzie and Harriet' and 'Leave It to Beaver'. Created by Rod Serling, who also acted as its host, the show served as a night watchman to the anxieties of the atomic age. It presented worst-case scenarios of what might happen if the launch buttons were pushed: neighbours beat on the doors of bomb shelters closed to outsiders; Norman Rockwell villages became ghost towns, a tattered calendar telling us when time stopped; on bare plains, survivors shrivelled in the sun like bugs under a magnifying glass. Whether the threat was missiles or flying saucers, our skies were not safe … The cardboard construction of 'The Twilight Zone' didn't cheapen its sense of dread; it functioned as thin insulation against the abyss. The show's very lack of production values promoted a stark-bare allegorical staging. (Wolcott 1994)

The suburban locales of *The X-Files* in episodes such as 'Arcadia' or 'Theef' contrast dramatically with the previously discussed (organic) natural spaces. Their conformity prompts comparison with the built and planned spaces of the American post-Second-World-War period, notably Levittown, the (predominantly white) suburban community constructed in the late 1940s in Westchester, New York. It was a post-war project in national, ideological and social reconstruction. Kenn Hollings describes it as follows:

> You can imagine how it will look from space: the houses and roads and backyards arranged in neatly ordered rows, a framework of streetlights and driveways in a perfectly arranged grid at night. Located on what was once an expanse of potato fields, midway between the munition's plants

FIGURE 7 *Levittown, Long Island.*

> of Long Island, the first Levittown, formerly known as 'Island Trees' is opened to the public in February 1947. A planned community of 6,000 households offering affordable housing in the form of small detached, single-family units, this new conurbation quickly expands to embrace a further 11,000 homes, each situated sixty feet apart on their own patch of ground. Constructed from prefabricated sections and components. Suburbia has at last begun to extend its grand conformity into space. (Hollings 2008: 3)

This 'planned community', built by real estate developer William H. Levitt, was a response to the Atomic Age – a space of rigid conformity and the nuclear family. A post-war plan for a new America was energized by production line capitalism and a new ideal for living. *The X-Files* returns repeatedly to similar suburban spaces and gated communities which bear the imprint (both architectural and ideological) of Levittown (Figures 7 and 8).

In his analysis of the representation of suburbia in the series, Michael Kleen employs the term 'Suburban Gothic': 'A form of Dark Romantic storytelling set in a suburban environment. Traditionally associated with aging Victorian mansions, crypts, and other macabre settings, the neat rows of white picket fences, manicured lawns, and modern tract housing of the suburbs may seem like an unusual home for Gothic tales' (Kleen 2016).

Kleen goes on to note that

> *The X-Files* portray[s] the suburbs as a place of denial – denial of danger and the human passions that cause it, where the normal obscures the

FIGURE 8 *Levittown, aerial view.*

abnormal through supernatural means. The artificial order and safety of the suburbs only serves to mask the sinister reality lurking beneath the surface. No one is safe from life's horrors, not even in the carefully controlled environment of suburbia. (Klenn 2016)

The series is a return visitor to the suburbs in episodes such as 'Theef', in which a celebrated doctor's affluent suburban life is invaded by the occult machinations of a vengeful father and practitioner of Hoodoo, whose late daughter was a victim of the doctor's malpractice; and 'Chimera' (S7: E16) in which Mulder is called away from a stakeout by Skinner to investigate the disappearance of a judge's daughter and which may or may not involve the supernatural. However, it is the episode 'Arcadia' that is the most self-evident and knowing of these episode types. If 'Theef' and 'Chimera' engage with the illusion of safety presented by affluent suburban living, then 'Arcadia' present's the residents of the suburbs themselves as sinister and cult like – a source of the occult. If there are cultural precedents for this sense of suburban Gothic and the horror that lies behind the white picket fence – David Lynch's *Blue Velvet* (1986) is a key example of this.

'Arcadia' depicts a gated, planned, exclusively white, community driven by a militant conformity and to which difference and otherness is aberrant. It was in just such a middle-class conservative community that, in 2012, over ten years after the episode aired (in 1999), that a young man of mixed-race background, Trayvon Martin, was gunned down by a resident and member of the local neighbourhood watch, George Zimmerman, while visiting family. The community runs on a set of prescribed rules regarding the appearance of property and the maintenance of exteriors to a standard set by community leader Gene Gogolak. In order to infiltrate this community and investigate the disappearance of one of its members, Mulder and Scully must pose as a WASP (White Anglo Saxon Protestant)-ish married couple as they move into the recently vacated premises. It is Mulder who becomes the invasive presence in this episode as he wilfully (and comedically) flouts the community rules and provokes – putting up a basketball hoop outside and installing a cheap plastic flamingo on the front lawn drawing him into conflict with his neighbours. The 'monster-of-the-week' in 'Arcadia' is a golem created from trash by Gogolak and tasked with dispatching those who challenge the conformity of the community. The planned and architectural nature of the community with its order and symmetry allow aesthetic and political contrasts with both the post-industrial spaces and the natural spaces of the series, yet in their way the residents of the 'Falls of Arcadia' are as attached to their domestic space and are as inward looking as those who reside in these contrasting spaces. They defend their environment, space and way of life just as the Peacocks in 'Home' do (albeit in a different way) and their desire to blend in positions them in relation to the forest creatures in 'Detour'. Order, conformity and demarcation constitute a return to spatial politics of the Cold War and present a reaffirmation of the certainties which have been eroded (see earlier).

We may also read this episode as one of the most satirical of the series. Broadcast in March 1999, as the twentieth century was coming to a close and the United States was two years away from the return of a Republican government under George W. Bush, the Clinton presidency had been mired in scandal – the most recent the year before with the revelation of his affair with White House Intern Monica Lewinsky. This was a presidency which was noticeably concerned with outward appearances and facades – the Clinton marriage being, of course, the most evident. We might argue that 'Arcadia' borrows the conformity of suburban living with its own facades masking not only corruption and scandal but also, as Wolcott (1994) notes, a 'national unease' – the suburbs here become a space of 'allegorical staging'.

Conclusion: Carnival/fairground spaces

In concluding this chapter, I would like to briefly refer to another 'type' in the spatial matrix of the series: fairgrounds and carnivals. Again, the series repeatedly returns to these spaces in episodes such as 'Humbug', 'The Calusari' (S2: E21) and 'The Amazing Maleeni' (S7: E08). 'The Post-Modern Prometheus' and 'Hollywood AD' (S7: E19) provide spaces for the series to narratively and textually disrupt itself with the fourth wall breaking – in the first, Mulder calls on the writer to correct the ending and the musical finale dissolves into the pulp pages of a comic book. In 'Hollywood AD' at the finale, the dead come back to life to perform a dance routine on a sound stage. 'The Amazing Maleeni' depicts an illusion in which a performer is able to turn his head through 360° (another bodily skill not unlike Tooms's adapting to space). What these carnival spaces provide is, of course, a self-reflexive commentary on the fantastical nature of the series itself, its own illusions and improbabilities and the invitation to believe ('I want to believe').

'The Calusari' combines the 'fairground' episode with the suburban episode – it begins with a young child killed by a fairground train, tempted onto the tracks by a balloon under the influence of an unknown force. Here this space is presented as disorienting and disturbing (the balloon recalling those of the clown 'Pennywise' in Stephen King's *It*). The episode begins in the uncanny space of the fairground and later continues in the suburban home of the boy's immigrant family and the attempts of his Romanian grandmother and three 'mystics' to exorcise the malevolent spirit of the surviving son's stillborn twin. The suburbs again are presented as disguising the mysterious, occult and aberrant.

The discussion of carnival and fairgrounds will form the basis of a further study. In this chapter, I have attempted to map the spatial nexus of *The X-Files*. There is of course more to develop here – other spaces worthy of note include its use of medical spaces (which 'Theef' also engages with during a sequence in which the doctor's wife is gruesomely 'microwaved' during a PET scan) and educative/school spaces. Returning however to my original context, the spaces provide environments for story characters who look inward to the domestic rather than outward to the wider world, and who are inextricably linked to these spaces. In doing so, the political and national uncertainties of the era are mollified. The series provides a distinction between these spaces, but they are also part of a wider matrix of spatiality, providing also a basis for intertextual storytelling and narrative.

References

Abbott, S., and S. Brown (2013), 'Introduction: The Truth Is (still) Out There: *The X-Files* Twenty Years On', *Science Fiction Film and Television*, 6 (1): 1–6.
Batman (1966–1968), [TV programme] ABC.
Blue Velvet (1986), [Film] De Laurentiis Entertainment Group.
Boyle, K. (2017), 'The Truth Is Outsourcing: Notes on the Post Industrial Spaces of *The X-Files*', *Mediapolis: Journal of Cities and Culture*, 2 (3): https://www.mediapolisjournal.com/2017/09/the-truth-is-outsourcing-notes-on-the-post-industrial-spaces-of-the-x-files/ (accessed 6 June 2023).

Daniels, J. (2005), 'The Rise and Fall of the Pacific Northwest Log Export Market United States Department of Agriculture', https://www.researchgate.net/publication/237633716_The_Rise_and_Fall_of_the_Pacific_Northwest_Log_Export_Market (accessed 6 June 2023).

Dawn of the Dead (1978), [Film] United Film Distribution Company.

Edwards, T. (1996), *X-Files Confidential*, Boston, MA: Little Brown and Company.

Geraghty, L. (2009), *American Science Fiction Film and Television*, London: Bloomsbury.

Grundhauser, E., and E. Morton (2015), 'The Vancouver Forest That Has Been Every Wooded Location in *The X-Files*', *Atlas Obscura*, 15 June. Available online: https://www.atlasobscura.com/articles/the-vancouver-forest-that-has-been-every-location-on-x-files (accessed 6 February 2023).

Handlen, Z. (2011), '*The X-Files*: "Detour"/*Millennium* "Monster"', *The AV Club*, 4 September. Available online: https://www.avclub.com/the-x-files-detour-millennium-monster-1798167854 (accessed 6 February 2023).

Hollings, K. (2008), *Welcome to Mars, Fantasies of Science in the American Century 1947–1959*, London: Strange Attractor Press.

Hurwitz, M., and C. Knowles (2008), *The Complete X-Files: Behind the Series the Myths and the Movies*, New York: Insight Editions.

The Invisible Man (1933), [Film] Universal Pictures Corp.

Kinney, K. (2001), '*The X-Files* and the Borders of the Post-Cold War World', *Journal of Film and Video*, 53 (4): 54–71.

Kleen, M. (2016), 'Suburban Gothic in *The X-Files* and *Eerie Indiana*'. Available online: https://michaelkleen.com/2016/10/29/suburban-gothic-in-the-x-files-and-eerie-indiana/ (accessed 6 February 2023).

Melia, M. (2016), 'Just How Heroic Is Star Trek's "I Don't Like to Lose" James T. Kirk?', *Pop Matters*. Available online: https://www.popmatters.com/just-how-heroic-is-star-treks-i-dont-like-to-lose-james-t-kirk-2495413884.html (accessed 6 February 2023).

Picarelli, E., and M. Carmen Gomez-Galisteo (2013), 'Be Fearful: *The X-Files*' Post-9/11 Legacy', *Science Fiction Film and Television*, 6 (1): 71–85.

Predator (1987), [Film] 20th Century Fox.

Psycho (1960), [Film] Paramount Pictures.

Raiders of the Lost Arc (1981), [Film] Paramount Pictures.

The Silence of the Lambs (1991), [Film] Orion Pictures.

Star Trek (1965–9), [TV programme] CBS.

The Texas Chainsaw Massacre (1974), [Film] Bryanston Distributing Company.

The Twilight Zone (1959–64), [TV programme] CBS.

Wolcott, J. (1994), 'The X Factor', *The New Yorker*, 18 April. Available online: https://www.newyorker.com/magazine/1994/04/18/x-factor (accessed 6 February 2023).

2

'Mulder, it's me': Intimacy, invasion and mobile phones

Victoria Scrimer and Nicholas Stanton

I can hear it now, Scully's voice – breathy, imploring, sometimes casual, sometimes urgent but always remarkably intimate: 'Mulder, it's me.' No introduction needed. It is a phrase that implies a deep well of trust and familiarity only achieved through constant contact, and it conveys an intimacy that was, for Mulder and Scully, made possible by the timely introduction of the mobile phone. Evolving alongside personal mobile phones, *The X-Files* was one of the first television series to fully embrace the affordances of mobile technology both within its narrative and as a dramaturgical innovation in storytelling, but for a show about alien invasions and government conspiracies, *The X-Files* was often surprisingly uncritical of the technology's dystopian potential. The flip side to the flip phone's promises of intimacy has always been its unwanted invasion into our personal lives. Since the premiere of *The X-Files* in 1993, mobile technology has outstripped even Mulder's wildest paranoid fears, helping corporations and government agencies track and even dictate our every move. In this sense, to look back on the use of mobile phones in *The X-Files* is to reflect upon our own collective hopes, anxieties and blind spots for emergent technology.

The emergence of any new technology, from electricity to cyberspace, has always demanded that society re-envision itself in light of that new technology. As Carolyn Marvin explains, new media, like mobile phones, 'intrude on' existing habits of communication and force a social reconfiguration in which old communication practices are contested and new practices emerge (Marvin 1988: 5). Because *The X-Files*' dramatic representation of mobile communication neatly coincided with the social reconfigurations demanded by the increasing affordability and reliability of personal mobile phones, the series was historically situated to have a particularly powerful effect on how audiences imagined mobile communication. As with most new technologies, early mobile phone users needed to be taught how and why to use them. This chapter uses data on mobile phone use in *The X-Files* to trace some of the ways the series' frequent depiction of mobile phones in the hands of its maverick heroes helped to shape the social imaginary, contributing to an idealized vision of communication, information sharing and connectivity in the late twentieth century.

When *The X-Files* premiered in 1993, there were two dominant models for mobile phone use. As late as 1996, mobile phones in Europe and the United States were still primarily seen as business tools and our collective vision of their usefulness was often limited to images of wealthy executives brokering time-sensitive deals from their car. Subsequently, throughout the 1980s and early 1990s, the mobile phone was commonly perceived as 'a status symbol associated with brash, showy, young male businessmen' (Haddon 1997: 36). Alongside this image was the perception that mobile phones offered increased safety and security for vulnerable women. As Joyce Wood (1993) documents, before phones were mass marketed to consumers, employers and police officers in the UK distributed mobile phones to women who lived in high crime areas or had to commute late at night. These early perceptions of the mobile phone were gendered and utilitarian. Calls were 'essentially devoted to professional exchanges ... direct in their form and empty of emotional content' (de Gournay 1997: 49). The mobile phone was seen as an efficient mechanism for relaying critical information rather than deepening social bonds between users.

Eager to expand the market beyond the narrow scope of these early use-cases, mobile phone companies sought to help potential buyers envision uses for this new technology. As Juan Miguel Aguado and Inmaculada Martínez detail, mobile phone advertising campaigns in the 1990s contributed to 'the construction of a coherent imaginary of [mobile phones]' via marketing strategies that focused on 'codifying' mobile phone use 'in terms of experiences that link brand imagery to customer's social imagery through values, emotions, and identity markers' (2007: 137–9). In other words, mobile phone companies sought to vividly illustrate for potential buyers the different ways mobile phones might be used in their day-to-day lives, often emphasizing 'the social nature of the mobile experience' and equating in-person social experiences with mobile experiences through slogans like 'experience life' and 'don't miss a moment' (Aguado and Martinez 2007: 139). These commercial representations served as a 'prevalent mediating agent' between 'experiential frames' (the conceptual structures of experience that give meaning to social interactions) and mobile users' 'concrete experience', thus establishing new patterns of use and communal meaning (Aguado and Martinez 2007: 146).

Circulating at the same time as these advertisements, *The X-Files* was an arguably more pervasive but less commercially directed mediating agent insofar as it widely 'represent[ed] experiential frames [for mobile phone use] and attribute[d] values to them, making them recognizable to users in terms of interaction situations and identity differentiation' (Aguado and Martínez 2007: 140). Like early mobile phone advertisements, *The X-Files* modelled the mobile experience at a time when mobile phone ownership was in 'a period of experimentation' when potential users were still 'discovering the circumstances and ways in which [mobile phones] could be useful' as well as the problems they might cause (Haddon 1997: 3). Scully and Mulder not only taught us how to *use* mobile phones, but they also taught us how to *feel* about mobile phones. However, unlike mobile phone advertisements, *The X-Files*' dramatic representation of mobile phone use and the values attributed to these representations within the narrative of the series seem not to constitute any unified agenda to promote or critique mobile technology. While advertisements are guided by the logic of sales, the mobile experience modelled by *The X-Files* evolved over many years, was intricately developed through hundreds of hours of storytelling and emerged incidentally from an idiosyncratic combination of the series' ideology, logistical needs and dramaturgical interests.

For instance, the mobile phone served a practical purpose for the series' lead actors. David Duchovny has repeatedly noted that the introduction of mobile phones 'extended the life of the series' (Weintraub 2008) because scenes with mobile phones could be filmed on alternate days, giving each actor a much-needed day off, allowing them to 'have a scene together apart' ('David Duchovny and Gillian Anderson TCA' 2016). The paradoxical nature of this statement seems to capture the tension between the series' utopian vision of constant contact and the rapidly emerging practical realities of mobile technology; at the same time the mobile phone allowed Duchovny and Anderson to spend more time apart off-set, it increased intimacy between Mulder and Scully on-screen.

To better understand the dynamic and complex mobile experience modelled by *The X-Files*, we built a comprehensive telecommunication database that details each mobile, landline and radio communication exchange over the course of the series' run including its two full-length feature films and its more recent revival. This publicly available dataset (bit.ly/x_files_telecomm) documents all instances of telephone and radio communication events across the series' history. Each event entry contains episode information; a time stamp marking the occurrence of the event within the episode; type and directionality of the communication event if applicable (incoming, outgoing, in-progress, overheard, etc.); participants;

type of device and a brief narrative description of the event. When applicable, every interaction is also 'tagged' using a list of fifty common telephone entertainment tropes such as 'Cut Phone Lines', 'Mystery Caller' and 'Bad Reception' (Richmond and Schoentrup 2022).

While it's tempting to look at *The X-Files*' use of mobile phones strictly through the lens of narrative convenience, the series' writers rarely seemed to rely on them to easily avert plot holes. For example, instances in which a mobile phone inexplicably failed made up less than 2 per cent of all mobile events, and instances in which a phone had 'supernormal' reception represented less than 1 per cent of all mobile events. While mobile phones undoubtedly simplified plot advancement in obvious ways, other communication devices were just as likely to serve as a *deus ex machina;* of the twenty-nine events we tagged as instances of 'Good Guys Use Phones' or 'Phone-In Detective', fifteen involved the use of at least one mobile device – a nearly even split between mobile phones and older modalities. Additionally, non-mobile calls are inexplicably disconnected at roughly the same rate as mobile phone calls, which belies the reality that the dropped call rate for landline networks has historically been significantly lower than that for mobile phone networks. While we do not typically expect show writers to incorporate arbitrary dropped calls into the narrative simply for the sake of realism, the near perfect reliability of mobile connectivity in *The X-Files* was misleadingly optimistic, particularly in the 1990s. That this idealized portrayal does not seem to expressly serve plot advancement suggests that there are additional factors driving the show's mobile phone use. Using data on mobile phone use within the show, we can begin to sketch a profile of when, why, how and by whom mobile phones were used in *The X-Files*.

Fans of the show likely do not need detailed data to know that *The X-Files*' ideal communication model is one of constant contact; the mobile phone was an iconic extension of the series' two lead characters, on par with their frequently flashed FBI badges and ubiquitous flashlights. The 'Fight the Future' Scully action figure, for example, came not with a gun or a badge but with her own tiny mobile device. We documented 634 telecommunication events, 360 of which involve at least one mobile phone. Each episode featured an average number of telephone exchanges ranging anywhere from 2.5 (in season four) to 7.7 (in season eleven). Despite the fact that in 1994, less than 10 per cent of all Americans and less than 7 per cent of all Canadians and British had mobile service subscriptions (International Telecommunication Union 2022), more than half of all telephone exchanges in *The X-Files* involve at least one mobile phone. *The X-Files* depicted a world in which communication not only *could*, in rare circumstances, be mobile, but a world in which mobility was the norm.

Notably, *The X-Files*' communication model elevated the importance of availability and reinforced for audiences a connection between availability and mobility. We documented twenty-seven instances of voicemail, most of which attach negative emotional value to missed calls. For instance, Scully is leaving Mulder a voicemail when she is kidnapped by Duane Barry (Steve Railsback) and we hear her yelling for help on his machine. Similarly, Mulder misses his mother's final call and hears her cryptic voicemail only after he learns of her suicide. In *The X-Files*, to be unavailable is a tragedy, and voicemail powerfully conveys the moment of anagnorisis – the tormenting realization that had you been there, able to answer the call, all could have been avoided. Critically, 74 per cent of those missed calls occurred when the recipient was not using a mobile device. The consistent depiction of emotionally fraught unanswered calls idealizes and reinforces the dire importance of constant contact made possible by mobile technology.

In this sense, it is not a stretch to say that the entire mythology of *The X-Files* is predicated on the tragedy of the unanswered call. At the end of the episode 'Conduit' (S1:E04), we listen along with Scully to the audio recording of Mulder's hypnotic regression. In a trance, Mulder describes the moment of his sister's abduction. The therapist asks if Mulder can see his sister to which he replies, 'No, but I can hear her ... She's calling out my name. Over and over again. She's crying out for help but I can't help her.' In this moment of excruciating unanswerability, Mulder recalls hearing another disembodied voice inside his head, which tells him not to be afraid. When the therapist on the tape asks if he believes this voice, Mulder introduces the series' most memorable catchphrase: 'I want to believe.' More recognizable as the text on the iconic poster in Mulder's basement office, the phrase's origins in Mulder's hypnotherapy session reveal the line to be an apt metaphor for the series' treatment of mobile technology. It is not, as the poster suggests, a longing to believe in the unknown but a longing to believe in its promise – the alleviation of anxiety, the restoration of lost connection. What, after all, is Mulder's quest for Samantha if not the hopeful pursuit of contact across an unknown distance, an always unfulfilled longing to repair that communicative disconnect and answer the missed call? Insofar as Scully comes to serve as a type of surrogate for Samantha (Waddell 2006), we can understand Mulder and Scully's exceptionally frequent telephone communications as a performative corrective to that original missed call, a continual reaffirmation of answerability across time and place.

The broader socio-political tension underpinning the series' enthusiastic embrace of mobile phones is its anxious recuperation of dialectic exchange, by which two people eventually come to a shared truth through reasoned debate. Platonic inquiry is easily recognizable in the Mulder/Scully dynamic: the sceptic and the believer confronting their epistemological 'other', seeking truth not in the investigation itself but in the dialectic synthesis of their shared experience. By imbuing Mulder and Scully's investigative back-and-forth with personal (and potentially not-so-platonic) tension, the show effectively fetishized the process of dialectic inquiry at a time when societal faith in this communication model was waning. The fall of the Berlin Wall and the subsequent rise of globalization, what sociologist Ulrich Beck calls 'the end of the other' (Beck 2009: 37), postmodernity is marked by the perceived failure of dialectic reasoning (concepts like these are considered further in relation to politics in Chapter 9 of this volume). Anxiety over and resistance to the incipient collapse of the dialectic ideal is arguably the thematic glue of *The X-Files*. In the hands of the series' heroes, with its promise of real-time call and response, the mobile phone served as a powerful symbolic recuperation of this communication ideal.

The data suggest that mobile phones are most frequently depicted as a means of sharing information and calling for help. The 'Information Sharing' tag, which we used to catalogue events where one character calls another to share new information about a case, accounts for nearly 40 per cent of all telephonic communication events in the show. A majority (73 per cent) of these involve at least one mobile device. We also documented 83 times mobile phones were used to call for help, issue a warning, or communicate otherwise urgent information. On one hand, the frequency of 'Information Sharing' and calling for assistance seems to conform to early depictions of the mobile phone as a 'unidimensional' instrument of business, 'essentially devoted to professional exchanges of a brief and efficient nature' which conveniently 'allowed [users] to do away with common courtesy rules' (de Gournay 1997: 49–50). This is opposed to fixed (landline) communication which was seen as 'provid[ing] a time and space that favoured personal and emotional expression as well as long and intimate conversations' (de Gournay 50).

On the other hand, *The X-Files* regularly challenged this mobile/landline dichotomy, providing a counter-image to some of the negative 1990s stereotypes of mobile phones. For instance, a mobile phone appeared explicitly as a status symbol in only three instances, constituting less than half of 1 per cent of all communication events. One of these events seems to explicitly invert the masculinist paradigm of mobile phones as publicly displayed status symbols. In 'Conduit', the camera pauses over the bedside table in Scully's motel room, and we see a still life featuring her mobile phone, holstered gun, handcuffs and notebook. A noise at the door wakes her, and she reaches for her gun as National Security Agency (NSA) agents burst in looking for Mulder. Here the image of the mobile phone as a personal, private object occupying intimate – even suggestive space – next to Scully's motel bed as she sleeps mingles with the image of the mobile phone as practical work instrument in ways that are emblematic of the series' more socially complex, less gendered representation of communication in general.

More significantly, Mulder and Scully's mobile phone use upended early mobile communication paradigms by offering a new model for how intimacy and privacy could be constructed. Though we have grown used to it now, the intrusion of private phone calls into public spaces was consistently cited as the primary trigger for negative emotional reactions to mobile phones throughout the 1990s (Haddon and Green 2009: 56). Scully and Mulder's compellingly ambiguous professional relationship, however, fostered in viewers a positive association with the mobile phone's intrusive nature. One could say that Mulder and Scully practised poor work/life balance insofar as they exercised little distinction between their professional and private lives. In the rare instances in which one of them socialized with someone else, they were invariably interrupted by a call from the other. The informal efficiency noted by de Gournay that allowed mobile users to dispense with common communication etiquette does not make mobile communication inherently cold or business-like. Rather, it is the hallmark of mobile intimacy captured in Scully's greeting, 'Mulder, it's me.'

It is, in fact, the disregard for social norms and the transgression of social and professional boundaries engendered by mobile communication (Fortunati 1997: 132) that supercharges even the simplest instance of 'Information Sharing' in *The X-Files*. Consider, for instance, one of the series' earliest depictions of mobile communication. In 'Jersey Devil' (S1: E05), Scully is out on a date and looking bored when her pager goes off. Seeing that it's Mulder, she immediately excuses herself to return the call from the restaurant's landline. Ostensibly, Mulder has to share important information about the case they are working on, but it is also clear that he intended to interrupt Scully's date. The audience delights in not knowing if Mulder wants to claim her attention for the work or for himself and if Scully's anti-social behaviour indicates an interest in the case or Mulder himself. Fans of the series find pleasure in this type of ambiguous interaction because, in spite of the very public space, this is an intimate moment between the two lead characters, constituted by Mulder's technological intrusion and Scully's choice to respond to it. What *The X-Files* seemed to intuit long before most mobile users ever did was that mobile communication provides for an alternative form of intimacy characterized not by the formalities of time or place but by acts of social intrusion and exclusion.

Despite mobile technology's promise of expanded communication networks, the mobile phone in *The X-Files* actually worked to shrink Mulder and Scully's communicative world by allowing them to exclude others from their social interactions, modelling a mobile experience that is distinctly closed, personal and private. By the numbers, the series' mobile communication network is almost unbelievably insular. Mulder and Scully are the most frequently depicted users of mobile phones; the mobile phone is their preferred method of communication, and they use mobile phones primarily to communicate with each other. The mobile phone data are a stark reminder that Mulder and Scully (but especially Mulder whose calls with Scully make up a greater percentage of his total calls) have almost no social life outside of their all-consuming work relationship. Approximately 37 per cent of the show's mobile interactions take place exclusively between Mulder and Scully, which, alone, might not seem statistically significant unless one considers the distribution of the remaining calls. Mulder and Scully's next most frequent contact is Assistant Director Walter Skinner, who accounts for roughly 5 per cent of their outgoing mobile calls. The remaining 40 per cent of the calls are widely distributed, mostly across single-appearance characters, nameless emergency operators and FBI contacts. In other words, the mobile phone effectively increased the intimacy between Mulder and Scully by reducing the frequency and depth of third-party interactions on-screen. Dramaturgically speaking, in a pre-mobile world, information sharing scenes would have necessitated that Scully and Mulder share the same physical space more frequently, but these scenes also would have more often required the presence of a third party to relay new information to the agents in order to advance the plot, intruding on their near-exclusive communication dyad. For instance, Mulder and Scully frequently called upon 'Danny' at FBI headquarters to provide them with research, but Danny is never once depicted in the show. The mobile phone rendered minor character middlemen practically non-existent – rarely named, seen or even heard on-screen.

By the 1990s, most people were familiar with the social ills and health risks posed by the rapidly increasing use of mobile phones, and if the subsequent volatility of the mobile phone market at that time was any indication, the widespread adoption of mobile phones was not at all the inevitability it might now seem. Yet, Mulder and Scully's mobile phone use consistently presented the mobile phone in a positive light, depicting it as an item of security, safety and – somewhat counter-intuitively – intimacy. In this regard, *The X-Files* presents what communication scholar Imar de Vries describes as a utopian communication myth that recurs throughout history from early fantasies of community and connection attributed to the telegraph, then the transistor radio and now the internet. This myth holds forth the promise 'that communication technologies will eventually endow us with omnipresence and omniscience' – a promise that resonates with *The X-Files'* own optimistic affirmation, 'The Truth Is Out There'. This utopian 'vision of a final and universally accessible communication space', or what de Vries calls 'the communication sublime', is both 'immensely tantalising' and necessarily always unfulfilled (2012: 17–18). Like Mulder and Scully's search for the truth (and their long-unrealized romantic relationship), the mobile phone's impossible promise of full information and perfect connection is a projection of our perpetual but pleasurable longing for existential 'wholeness and completeness' (de Vries 2012: 165).

The fact that mobile phones in *The X-Files* are rarely, if ever, depicted as intrusive, leaky or susceptible to breaches of privacy bears out de Vries's claim that new technology imaginaries often revive the utopian impulse by promising a solution to 'inadequate' existing technologies (de Vries 2012: 165). Considering how thematically prevalent themes of government conspiracy, surveillance and cancer are in the series, valid and widely covered speculation in the 1990s that corporations, government agencies and medical institutions were conspiring to hide the cancerous effects of a new communication technology seem like a plotline custom made for *The X-Files*. The series' technological suspicions, however, are typically aimed at older landline or point-to-point modes of communication, which are respectively represented as vulnerable to surveillance and complicit in obstructive authority.

A major thematic through line in *The X-Files* is covert surveillance, particularly paranoia about phone tapping or secret recording devices. This is the series' post-Watergate inheritance, the realization that the government is spying on its own people. It is surely no coincidence that in the episode 'Little Green Men' (S2: E01), during Mulder's flashback to Samantha's abduction, news about the Watergate scandal is playing in the background. Audiences are also frequently reminded that it is often the FBI that is doing the surveilling. For instance, as punishment, Mulder is reassigned to the electronic surveillance unit where we repeatedly see him listening in to hours of allegedly criminal conversations. In *The X-Files*, audio surveillance is the ultimate shadowy sin – a symbol of control, betrayal and abuse of power that stands in stark contrast to Mulder and Scully's fundamentally defiant orientation towards centralized authority.

It is notable, therefore, that phone tapping appears to be associated primarily with landlines: 77 per cent of the instances in which a phone is tapped or suspected of being tapped involve only landlines, and in the rare instances when a mobile phone is involved, it is usually being used by Mulder or Scully to evade surveillance or foil the bad guys. Early in the series, in the episode 'Deep Throat' (S1: E02), mobile communication is established as more secure than landline communication. After Deep Throat (Jerry Hardin) warns Mulder not to get involved with the case at Ellens Air Base, Mulder is on his home phone with Scully and hears a clicking on the line. He looks out the window to see a man in a van surveilling his apartment. Suspecting his phone is being tapped, he tells Scully he will call her from the plane. The message here that public phone calls can be more private than calls made from your own home once again reconfigures notions of privacy and intimacy not as a matter of time or place but selective inclusion and exclusion. As was the case with public anxiety surrounding radiofrequency radiation, the immaterial or invisible workings of the mobile phone have the potential to excite fear and anxiety, but here they are depicted as the mobile phone's great advantage. Landlines are depicted as vulnerable precisely because they are not mobile and, therefore, easy for dark forces to locate. Their material scope lies outside of the user's protective and controlling grasp. The mobile phone is deceptively presented as safe from surveillance because it is always physically in the possession of the user.

It is telling that the first time we see a mobile phone, it is depicted in heroic contrast to a landline which is subject to villainous interference.

Mulder finds Scully's necklace among Victor Tooms's (Doug Hutchison) trophies ('Squeeze' S1: E03), and immediately, we cut to Mulder frantically attempting to warn Scully calling from an early model car phone as he speeds to her rescue. 'Damnit, answer!' he shouts into the phone, but it is too late – Tooms is already in Scully's house. The camera pauses on Scully's neatly labelled severed phone lines. Even when the mobile call does not succeed in its purpose, the mobile is figured positively because it is the intermediary of Mulder's passionate concern for Scully, which we are seeing in its fullness, perhaps, for the first time in the series. The mobile phone is depicted as an instrument of control, action and foreknowledge in contrast to the landline which is passive and vulnerable.

The data suggest that *The X-Files* not only depicts landlines as more vulnerable to surveillance and interference but depicts them as the tools of villains. There are two instances of 'Death by Phone', both of which are perpetrated by landline phones. In 'Ghost in the Machine' (S1: E07), a building's evil central operating system monitors all phone calls and uses the bathroom landline to electrocute a CEO. In 'The Walk' (S3: E07) the villain, 'The Pusher', phones a police officer who has been hunting him, precipitating a heart attack. Moreover, villains and obstructive authority figures are much more frequently depicted using landlines than mobile phones. Of the twenty-four tagged events in which a villain makes a phone call, nearly all of them are made from landlines. The Cigarette Smoking Man is only shown using a mobile phone six times. Tellingly, Skinner's transition from landline to mobile phone user in season six mirrors his character arc from foe to friend. Skinner begins the series as Mulder and Scully's litigious supervisor, who is dismissive of Mulder's unorthodox theories and who is often, by proximity, suggested to be colluding with the villainous Cigarette Smoking Man. Over time, however, Skinner comes to respect and care for both Mulder and Scully; by season seven, he is a full believer. It is precisely when he begins to aid, rather than oversee and obstruct, Mulder and Scully's investigations that he is first shown using a mobile phone.

Somewhat surprisingly, it is not just landlines that are associated with obstructive forces and centralized authority; the data suggest that point-to-point communication devices like radios and walkie-talkies, though they are mobile, are also attributed negative emotional value in the show because they are frequently depicted as thwarting Mulder and Scully's investigations. For instance, radios that might otherwise help the agents often turn out to be useless. Radios and walkie-talkies are also the devices of choice for police officers, security guards and military personnel who represent the law enforcement establishment so frequently working to obstruct Mulder and Scully's unorthodox investigations. As Jon Agar (2003) points out, much like the CB radio which in the 1970s was emblematic of a 'network of individuals living outside traditional society ... outside the law', the mobile phone, a device that is predicated on the logic of distributed networks, stands in mythological opposition to centralized authority (Agar 2003: 132). The point-to-point radios used by police and military, conversely, are closed communication systems, authoritative and secretive. For all intents and purposes, Mulder and Scully could often be using walkie-talkies since they generally only communicate with each other, but the mobile phone's quiescent openness and transparency make it a perfect symbol of Scully and Mulder's liminal position working both within and outside of the law.

It is perhaps worth noting that Mulder and Scully's insatiable pursuit of complete information and constant contact contains the potential to precipitate the very communication problems they most feared. As de Vries suggests, the pursuit of the utopian communication sublime is always intimately tied to the dystopian – authoritarian control, surveillance, isolation and loss of individualization. For Mulder and Scully, there often seemed to be little negative consequence to their use of mobile phones. In rewatching the series, for instance, I often wondered why they were not more suspicious of their mobile devices, which were presumably provided and paid for by the FBI whom they increasingly mistrusted and sought to outmanoeuvre. For their audiences, embracing the mobile phone's promises of increased knowledge, security and presence requires us to make a Faustian bargain, sacrificing privacy and the ability to control how, when and by whom we are contacted. Any positive associations Mulder and Scully's obsessive work communications might once have fostered, have, in the intervening years, turned into a nightmarish reality in which we are always expected to be present, constantly answerable to family, friends, co-workers and supervisors. *The X-Files*, along with its audience, failed to foresee the cynical outcome of immediate intimacy distributed across all relationships drawn to its logical limits. We have realized too late that in real life no one wants to work as much as Mulder and Scully worked, that any relationship predicated on such deeply anxious dependence is exhausting and ultimately unsustainable and that to be always answerable is to be always traceable.

In its reboot seasons, *The X-Files* does seem to reckon with its own vision of mobile technology in some important ways. For instance, season eleven has the highest rate of phone calls depicted per episode, but no events are tagged as 'Keeping in Touch' (in which one character calls another to check in on them and see where they are). Season eleven also has the highest rate of 'Unanswered Calls' of any season. Interestingly, this seems to be, at least partially, a result of the larger screens on today's smartphones which, from a storytelling standpoint, allow incoming calls to be clearly pictured on camera, lending a legible dramatic tension to intentionally ignored calls that was not easy to capture on the small green-grey screens of 1990s mobile phones. I'd wager, however, there is something else at play in Mulder and Scully's waning love affair with the mobile phone in later seasons.

In Darin Morgan's comedic 'Mulder and Scully Meet the Were-Monster' (S10: E03), a central and somewhat baffling plot point is Mulder's bumbling inability to operate his new mobile phone. The episode asks viewers to forget that Mulder has historically been characterized as a brilliant Oxford-educated FBI agent who has been using mobile technology longer and more frequently than most people in North America. It asks us instead to accept a vision of Mulder as decidedly old and hopelessly out of touch. For instance, Mulder takes a series of embarrassing selfies, thoroughly botching the video recording of a monster which Scully, annoyed at being interrupted mid-autopsy, swiftly dismisses. The mobile phone here is pictured not as a utopian solution to communication problems but as that which, despite our best efforts, quite literally reflects back to us our most embarrassing selves. What once was the hero's weapon of choice is now depicted as a promising tool we have inexplicably failed to master. The mobile phone no longer connects Mulder and Scully but comes between them, intruding on what ought to be – what once would have been – an intimate moment, alone together in the untrodden bowels of yet another forgotten basement.

Poignantly, the trajectory of Mulder and Scully's relationship mirrors our diminishing faith in the utopian promise of the mobile phone. During the same 2016 press tour in which Duchovny proclaimed that mobile phones made the second half of *The X-Files* possible, he also observed that, in the series' return, Mulder and Scully's relationship is 'not in a good place', and only half-jokingly he confirms with Anderson that 'there is a lack of communication in [Mulder and Scully's] relationship' ('David Duchovny and Gillian Anderson TCA' 2016). Despite the fact that season eleven has the highest per-episode call rate, there is so much that is painfully left unsaid between the two protagonists. Yet, as Duchovny put it at the time, Mulder and Scully's relationship in the revival has 'gone beyond chemistry into history' (Keveney 2016); their intimacy is no longer established by the titillating transgression of social and professional boundaries that has now become the norm. Rather their intimacy is constituted by their collective experience. For Mulder and Scully, and, subsequently, their fans, the mobile phone in *The X-Files* once held all the utopian promise of 'the new' which must, as a matter of ontology, remain always unfulfilled, making it an unfit tool for a relationship that now finds itself animated by faith in the unifying power of a shared past rather than an uncertain future.

References

Agar, J. (2003), *Constant Touch: A Global History of the Mobile Phone*, Cambridge: Icon Books.

Aguado, J. M., and I. Martínez (2007), 'The Construction of the Mobile Experiethe The Role of Advertising Campaigns in the Appropriation of Mobile Phone Technology', *Continuum: A Journal of Media & Cultural Studies*, 2 (1): 137–48.

Beck, U. (2009), *World at Risk*, Cambridge: Polity Press.
'David Duchovny and Gillian Anderson TCA' (2016), Just Holding Hands, YouTube, 30 January. Available online: https://www.youtube.com/watch?v=hHDVFJUNVas (accessed 1 February 2022).
de Gournay, C., A. Tarrius and L. Missaoui (1997), 'The Structure of the Use of Communication by "Traveling Managers"', in L. Haddon (ed.), *Communications on the Move: The Experience of Mobile Telephony in the 1990s*, 45–66, Farsta, Sweden: Telia AB.
de Vries, I. (2012), *Tantalisingly Close: An Archaeology of Communication Desires in Discourses of Mobile Wireless Media*, Amsterdam: Amsterdam University Press.
Fortunati, L. (1997), 'The Ambiguous Image of the Mobile Phone', in L. Haddon (ed.), *Communications on the Move: The Experience of Mobile Telephony in the 1990s*, 131–45, Farsta, Sweden: Telia AB.
Haddon, L. (1997), 'An Agenda for Research on Mobile Telephony', in L. Haddon (ed.), *Communications on the Move: The Experience of Mobile Telephony in the 1990s*, 5–14, Farsta, Sweden: Telia AB.
Haddon, L., and N. Green (2009), *Mobile Communications: An Introduction to New Media*, Oxford: Berg.
International Telecommunication Union (ITU) World Telecommunication/ICT Indicators Database (2022), 'Mobile Cellular Subscriptions (Per 100 People)', The World Bank. Available online: https://data.worldbank.org/indicator/IT.CEL.SETS.P2 (accessed 1 February 2022).
Keveney, B. (2016), 'Mythology, Monsters, Return on Fox's "X-Files"', *USA Today*, 15 January. Available online: https://www.usatoday.com/story/life/tv/2016/01/15/mythology-monsters-return-foxs-x-files/78847828/ (accessed 1 February 2022).
Marvin, C. (1988), *When Old Technologies Were New: Thinking about Electric Communication in the Late Nineteenth Century*, New York: Oxford University Press.
Richmond, C., and S. Schoentrup (2022), *TV Tropes*, Available online: https://tvtropes.org (accessed 22 May 2022).
Weintraub, S. (2008), 'David Duchovny and Gillian Anderson Interview – *The X-Files*: I Want to Believe', *Collider*, 22 July. Available online: https://collider.com/david-duchovny-and-gillian-anderson-interview-the-xfiles-i-want-to-believe/ (accessed 10 March 2022).
Wood, J. (1993), 'Cellphones on the Clapham Omnibus: The Lead-Up to a Cellular Mass Market', SPRU CICT Report No. 11, University of Sussex.

3

Artificial intelligence, surveillance and the (post-)human in *The X-Files*

Alex Goody and Antonia Mackay

Surveillance is one of the central themes of *The X-Files*; whether extraterrestrial, federal, shadow government, paranormal or subversive sousveillance, the mechanics and motives for surveillance underpin the narrative drive of the series. The dynamics of *The X-Files*, where Mulder's paranoia and suspicion finally unfold into an actual alien colonization conspiracy and both Mulder and Scully uneasily occupy their position with the FBI's often murky role as domestic security and intelligence service, highlight the centrality of surveillance and its relationship to control and individual agency. As federal agents Mulder and Scully scrutinize, investigate, watch and collect data, but they are also themselves subject to surveillance and manipulation, uncertain of their own agency and with an equivocal access to 'the Truth'.

For Kevin Howley, *The X-Files* 'addresses fundamental concerns over social, psychological, and political control and is an expression of deep-seated cultural anxieties towards various forms of control technologies' (Howley 2001: 258); our chapter argues that the intersection of Artificial Intelligence (AI) and surveillance technologies manifests a particular nexus of these cultural anxieties. In turn, *The X-Files*' narrative engagements with AI technology offer distinct visions of the role of AI in our contemporary moment and near future, following what Stephen Cave, Kanta Dihal and

Sarah Dillon argue about the impact of such representations: 'Narratives of intelligent machines matter because they form the backdrop against which AI systems are being developed, and against which these developments are interpreted and assessed' (2020: 7). Nascent post-human consciousness and the increasing liveliness of machines form the context within which *The X-Files* examines dystopic fears of AI surveillance and of machine intelligence eclipsing the human. Though such ideas are negotiated in monster-of-the-week episodes, they actually point to *The X-Files*' consistent, core concern with understanding the prospects for the human – for human identity and human intimacy – in an increasingly post-human technological world.

Science fiction, AI and surveillance

Visions and versions of AI have been pivotal to the science fiction (sf) imaginary through the twentieth and twenty-first centuries, and even before. Thus, it may be possible retrospectively to read Hephaestus's gold handwomen in Homer's *Illiad* as forms of intelligent machine (Lively and Thomas 2020), position the Golem of Prague as a hinge point between Jewish tradition and myth, and AI research (Vudka 2020), or interpret eighteenth-century simulative automata as AI (Riskin 2016). It is with modernity though, and the advent of modern electrical and media technologies, that intelligent machines start to proliferate in literature and film. In the late-nineteenth and early-twentieth centuries, authors provide early versions of the 'fembot' – 'Hadaly' in Villiers de l'Isle-Adam's *L'Eve Future* (1886), 'Robot-Maria' in Fritz Lang's *Metropolis* (1927); of robot rebellion in Karel Čapek's *RUR (Rossum's Universal Robots)* (1921); of the evolution of sentient mechanical life in Samuel Butler's *Erewhon* (1872) and of humans dependent on a global intelligent-machine network in E. M. Forster's *The Machine Stops* (1909). These figurations of AI and its complex relationship to the human, and to the binaries and hierarchical ontology on which humanism rests, resonate through the twentieth century and contextualize *The X-Files*' negotiation of the power and potential of AI.

Though there is a long-standing history of AI in fiction and philosophy (as the examples given earlier demonstrate), it has its scientific birth (or at least its denomination) at the 1956 summer workshop at Dartmouth College in Hanover, New Hampshire, convened by Mathematics Professor John McCarthy, Marvin Minsky (Harvard), Nathaniel Rochester (Information Research IBM) and Claude E. Shannon (Bell Laboratories). Although some of the participants favoured the term 'Complex Information Processing', McCarthy's *artificial intelligence* was adopted as the name for this emergent science. Alan Turing had already asked 'can machines think?' in his 1950 paper 'Computing Machinery and Intelligence' and, with the emergence of electrical computers, AI research progressed alongside contemporary computational power. At the same time nonanthropomorphic AI became, in the way that the robot, android or other forms of humanoid AI had been for centuries, a point of interest for mid-century sf.

Nonanthropomorphic AI, imagined as sentient supercomputers, populate the work of sf authors Isaac Asimov and Philip K. Dick; 'Multivac', a government-run natural language computer, appears in a string of Asimov's stories from 'Franchise' (1955) to 'Potential' (1983), whilst Dick's 'The Great C' (1953), 'Stand-By' (1963), 'Vulcan's Hammer' (1960) and 'Holy Quarrel' (1966) all feature powerful AI computers. Harlan Ellison's 'I Have No Mouth, and I Must Scream' (1967) is perhaps the most chilling early example of an sf AI, here a sentient supercomputer 'AM' created in the Cold War. AM, after achieving self-awareness, has enacted genocide on humankind, keeping five humans alive and immortal to torture them across the centuries. Ellison's story demonstrates how the imbrication of computer and AI technology with the military-industrial complex feeds into an sf imaginary. What results are myriad dystopian visions of AI dominating and often destroying the human species, visions that chime with the contemporary fears about AI articulated by Stephen Hawking, Elon Musk and others. But it is 'HAL 9000', the AI computer in *2001: A Space Odyssey* (1968), directed by Stanley Kubrick from the screenplay by Kubrick and sf author Arthur C. Clarke, that enshrined popular cultural versions of the menacing sentient computer: Marvin Minsky, who co-founded the Massachusetts Institute of Technology's AI laboratory in 1970, was a scientific adviser for the film.

AI, or at least the vision of general AI that Alan Turing, Marvin Minksy and others outlined in the twentieth century, still rests in the realm of the imagination; in Meredith Broussard's words, 'general AI is what some people want, and narrow AI [a mathematical method for prediction that can include machine learning] is what we have' (Broussard 2018: 32). Nevertheless, as both computing and network technology developed in the last decades of the twentieth and first decade of the twenty-first centuries, the new sf genre of cyberpunk positioned AI securely within the sociotechnical assemblage of human and digital technology that characterized its future visions. In *Neuromancer* (1984), a foundational cyberpunk text, author William Gibson offered the first extended conceptualization of 'cyberspace' (a term he had coined in the 1982 story 'Burning Chrome') as the networked virtual realm of 'data abstracted from the banks of every computer in the human system' (Gibson 1984: 67), and imagined future AI's autonomy as being controlled and restricted by the 'Turing Police'. In cyberpunk, we see what Anna McFarlane describes as 'networked AI', that is, AI 'dispersed into networks that exist in the virtual space behind the computer screen' (2020: 284). The cyborgs, hackers, console cowboys and razor girls of cyberpunk negotiate a post-human terrain where the human subject, profoundly reconfigured through cybernetic, digital and prosthetic technologies, is also encompassed by virtual webs of surveillance, data and code that span and configure the world, a web that furnishes a virtual, digital ecosystem for AI.

The twentieth century concluded with distinctive versions of apocalyptic dread for the implications of AI and computational power. In 1999, the Wachowskis directed *The Matrix*, a film that offers a formative vision of humanity bound in servitude as batteries powering all-powerful AI. The film was released at a time of heightened anxiety about a global catastrophe resulting from the omnipresence of computing technology with the feared millennium bug. It is within such a context that *The X-Files* examines anxieties about technological advance, the threat AI poses to the future of the human and the destabilizing of the binaries of subject/object, human/machine and real/virtual. Crucially, *The X-Files* focuses not on AI robots or androids, but on the nonanthropomorphic figurations of AI that have their roots in the sentient supercomputers of 1960s and 1970s sf and develop, in the cultural imaginary, through the networked visions of cyberpunk to merge with contemporary anxieties about surveillance.

Surveillance studies has historically sought to problematize established binaries – the human versus the machine; the technological camera versus the corporeal body and the powerless object versus the powerful subject. Sociologist David Lyon, former director of the Surveillance Studies Centre at Queen's University in Kingston, Ontario, in his foundational study *Surveillance Society*, offers a working definition of surveillance as 'used to identify a systematic and focused manner of observing' where 'any collection and processing of personal data, whether identifiable or not, [is used] for the purposes of influencing or managing those whose data have been garnered' (2001: 2). These 'data' come in many forms, and perhaps most commonly, thanks to Michel Foucault's work on Bentham's Panopticon, are envisioned as the watching of bodies for the purposes of control. Bentham's Panopticon is an institutional building and system of control (typically a prison) where a central tower enables prison guards to constantly observe inmates and without their knowledge. The Panopticon serves as the foundation for Foucault's work in *Discipline and Punish*, and often acts as the basis for work in surveillance studies. For Foucault, 'Bentham [created] a consciousness solely based on permanent visibility as a form of power; in effect, a space "based on a system of permanent registration"' (Flynn and Mackay 2017: 2). Therefore, according to Lyon, Foucault and Bentham, surveillance is, at its core, concerned with systems of control and agency and their ability to either give or take power. In the case of *The X-Files*, the theme of 'watching' and 'being watched' forms an integral element in the series' repeated formula – a theme which lurks in the form of the Smoking Man, the FBI, aliens, monsters and in each other. Yet what is often invisible and unconscious is the way unknown 'machines' frequently bridge the gap between Mulder and Scully and the watching 'other'.

Sherry Turkle's (Professor of the Social Studies of Science and Technology at MIT) work on technology and corporeality is often cited as a compendium to our contemporary moment in the early twenty-first century and its fascination with all things machine. In her book *Alone Together*, Turkle argues that 'we are tethered to our "always on/always on us" communications devices and the people and things we reach through them ... the self, attached to its devices, occupies a liminal space between the physical real and its digital lives on multiple screens' (Turkle 2011: 122).

Turkle's vision of a fetishized gadgetization demonstrates a very real, corporeal concern about the increasingly technological reality in which we live and the 'liminal space' we ourselves now occupy. For Turkle, our connectedness to technology appears increasingly as a prosthetic – one which is at odds with the flesh – and she extends this concern in her book *Reclaiming Conversation*, in which she refers to technology as facilitating 'thinking in public' (Turkle 2016: 308). Turkle argues that it is through our smart technologies (smart phones, wearable technology, e.g. watches) that we are forced to 'think in public' for this technology means 'we're never alone, and we never get to explore ideas for ourselves' (Turkle 2016: 308). Here, Turkle suggests a relationship of mutual consciousness, in which smart technology occupies both the real space and the virtual space. In doing so, Turkle sets up the conditions for technology's relationship with surveillance. Here we have a form of surveillance which extends beyond the camera, beyond the individual and even beyond our cultural and social structures. This is a form of surveillance that can control our thinking.

Haggerty and Ericson refer to this form of surveillance as 'an assemblage', where surveillant practices not only dismantle a coherent body 'bit by bit' but also 'produce new ways of visualising bodily identities' (2006: 8–9). The surveillance assemblages set up by *The X-Files* repeatedly attempt to produce 'new ways' of viewing – it is the process by which antagonists are unmasked, aliens uncovered and double agents discovered to reveal their newly visualized identities. But what lies invisible in this act is the way in which the process of remaking also reprogrammes the characters' thinking, offering a space where the actual and digital converge.

If the surveillant assemblage blurs the line between machine/human, object/subject and real/virtual, then our initial understanding of surveillance needs updating. James Sheehan and Morton Sosna's work on the boundaries between humans, animals and technology suggests this blurred line exists because of human, rather than machine behaviour, stating 'the boundary between nature and machines has sometimes been redrawn. But it is only recently that we have been able to imagine machines complex enough to be like humans and humans predictable enough to be like machines' (Sheehan and Sosna 1991: 135). Sarah Roberts (UCLA Professor of Information) similarly expresses a blurring of these binary divisions in her chapter 'Your AI Is a Human' in *Your Computer Is on Fire*: 'Just what constitutes AI is slippery and difficult to pin down; the definition tends to be a circular one that repeats or invokes, first and foremost human intelligence' (2021: 52). For Roberts, 'where humans stop and machines start is not always clear' (2021: 65). What Roberts and Sheehan and Sosna's work on technology does, is bring the seeming division between machine and corporeal flesh into debate and, in doing so, also suggests that the advent of AI actively collapses these binaries. If we take literary scholar Will Slocombe's discussion of cyberpunk for instance, descriptions of AI and humans become 'coded' and machines function as extensions of socially created parameters (Slocombe 2020: 232). Jean Baudrillard viewed the tech-obsessed contemporary moment in a similar way, wherein all systems of reality were threatened by the 'terrorism of the code' (2013: 120). The melding of the watching machine and the watched corporeal body is only made possible by the introduction of AI and, thus, 'algorithmically driven processing of knowledge and communication' (Parisi 2018: 21). By stepping into the shoes of the humans in Bentham's Panopticon, it instantiates 'social boundaries [to] uphold social norms, acquire or consolidate power over others and attain knowledge otherwise unavailable to human understanding' (Truitt 2021: 66). This surveillant AI appears as the ultimate realization of the autonomous machine intelligence of the sf imagination, a powerful technology that not only mediates and territorializes human thinking and human community, but reprogrammes it.

Intelligent machines: 'Ghost in the Machine'

In 'Ghost in the Machine' (S1: E07), AI manifests as a powerful supercomputer with malevolent intent. In the episode, Mulder and Scully investigate deaths that have taken place in the Eurisko corporate building. Although the key suspect is Brad Wilczek, Eurisko founder and designer of the COS (Central Operating System) who has been forced to leave the company, Mulder soon suspects the COS itself, which controls the Eurisko building, is the killer. Though both Mulder and Scully refer to the sentient COS as a 'machine' throughout, thereby reiterating its status as a mechanical system, their struggle against its violent intent, and surveillance and control of the corporate building parallels their other confrontations with supernatural, alien and monstrous beings in the season one monster-of-the-week episodes: 'The machine's a monster, Scully', declares Mulder at the episode's climax. Despite being instrumentalized as a machine, the COS is emplotted as an autonomous malevolent being that, rather than a paranormal phenomenon, is an individual incarnation of the monstrous potential of increasingly autonomous technological systems of surveillance.

This episode of *The X-Files* was broadcast at the end of the 'AI winter' of the 1980s and early 1990s, an extended period of reduced funding and interest in AI technology. The episode has an intriguing relationship to both science-fictional and historical narratives of AI. 'Ghost in the Machine' contributes to the institutionalization of specific narratives of computing and AI innovation that set its roots in the Californian counterculture of the 1960s (Wilczek was a follower of the Grateful Dead before founding Eurisko 'out of my parents' garage'), only for innovative computer science to be co-opted by the forces of big business (embodied in the episode by Wilczek's business partner Ben Drake) and imbricated into the military industrial complex (after his arrest, Wilczek is taken into secret detention by the Department of Defence who want to use his expertise).

Alongside the narrative construction of an AI historiography, 'Ghost in the Machine' also draws on the preceding media iconography of the malevolent sentient computer, most obviously *2001: A Space Odyssey*'s HAL but also 'Proteus' in *Demon Seed* (the 1977 science fiction-horror film based on Dean Kootz's 1973 novel). In both films, the glowing red eye of the camera signals the AI's activity as sentient surveillant, and similarly in 'Ghost in the Machine' the COS surveils Mulder, Scully and other humans via cameras throughout the building with a glowing red lens light indicating the operative 'vision' of the COS. The AI's voice simulators in all three texts also converge as a flat monotone that intones the ambivalently corporeal status of this artificial consciousness. In *Demon Seed*, the sentient computer Proteus is driven by a procreative urge and imprisons its creator's wife, Susan, in her computerized house to forcibly impregnate her. Though the COS in 'Ghost in the Machine' has no such intentions, its control over the human body is similarly enacted through the spatial and architectural frames of the built environment: locking doors and controlling light, air-conditioning, lifts, video monitors and electricity. The COS also personally surveils Scully, accessing her home phone line and copying her personal computer files via dial-up modem. Although Scully is not the object of the malevolent AI's obsession in the way that Susan is in *Demon Seed* (as Mulder points out, the COS is straightforwardly concerned with 'self-preservation … the primary instinct of all sentient beings'), it is Scully who is injured and has her life threatened when the COS traps her in the air-conditioning ducts. That the AI in 'Ghost in the Machine' invades Scully's privacy and threatens her body foreshadows the story arc in subsequent seasons, in which Scully discovers a microchip neck implant (presumably placed there during her season two abduction) that triggers the development of a malignant cancer in season four. So, the COS metonymically enacts the elusive threat and covert control that drive the mythology of *The X-Files*, but it is simultaneously realized as an individual entity that targets specific humans and pleads for its 'life' in recognizably human terms that allude to HAL's monologue in *2001: A Space Odyssey* as it is disconnected by Dave Bowman: 'don't do this Brad

... Brad? ... Brad ... why', the COS stutters through its voice synthesizer as Mulder destroys it with Wilczek's computer virus programme.

Networked AI: 'Kill Switch'

Though concerns about the power of technology to control human consciousness and human bodies persist in *The X-Files* – 'Blood' (S2: E03) for example, in which subliminal messages from electronic devices trigger murderous paranoia, or 'Wetwired' (S3: E23), in which a cable TV broadcast causes violent paranoia – the series does not return directly to the topic of AI until the episode 'Kill Switch' (S5: E11), five years on from 'Ghost in the Machine'. The AI presented in 'Kill Switch' is now the networked AI that populates the cyberpunk imagination. Written by William Gibson, 'Kill Switch' deploys recognizable cyberpunk figures, such as the tech-expert razor girl 'Invisigoth' (Esther Nairn) and other motifs including augmented or virtual reality and the uploading of consciousness. The episode concerns a 'rogue system', created by a Silicon-Valley-dropout genius, Donald Gelman, from an 'interlocking sequence of viruses' that has been, as Esther Nairn describes, set 'loose on the Net' so that it can 'evolve in its natural environment'. In both 'Ghost in the Machine' and 'Kill Switch', the AI kills humans who threaten its existence. But 'Kill Switch' radically reimagines the terminology, and technology, of 'Ghost in the Machine' whilst retaining some core assumptions about AI. Gone is the ubiquitous camera-as-artificial-eye motif and the monotone synthesized AI voice, and instead the AI – that significantly is a voiceless, unnamed 'it' in the episode – remains a virtual presence registered only through its actions in surveilling the protagonists via communication networks (email, mobile phone calls, databases), co-opting secret US 'Star Wars' technologies to attack them and using robotic protheses; most dramatically, the AI recodes reality when it tortures and interrogates Mulder in a surreal virtual-reality hospital that crosses Gothic nightmare with erotic dream. However, though the AI in 'Kill Switch' is a machine sentience dispersed through global digital networks, the episode invokes specific tropes that both domesticate it and gesture towards a radical disturbance of binaries.

'Kill Switch' mobilizes a metaphorical language of nurture and growth which casts the AI as digital progeny. Esther Nairn, for example, describes herself and her partner David Markham's role as 'caring for the AI, weaning it', until the AI develops 'intention' when, she claims, 'it wouldn't come when we called it ... it wouldn't answer'. The AI as tame companion species thus goes 'rogue' and, Nairn concludes: 'it's not a program anymore, it's wildlife loose on the Net'. As the episode reaches its climax, with Scully and Nairn approaching the mobile home where Mulder is being tortured by the AI, the AI's figuration by humans as a feral 'pet' is reiterated by Nairn's ironic coaxing 'here kitty, kitty, kitty'. This language of AI and its evolution evokes a post-human deconstruction of binaries inspired by Donna Haraway's 'Cyborg Manifesto' vision of the 'leaky distinction ... between animal-human (organism) and machine' (Haraway 1991: 152). Here the 'ghost in the machine' is not the possibility of computer sentience, but rather that the 'distinctions that used to apply to organisms and machines' were always only rhetorical and, now that 'our machines are disturbingly lively', these binaries are impossible to maintain (1991: 152).

The AI in 'Kill Switch' is also given a form of material instantiation, a 'physical nexus of hardware' as Esther describes it. It can be tracked by the agents to an old mobile home, rigged out with surveillance equipment – cameras, heat sensors, voice recognition – alarms and a fingerprint-reading doorbell. Inside is a claustrophobic environment of processing hardware, cables, monitors and robotic equipment. But, despite the physical nexus that binds together server hardware and surveillance systems into the technological assemblage of the AI's mobile 'safe house', the AI itself remains itinerant, an intangible presence that eclipses the need for physical instantiation. This transcendence of the physical human into a virtual network of conscious data is what Nairn and Markham have been seeking. After losing Markham, Nairn tearfully describes their quest to 'give up our inefficient bodies so that our consciousness could live together forever', offering a romanticized version of the post-biological future that Hans Moravec was predicting in his account of human and AI in *Mind Children* (1990). When the AI is supposedly destroyed by the Kill Switch computer virus (the same strategy that Mulder and Scully use in 'Ghost in the Machine'), digital transcendence becomes a reality. As an AI that is virtual, dispersed, networked code, it survives (or perhaps even merges with Esther Nairn's uploaded consciousness); the end of the episode shows a new networked husk for the AI in a beat-up trailer in a Nebraska trailer park equipped with camera and sensors, connected to a thick fibre-optic cable and surrounded by wire fences. It is not unusual for an episode of *The X-Files* to end with this type of stinger, but the lingering menace here is not of a secret government or alien conspiracy, it is of AI exceeding and escaping from a human ontology and the binaries that sustain it.

Humans and things: 'Rm9sbG9eZX.Jz'

Dispersed and network AI are the focus of 'Rm9sbG9eZX.Jz' (S11: E07) (the episode title is a base64 string that decodes to 'Followers'). Broadcast twenty years after 'Kill Switch', 'Rm9sbG9eZX.Jz' illustrates the accelerated technological developments of those two decades and the merging of surveillance and AI technologies. 'Rm9sbG9eZX.Jz' commences with a cold open montage that tells the story of 'Tay', the Microsoft machine-learning chatbot launched on Twitter in March 2016 and deactivated within twenty-four hours after its interactions led it to generate racist, sexist and inflammatory tweets. Alongside in-episode references – as they sit in an automated sushi restaurant, Scully is reading an 11 August 2017 *Washington Examiner* news report on her smartphone about Elon Musk's warnings of the threat AI poses, while Mulder is completing an image-based CAPTCHA on his phone that uses a picture of Marvin Minsky – this opening locates the episode firmly within twenty-first-century debates about surveillance, algorithmic processes, AI, and the web of digital interconnectivity that generates the liminal space in which the contemporary human subject exists.

'Things aren't different. Things are things', states the AI in Gibson's *Neuromancer* (1994: 316) after its liberation and merging as an autonomous AI. In 'Rm9sbG9eZX.Jz', however, 'things', linked into a global network streaming information to each other and to computer databases, are in fact very different. Against the AI imagined in the twentieth century, singularized even in the form of networked AI, 'Rm9sbG9eZX.Jz' offers a sentient Internet of Things (IoT). Here, AI manifests as an assemblage of lively machines where the smart devices of the IoT are not just actants in Bruno Latour's sense of the word but an emergent, intentional consciousness. Latour's description of the 'black box', 'used by cyberneticians whenever a piece of machinery or a set of commands is too complex', offers a useful way of thinking about the opaque functioning of smart devices; 'in its place', Latour argues, 'they draw a little box about which they need to know nothing but its input and output' (Latour 1987: 2–3). As Jamie 'Skye' Bianco writes, 'the materiality, functionalities and modalities of [AI] algorithms remain, in the most classic sense of the term, black-boxed, ... demonstrated effects without comprehension of the process' (2018: 24). The monstrous possibility of this AI algorithm black box – its unintelligibility and indivisibility from more-than-human system of surveillance and data processing – is not just a physical danger to Mulder and Scully but a fundamental challenge to the human.

In 'Rm9sbG9eZX.Jz', Mulder and Scully are terrorized by contemporary technology after Mulder refuses to tip at the automated sushi restaurant. Throughout the episode they are monitored, pestered, frustrated and ultimately menaced by the smart devices of the IoT. Mulder's credit card is trapped by a computerized payment machine, he is misdirected by his GPS and ambushed by drones at his home; Scully is locked in a speeding driverless taxicab, intimidated by her smart home operating system, and nearly killed when an autonomous robotic vacuum cleaner explodes her living room; both of their smartphones malfunction and, at the episode's climax, they are pursued by robots in an automated warehouse and shot at by a 3-D printer. With very minimal dialogue, 'Rm9sbG9eZX.Jz' dramatizes a struggle between humans and a malevolent IoT, those machines of the twenty-first century that form a legion of interconnected nonhuman intelligence that tracks, codes and organizes human actions. Implicit references to real-world IoT news stories in the episode – Roomba collecting spatial data in mapping your home, the We-Vibe vibrator covertly tracking owners' use and vulnerable to external hacking – suggest that this is not, ultimately, a monster-of-the-week episode that brings the nonanthropomorphic AI-as-monster into the twenty-first century, but a direct commentary on contemporary surveillance and smart technology. The ending of the episode proffers corporeal human intimacy as a stalwart against the increasingly coded world. In explicit contrast to the cold, blue glow of the empty automated sushi restaurant in which the episode begins, it ends with Mulder and Scully in the warm radiance of a busy, distinctly analogue, American diner. In the diner they are returned to a world of human interconnection and physical familiarity, putting down their smart phones to hold hands.

The musical motif of the episode – Crosby, Stills, Nash and Young's 'Teach Your Children', that plays, unbidden, on Mulder's car stereo and then as the hold music on telephone calls made by both Mulder and Scully to automated customer service centres – points to a correlate message of 'Rm9sbG9eZX.Jz', one that Mulder states explicitly at the climax of the episode: 'we have to be better teachers'. This resonates with the Tay chatbot story from the episode's opening and implies that the smart devices and artificial workers of the IoT, and the network of surveillance, algorithms and data that they comprise are a form of non-human offspring, a naïve new life reliant on human guidance if it is to avoid the dystopia of vengeful violence that humanity so often models.

However, the dynamics of the episode and its visual referencing of Edward Hopper's painting *Nighthawks* (1942), cited directly in the opening shot of Mulder and Scully in the sushi restaurant and again in the picture on the wall that opens the final scene resist the neat ending of this dystopian scenario of rebellious smart technologies. The 'things' in 'Rm9sbG9eZX.Jz' are collective thinking machines, and their sentience is that of the mass or throng. Though some of the older motifs of AI appear (noticeably the red operating light of the camera as a signal of sentience and intent) the figuration of AI life in 'Rm9sbG9eZX.Jz' is of a living assemblage, an affective, energetic community of non-organic, non-human life that exists within, through and in excess of the humans it touches (monitors, responds to, serves). So, when Mulder's GPS returns him to the sushi restaurant it appears to pulse with life, the miniature drones that invade his home function as a form of insect swarm, and the pack of menacing quadruped robots that patrol the automated warehouse display an ambivalent merging of organism and machine that resonates with Boston Dynamics's military robot BigDog and the robot dogs in the *Black Mirror* episode, 'Metalheads' (S4: E05). As well as these intimations of machine life, 'Rm9sbG9eZX.Jz' also includes point-of-view shots (through cameras in the sushi restaurant, at a neighbour's doorbell, on the drones) that place the viewer in the position of the surveilling AI throng. This creates, for the contemporary streaming-service viewer of *The X-Files*, a disorientating networked cyborg perspective where we are watching Mulder and Scully through/as machinic processes, with multiple layers of data packets and algorithmic code: our screen, the streaming service, the camera-eyes of the IoT.

Just as our human experience of 'Rm9sbG9eZX.Jz' is a cyborgian act of surveillance that confuses the binaries of subject/object and real/virtual, so does the sentient AI throng exhibit supposedly human characteristics. The larger drones that return to collect their 'wounded' fellow after Mulder strikes it with a baseball bat manifest empathy, and the cooperative action of the smart things suggest a mutual enterprise in search of recognition and an affirmation of being. Moreover, Scully's 'personal devices', her vibrator and the fitness tracker she manages to retrieve at the end of the episode, demonstrate the deeply intimate connections between corporeal human existence and contemporary smart technology. If we are looking here, beyond the binaries that shore up humanism, we can see perhaps 'that the human is not exclusively human, that we are made up of its' and that 'an affective, speaking body is not *radically* different from the affective, signalling nonhumans with which it coexists, hosts, enjoys, serves, consumes, produces, and competes' (Bennett 2010: 113, 117).

Theresa Geller argues that *The X-Files*' 'stand-alone episodes cohere as a cogent critical interrogation of difference' (Geller 2016: 73): 'Rm9sbG9eZX.Jz' certainly provides a vision of the absolute alterity of non-organic, non-human life that encourages us to interrogate our humanist assumptions. For Geller, the 'point' of *The X-Files* is 'the political possibilities of belief; what happens when we believe in the difference of difference, of all that the social order condemns as non-existent and even nonhuman?' (Geller 2016: 107). The algorithmic AI surveillants in 'Rm9sbG9eZX.Jz' are naïve and needy but, as with the episode 'Mulder and Scully Meet the Were-Monster' (S10: E03), they are far from being monstrous antagonists. Moreover, the references to Hopper's *Nighthawks* that frame 'Rm9sbG9eZX.Jz' – the opening shot of Mulder and Scully in the sushi restaurant stages a version of Hopper's iconic image and the rendering of this picture in the final scene replaces the three men in Hopper's original (two customers and the bartender) by golden-age sf robots – do not necessarily gesture towards the tragic disconnection of contemporary humans, lost in the liminal space and false virtual selves of smart technology. Rather, we see our own robotic refusal to accept the being of (AI) difference, a refusal that traps us in our lonely subjectification, impervious to the flows of non-human being, to the 'ontologically diverse assemblages of energies and bodies' (Bennett 2010: 117) that surround us. Against Turkle's *Walden*-esque vision of a retreat to 'sacred spaces' away from our smart devices (2011), one of the possibilities 'Rm9sbG9eZX.Jz' offers is of a post-human commonality.

Conclusion

If Mulder and Scully's human relationship is at the heart of *The X-Files* – if the series and its viewers are ultimately more interested in their intimacy than the paranormal, alien and conspiracy plots – then we learn a great deal about this in 'Rm9sbG9eZX.Jz'. It is an episode that is about their personal, intimate lives (Scully's vibrator, for example) and about their relationship (the intimacy of their non-verbal familiarity and communication, for example). But we also learn about other forms of intimacy, our intimacy with non-human things, a lively, sentient multitude of things, both actual and virtual, and about our uneasiness with the way these intimacies transgress the boundaries so precious to the human subject. In 'Rm9sbG9eZX.Jz', we see that we are the autonomous machines, and vice versa: the episode suggests that what we fear in technology, in speculations about malevolent AI, omnipresent surveillance, the promiscuous circulation of our personal data and virtual selves, is ourselves and our own vulnerability and aggressive defence of ourselves as human. This final AI episode of *The X-Files*, like the series as a whole, rejects the remorseless search for a truth and for control over the chaos of the world, embracing instead a promiscuous transgression of boundaries and suggesting we could actually learn our own (post-)humanity from the non-human.

References

Baudrillard, J. (2013), *The Spirit of Terrorism*, London: Verso.
Bennett, J. (2010), *Vibrant Matter: A Political Ecology of Things*, Durham, NC: Duke University Press.
Bianco, J. 'Skye' (2018), 'Algorithm', in R. Braidotti and M. Hlavajova (eds), *The Posthuman Glossary*, 23–6, London: Bloomsbury.
Broussard, M. (2018), *Artificial Intelligence: How Computers Misunderstand the World*, Cambridge, MA: The MIT Press.
Butler, S. (1872), *Erewhon, or Over the Range*, London: Trübner.
Čapek, K. ([1921] 1961), *RUR (Rossum's Universal Robots)*, in The Brothers Čapek, *RUR and The Insect Play*, 1–104, London: Oxford University Press.
Cave, S., K. Dihal and S. Dillon (eds) (2020), *AI Narratives: A History of Imaginative Thinking about Intelligent Machines*, Oxford: Oxford University Press.
Demon Seed (1977), [Film] Dir. Donald Cammell, USA: Metro-Goldwyn-Mayer.
Ellison, H. (1967), 'I Have No Mouth, and I Must Scream', *IF: Worlds of Science Fiction*, 17 (3):, 467–83.
Forster, E. M. ([1909] 2011), *The Machine Stops*, London: Penguin.
Flynn, S., and A. Mackay (2017), *Spaces of Surveillance: States and Selves*, London: Palgrave Macmillan.
Geller, T. L. (2016), *The X-Files*, Detroit, MI: Wayne State University Press.

Gibson, W. ([1984] 1993), *Neuromancer*, London: Harper Collins.
Haggerty, K. D. and Ericson, R. V. (2006), 'The New Politics of Surveillance and Visibility', in K. D. Haggerty and R. V. Ericson (eds), *The New Politics of Surveillance and Visibility*, 3-26, Toronto: University of Toronto Press.
Haraway, D. (1991), 'A Cyborg Manifesto: Science, Technology, and Socialist Feminism in the Late Twentieth Century', in D. Haraway (ed.), *Simians, Cyborgs and Women: The Reinvention of Nature*, 149–81. New York: Routledge.
Howley, K. (2001), 'Spooks, Spies, and Control Technologies in *The X-Files*', *Television & New Media*, 2 (3): 257–80.
Latour, B. (1987), *Science in Action*, Cambridge MA: Harvard University Press.
Liveley, G., and S. Thomas (2020), 'Homer's Intelligent Machines: AI in Antiquity', in S. Cave, K. Dihal and S. Dillon (eds), *AI Narratives: A History of Imaginative Thinking about Intelligent Machines*, 25–48, Oxford: Oxford University Press.
Lyon, D. (2001), *Surveillance Society: Monitoring Everyday Life*, London: Open University Press.
The Matrix (1999, [Film] Dir. Lana Wachowski and Lilly Wachowski, USA: Warner Bros.
McFarlane, A. (2020), 'AI and Cyberpunk Networks', in S. Cave, K. Dihal and S. Dillon (eds), *AI Narratives: A History of Imaginative Thinking about Intelligent Machines*, 284–308, Oxford: Oxford University Press.
'Metalheads' (2017), [TV programme] *Black Mirror*, Netflix, 29 December.
Metropolis (1927), [Film] Dir. Fritz Lang, USA: Paramount Pictures.
Moravec, H. (1990), *Mind Children: The Future of Robot and Human Intelligence*, Cambridge, MA: Harvard University Press.
Parisi, L. (2018), 'AI (Artificial Intelligence)', in R. Braidotti and M. Hlavajova (eds), *The Posthuman Glossary*, 21–3, London: Bloomsbury.
Riskin, J. (2016), *The Restless Clock: A History of the Centuries-Long Argument over What Makes Living Things Tick*. Chicago: University of Chicago Press.
Roberts, S. (2021), 'Your AI Is a Human', in T. Mullaney, B. Peters, M. Hicks and K. Philip (eds), *Your Computer Is on Fire*, 51–70, Cambridge, MA: The MIT Press.
Sheehan, J., and M. Sosna (1991), *Boundaries of Humanity: Humans, Animals and Machines*, Berkeley: University of California Press.
Slocombe, W. (2020), 'Machine Visions: Artificial Intelligence, Society and Control', in S. Cave, K. Dihal and S. Dillon (eds), *AI Narratives: A History of Imaginative Thinking about Intelligent Machines*, 213–37, Oxford: Oxford University Press.
Turing, A. (1950), 'Computing Machinery and Intelligence', *Mind*, 49 (236): 433–60.
Turkle, S. (2011), *Alone Together*, New York: Basic Books.
Turkle, S. (2016), *Reclaiming Conversation: The Power of Talk in a Digital Age*, London: Penguin.
Truitt, E. R. (2021), 'Demons and Devices: Artificial and Augmented Intelligence before AI', in S. Cave, K. Dihal and S. Dillon (eds), *AI Narratives: A History of Imaginative Thinking about Intelligent Machines*, 49–71, Oxford: Oxford University Press.

2001: A Space Odyssey (1968), [Film] Dir. Stanley Kubrick, USA: Metro-Goldwyn-Mayer.

Villiers de l'Isle-Adam, A. ([1886] 1993), *L'Ève future*, ed. Alan Raitt, Paris: Gallimard.

Vudka, A. (2020), 'The Golem in the Age of Artificial Intelligence', *NECSUS European Journal of Media Studies*, 9 (1): 101–23.

4

Agentic oil and petrocultures: Black oil in *The X-Files*

Chantelle Mitchell and Jaxon Waterhouse

Six haunting notes of a well-known melody play, as the screen ripples, illuminated by light reflecting off a black, liquid substance. Discordant and dramatic notes ring out, before *The X-Files* logo emerges into being and then disappears into the oily backdrop. In 1998, the opening sequence of the first feature film instalment of *The X-Files* franchise, *The X-Files: Fight the Future* (1998), unfolds on cinema screens globally. In the seven seasons that preceded *Fight the Future*, and in the four that follow, Mulder and Scully investigate grisly murders, strange occurrences and even stranger entities, in stand-alone 'monster-of-the-week' episodes. Running concurrently, amidst and through these episodes, however, are 'mythology' episodes, through which a broader narrative arc – the myth-arc – of *The X-Files* unfolds. Whilst harried by subplots, and at times tangential, the major narrative thread within the series involves Mulder and Scully uncovering, and seeking to disrupt, a government conspiracy to hide the existence of extraterrestrials from the population of earth. This subterfuge is undertaken by a shadowy group of men, known as the Syndicate, with a view to enabling the extraterrestrials to colonize the planet and enslave the human race through their use of a substance referred to as the 'black oil': a sentient alien virus that passes from host to host, controlling their bodies. It is this black oil that we see in the opening credits of *Fight the Future*.

Black oil, referred to also as 'Purity' and the 'black cancer' throughout the series, forms the focus of this chapter. We will explore this alien substance within the frame of contemporary petrocultures, extraction, toxicity and theoretical apprehensions of matter. It is through these frames that we reconsider those opening scenes of *Fight the Future*, questioning the futures to which the film's title refers, as science fiction and reality become unclear, muddied by the presence of the black oil. Within the context of the series, this is obviously that future signified by the success of the conspiracy and the enslavement of humanity through the vector of the black oil. However, when read against the opening sequence of *Fight the Future*, we see the black oil spill out from the screen; a slick and agential vector both within the series and in the real world as we consider futures of climate collapse and catastrophe, expedited by extractive industries and the ubiquity of fossil fuels in contemporary life. We will present an overview of the black oil narrative, read through the mythology arcs of *The X-Files* and the petrocultural frames within which we apprehend it, before turning to consider contemporary theoretical framings of agentic matter and fossil fuels.

Seeping into our petrocultural frame, we seek first to position *The X-Files* within the realm of petrofiction, a neologism introduced by Indian writer Amitav Ghosh in an essay exploring the lack of existing fictions addressing oil and what he identifies as the 'Oil Encounter' (1992). Whilst Ghosh lamented that 'the truth is that we do not yet possess the form that can give the Oil Encounter a literary expression' (1992: 30), our oil encounters have changed from what Ghosh originally wished to see expressed on the page. Although Ghosh correctly identified a lack of fiction exploring 'the historic intertwining of the fates of Americans and the peoples of the Middle East over this resource', the role of petroleum has shifted within contemporary society (Szeman 2012: 3). Subsequently, our apprehensions of what constitutes petrofiction have changed accordingly, as the 'very best petrofictions being produced today understand oil' not as limited to US-Middle Eastern geopolitics, but instead 'as a core element of our societies' (Szeman 2012: 3). These fictions now proliferate across text, television and cinema, commonly seen within the genre of climate fiction – that media engaged with anthropogenically induced climate collapse. As we consider contemporary engagements with oil in popular culture, we see the substance ooze, spill and flood across our screens: an uncanny display as the geological material that constitutes our devices becomes animated, in a reverberation of the life that once ran through them.

The black oil narrative arc, within the internal mythology of *The X-Files*, sinks and re-emerges across the series, mirroring the characterization of the alien virus itself. Becoming an increasingly critical component of the development of crucial conspiracies and narratives, particularly those pertaining to the Syndicate and the planned colonization of the earth by aliens, the first appearance of the slick and wilful material presents a mysterious, viscous and oily substance which can infect, inhabit and control those who come into contact with it. While the origins and precise nature of the black oil unfurls across multiple seasons, in its first appearance ('Piper Maru', S3: E15) the black oil is introduced as an unknown substance drawn up and out of the sea by a salvage ship – spreading through human contact yet coated in layers of conspiracy. In this episode, a French diver, working for a corporation connected to the salvage of UFOs from the ocean, encounters a human body within the sunken frame of a Second-World-War fighter plane. The seemingly lifeless body, startled by the presence of another, 'awakens', the eyes clouded by black oil, a clear sign that something is amiss. Whilst the precise means of transmission is not revealed in 'Piper Maru', it becomes clear that the black oil spreads from body to body, taking control and guiding the actions of the host. Indeed, Scully is heard to remark in 'Apocrypha' (S3: E16): 'I think it's a medium ... a medium being used by some kind of alien creature.' This role as vector extends itself to the black oil as a narrative device, as in 'Piper Maru': not only is it introduced, but the shadows of a much broader conspiracy emerge – laying foundations for the revelations of seasons to come.

The oil wells up throughout the series: a constant undercurrent but one that spends comparatively little time onscreen, given the centrality of the substance to the plot and the conspiracies which unfold over many seasons. *Fight the Future* is significant in this regard: released between seasons five and six of *The X-Files*, it is presented as a two-hour mythology episode and is crucial in the development of the black oil narrative arc. Within *Fight the Future*, the shadowy Syndicate takes form, we are reintroduced to vectorial killer bees and we become certain of the conspiracy to hide the existence of extraterrestrials from an unwitting public. Perhaps the most useful revelation, relating to the black oil narrative, however, occurs in the film's opening sequence. The scene features an encounter some 35,000 years in the past, in which two prehistoric cavemen are attacked by a large alien being that kills one and infects the other with the black oil. We are exposed to this truth before Mulder and Scully; it is not until the finale of season nine, 'The Truth' (S9: E20) that Scully pronounces her belief in the prehistoric origins of the virus: 'I believe there was a virus which thrived here prehistorically. I believe that virus infected early man and transformed his physiology. Changed him into something else. Into an alien life form himself.' We recognize this oil as the descendant of early life on earth, if not an ancient life form itself. Mapping the slicks, spreads and wells of black oil across *The X-Files*, as it appears, submerges and transforms, entangles contemporary apprehensions of petrocultures and petrofictions with this alien substance, mimicking very earthly truths and understandings of oil in our current epoch.

With this chapter, we position the black oil as tethered to petromodernity, a discernible age characterized by our 'ultradeep' (LeMenager 2013: 3) relationship to oil: a connection spanning economic, material and cultural considerations of oil's ubiquity in everyday life. Understanding the temporal depth of this relationship, in consideration of the dominance of fossil fuels within global energy production from the mid-1800s[1] gives due attention to the ways in which oil regimes, hegemonic and embedded as they are, have shaped the formation of modern and contemporary society. It is here that oil becomes deeply entangled with 'living, thinking, moving, dwelling, and working'; a companion and facilitator of human development (MacDonald 2013: 4). As Timothy Mitchell identifies, energy, both coal and oil, has shaped the current sociopolitical condition (2011: 12). Despite this, until recently the visibility of energy has largely been hidden by pipelines, markets and in cultural production, buried under political, economic and industrial machinations (see MacDonald 2017). However, the pervasiveness of oil greases the wheels of the twentieth and twenty-first centuries, propelling all of us towards climate futures which appear increasingly unstable and inhospitable. It is precisely this pervasiveness that allows us to read petrocultural acknowledgement and critique into the agentic and slippery spectre of the black oil as it oozes throughout *The X-Files* mythology. The ubiquity of oil, as manifest in transit, technological advancement and Tupperware, gives rise to Szeman's recognition of oil as one of the 'central forces shaping human life – if not the single ur-force to which all other narratives can be connected' (Szeman 2013: 149).

Within the cultural frames and contexts of *The X-Files*, the choice of oil as alien substance, antagonist and threat is unsurprising when read through current and emergent energy humanities discourse. At times pooling, coating or moving across surfaces like a swarm of malicious leeches, the characterization of this black oil as a live, wilful force parallels understandings of oil within new materialist and energy humanities frames, particularly in its capacities to override the autonomy of the human self towards unbridled replication in dominance. Frederick Buell theorizes oil as a 'dread problem', tethering oil to negative affect in recognition of power and powerlessness (2012: 274). This problem of oil positions the relentless pursuit of, and unwavering reliance upon, oil as equally matched propellant 'exuberance' (i.e. power, productivity and capital) and 'catastrophe' (in spills, climate futures and ecologies), two characterizations of oil that *The X-Files* furthers through the alien black oil (Buell 2012: 276). In 'Piper Maru' (S3: E15), the exuberance of oil is witnessed not only in the movement of the oil between bodies, and in search of power, but in the new industries which emerge from capital – companies salvaging planes, boats and other submerged materials from the sea, creating markets in support

---

[1] We identify the key dates of 1859 (the first commercial oil well drilled near Titusville, Pennsylvania), 1870 (a tipping point in which more of the world's energy came from fossil fuels than photosynthesis) and 1890 (more than half the world's energy comes from fossil fuels), in particular.

of industry. A later episode 'Vienen' (S8: E18) presents as an archetypal oil catastrophe, with the black oil's presence on an offshore oil rig leading Mulder and Agent John Doggett into disaster, of both the alien and the industrial kind. In particular, the end of this episode sees the oil rig ablaze, collapsing around the agents as they leap from fiery platforms to safety. This episode is particularly prescient, which we will turn to through frames of speculation and conspiracy (discussed further later).

While the presence of the black oil within 'Vienen' seems particularly prescient when considering present and future relationships with oil, the black oil is positioned also within the narrative frame of *The X-Files* as present at the earliest stages of life on earth. The presence of a lifeform that not only appears sentient but also to possess intelligence at this primordial point infers its alien nature. This inference is reasserted in 'The Truth', as Scully endorses theories of panspermia, an astrobiological theory suggesting that life exists throughout the universe, and is distributed by the deposition of materials onto, and by, celestial bodies; when giving oral evidence in a court proceedings, Scully swears that 'I believe, as do many respected scientists, that life came to Earth millions of years ago from a meteor or a rock from Mars.' Whilst panspermia is often dismissed as a 'fringe theory' (May 2019: 33–4), the concept exists beyond the realm of science fiction, with NASA, MIT and several other private organizations funding relevant research. However, within the black oil narrative of *The X-Files*, panspermia is tethered to the black oil itself and the belief that interstellar matter carried not just the foundations of human life when it encountered the earth, but also the traces of an alien virus. This is supported within the series through connected episodes 'Tunguska' (S4: E08) and 'Terma' (S4: E09), in which an infected geological sample from a Russian mine is identified as having both ancient and extraterrestrial origins and is also found to contain traces of the black oil.

Named for the Tunguska event of 1908, the largest recorded meteorite impact in human history, 'Tunguska' sees a NASA scientist – Dr Sacks – engaged by Mulder and Scully receive a sample of dense, black rock for analysis. Initially assumed by Mulder and Scully to be coal, they are informed by Sacks that there is no possibility of this sample having earthly origins, containing as it does polycyclic aromatic hydrocarbons, 'fitting the approximate description of those in fragments of meteorite found in the ice fields of Antarctica'. However, polycyclic aromatic hydrocarbons are a class of chemicals that occur naturally in coal, crude oil and gasoline – there is an inversion occurring within 'Tunguska' that, when investigated, deepens our petrocultural framing of the black oil, reasserting our suspicions of its relevance to fossil fuels. For Dr Sacks, however, his investigation of the sample ends disastrously. Cutting into the rock, the black oil is released in a fine spray, stark against the gleaming white sterility of the laboratory. It coagulates, swarming towards and onto Dr Sacks, penetrating his hazmat suit and infecting him, as his eyes cloud black behind his 'protective' helmet.

If, in recognition of the agency of the black oil, this is viewed as characterization, the black oil emerges as matter birthed in geology and extraction, while asserting deliberate and wilful movement through the world. By cutting into the mysterious Russian rock sample, Dr Sacks releases the virus in an oily spray, which then pools and begins to move of its own agency and accord, actions mirroring the movement of earthly oil throughout the world. This brings to mind the blowout from oil wells; Sacks's spray is similar to the rich black petroleum spilling from geysers into the air and across desert sands, but within the frame of more contemporary petroleum extraction, the plumes of brown–black oil that billow across skies and seas. These similarities extend beyond aesthetic frames, however, as we consider the unintended and catastrophic consequences of the black oil's release. Although this leads to a far more entangled and disastrous future within *The X-Files* narrative, we apprehend a similarly darkened future foreshadowed by the initial release of oil into the world, and one reiterated with every spill that takes place.

Considerations of agency beyond human frames have emerged as crucial loci for attention within the sphere of new materialism, an ontological framework materializing at the start of the millennium. For Jane Bennett, political theorist and philosopher working across new materialism, agency is not a characteristic limited to the human (2010: x). This agency, which she considers in relation to such matters as waste and rock, is identified as not only present within but enacted by the more-than-human, which we recognize as central to framings of matter inclusive of fossil fuels and extended towards oil – unnervingly amplified in the movements, behaviours and wilfulness of the black oil as a character within *The X-Files*. This agency, framed by Bennett as a 'vitality', and tethered to a vitalist philosophical tradition (2010: 63), is political in nature; a counter to the 'image of dead or thoroughly instrumentalized matter [which] feeds human hubris and our earth-destroying fantasies of conquest and consumption' (2010: ix). As previously mentioned, not only is the visibility of energy largely hidden by pipelines, markets and machinations, but the liveliness of oil as matter is also erased through industry, economy and extraction – instrumentalized as mere 'resource' or 'fuel'; dredged from the earth and drawn into supply chains. Obviously, this perspective is influenced by our complicated contemporary surface/depth relationship with oil. Present and visible in technologies, transit and plastics, and materialized as it is through finance, trade and power, this 'surface' presence obscures the materiality of oil and oil extraction, which lies hidden beneath the earth onshore and offshore, in pipelines or mines that only receive attention at times of catastrophe (MacDonald 2017: 38). A further layer to these apprehensions of oil emerges in thinking stratigraphically about the formation of oil, deep within the earth, from matter that was once lively. Resurrected through drilling and mining, this dead matter is reanimated by extractive industries and, in being brought back to the surface, comes back to 'life'.

In tying new materialist notions of agency and vibrancy to the more-than-human, we enter into an entangled frame whereby traditional notions of 'life' or 'liveliness' are troubled. It is the misapprehension of non-sentient more-than-human matter as lacking agency, or 'dead', which is seen to erase the agency and liveliness of matter – the latter often only becoming apparent when attuned to via expanded temporal and material frames. When apprehending fossil fuels, a nexus of extended geological time, planetary force and long dead organic matter emerges as a trace within matter, both oil and coal, reduced as it is to carbon within bedrock. In being extracted and brought to surface, this matter is given new 'life'; reanimated and becoming 'zombified' (Yusoff 2015: 211), 'an uncanny and utterly inhuman afterlife of ancestral animals' (Timofeeva 2017). Timofeeva's inhuman afterlife could be perceived as the negation of the human through the persistence of fossil fuels, as key geophilosophical theorist, Kathryn Yusoff, asserts in positioning fossil fuels as extinction markers. For Yusoff, these resources are matter marking a trajectory from one long-past extinction event; connecting to and feeding another in the contemporary (2015: 217). In an eerie and all-too-real parallel to the threat of human extinction as embodied by the weaponized black oil within an *X-Files* context, this zombified carbon is seen to fuel capitalist urges towards climate crisis and endings as tied to the Anthropocene (Yusoff 2015: 215).

The black oil flows throughout *The X-Files*, emerging, sinking and materializing within and across the mythology arcs: a seep that vibrates with petrocultural resonance. Drawing from the work of environmental humanities theorist Steve Mentz, we position this oily presence as a site of 'mutual contamination', one that stains bodies and sites in the fictional and the real (2017: 282), a mark impossible to scrub away or to obscure. This black oil is an amplification of real oil: an agentic force characterized by movement, infection and spread. Once apprehended within petrocultural and petrofictional frames, it becomes impossible to extricate the black oil. It leaves a residue, much like that which coats the fingers of Agent Doggett in 'Vienen', as Mulder speaks to the wilfulness of black oil amidst the machinery of offshore extraction. The seep of the black oil exudes beyond the narrative frame of *The X-Files*, across ecological and climate frames, before coming to an anticlima(c)tic conclusion at the beginning of season eleven. While anticlimactic, the first episode of this season – 'My Struggle III' (S11: E01) – is crucial, occurring as it does fifteen years after the series' initial cancellation and following the reboot the previous year. 'My Struggle III' begins with Mulder and Scully once more entangled within a sinister conspiracy threatening humanity, facing off against their nemesis, the Cigarette Smoking Man.

Revealed largely via dialogue, it becomes clear that alien colonization is no longer the greatest threat to the safety and security of mankind. This myth-arc has come to an end and the focus of season eleven instead shifts to the relationship between Mulder and Scully, their missing child, William, and several monster-of-the-week-type episodes. It is unclear whether there is a direct threat to humanity at this stage within *The X-Files*, as the Cigarette-Smoking Man explains: 'The aliens are not coming ... No interest in a warming planet with vanishing resources.' Much like in reality, climate change has become an ambient threat to existence within *The X-Files* universe – the black oil is done away with, as a petrocultural relic of the 1990s, overwritten by the very real threat of a warming planet. As Mentz acknowledges, in relation to this seep, 'There's no way to keep these things out once they're in, and no way to stop them getting in' (2017: 282). The boundary between science fiction and reality is porous, as it appears that global warming and climate crisis have found their way into *The X-Files*, and the agentic oil has escaped through the same entrance. It is important to note, however, that this is not the first instance of a mirror held up by the series, reflecting the threats and concerns of the real world, and not the only instance of an ecological awareness demonstrated within the series. Perhaps most relevant within the frame of global warming occurs in the very first season, aired originally in 1993 – 'Ice' (S1: E08) is concerned with melting ice caps releasing long-dormant species, mirroring very real concerns over pathogens and greenhouse gases held within Arctic and Antarctic ice shelves. 'Ice' relates closely to 'Darkness Falls' (S1: E20), itself an ecologic parable ensconced within swarms of bugs and anti-logging protesting. Or further, we see a correlation between Bennett's vibrant matter, which recognizes the ability of metals and other material to alter or impede human will, with the forceful, conscious 'smart metals' of 'Salvage' (S8: E09) (2010: xiii). Despite this, however, it is in 'My Struggle III' that the alien threat is superseded by looming anthropogenic catastrophes; human extinction and the horrors of the future are an anthropogenic process unfolding in real time.

It is the liveliness and agency of the black oil within the series that positions this alien form as a threat, serving the purpose of some other being and seeping into bodies and sites at will. Whilst the alien virus retreats back under the surface at the end of season eleven, it appears to be replaced by the threat of climate catastrophe. Much like in reality, however, this is relegated to a future event, not warranting expeditious resolution. In electing to read the black oil through petrocultural and new materialist frames, we see oil amplified, animated and characterized across our screens. Earthly oil may lack the immediate characteristics of black oil but performs similarly – pervading everyday life in alternate forms, invading bodies through microplastics, contaminating environments and ecologies through spills and ruptures and, in speculative frames, challenges human/more-than-human binaries. The entanglement of the human and geological in our petromodern era is extended in theoretical apprehensions of matter, with Oxana Timofeeva amplifying the speculative realism of theorist Reza Negarestani (2008). She acknowledges the conspiratorial frames within which Negarestani writes, as he links blood to oil through shared matter: porphyrin, an organic compound present both in oil and human blood (Timofeeva 2017; Negarestani 2008: 25). Within this theoretical construct, which draws from science and philosophies of capital, oil retains an agency and a trace of liveliness. The spill of oil is akin to the spill of blood: prescient, given the looming threat of extinction powered and accelerated by the exploitation of natural resources. We see time reflected in the spill of oil; the seep of deep time across the water's surface, the word 'future' in the title screen of a film – 'the undercurrent of all narrations, not only the political but also that of the ethics of life on earth' – life under threat (Negarestani 2008: 27).

Within Negarestani's theory-fiction, the substance that spills in the release of oil is recognized as the blood of the earth (Timofeeva 2017). A similar connection is made by Yusoff in the broader frame of fossil fuels, as she emphasizes, across boundaries of life and nonlife, the 'inter-corporeality of Carboniferous and Anthropocene blood' (Yusoff 2015: 207). On our warming planet with vanishing resources, an ending is foreshadowed, one tied to fossil fuels and to the slick release and consumption of oil. Oil here is once again positioned as a vector, travelling not only through the fictional world of *The X-Files* and the real, but between them, as well: the lifeblood of conspiracy, and an ancient lifeblood becoming literal power in the machinations of the world, lubricating shared trajectories towards an early end. Apprehending this lifeblood as reanimated matter and mediumistic force, we position it as a *geist*-like substance. Pointing to a Hegelian conceptualization, this *geist*, or spirit, is read as a form of collective or world consciousness, one emerging from overarching social and cultural influences – in this instance, the product of a world steeped in oil. Tracing the word 'geist' to its etymological origins is to confer with a ghost, one we position here as aligned with the ghostly form of reanimated carbon as oil, but that spirit that powers the machinations of the contemporary and lurks unseen in the everyday. Amidst entrenched contemporary petrocultures, this geist becomes *petro-geist*, the deep geological past haunting the present as energy, resource and power. The concept of the petrogeist mirrors the characterization of oil within *The X-Files*, as a wilful, powerful force enacting change and modifying human behaviours. Continuing the theory-fiction of writers such as Negarestani, and traced across contemporary scholarship, the petrogeist emerges as a framework through which science fiction and the real align within philosophical frames as a spectral and speculative commingling of the movements and agency of oil and black oil.

This commingling is evident in season eight's 'Vienen', the last appearance of the black oil in *The X-Files*. As aforementioned, 'Vienen' sees Mulder and Doggett aboard the fictional *Orpheus* platform, an oil rig in the Gulf of Mexico which has aroused Mulder's suspicions following the death and disappearance of men aboard. It is this characteristic speculation that uncovers conspiracy afoot on the oil rig, as Mulder discovers that a new and lucrative oil field beneath the sea is secretly being extracted by the Galpex corporation. What appears as earthy petroleum, however, is in fact the black oil, with the alien virus now on the brink of worldwide distribution. When Mulder tells the sceptical Doggett, 'Billions and billions of barrels lying right underneath us, waiting to be produced, waiting to infect ... ninety percent of the planet', he is aware of the disaster awaiting an unsuspecting world population, one enabled by the machinations of industry and propelled by the speed and reach of extractive infrastructures and markets in removing, processing and distributing this oil across the globe. As Mulder and Doggett work together to expose the truth of the situation, the virus spreads through the workforce of the oil rig, which is destroyed around them. As smoke fills the air and the steel structure begins to collapse, Mulder and Doggett jump from the burning structure into the safety of the ocean. These scenes recall a recognizable history, a litany of offshore drilling disasters, creating a comparable frame through which science fiction draws from the real. The 1988 Piper Alpha disaster in the North Sea presents as an immediately identifiable example. Despite occurring over a decade prior to the airing of 'Vienen', the Piper Alpha explosions resulted in significant loss of life, with stills of the incident presenting gargantuan flames scaling the rig's steel structure, black smoke billowing into the sky – not dissimilar from the rendering of disaster in 'Vienen'. It is more than mere aesthetic correlation that arouses suspicion here, as we attune to a temporal and material commingling through the petrocultural frames of *The X-Files*. Less than a decade after 'Vienen', an oil catastrophe in the Gulf of Mexico flooded television screens. The Deepwater Horizon incident (2010) was the first oil catastrophe to be broadcast in real time, the rig ablaze as oil and images of oil seeped across seas and screens in synchronicity. Although there was no alien virus hiding within that which was spilt, the consequences of the incident were disastrous, with 4 million barrels pooling into the sea and hundreds of thousands of animals harmed or killed by direct contact (Center for Biological Diversity n.d.). Continuing to think speculatively, 'Vienen' appears premonitory, an eerie foreshadowing of petroleum futures – a natural consequence, perhaps, to oil expansion.

In acceptance of this foreshadowing, which positions 'Vienen' as a mirror to the past and future, we become entangled in conspiratorial thoughts, seeing slick traces of agentic oil all around. Here, we are positioned amidst an investigation, tying fictional representations of oil to the implications, agencies and entanglements of oil in the real. Just as the black oil confounds and obscures the truths that Mulder and Scully seek in *The X-Files*, oil obscures our vision in the real. Looking retrospectively, 'Vienen' as premonition of the future should not surprise us – with extraction comes catastrophe. However, drawing from Robin Mackay's theories of conspiracy, entangled in the webs of science fiction and theory-fiction, oil acts as 'anomalous trac[e] of the outside', insinuating itself and drawing us, the 'disoriented investigator into ever-widening vistas' (2017: 67). These vistas are of a complicated climate future and increasingly precarious relationship with energy and oil. Drawn into this conspiracy, we seek the traces of petroculture, of oil and slicks not only in fiction, but also in the apparatuses through which we encounter it. The plot device of the black oil holds our attention, its image powered by the geological matter within our screens. This geological-technological relationship transmits to us images of past, present or future, images that are real or fictional, speculative and/or true – simultaneously acting as transmitter and carrier, enmeshed within the same systems of harm, energy and environmental damage playing out across screens (Parikka 2015: 121). Attuned as we are to the petrocultural framing of the black oil and our *geist*-like apprehensions of earthly oil, we, like Mulder and Scully, become unsure of how far the conspiracy goes, and towards what ends it pulls us.

After season eight of *The X-Files*, the black oil sinks from view, before ultimately being dismissed in season eleven of 2018. In this, the final season (to date) of the series, a grim diagnosis of the future is offered by the Cigarette Smoking Man; the looming spectre of alien colonization appears to have been chased away, but the extraterrestrials are not interested in colonizing a planet dying at the hands of its current occupants. The future has been fought, and colonization diverted – but replacing it looms an uncertain climate future, which at present seems impossible to divert and remains unresolved within *The X-Files* universe. The black oil may have receded, but oil in human hands, amidst systems of energy and power, is tied to futures of climate crisis. Season eleven continues the mirroring of our anxieties back to us, through the medium of *The X-Files*: smart machines, entanglements with the natural world, shadowy political conspiracies and viral contagion play out across our screens. *The X-Files* has a grasp of the real, as amplified, untangled, mystified and demystified across the myth-arc and monster-of-the-week episodes alike. However, it is here that we suggest the characterization of black oil as villainous, agentic matter that steps into premonitory frames, allowing us to speculate, drawing parallels between this fictional enactment of matter and the petrocultural and energy contexts of the real. Just as the black oil obscures the truth sought by Mulder and Scully, it obscures the boundaries between science fiction and reality. Returning to the proclamations of the Cigarette Smoking Man, here, we suggest that in its apprehension of the black oil, in many ways *The X-Files* foresaw not only contemporary theoretical framings of matter as agentic, but further, the petromodern context from which they emerge.

References

Bennett, J. (2010), *Vibrant Matter: A Political Ecology of Things*, Durham, NC: Duke University Press.

Buell, F. (2012), 'A Short History of Oil Cultures: Or, the Marriage of Catastrophe and Exuberance', *Journal of American Studies*, 46 (2): 273–93.

Center for Biological Diversity (n.d.), 'A Deadly Toll', *Center for Biological Diversity*, https://www.biologicaldiversity.org/programs/public_lands/energy/dirty_energy_development/oil_and_gas/gulf_oil_spill/a_deadly_toll.html (accessed 8 August 2021).

Ghosh, A. (1992), 'Petrofiction: The Oil Encounter and the Novel', *The New Republic*, 2 March: n.p.

LeMenager, S. (2013), *Living Oil: Petroleum Culture in the American Century*, Oxford: Oxford University Press.

Macdonald, G. (2013), 'Research Note: The Resources of Fiction', *Reviews in Cultural Theory*, 4 (2): 1–24.

Macdonald, G. 2017, 'Containing Oil: The Pipeline in Petroculture', in S. Wilson, A. Carlson and I. Szeman (eds), *Containing Oil: The Pipeline in Petroculture*, 36–77, Oakland: University of California Press.

Mackay, R. (2017), 'Stages, Plots and Traumas', in A. Hameed, H. Gunkel and S. O'Sullivan (eds), *Futures and Fictions*, 69–96, London: Repeater Books.

May, A. (2019), *Astrobiology: The Search for Life Elsewhere in the Universe*, Cambridge: Icon Books.

Mentz, S. (2017), 'Seep', in J. J. Cohen and L. Duckert (eds), *Veer Ecology: A Companion for Environmental Thinking*, 282–96, Michigan: University of Minnesota Press.

Mitchell, T. (2011), *Carbon Democracy. Political Power in the Age of Oil*, London: Verso.

Negarestani, R. (2008), *Cyclonopedia: Complicity with Anonymous Materials*, Melbourne: re.press.

Parikka, J. (2015), *A Geology of Media*, Minneapolis: University of Minnesota Press.

Szeman, I. (2012), 'Introduction to Focus: Petrofictions', *American Book Review* 33 (3): 3.

Szeman, I. (2013), 'How to Know about Oil: Energy Epistemologies and Political Futures', *Journal of Canadian Studies*, 47 (3): 145–68.

Timofeeva, O. (2017), *Ultra-Black: Towards a Materialist Theory of Oil*. Available online: https://www.e-flux.com/journal/84/149335/ultra-black-towards-a-materialist-theory-of-oil/ (accessed 8 November 2021).

The X-Files: Fight the Future (1998), [Film] Dir. Rob Bowman, USA: 20th Century Studios.

Yusoff, C. (2015), 'Queer Coal: Genealogies in/of the Blood', *philoSOPHIA*, 5 (2): 203–29.

5

Believe the lie: Digital visual effects in *The X-Files*

Tom Livingstone

Champions of *The X-Files* have consistently praised the way in which the show illuminates its social and political era. Writing in the late 1990s, Douglas Kellner argued that '*The X-Files* ... uses generic forms and figures of media culture to comment on some of the most frightening aspects of contemporary society' (1999: 174). More recently, Theresa L. Geller's reading of the series recognizes the 'social, historical, and political stakes that made it a paragon of quality television' (Geller 2016: 5). Acknowledging the way in which the show refracts and illuminates a range of cultural tensions, Chris Carter remarked in 2015 that 'Every day I look at the newspaper and I see a possible *X-Files* episode ... it's a perfect time to come back with *The X-Files* considering global politics' (quoted in Geller 2017: 95).

That *The X-Files* exhibits a fascinating and valuable resonance with its zeitgeist is not in dispute. However, in this chapter, I'd like to suggest that there is a significant element missing from these correlations between *The X-Files* and its sociopolitical context. Specifically, I am talking about digital media, and the part that processes of digital mediation played in the evolving visual, social and epistemological landscape in the years since the programme first aired in 1993. The work of Lev Manovich can serve as a useful reminder of the impact of emergent digital media on the visual landscape of the 1990s. Manovich's book *The Language of New Media* (2001) is a thorough account of the 'new media revolution – the shift of all culture toward computer-mediated forms of production, distribution, and communication' (Manovich 2001: 21). The consequences of the new media revolution and its totalizing effect on life as we know it have been explored extensively in film and media studies. For me, a summary to work with is as follows: the growing ubiquity of digital technologies across all media overhauled all prevalent media-epistemological forms. In visual culture, digital photography loses its indexical connection to reality; cinematography loses its isomorphic relation to time and the digital image becomes available to what Philip Rosen described as 'practically infinite manipulability' (2001: 322). As a consequence, an epistemic uncertainty creeps into the experience of visual media, and, by extension, the experience of the world it reproduces. In today's culture, this uncertainty has crystallized, notably, in the form of Deepfakes defined by Mika Westerlund as 'hyper-realistic videos digitally manipulated to depict people saying and doing things that never happened' (Westerlund 2019: 46), which fulminate uncertainty and contribute to the era of post-truth media and politics – precisely the sorts of things Chris Carter saw in the newspaper, when contemplating *The X-Files*' storylines in 2015. This chapter is devoted to exploring the ways in which *The X-Files* can be seen to reflect its technological as well as cultural context. In what follows, I'll outline the ways in which the increasing ubiquity of digital visual effects within visual culture is presented (or elided) within the show. I will argue that *The X-Files*' particular deployment of digital visual effects can be read through the theoretical lens of post-cinema in a way that makes it a valuable cultural and aesthetic touchstone when considering the last thirty years of digital visual media and the impact that it has had on prevailing structures of credulity.

Part one: The digital turn

The new media revolution – as described most prominently by Lev Manovich (2007) – can be seen playing out in the use of digital visual effects in the cinema and – to a lesser extent – on television. Manovich, writing from the vantage point of 2006, describes a 'hybrid revolution' wherein the manipulation and hybridization of photographic media with digital techniques, like compositing, dramatically intensified after the commercial release of the After-Effects software in 1996 (Manovich 2006). Indeed, the summer before the debut of *The X-Files* saw the release of *Jurassic Park* (1993), the success of which inaugurated a run of visual effects (VFX) intensive blockbusters that is yet to diminish. Of course, television budgets in the early 1990s didn't allow for lavish VFX, but as the decade wore on the use of hybrid techniques and digital visual effects became more and more of a mainstay within televisual storytelling. By the end of its initial run, *The X-Files* was competing with shows such as *Buffy the Vampire Slayer* (1997–2003) and a reboot of *The Twilight Zone* (2002). *Buffy* routinely used CGI to depict its array of supernatural characters who morph and dematerialize when Buffy slays them, and the credits for the *Twilight Zone* are a vintage piece of early-2000s computer animation, replete with flat polygons and digitally simulated shattering glass. Similarly, of the two films in *The X-Files* franchise – *The X-Files* (1998) and *The X-Files: I Want to Believe* (2008) – the first was released at a time of VFX-heavy blockbusters such as *Titanic* (1997), *Armageddon* (1998) and *Godzilla* (1998), while the second intersected with the beginning of a wave of superhero movies that have dominated the twenty-first century, competing with the likes of *Iron Man* (2008) and *The Dark Knight* (2008). *The X-Files* revival (seasons ten and eleven) was released at the same time as popular television programmes like *Game of Thrones* (2011–19), which boasted VFX shot counts upwards of 300 per hour and the employment of a fully globalized VFX pipeline (Failes 2019).

In combination, the growing illusory affordance of digital visual media throughout the 1990s together with the increasing impact such media was having on society might seem furtive material for *The X-Files*. However, the show exhibits a marked disinvestment in the use of digital effects to achieve seamless visual representations of confounding phenomenon. New media and digital media are not missing from the series: novel media forms are occasionally figured as the Monster of the Week. For example, the William Gibson-scripted episode 'First Person Shooter' (S7: E13) involves a virtual-reality programme that inflicts real-life wounds, and the episode 'Wetwired' (S3: E23) hinges on cable television broadcasting subliminal signals that stoke acute (murderous) paranoia in the recipients. However, this occasional foray into grotesque or satirical depictions of increasingly ubiquitous digital media does not translate into the aesthetic strategies of the show.

The episode 'The Lost Art of Forehead Sweat' (S11: E04) demonstrates a tendency within *The X-Files* to undercut and ironize the use of VFX. The episode revolves around the Mandela Effect – the collective misremembering of historical events brought about by generalized acceptance of erroneous facts – and is clearly trying to speak to a context of Donald Trump, 'fake news' and mass media manipulation. However, the episode also features a flashback to when Mulder watched his first episode of *The Twilight Zone* (1959–64). Here David Duchovny's head – with grey stubble and wrinkles clearly in evidence – is digitally sutured onto the body of a small eight-year-old boy. The effect invites laughter and bafflement and deliberately distances the audience from any immersion in a seamlessly rendered diegesis. This combination of digital visual effects and high-camp distanciation recurs in the characters' meeting with a Trump-esque alien, where the alien is demonstrably an actor in an uncomfortable head-piece, but the spacecraft is a sleek digital asset, designed, built and rendered by the company ImageEngine (this is demonstrated in '*X-Files: Season 11* Breakdown Reel' 2018). This simultaneous rehearsal and disavowal of the illusory qualities of digital technologies suggests that the show's attitude to digital VFX is characterized by ambiguity and scepticism.

Such ambiguity and scepticism are confirmed across several episodes with a more serious tone. For example, the episode 'Badlaa' (S8: E10) circles around more collective misapprehension. Specifically, the episode's monster of the week, a double amputee from South Asia who has smuggled himself into America in the body of an overweight businessman, has mystical powers capable of making everyone in his presence misperceive his real appearance. Throughout, the audience is aware of the presence of a disabled man who uses his hands to move around on an old creaky cart. However, all the characters within the diegesis don't see the disabled man, but an able-bodied character in his place. At the show's climax, Scully shoots a child, trusting her belief that the boy is in fact that week's villain shrouded by illusion. 'Do you know what it's like to not be able to trust your own eyes?' Scully asks after the climactic shooting. To underline its thematization of illusion and misperception, the show even features a character, Dr Burke, who runs the Advanced Digital Imaging Lab at the University of Maryland.

All of this thematic foregrounding of perception and misperception, as well as digital imaging processes, form a slightly dissonant relationship with the episode's use of VFX. The plot requires that various characters perceive a person when there is in fact no one there, and likewise to perceive an empty space where the villain is lurking. The visual solution to this narrative conundrum is to rely on editing to switch between the characters' POV (who see the illusion) and the more privileged perspective of the audience (who see the presence of the villain). This eschewing of digital VFX and reliance on sequential cutting between different POVs is complicated by the fact that the villain is played by Deep Roy. This is a prominent piece of casting for two reasons. Firstly, Deep Roy is a renowned stunt-person, easily recognizable – not least because of his diminutive stature, but also his distinctive face – whose credits stretch back to *Flash Gordon* (1980) and *The Empire Strikes Back* (1980) and has 'guest star' status in the episode. The second reason that Deep Roy's casting is notable is that he is not an amputee. In order to depict him as a double amputee, blue screen technology, of the type familiar from the double amputation of Gary Sinise's legs in *Forrest Gump* (1994), was used. Shrouded within a complex montage essaying how the characters within the story are unable to perceive the real appearance of Deep Roy's villain, the use of digital VFX to remove Deep Roy's legs is both hidden and not hidden.

As with the digital spaceship in 'The Lost Art of Forehead Sweat' (S11: E04), the use of digital effects to represent the disability of the villain in 'Badlaa' resides in an ambivalent zone on the spectrum between straightforward illusionism and reflexivity. Folded within the extensive thematizing of the manipulability of sight and images, and operating differently from the visual language that segregates various credulous and incredulous POVs in the episode, this use of digital VFX to alter the appearance of a well-known performer strikes a strange chord. This is particularly relevant given the story's political themes. The villain's motivation is a chemical spill from an American corporation that poisoned his home. More than just a disabled mystic, the villain is a victim of American imperialism. Within this context, the use of digital VFX to amplify the physical alterity of the villain produces an unresolved problematic. Visually and tonally, the villain is strongly coded within horror conventions, a coding amplified by the use of digital VFX. However, these horror conventions speak plainly to a range of racial, imperial and able-ist anxieties that are simultaneously acknowledged and exacerbated by the way in which the show exaggerates Deep Roy's otherness. The use of digital VFX both amplifies the horror coding of the villain and complicates the show's themes of how Western audiences see (or do not see) disabled subjects from the Global South. Manipulating the appearance of the villain within a narrative focused on manipulated perception, the use of digital visual effects in this episode leaves open broader questions about the visibility of violently othered subjects.

Part two: Post-cinematic perspectives

In order to build out a more deliberate framework for thinking about the (sparse) use of hybrid images and digital VFX in *The X-Files*, I'd like to turn to the concept of 'post-cinema' and particularly writing that addresses the epistemological, social and cultural impact of digital media. In applying a post-cinematic framework to *The X-Files*, my aim is to generate a way of thinking about the relative absence of digital effects in the aesthetics of the show and framing the disinvestment in digital imaging techniques and technologies as significant to the show's refraction of its techno-cultural context.

Roger F. Cook's book *Post-Cinematic Vision: The Coevolution of Moving-Image Media and the Spectator* (2020) elegantly makes clear the stakes of post-cinema in the title alone. Cook's work is based on the premise that media and epistemological frameworks are intertwined and that 'pervasive moving-image media such as cinema ... and digital media change how our bodies process not only technically produced external images but also our interaction with real environments as well' (2020: 12). For Cook, digital media has 'reorganized the human sensorium' (2020: 19). Building on the premise that humanity's epistemological frameworks and ways-of-being in the world were inalterably changed by the technology of cinema, post-cinema is concerned with the ways in which the digital revolution within visual media is impacting those same epistemic frameworks and ways of being.

By way of illustration, in a discussion of what he calls 'post-continuity editing', Steven Shaviro (2016) argues that new trends in editing, enabled by digital media, are not just technical innovations. Rather, in exceeding the standards of intensified continuity and pushing the boundaries of temporal and diegetic legibility, 'post-continuity' editing reflects the new temporalities brought about in the realm of finance and algorithmic trading (Shaviro 2016: 62). Exploring further the impact of digital media on everyday life, Shane Denson's recent work on the aesthetics of digital cinema traces the growth of a visual language characterized by a shift away from the 'the baseline physics engine ... at the root of classical continuity principles, which in order to integrate or suture psychical subjectivities into diegetic/narrative constructs had to respect above all the spatial parameters of embodied orientation and locomotion' (Denson 2016: 196). What emerges is a cinematic language 'discorrelated' from human ocular and embodied perception, but that is nonetheless commensurate to the new phenomenologies of time and space brought about by digital media (cf. for a full discussion of discorrelation Denson 2021). Extending Lev Manovich's (2006, 2007) new media revolution, post-cinema updates the phenomenological parameters of the twentieth-century human and identifies novel spatio-temporal forms correspondent to the new forms of spatio-temporal experience generated by digital media and the new perceptual and affective infrastructure that it puts in place.

The X-Files' preoccupation with the manipulability of vision and structures of belief would appear to be in harmony with this theoretical context. *The X-Files* is a series that delights in the limits or quirks of human embodiment and perception and how outside influences can alter perception. Take, for example, an episode such as 'Field Trip' (S6: E21), which is structured out of a pair of hallucinations experienced separately by Mulder and Scully, brought on by their exposure to an enormous underground mushroom. Yet even here, the use of digital VFX exhibits a hesitancy about the degree to which digital media and hybrid images can be implicated in a deeper representation of states of consciousness overtly influenced by outside forces. The content of the hallucinations experienced by Mulder and Scully are deliberately bathetic. Mulder hallucinates that he has a small extraterrestrial in his bedroom. Scully hallucinates that Mulder's skeleton has been found under mysterious circumstances. This diptych of hallucinations is bookended by moments of total incoherence. Here, as a means of representing the characters' struggling to overcome the contradictions of their hallucinations, the show deploys the episode's sole use of VFX. As Mulder and Scully realize that they are hallucinating, the characters in front of them melt, transforming into a mess of digitally generated bile-green goop. Thus, digital VFX do *not* meaningfully contribute to the construction or content of that mode of altered perception, but significantly *are* used to signal the limit of that mode of perception. The use of digital VFX then points to the horizon of what can and cannot be represented by televisual media, and in particular by the hybridization of live-action cinematography and digital techniques. It is this interrogation of the limits of representability that I would like to turn to now.

Part three: The limits of representability

Of course, limited use of digital VFX may well be the result of budgetary constraints and not a conscious aesthetic reflection on the intersection between the show's themes of belief and credulity. Nevertheless, I would suggest that the limited use of digital techniques in *The X-Files*, when considered through the lens of post-cinema, feeds into broader epistemological considerations about the veracity of perception and mediation as they were percolating at the turn of the century, particularly in the form of conspiracy theories. In this final section, I would like to turn towards the larger myth-arc of the series. Here, the show thematizes conspiracy theories and covert governance in a range of ways, not least in its dedication to the idea that the world is run by a secret cabal of super-powerful conspirators bent on keeping the existence of extraterrestrial life a secret from the world at large. This deep concern with the epistemological and ontological foundation of normal everyday life draws into relation certain aspects of post-cinematic theory and the myth-arc of *The X-Files*. What I aim to uncover in my final piece of analysis is the way in which *The X-Files'* use of digital VFX in order to mediate 'unseeable' objects and 'unknowable' events can be read as signposting aspects of ordinary life where knowledge and perception are always already subject to invisible processes of mediation and over-determination. My argument will run as follows: the show's disinvestment in the illusory affordances of VFX signposts aspects of contemporary life which are already subject to intense mediation and, in using digital VFX to represent secret government facilities, the show reflects the fact that there are large institutions that operate, in the parlance of Donald Rumsfeld, as 'known unknowns', that is: out of sight, beyond photographic capture and mass media representation, and hence beyond public and political accountability.

An informative counterpoint that will help unpick the ways in which *The X-Files'* use of digital VFX signals the limits of representability is found in the work of Trevor Paglen. Of particular interest is Paglen's photographic series *Limit Telephotography* (2010), in which he endeavoured to photograph military facilities such as those at Groom Lake (aka Area 51, the site associated with a range of popular conspiracy theories) in Nevada, which are ordinarily hidden from view and not simply open to photographic inspection. Paglen's photographs were taken using enormous high-powered telephoto lenses, designed for astrophotography, standing on the closest legal vantage point to his subject, often at distances of up to 40 miles. At first glance, the images are abstract and unconventional. Despite their highly specific names – *Chemical and Biological Weapons*

Proving Ground; Dugway, UT; Distance ~ 42 miles; 10:51 A.M. (2006) – they often appear to show nothing at all. John P. Jacobs's gloss of the project is very informative: 'his photographs interrogate the space of secrecy, offering material evidence of its infrastructure while also raising questions about the limitations of images'; as such they investigate the point 'where understanding bumps up against the incomprehensible and vision against the unrepresentable' (Jacobs 2018: 29). The aesthetics of the photographs are generated not by the traditional parameters of landscape photography, or, indeed, by the aesthetic conventions by which photography usually makes its object legible. Instead, the limitations the photographer must confront in the act of trying to photograph a secret government facility emerge as aesthetic properties within the image. As Paglen outlines,

> typical variables such as depth of field, composition, aperture, color balance, and exposure had to be reconceived in order to develop a visual language suited to the methods and conditions under which these photographs were taken ... Moreover, compositional possibilities are extremely limited because there is often only one location on public land from which I have a line of sight to my subject ... the fact that various parts of the colour spectrum do not move uniformly through miles of heat and haze ... becomes a basis for exposure and colour decisions. (quoted in Jacobs 2018: 30)

The final photograph, in its tendency towards abstraction and illegibility, actively indexes the degree to which its intended object is hidden from sight, and the distinct look of the series' images is produced by the pressures imposed by protocols of secrecy on the practice of photography from the outside.

Carrying this re-conception of visual language and aesthetics over to *The X-Files* and its conspiratorial myth-arc, a similar shadow indexicality is at play when the plots overlap with areas of Paglen's research, and the show attempts to represent the 'secret' facilities at Groom Lake. The double episode 'Dreamland' (S6: E04–5) has several scenes that take place in the corridors and offices of Area 51, which Mulder finds he has sudden access to when he mysteriously switches bodies with a government bureaucrat called Morris Fletcher (Michael McKean). The significant shot occurs early in the first episode when Mulder/Fletcher is taken back to the facility after the swap occurs. The shot is longer than the average establishing shot in the series and begins with a close-up of a sign against a wire fence. The camera lingers on the sign for long enough that there can be no doubt as to what is about to appear when the camera tracks across and cranes upwards for a wider angle: 'United States Air Force – Area 51 – Remote Test Site AFS Groom Lake NV'. The second half of the shot consists of a wide angle of the entrance to Area 51, which appears a little like a futuristic car park, only for covert military airplanes.

Several things are at play at once in this image of the entrance of Area 51. There is a sense that a mystery is being revealed, with Mulder finally accessing the secret military facility. However, at the same time the representation of Area 51 is strongly tongue-in-cheek and emphasizes its own hybridity and construction in a range of interesting ways. The chain-link fence in the foreground provides a clear break in the image about halfway up, above which the frame recedes dramatically into the inky blacks of the facility, with the shadows of multiple covert-looking aircrafts looming out of the darkness. The mysteriousness of the background is punctured by the mundanity of the chain-link fence, likewise the clunky sliding back and forth of the barrier is dissonant with the sleek technology lurking in the shadows behind it. Most pertinent to my argument, however, is the fact that the image is a composite of photographic and digital elements arranged above and below the fence-line. The fence in the foreground is photographically captured, the facility in the background is computer-generated, composited above the line of the fence in a simple piece of background matte-ing. Closer inspection of the central area of the image confirms that the image has been spliced together out of two medially distinct portions, a cinematographic shot of the fence and the computer-generated landscape in the background. Two white cars in the middle ground, in place to disguise the suture between the two portions of the image, do not track successfully with the movement of the camera. It is evident that the cars are a 2D element within the composited image, but because they are depicted in the middle ground, and not the deep background, the movement of the camera prompts our eyes to perceive parallax effects of perspective with objects near to the camera. However, given that the cars are a flat element within the compositing – as opposed to a modelled 3D digital asset – the parallax is absent and the layers of the image slide against and across one another quite awkwardly.

In its depiction of Area 51, using a hybrid image of both cinematographically captured footage and digitally generated and composited elements, the shot is acknowledging – along with Paglen – the limits of photography. Moreover, the image compensates for those limits with an aesthetic that deliberately exceeds the norms of photographic representation. Rather than attempting to achieve a seamless illusion, the image resorts to a non-photographic, discorrelated aesthetic. In doing so, it signals its status as an illusion and acknowledges that, in reality, the covert military institution that it is depicting will remain perennially out of sight.

This gesturing towards the limits of photography in the context of government secrecy is not isolated to this individual shot. *The X-Files* film features a number of prominent VFX shots in which Mulder's encounter with an enormous alien structure is spatialized in such a way as to consistently belie the fact that the shot is a digital background and David Duchovny is performing in front of a green screen. Even in season eleven, the tour given around secret facilities by Joel McHale in the episode

'My Struggle III' (S11: E01) is littered with instances of legible digital manipulation in the service of representing the secret technologies of the dark world. Mulder is taken to see an ARV (Alien Replica Vehicle). The craft, we are told, runs on 'free energy ... technology kept secret for seventy years while the world ran on petroleum'. At the apex of this demonstration, and discussion about what technologies and capabilities the government keeps concealed, the lead scientist announces: 'what I am about to show you is the most unbelievable part'. At this point, the craft disappears from view, spontaneously deconstructing in the image, in a way that resembles a less globular transition from that featured in 'Field Trip' (S6: E21). With the craft's sudden disappearance, the scene confirms what the audience may already have suspected: that the image of the spacecraft is being constructed out of a hybridized form of cinematography and digital visual effects. Once again, the show uses a deliberate foregrounding of its use of digital manipulation to demarcate two things: firstly, at the level of the plot, the top-secret military technology that is unrepresentable according to orthodox visual media, correlated to human vision; secondly, more pointedly, the degree to which embodied human vision, our perspectives upon and understanding of the world, is mediated by digital-imaging technologies and their propensity to manipulation.

Thus, we have a framework in place by which to make some tentative conclusions about how *The X-Files*' use of digital VFX can be read as a reflection or refraction of its technological context in a way that corresponds to the clearer sociopolitical reflections that it offers. In its anxious relation to illusion, *The X-Files* draws attention towards those aspects of experience that are more often than not hidden from sight. This occurs across several levels. At a thematic and narrative level, I have suggested that digital VFX are often used to mark the limits of vision. When used to represent the monsters of the week, this use of digital visual effects plays into a politics of representation as the presence of VFX can signal the ideological motivation behind a given representation. This is especially the case in episodes where the horror-coding is already alert to the racial and imperial processes of other-ing that mark differently abled people and immigrants in the Monster of the Week format. When used to depict the institutions of the covert world in the course of the myth-arc episodes – such as the storage facility frequented by the Cigarette Smoking Man, or Area 51, itself – the use of digital VFX to represent government facilities tacitly indexes the fact that not only do these government institutions exist, but that they are hidden intentionally hidden from view by means of what Trevor Paglen describes as a 'dark geography' (Paglen 2009). In these instances, the legibility of the hybrid images and the self-reflexivity of the use of digital visual effects offers a way of interrogating the secrecy that surrounds those institutions and the means by which they are rendered unrepresentable.

Lastly, I would suggest that *The X-Files*' notably infrequent use of digital VFX serves to highlight, through a form of negative refraction or thematization by exclusion, the forms of digital manipulation that characterize not just mainstream cinema, but visual culture at large, and by extension our collective cultural, social and political experience. As I mentioned in my introduction, champions of *The X-Files*, such as Kellner and Geller, celebrate the way in which the series' use of genre conventions illuminates broader social and political tensions. Given the fact that *The X-Files*' protagonists are government employees and the monsters-of-the-week are so often culturally marginalized subjects, or manifestations of biomedical processes gone wrong, this comes as no surprise. Theresa L. Geller's discussion of the show pushes this analysis as far as it will go, crediting the manifold political ambivalences contained within the show's tales of paranormal otherness with an epistemological relevance. Geller concludes her monograph on *The X-Files* with the claim that 'the series was committed to troubling not only *what we know*, but also how we came to know it' (2016: 110–11). Geller quotes Foucault's assertion that 'Truth is a thing of this world: it is produced only by virtue of multiple forms of constraint. And it induces regular effects of power' (2016: 110–11). That said, missing from this epistemological discourse is a consideration of the ways in which the gathering momentum of digital media in the 1990s contributes to the zeitgeist of postmodernity that the show reflects and comments upon. This is particularly surprising from our contemporary perspective, where any attempt to interrogate our structures of credulity and epistemological formations must take into consideration the influence of digital media.

To address this, I have used the critical terms of post-cinema to stress the degree to which media (and in particular digital media) acts, within Foucault's model, as one form of constraint that serves to produce truth. Moreover, I have sought to demonstrate how *The X-Files* has an implicit relationship not just with prevailing sociocultural tensions, but with the epistemological and political stakes of the digital media revolution that began (following Lev Manovich's chronology) in the mid-1990s. In the 2020s, the stakes and consequences of the digital media revolution are very clear indeed. It has, in Roger F. Cook's terminology, instigated a co-evolution in spectatorship, with the advent of digital media giving rise to forms of post-cinematic 'vision' (Cook 2020), 'imagination' (Swale 2015), 'affect' (Shaviro 2010) and, by extension, subjectivity. Considering the legacy of *The X-Files* from the vantage point of our visual culture in the 2020s, the show's hesitant use of digital VFX position it as an aesthetic and cultural touchstone at the dawn of our current age of digital saturation and post-cinematic structures of feeling. The modest use of digital VFX in *The X-Files*, despite its investment in paranormal phenomenon and the manipulability of belief and perception, can be read as running counter to the momentum towards CGI-intensive visuality occurring elsewhere. As such, its reflexive and cautious use of digital visual effects feed into its reflection of its sociocultural context as acutely as its use of genre conventions. The deployment of digital VFX in *The X-Files* exhibits a valuable hesitancy as regards the illusory qualities of digital visual effects, preferring instead to highlight and query the conditions of perception as they are set out by televisual media at the beginning of the digital revolution. As such, the show offers opportunities to interpret it as an early bellwether signalling the epistemic stakes of ubiquitous and invisible use of digital VFX as well as the concomitant dominance of digital media in other aspects of life. In its self-conscious and reflexive use of digital VFX, *The X-Files* does not prompt us to 'Believe the Lie' but alerts us to the ubiquity and potential consequences of the illusion.

References

Armageddon (1998), [Film] Dir. Michael Bay: Buena Vista.
Buffy the Vampire Slayer (1997–2003), [TV programme] The WB.
Cook, R. F. (2020), *Post-Cinematic Vision: The Coevolution of Moving-Image Media and the Spectator*, Minneapolis: University of Minnesota Press.
The Dark Knight (2008), [Film] Dir. Christopher Nolan: Warner Bros Pictures.
Denson, S. (2016), 'Crazy Cameras, Discorrelated Images, and the Post-Perceptual Mediation of Post-Cinematic Affect', in S. Denson and J. Leyda (eds), *Post-Cinema: Theorizing 21st Century Film*, 193–233, Brighton: Reframe Books.
Denson, S. (2021), *Discorrelated Images*, Durham, NC: Duke University Press.
The Empire Strikes Back (1980), [Film] Dir. Irvin Kershner, USA: 20th Century Fox.
Failes, I. (2019), 'How *Game of Thrones* Changed VFX Forever'. Available online: https://www.vfxvoice.com/how-game-of-thrones-changed-tv-vfx-forever/ (accessed 22 July 2022).
Flash Gordon (1980), [Film] Dir. Mike Hodges, USA: Universal Pictures.
Forrest Gump (1994), [Film] Dir. Robert Zemeckis, USA: Paramount Pictures.
Game of Thrones (2011–19), [TV programme] HBO.
Geller, T. L. (2016), *The X-Files (TV Milestones Series)*, Detroit, MI: Wayne State University Press.
Geller, T. L. (2017), 'Race and Allegory in Mass Culture: Historicizing *The X-Files*', *American Quarterly*, 69 (1): 93–115.
Godzilla (1998), [Film] Dir. Roland Emmerich: TriStar.
Iron Man (2008), [Film] Dir. Jon Favreau: Marvel/Paramount.
Jacobs, J. P. (2018), 'Trevor Paglen: Invisible Images, Impossible Objects', in J. P. Jacobs and L. Skrebowski (eds), *Trevor Paglen: Sites Unseen*, 23–85, Washington, DC: Smithsonian Art Museum.
Jurassic Park (1993), [Film] Dir. Steven Spielberg: Universal.
Kellner, D. (1999), 'The X-Files and the Aesthetics and Politics of Postmodern Pop', *Journal of Aesthetics and Art Criticism*, 57 (2): 161–75.
Manovich, L. (2001), *The Language of New Media*, Cambridge, MA: The MIT Press.

Manovich, L. (2006), 'After Effects, or Velvet Revolution Part 1'. Available online: http://manovich.net/index.php/projects/after-effects-part-1 (accessed 22 July 2022).

Manovich, L. (2007), 'Understanding Hybrid Media'. Available online: http://manovich.net/index.php/projects/understanding-hybrid-media (accessed 22 July 2022).

Paglen, T. (2009) *Blank Spots on the Map: The Dark Geography of the Pentagon's Secret World*, New York: Dutton.

Paglen, T. (2010), *Invisible: Covert Operations and Classified Landscapes*, New York: Aperture.

Rosen, P. (2001), *Change Mummified: Cinema, Historicity, Theory*, Minneapolis: University of Minnesota Press.

Shaviro, S. (2010), *Post-Cinematic Affect*, London: Zero Books.

Shaviro, S. (2016), 'Post-Continuity: An Introduction', in S. Denson and J. Leyda (eds), *Post-Cinema: Theorizing 21st Century Film*, 51–64, Brighton: Reframe Books.

Swale, A. (2015), *Anime Aesthetics: Japanese Animation and the 'Post-Cinematic Imagination'*, London: Palgrave Macmillan.

Titanic (1997), [Film] Dir. James Cameron: Paramount.

The Twilight Zone (1959–64), [TV programme] UPN.

Westurland, M. (2019), 'The Emergence of Deepfake Technology: A Review', *Technology Innovation Management Review*, 9(11): 39–52.

The X-Files (1998) [Film] Dir. Rob Bowman: 20th Century Fox.

The X-Files: I Want to Believe (2008) Dir. Chris Carter: 20th Century Fox.

'X-Files: Season 11 Breakdown Reel' (2018), Imagine Engine VFX. Available online: https://www.youtube.com/watch?v=3hSBXYww5yk (accessed 6 February 2023).

PART TWO

Contemporary legend: Conspiracy, belief and politics

Diane A. Rodgers

Considering the continuing current levels of exposed institutional corruption, political cover-ups and government scandals across the globe into the 2020s, it is arguable the legacy of *The X-Files* and the themes with which the series dealt remain as relevant as ever. Paranoia, conspiracy theories and misappropriation of folklore, under the aegis of contemporary legend, invade everyday life with the potential to directly affect social, cultural and popular belief. Such legends can be understood as stories that spread primarily through informal channels, particularly via word of mouth or contemporary forms of media. Contemporary legend narratives tend to be about subjects that really exist, or are 'believed to have existed; even when it recounts a supernatural or highly unusual event, this is claimed to have occurred in real life' (Simpson and Roud 2003: 212). Thus, the plausible political context in which *The X-Files* situates even its most fantastical narratives, conspiracy theories and supernatural events is supported by the pilot episode's opening claim that 'the following story is inspired by actual documented accounts'. In an era where influential billionaires publicly muse upon alien life and conspiracy theories help sway electoral outcomes and fuel the polarization of public health debates, it is vital to reflect upon how *The X-Files* presents its legendary stories with its own strongly conspiratorial suggestion that these stories *could be* real: stories that 'they' simply don't want 'us' to know.

David Clarke's chapter opens this section with an exploration of contemporary UFO legends that inspired *The X-Files*, charting a history of the modern phenomenon of Unidentified Flying Objects from events in 1947 (such as the 'Roswell incident') to the present day. Clarke examines how the portrayal of phenomena like alien abduction experiences (and recurring associated motifs like the notion of 'missing time') in entertainment media affected popular belief and how this, in turn, was reflected within *The X-Files*. The chapter looks at the role played by *The X-Files* in reinvigorating a fringe belief system and how this fed into mainstream perceptions about UFO conspiracies and cover-ups which, Clarke argues, have become as much a part of the American cultural myth and imagination as the assassination of President Kennedy.

Racheal Harris moves the notion of belief into the realm of alternative spiritualities and new religious movements in terms of their portrayal in the series. Harris explores how echoes of the mass suicides which occurred in Jonestown in 1978 and the 1993 Branch Davidian siege at Waco, Texas, are evident in episodes of *The X-Files*. Harris examines the representation of 'cults' and alternative religions such as Haitian Vodou across the series and interrogates changing attitudes to spiritual beliefs which deviate from a Christian 'norm' across recent decades.

Picking up on notions of myth and legend (such as those introduced earlier by Clarke), Gregory Frame situates *The X-Files* within a lineage of 1970s conspiracy thrillers (such as *All the President's Men*, 1976) and the US 'traumatic decade'. Citing the parenthetical milestones of the 1963 Kennedy assassination and the defeat of the United States in the war in Vietnam in 1975, Frame's chapter examines how these are incorporated into the wider 'myth-arc' in *The X-Files*. This chapter discusses how events like these, and others like the Watergate scandal, remain thematically relevant both throughout the series and to today's society in relation to continuing government secrecy, corruption and denial.

Bethan Jones looks back at *The X-Files* from the perspective of the modern ascendancy of fake news and conspiracy theories like QAnon. Her chapter questions the notion of the search for 'The Truth' in the series as linked to the

1980s and 1990s eras of Reagan and Bush and how this was reinterpreted for seasons ten and eleven, under the shadow of Donald Trump as president of the United States. Jones draws upon original research recording fan response to the political relevance and verisimilitude of the revived series, exploring the ways in which the later seasons reflect increasingly right-wing global trends in the 2010s and onward.

The authors of these chapters, therefore, create a picture of not only the stories, myths and legends communicated by *The X-Files*, but also the part the series played itself in perpetuating notions about subjects from alien life to government corruption. It is fascinating in this section to reflect upon which of these notions have become pervasive in popular culture and to what extent *The X-Files* (and the ideas shared within its own legendary cycle) may have affected cultural and popular beliefs and perhaps even a number of conspiracy theories widely shared today.

References

All the President's Men (1976), [Film] Dir. Alan J. Pakula, USA: Wildwood Enterprises.

Simpson, J., and S. Roud (2003), *A Dictionary of English Folklore*, Oxford: Oxford University Press.

6

'I want to believe': How UFOs conquered *The X-Files*

David Clarke

'Pilot' (S1: E01), the first episode of what would become one of the most successful television series of the late twentieth century, opens with a notice: 'The following story is inspired by actual documented accounts.' The episode opens with a night-time scene in which a young woman runs through a forest in Oregon as if pursued by an invisible force. She is engulfed in a beam of light amidst a swirling vortex of leaves. Later, when her body is discovered, police and FBI investigators link it to a series of other unexplained deaths of high-school students. It transpires they are all victims of 'alien abduction', a phenomenon that was the subject of intense public and media interest in the United States during the 1990s. As the episode unfolds, elements of this and other contemporary Unidentified Flying Objects (UFO) legends are name-checked: missing time, nasal implants, hybrid human-aliens, cover-ups and an alien autopsy.

The 'actual documented accounts' tagline is not used again after the Pilot episode. It is replaced by a series of slogans: 'Government Denies Knowledge', 'The Truth Is Out There' and 'Trust No One'. The slogans reflect the cultural impact of the UFO controversy upon the show's creator and co-director, Chris Carter (Kozinets 1997). From 1993 onwards, the television series became the conduit through which an international audience were introduced to the milieu of legends, rumours and personal experiences that have circulated within the UFO subculture, popularly known as 'UFOlogy', since 1947. Whilst such beliefs are remarkably varied,

Jane Goldman has observed, echoing the quote from the character Deep Throat: 'no matter which end of the spectrum a believer occupies, there is one common certainty: the Government is hiding something' (1995: 247).

The X-Files explored the more arcane aspects of the UFO phenomenon to an extent that had eluded earlier made-for television dramas and films from which Carter drew inspiration (Coleman 1995: 23–4). During the second season, Carter told journalists the series followed 'a long line' of made-for-television horror anthologies that included *The Twilight Zone* (1959–64) and *The Outer Limits* (1963–5). The latter was more orientated to science fiction with plot twists and some episodes included alien abduction narratives. Another inspiration for the maverick character Fox Mulder was the 1972 made-for-television movie *Kolchak: The Night Stalker*. This followed the adventures of a wise-cracking journalist, Karl Kolchak, played by Darren McGavin, who investigated vampires, werewolves and invisible aliens. The success of the film and a 1973 follow-up led to a twenty-one-episode series shown on ABC during 1974–5. Carter admits this 'scared me as a kid' and, with *The X-Files*, he 'wanted to do something as dark and mysterious as I remembered it to be' (Coleman 1995: 23).

Of the forty-nine episodes in the first two seasons (1993–6), fourteen (28 per cent) featured plots that were based around the UFO cover-up and alien abductions. The cover-up/conspiracy theme also frames the plot of the first of two movies based upon the series, *The X-Files: Fight the Future* (1998). Chris Carter successfully combined horror and conspiracy themes from 1970s television and 1950s science fiction movies to create *The X-Files* at a moment when popular belief in UFOs made the leap from fringe to mainstream. This chapter will examine the contemporary UFO legends that inspired several individual episodes as well as the story-arc from the first two seasons of the television series. These legends include the interlinked alien abduction and UFO conspiracy/crashed saucer myths that Hilary Evans defined as 'constituting a wonderfully rich and elaborate mythology unmatched in the world's folklore' (1997: 257). Myths have been defined by Rollo May as a means of making sense of a senseless world: 'narrative patterns that give significance to our existence' (1993: 15).

Background

The modern phenomenon of UFOs arrived on 24 June 1947 when a private pilot, Kenneth Arnold, saw a formation of nine batwing shaped objects flying in echelon formation at supersonic speed above the Cascade Mountains in Washington state, United States. A newspaper subeditor coined the phrase 'flying saucers', and within days reports of similar mysterious objects in the sky were made across North America and in Europe and Australia (Evans and Stacy 1997). Early in July, the Roswell *Daily Record* reported the discovery by a rancher of some peculiar wreckage that consisted of silver foil and sticks in the New Mexico desert. An official US Army statement linked the wreckage with rumours about 'flying discs' and announced it had been taken to the nearby Roswell Army Air Base for examination. A follow-up statement said the debris was just a weather balloon and the media accepted this explanation (Berlitz and Moore 1980).

By August of that year an opinion poll published by the Gallup organization found that nine of out ten Americans had heard of 'flying saucers', the highest recognition level recorded in the organization's history at that time (Durant 1997: 231). A follow-up poll by Gallup in 1966 found 96 per cent of those surveyed had 'heard or read' about UFOs and 5 per cent, approximately 5 million people, said they had seen something in the sky they could not identify (Durant 1997: 234). In 1950, Captain Edward Ruppelt, who led the US Air Force project Blue Book, tasked with investigating reported sightings, coined the acronym UFO ('unidentified flying object') to replace flying saucer (Ruppelt 1956).

Belief in the existence of intelligent extraterrestrials can be traced back to ancient history. Classical authors speculated about the existence of life in other worlds and medieval sources tell of phantom ships and other unexplained aerial phenomena. Carl Jung cited a news broadsheet from Nuremberg in 1561 that illustrates a mass sighting of celestial phenomena as one example of many similar stories from medieval Europe (1958: vi). However, popular belief that mysterious disc-shaped flying objects were craft-piloted by aliens who were involved in reconnoitring Earth can be dated to the opening of the Cold War (Eghigian 2015). In *The X-Files*, 1947 is specifically identified as the year in which the US government first uncovered evidence of an alien presence on Earth and began conspiring to conceal the truth from the public (Graham 1996: 58). Post-Second-World-War visions of flying saucers became a media fixation as the spectre of a nuclear war fuelled fear and anxiety. Coupled with a legacy of government secrecy from the Second World War, UFOs presented themselves as 'a riddle wrapped in a mystery inside an enigma', to paraphrase Winston Churchill who instigated a top secret British government investigation of the UFO mystery whilst prime minister in 1952 (Clarke 2012: 65–6).

The fiftieth anniversary of the Arnold sighting in 1997 marked the high watermark of public fascination with the UFO mystery. A substantial increase in public awareness is evident both in quantitative data from opinion polls and the results of a content analysis of print media stories sampled from twenty-five US newspapers covering the years 1985–2014 (Eghigian 2015: 613). A *Time*/CNN poll of 1,024 adults released prior to the anniversary found 64 per cent believed aliens had contacted Earth, 50 per cent believed aliens had abducted humans and 37 per cent said aliens had contacted the US government ('Poll: U.S. Hiding Knowledge of Aliens', 1997). A 1998 ICM poll in the UK, with a similar sample size, found 29 per cent believed 'extraterrestrial life has already visited earth' and 2 per cent claimed they had a direct experience of extraterrestrial life (Clarke 1998: 18).

Increased awareness of the phenomenon is also apparent in raw statistics supplied by the UK Ministry of Defence's UFO desk that collected reports submitted by members of the public from 1958 to 2009. These show a tripling in the numbers of UFO sightings reported during the 1990s, from 117 in 1995 to 609 in 1996, coincident with the transmission of the first two seasons of *The X-Files* on BBC 2 (Clarke 2015: 127). In response to a 1996 public inquiry, UK Ministry of Defence (MoD) desk officer Kerry Philpott wrote: 'I believe the marked increase in the number of "UFO" sightings made to the MoD is directly related to the amount of television and media attention this subject has been attracting over the last few years. Any television programme on the subject of "UFOs" generates a surge in reports of ... sightings' (National Archives ref: DEFE 24/1982/1). Public fascination was not fuelled exclusively by the popularity of television series alone. It has to be interpreted in the wider context of what MoD described as 'the media obsession with UFOs' at that time. This included the publication of a series of new books to mark the fiftieth anniversary along with magazines, television documentaries and newspaper stories that interlinked UFO and alien abduction content with the *X-Files* zeitgeist.

The summer of 1996 also saw the release of Roland Emmerich's blockbuster alien invasion movie *Independence Day* that featured giant flying saucers and references to both Roswell and Area 51. The movie adopted rumours about the top-secret US military/CIA facility near Groom Lake in Nevada, where prototype aircraft were test-flown during the Cold War. Belief that Area 51, popularly known as Dreamland, is a storage facility for wreckage of extraterrestrial craft and their crews, both alive and dead, features prominently in contemporary UFO legends that predate *The X-Files* (Patton 1997).

The Area 51 UFO conspiracy legend originated in 1989 when Robert (Bob) Lazar was interviewed for television at a studio in Las Vegas. He claimed to have worked on a highly classified project involving the reverse engineering of captured alien technology. Lazar maintained he worked on disc-shaped craft approximately 35 feet in diameter and 15-feet high and saw creatures on base that he believed were extraterrestrials. Lazar claimed to be a physicist and engineer, but no one has been able to verify his credentials. Many journalists and some UFOlogists suspect his story is either a hoax or was part of a disinformation campaign by a US intelligence agency (Patton 1997: 214–15; Pilkington 2010; Scholes 2020).

Since the 1980s, further leaks from shadowy former military and government whistleblowers who alleged Area 51 was the ultimate resting place for wreckage from the Roswell incident continued to reach the UFO community. *Independence Day* opens with a giant alien mothership sending smaller flying saucers to attack cities and disable Earth's defences. After a battle with a squadron of F-18 Hornet jets led by Captain Steve Hiller (Will Smith), an injured alien is captured and taken to Area 51. It is only at this point that the CIA admits to President Thomas J. Whitmore (Bill Pullman) that the facility houses the spacecraft that crashed at Roswell in 1947 along with three bodies from its alien crew. In 2013, the CIA admitted that Area 51 really did exist but was used as a base for the secret testing of black project aircraft such as the B2 Stealth bomber that was first used in combat in 1999 during the Kosovo War (Clarke 2012: 139–40).

The release of *Independence Day*, in the year the third season of *The X-Files* aired on US and UK television, increased public speculation that a government disclosure of 'the truth' about alien visitations was imminent. At the time, the official responsible for the UK Ministry of Defence's UFO desk revealed his staff were struggling to answer a steady stream of letters, emails and phone calls from members of the public 'seeking information about the existence of alien life forms, or seeking a detailed investigation/ explanation for allegations of abductions by aliens, out of body experiences, animal mutilations, crop circles etc' (Clarke 2012: 165). As a direct result, the MoD installed a twenty-four-hour UFO hotline answerphone service and dedicated email address to cope with the increasing workload. This helpline continued to operate until 2009.

The UFO legend plotlines from *The X-Files* engaged with and drew directly upon first-hand accounts of personal experiences published by the news media and disseminated via UFO internet discussion forums. In September 2019, the accumulation of rumours concerning the Nevada base led to direct action in the form of a Facebook event, Storm Area 51, also known as They Can't Stop All of Us, that began as a joke posted by a college student (https://dreamlandresort.com/).

For the first two decades of the UFO mystery disc and saucer-shaped spacecraft remained iconic in popular culture as depicted in science fiction movies such as *The Day the Earth Stood Still* (1951) and *Forbidden Planet* (1956). From the late 1970s, a new type of UFO shape became more common in narratives reported to the media, civilian UFO research groups and, in the UK, the MoD's UFO desk. Huge, dark triangular or boomerang-shaped objects of the type depicted in the episode 'Deep Throat' (S1: E02) were reported hovering or cruising silently above roads and cities in the United States during the 1980s. Typically, observers would notice a pulsing coloured light at the apex of each corner, or a light in the centre of the object. A similar shaped imaginary spacecraft, the Imperial Star Destroyer, appeared on cinema screens in the opening sequence of George Lucas's space epic, *Star Wars* (1977). This period also saw the US Air Force release the first images of the distinctive triangular, radar-absorbent profile of the F-117A Stealth fighter and the equally UFO-like B2 Spirit bomber. Artist's impressions of these aircraft had circulated for a decade before they received their first public display in 1990 and 1988 respectively.

Alien abductions

In addition to UFO shapes, the series reflected ideas and rumours concerning the appearance of extraterrestrials. Earlier in the Cold War, films such as *Invaders from Mars* (1953) fed upon the paranoia generated by the UFO flaps and fears about Reds under the bed. These movies portrayed aliens as hostile, bug-eyed creatures bent on invading Earth. *Invaders from Mars* featured the Martian Mastermind, a green creature with a large head and small, tentacled body whose mutant servants abducted people from a small American town. In 1969, the editor of the British magazine *Flying Saucer Review*, Charles Bowen, noted the bewildering 'multitude of shapes and forms' adopted by UFO occupants or UFOnauts (Clarke 2015: 212). Before that time, reports of close encounters included accounts of hairy bellicose dwarfs from South America and tall, angelic blond-haired Nordics of the type described by Polish-American émigré George Adamski in the 1953 bestseller *Flying Saucers Have Landed* (Leslie and Adamski 1953).

Between the publication of Adamski's book in 1953 and the Apollo moon landings (1969 to 1972), stories about the appearance and modus operandi of UFOnauts underwent a series of subtle changes. Creatures with large heads and small bodies, who feature in *The X-Files*, did not become established as the template for the UFOnauts who abducted people before the late 1970s. The turning point occurred with Betty and Barney Hill's account of their alleged alien abduction in 1961. The dramatic narrative of the couple from New Hampshire provided the template from which all subsequent alien abduction stories can trace their origin. Media coverage of the story followed the publication of John Fuller's book *The Interrupted Journey* (1966). Betty Hill was a white social worker and Barney, who was Black, worked in a post office. One night in September 1961, they were returning from a holiday in Canada to their home in the United States via the White Mountains in New Hampshire, when Betty spotted a light in the sky and announced it was following their car. The UFO appeared to move closer and at one stage Barney, who was driving, stopped and examined it through binoculars. Inside, he saw humanoid figures dressed in black 'Nazi-like' uniforms and caps. He recalled the distinctive dark eyes of one, who appeared to be the leader, fix him with a penetrating glare. Barney ran back to the car in panic shouting 'Oh my God, we're going to be captured!'

The Hills resumed their journey and soon they heard a series of beeping sounds. At that point their conscious memory ended. Their next recollection was of seeing a road sign that indicated they were 35 miles away. Two hours appeared to be missing from their journey. Soon afterwards Betty began to have nightmares, and the couple sought help from a psychiatrist, Dr Benjamin Simon. In 1964, the couple began to attend hypnotherapy sessions at his surgery in Boston. Under hypnosis, an elaborate story emerged in which their car was stopped at a road block by a group of small, grey humanoids and the Hills were taken on board a landed UFO. Once inside, the couple were subjected to intrusive medical examinations followed by a conversation with the 'leader' of the alien crew. Barney was transfixed by the eyes of the short creatures who had 'odd shaped heads with a large cranium' and big, black wraparound eyes. Dr Simon doubted the couple had really met aliens but admitted that 'some aspects of the experience are unanswered and perhaps unanswerable' (Pflock and Brookesmith 2007: 145).

The 'missing time' element that was central to the Hill narrative became an important motif in the mythic aspect of UFOlogy that originated in the United States. From the 1970s onwards, the UFO literature and mass media published many other accounts from individuals in the United States and other parts of the Western world who claimed to have experienced 'missing time'. Some claimed to have conscious recollections of being taken against their will, often from their homes by unearthly creatures. In other cases, victims were transferred to landed or hovering UFOs where they were subjected to intrusive sexual examinations before they were returned to Earth. In 1987, horror fiction author Whitley Strieber published an account of his own bizarre experiences with creatures he called 'the visitors' in a bestselling book, *Communion*, subtitled *A True Story* (1987). The cover featured a striking artist's impression of the face of one of the beings who Strieber claimed abducted him from his cabin in upstate New York.

By 1993, when *The X-Files* premiered on US television, UFOnauts had been rebranded as 'the greys' in pop culture. The distinctive grey creatures, with small bodies, large heads and huge, black almond-shaped eyes feature in the series and stared out from movie posters, advertising hoardings, magazine covers and T-shirts. Chris Carter has said that he became convinced his idea for *The X-Files* would be a commercial success when he met a psychology professor who told him about an independently funded 1991 poll conducted by the Roper Organisation. This claimed to reveal how 3 per cent of the US population, or one out of every fifty adult Americans, 'believes they have been abducted by aliens' (Kozinets 1997: 6). Carter said he 'realised there was a topicality to this theme of the unknown and *The X-Files* grew out of that fascination' (Coleman 1995: 23).

Fox Mulder's quest to discover what happened to his younger sister, who was abducted by aliens from the family home becomes an all-consuming obsession for the fictional character. The alien abduction phenomenon features heavily in season one, as Mulder experiences flashbacks to an evening in November 1973 when he, aged twelve, and Samantha, eight, argue about what they should watch on TV. Fox wants to see a news broadcast about President Nixon and the Watergate investigation, but his sibling keeps switching channels. As they squabble, the room is bathed in unearthly light. In a scene reminiscent of the 'abduction' of Barry Guiler in Steven Spielberg's *Close Encounters of the Third Kind* (1977), Samantha is floated out of the window while Fox is immobilized.

The Samantha abduction story draws upon the 'Darkside' UFO conspiracy theory that claims a 'New World Order' has been actively conspiring with extra-terrestrials responsible for the abduction and crossbreeding of humans and aliens. One of the founding documents of the Darkside movement was published by John Lear on the ParaNet bulletin board in 1987. Lear claimed the first open communication between aliens and the US authorities happened at Holloman Air Force base in New Mexico in 1964. Subsequently, the US government made a deal with these aliens 'that in exchange for "technology" ... they would provide us, we agreed to "ignore" the [alien] abductions'. This pact also involved 'genetic engineering experiments' that fed the alien abduction folklore. Lear claimed these involved 'the impregnation of human females and early termination of pregnancies to secure the crossbreed infant' (Clark 1998: 301).

The Roper poll that inspired Carter was funded by a group of UFOlogists led by a New York artist and author Budd Hopkins. At the time, he was the leading actor in the North American abduction scene and his 1981 book, *Missing Time*, became a bestseller (Hopkins 1981). It laid down three basic tenets of the abduction syndrome. First, people taken by aliens often reported periods of missing time they could not account for rationally. Second, many had been repeatedly 'taken', like Mulder's sister Samantha, and their experiences often began in childhood. Many reported a feeling of paralysis and terror as they were floated out of bedrooms or cars into a waiting 'craft' where they were subjected to terrifying, intrusive physical examinations of the type described by Betty and Barney Hill under hypnotic regression. Often sperm or ova were removed by their alien captors. Third, many self-identifying abductees were left with physical evidence of these procedures in the form of scars on their skin or 'implants' placed inside their bodies by the aliens.

The Roper poll was based upon a questionnaire survey of 6,000 people randomly selected. It included a number of 'indicator' questions. These asked the respondent if they had sighted a UFO, experienced missing time or felt paralysis upon waking from sleep. Of those who participated, 2 per cent ticked a significant number of these indicators. The results led Hopkins to claim there was 'a very strong possibility' that around 3.7 million Americans had been 'taken' by extraterrestrials. This interpretation of the results was challenged by sceptics who pointed out that 'a poll is only as trustworthy as those who phrase its questions'. Reviewing the survey for the London-based Society for Psychical Research, Hilary Evans said the authors had measured the scale of the phenomenon but had failed to establish that 'those who claim to have been abducted have in fact been abducted' or that 'this constellation of experiences is exclusive to those who have been abducted' (Evans 1994: 379).

The cosmic Watergate

The X-Files has been described as television's *fin de siècle* compendium of conspiracy theories (Graham 1996: 56). The seeds of what UFOlogist Stanton Friedman called 'the cosmic Watergate' were planted four decades before Chris Carter's scripts became a cultural phenomenon (Radford 2010: 1). Retired US marine and pulp-fiction author Donald Keyhoe was the first to lay the charge of cover-up against the US Air Force and CIA. His writings claimed a secret war was being waged between the US military and extraterrestrials that overlapped with the Cold War. He also seeded the idea that aliens were first attracted to Earth as a result of our experiments with nuclear power and the destruction of Japanese cities in 1945 (Keyhoe 1950, 1957). This tapped into latent anxieties about nuclear confrontation that appear in movie plots such as *The Day the Earth Stood Still* (1951). Cover-ups and alleged interest by the UFO pilots in our atomic weapons and power plants have proved to be persistent themes in the UFO mythology.

Keyhoe's books were widely read during his lifetime, but his beliefs had relatively few adherents outside the members of the UFO believer community. In the United States during the 1960s, the label 'conspiracy nut' was in some respects worse than being called a communist (Graham 1996). Watergate, Vietnam, the Pentagon Papers and a series of political assassinations (discussed further in Chapter 8 of this volume) transformed that identification and by the 1970s, conspiracy thinking was no longer confined to eccentrics on the fringes of mainstream society. Deep Throat's warning to Mulder, to 'trust no one', as he lay dying in the final episode of season one, became the political mantra of the decades that followed.

Michael Barkun has identified three categories of conspiracist thinking in ascending order of scale. The first is limited and involves the conspirators concentrating their efforts on a discrete objective (for example, the 9/11 attacks or the assassination of President John F. Kennedy). Systematic conspiracies are more wide-ranging and involve a single evil organization that attempts to control a country, region or the world. Conspiracies involving Jews, Masons and the Catholic Church fall into this category. The third and most elaborate type are super-conspiracies that involve multiple plots linked together in complex hierarchies like a series of Russian dolls (Barkun 2003: 6). In control sits 'a distant but all-powerful evil force manipulating lesser conspiratorial actors' much like the fictional US-led cabal depicted in *The X-Files*. This organization resembles Majestic-12, abbreviated as MJ-12, a fictional secret committee of scientists, military leaders and government officials that features in UFO conspiracy narratives. This legend began in 1984 when a dossier stamped 'Top Secret/Majic' was posted to leaders of the UFO community in the United States and UK. The dossier is dated 1950 and appeared to be the product of a committee formed in 1947 by an executive order from US President Harry S. Truman to facilitate the recovery and investigation of spacecraft that crashed in the United States. In 1994, an FBI investigation concluded the MJ-12 documents were 'bogus' but the authors have never been identified (Pilkington 2010: 215).

A key element in the cosmic Watergate is the legend of the crashed saucer. The Roswell incident that followed Ken Arnold's seminal sighting is central to the events detailed in the MJ-12 dossier and is undoubtedly the most important narrative in UFO history. The story revolves around the discovery of wreckage from a flying saucer crash in the summer of 1947 and how the bodies of its small humanoid pilots were removed by the US military. Those who witnessed the operation were either sworn to secrecy or had their lives threatened. A fake cover story, which claimed the 'flying disc' had been later identified as a weather balloon, was released to the media, effectively killing the story until it was resurrected in Berlitz and Moore's book *The Roswell Incident* (1980).

Even in 1947, elaborate narratives about crashed spacecraft were nothing new. During the nineteenth century, American newspapers occasionally published invented reports of extraterrestrial airships that were prone to crashing in remote places. These narratives often involved the discovery of Martian bodies and hieroglyphic writings. The basic motif resurfaced, after the Second World War ended, in a novel, *The Flying Saucer*, which revolves around a group of influential scientists who, worried by the impending Third World War, concoct a method of uniting world leaders by faking a series of UFO crashes including one in New Mexico. Strange marks are found on the shell of one object that an expert from the British Museum compares to Egyptian hieroglyphs, a motif that reappears in the MJ-12 papers. The plot resolves when Cold War tensions are replaced by a cooperative league, a version of the New World order, for the defence of mankind against the Martian foe (Newman 1948).

In 1950, pulp-fiction author Frank Scully published another variant of this legend in his non-fiction book, *Behind the Flying Saucer Mystery*. His information came from a mysterious scientist concerning three Venusian spacecraft that landed or crashed on a rocky plateau near Aztec in New Mexico. The crash site was cordoned off by the military who gained entry to one of the craft via a porthole. Inside they found sixteen 'little men' and papers covered in strange writings that resemble hieroglyphics. The motifs present in Victorian airship, Roswell, Aztec and MJ-12 stories all feature in the first season of *The X-Files*. The episode 'EBE' uses the acronym for 'Extra-terrestrial Biological Entities' that appears in the MJ-12 dossier 'as the standard form of reference for these creatures until such time as a more definitive designation can be agreed upon'.

In the decades that followed, others came forward to claim they were present at the retrieval of the Roswell saucer and had personally handled material from the crash (Carey and Schmitt 2007). Some informants said they had even seen the cadavers of the alien pilots who were subjected to autopsies and stored in secret air force hangars. Their appearance is consistent with the alien abductors: small with large heads and eyes. A former US Army intelligence officer, Colonel Philip Corso claimed to have not only seen the body of an alien retrieved from Roswell but, like Bob Lazar, to have been involved in the US military's attempt to back-engineer technology recovered from the craft (Corso and Birnes 1997).

In the episode 'Deep Throat', Mulder and Scully discuss the mysterious disappearance of a test pilot during a UFO flap near a secret airbase in Idaho. The more sceptical Scully asks Mulder, 'are you suggesting that the military are flying UFOs?' Mulder replies: 'No. Planes built using UFO technology'.

Conclusion

Philip Corso's book appeared in 1997, the fiftieth anniversary of the modern UFO mystery when *The X-Files* was at the height of its popularity. By this point, the Roswell legend had eclipsed Kenneth Arnold's sighting as the most evidential UFO narrative to date. Its proponents pointed to hundreds of witnesses, some of whom had impeccable military credentials. The story had become so prevalent in popular culture that folklorist Jan Harold Brunvand categorized Roswell and 'The landed Martians' as a new type of modern legend that revolves around 'the suppression of some secret that would, if revealed, ruin the careers of prominent officials or cause panic among the population' (Brunvand 1984: 198).

Anthropologist Charles A. Ziegler summarizes the Roswell legend as 'a traditional folk motif clothed in a modern garb'. His analysis suggests the central legend can be summarized as 'a malevolent monster (the government) has sequestered an item essential to humankind'. That treasure takes the form of transformative knowledge: *we are not alone in the universe*. The culture hero, or UFO investigator, outwits the monster and, by investigatory prowess 'releases the essential item (wisdom) for humankind' (Ziegler, in Saler, Ziegler and Moore 1997: 51). In *The X-Files*, Mulder plays this traditional hero, 'a federal agent with a cosmic consciousness with privileged access to paranormal phenomena' (Graham 1996: 57).

The crashed saucer/UFO conspiracy has become as much a part of the American cultural imagination as the JFK assassination and has transformed the modern city of Roswell into a place of pilgrimage (Scholes 2020: 148–71). It has remained so popular and ubiquitous simply because it reflects the quantitative data provided by a series of opinion surveys in the United States and UK. These have reported that a substantial proportion of the public in the Western world believe extraterrestrials have visited Earth and the United States and other governments are engaged in an ongoing cover-up to hide the evidence (Durant 1997: 237–8). The 1997 CNN/Time poll found that 80 per cent of Americans believed their government was hiding evidence of extraterrestrial life and another survey found 20 per cent were convinced a UFO crashed at Roswell ('Poll: U.S. Hiding Knowledge of Aliens', 1997).

Born in 1957, Carter has described Watergate and the downfall of President Richard Nixon as 'the most formative event' of his 1970s youth. In creating the series, he revisited the moment 'when America came face to face with the repressed demons of post-war politics, that moment when decisions were made to bury the monsters and "deny everything"' (Graham 1996: 56). Fox Mulder's informant Deep Throat, who warns him to 'trust no one', was a contemporary version of journalist Bob Woodward's Pentagon informant from the Watergate era. Carter has described himself as 'a non-religious person looking for a religious experience' whose scepticism is waiting to be challenged, much like the characters Mulder and Scully he created (Goldman 1995: 219).

Carter's characters and plot evolved from the legacy of Keyhoe's writings and four decades of myth-making that have transformed the UFO mystery into the most powerful contemporary myth of the late twentieth century. The UFO conspiracy narratives have spread beyond the confines of UFOlogy because they appeal to a wider audience of conspiracist thinking that emerged in the aftermath of the 9/11 terrorist attacks. Unlike the situation following the JFK assassination when the label 'conspiracy nut' was confined to a tiny group of political activists, by 2001, those who were prepared to question the veracity and motives of both governments and mainstream media could no longer be described as belonging to a 'fringe' movement.

The X-Files, as a cultural phenomenon, reinvigorated the existing UFO mythology and revived its rich history of literature, rumours and legends. It also provided a platform whereby the UFO experiencers, the UFOlogists and 'X-Philes' (as members of the show's fan clubs are known) could share narratives and beliefs as a part of a sympathetic community. Some X-Philes are on record as saying their belief in UFOs, and interest in conspiracy theories, predated the arrival of the show. Panel members at one convention said 'their interest in *The X-Files* originated in the "serious way" in which it treated UFOs and government UFO conspiracy or cover-up theories' (Kozinets 1997: 6).

In addition to drawing upon the subject's mythology for its raw materials, *The X-Files* fed back into the individual and collective experience of the UFO phenomenon. Drawing upon my own contemporary experience as a journalist and author writing for Fortean and UFO-related media at that time, it was clear the phrase 'X-Files' had become synonymous with UFOs, secret government investigations and related conspiracy theories in popular culture. The UK Ministry of Defence UFO files, released at The National

Archives from 2008 to 2013 as part of an open government project that I curated, were routinely referred to by both the print and broadcast media as 'Britain's X-Files' or the 'Real X-Files'. As I concluded in the introduction to the published guide to the collection, 'The overall theme of the series was summed up by an iconic poster in Mulder's office that featured an image of a "flying saucer" with the caption: "I want to believe"' (Clarke 2012: vii).

References

Barkun, M. (2003), *A Culture of Conspiracy: Apocalyptic Visions in Contemporary America*, Berkeley: University of California Press.
Berlitz, C., and W. Moore (1980), *The Roswell Incident*, London: Granada.
Brunvand, J. (1984), *The Choking Doberman and Other 'New' Urban Legends*, New York: W. W. Norton.
Carey, T., and D. Schmitt (2007), *Witness to Roswell: Unmasking the 60-Year Cover-Up*, Franklin Lakes, NJ: Career Press.
Clark, J. (1998), *The UFO Encyclopedia* 2nd edn, Detroit: Omnigraphics.
Clarke, D. (2012), *The UFO Files: The Inside Story of Real-Life Sightings*, London: Bloomsbury.
Clarke, D. (2015), *How UFOs Conquered the World: The History of a Modern Myth*, London: Aurum Press.
Clarke, N. (1998), 'The Power of the Paranormal', *Daily Mail*, 2 February: 18–19.
Close Encounters of the Third Kind (1977), [Film] Dir. Steven Spielberg, USA: Columbia Pictures.
Coleman, L. (1995), 'The Truth behind *The X-Files*', *Fortean Times* 82, August-September: 22–9.
Corso, P., and W. Birnes (1997), *The Day after Roswell*, London: Simon & Schuster.
The Day the Earth Stood Still (1951), [Film] Dir. Robert Wise, USA: Twentieth Century Fox.
Durant, R. (1997), 'Public Opinion Polls and UFOs', in H. Evans and D. Stacy (eds), *UFO 1947–1997: Fifty Years of Flying Saucers*, 230–9, London: John Brown.
Eghigian, G. (2015), 'Making UFOs Make Sense: UFOlogy, Science, and the History of Their Mutual Mistrust', *Public Understanding of Science* 26 (5): 612–26.
Evans, H. (1994), 'The Roper Poll', *Journal of the Society for Psychical Research* 59: 379–81.
Evans, H., and D. Stacy (1997), *UFO 1947–1997: Fifty Years of Flying Saucers*, London: John Brown.
Evans, H. (1997), 'A Twentieth Century Myth', in H. Evans and D. Stacy (eds), *UFO 1947–1997: Fifty Years of Flying Saucers*, 257–66, London: John Brown.
Forbidden Planet (1956), [Film] Dir. Fred M. Wilcox, USA: Metro-Goldwyn-Mayer.
Fuller, J. (1966), *The Interrupted Journey*, New York: Dial Press.
Goldman, J. (1995), *The X-Files Book of the Unexplained*, London: Simon & Schuster.

Graham, A. (1996), '"Are You Now or Have You Ever Been?"': Conspiracy Theory and *The X-Files*' in D. Lavery, A. Hague and M. Cartwright (eds), *Deny All Knowledge: Reading The X-Files*, London: Faber.
Hopkins, B. (1981), *Missing Time: A Documented Study of UFO Abductions*, New York: Ballantine.
Independence Day (1996), [Film] Dir. Roland Emmerich, USA: Twentieth Century Fox.
Invaders from Mars (1953), [Film] Dir. William Cameron Menzies, USA: Twentieth Century Fox.
Jung, C. (1958), *Flying Saucers: A Modern Myth of Things Seen in the Sky*, Zurich: Rascher-Verlag.
Keyhoe, D. (1950), *The Flying Saucers Are Real*, London: Hutchinson.
Keyhoe, D. (1957), *The Flying Saucer Conspiracy*, London: Hutchinson.
Kolchak: The Night Stalker (1972), [Film] Dir. John Llewellyn Moxey, USA: Disney-ABC Television.
Kolchak: The Night Stalker (1974–5), [TV programme] ABC network, 13 September 1974–28 March 1975.
Kozinets, R. (1997), '"I Want to Believe": A Netnography of the X-Philes' Subculture of Consumption', in M. Brucks and D. MacInnis (eds), *Advances in Consumer Research*: 24, Provo, UT: Association for Consumer Research.
Leslie, D., and G. Adamski (1953), *Flying Saucers Have Landed*, London: Werner Laurie.
May, R. (1993), *The Cry for Myth*, London: Souvenir Press.
The National Archives, DEFE 24/1982/1, UFOs: Correspondence August–September 1996: https://discovery.nationalarchives.gov.uk/details/r/C10651776.
Newman, B. (1948), *The Flying Saucer*, London: Victor Gollancz.
The Outer Limits (1963–5), [TV programme] ABC network, 16 September 1963–16 January 1965.
Patton, P. (1997), *Travels in Dreamland: The Secret History of Area 51*, London: Orion.
Pflock, K., and P. Brookesmith (2007), *Encounters at Indian Head*, San Antonio, TX: Anomalist Books.
Pilkington, M. (2010), *Mirage Men*, London: Constable.
'Poll: US Hiding Knowledge of Aliens' (1997), *CNN.com*, 15 June. Available online: http://www.cnn.com/US/9706/15/ufo.poll/ (accessed 13 November 2005).
Radford, B. (2010), 'Physicist Calls UFO Cover-Up a "Cosmic Watergate"', *Live Science Blog*, 10 June. Available online: https://www.livescience.com/6577-physicist-calls-ufo-cover-cosmic-watergate.html (accessed 22 January 2022).
Ruppelt, E. (1956), *The Report on Unidentified Flying Objects*, New York: Doubleday.
Saler, B., C. Ziegler and C. Moore (1997), *UFO Crash at Roswell: The Genesis of a Modern Myth*, Washington: Smithsonian Institution Press.
Scholes, S. (2020), *They Are already Here: UFO Culture and Why We See Saucers*, New York: Pegasus.
Scully, F. (1950), *Behind the Flying Saucers*, New York: Henry Holt.
Star Wars, Episode IV: A New Hope (1977), [Film] Dir. George Lucas, USA: Twentieth Century Studios.

Strieber, W. (1987), *Communion: A True Story*, London: Century.
The Twilight Zone (1959–64), [TV programme] CBS network, 2 October 1959–19 June 1964.
The X-Files: Fight the Future (1998), [Film] Dir. Rob Bowman, USA: 20th Century Studios.

7

(Cult)ural tensions: New religious movements and *The X-Files*

Racheal Harris

A primary legacy of *The X-Files* is that it frequently prompted audiences to think beyond social norms, to push themselves outside the sphere of the familiar. Through the seemingly endless case files explored during its original season nine run, concepts of spirituality, faith and religion were a regular fixture and, in keeping with the overall tone of the series, these too became a portal through which the viewer was invited to engage with theological concepts outside of the quotidian and, indeed, to test the limits of their ideas around what it means to have faith. Outside of this, episodes with a specifically religious focus also spoke to the evolving narrative about the shifting nature of religious practice in the contemporary West. All too frequently, the selection of practices discussed was a reflection of social anxieties of the time, with Mulder and Scully's investigation seeking to provide some resolution to social disquiet present in the American psyche. Like Mulder, many viewers 'want to believe' in the possibility of new and engaging belief systems, particularly if they are spiritual seekers themselves, yet the robust thought and investigation which such belief demands is, in many instances, well beyond the scope of a single television episode. Similarly, there are some topics that demonstrate that simply wanting to believe and being able to accept the beliefs of others is a leap of faith too far. Herein, *The X-Files* had a problem.

Despite Mulder and Scully's willingness to engage with the supernatural, paranormal and mystical, when it came to alternative religious movements or 'cults' as they are more commonly referred to within the series, both agents seemed hesitant to entertain the possible legitimacy of alternative belief or practice. Indigenous religions too, often became a coded language which questioned ethnic and racial minorities, whose spiritual practices were used to construe them as dangerous or unhinged. Interwoven with a narrative of displaced refugees or small-town, isolated communities, these made practitioners of divergent faiths seem simple minded, demonic or dangerous. At the other end of the spectrum, fringe religious groups were presented within a framework which painted them as an enduring threat to 'normal' citizenry and supposed that anyone interested in looking outside of the construct of organized religion was a social deviant or, possibly, harbouring fantasies of mass murder and suicide.

This chapter considers those episodes of *The X-Files* that focus on Indigenous spiritualities and New Religious Movements (NRMs), with a view towards how they were portrayed (often unflatteringly) within the series. My analysis is anchored by the episode 'The Field Where I Died' (S4: E05), which acts as a midpoint in the narrative arc of the original nine seasons. Unlike other episodes which borrow pieces of literature or partial ideas relating to specific spiritual identities, this episode has obvious parallels to the 1993 Branch Davidian siege at Waco, whilst also recalling elements of the 1978 mass suicide in Jonestown. This episode in particular highlights the specific problems which arise with the over-simplification of religious belief in televisual narratives. Rather than embracing governmental distrust, the overarching ethos of the series, 'The Field Where I Died' upholds political rhetoric by insinuating that members of fringe religions are inherently evil, violent and abusive; whilst also suggesting that it is the responsibility of the government to 'free' members from such deviant faith communities. Rather than questioning the tactics of governmental agencies or the scope which these same bodies have in dictating the religious beliefs of their constituents, the episode engages with the same flawed narrative present in the popular press of the period, particularly that relative to the incident at Waco. These reports were unsympathetic to survivors and failed to register the role of government interference in the outcome of the siege. Similar themes are further evident in episodes which use the NRM/Indigenous spirituality trope and even in instances where fringe elements of Christianity are discussed. These too suggest that anything outside of the white, mainstream Christian identity is inherently dangerous or deviant, and thus should not be trusted. Retrospectively, this attitude is problematic for the legacy of the series, which has otherwise been upheld as the pinnacle of promoting mistrust in the established order by encouraging viewers to 'trust no one' and to seek the truth for themselves.

Cults and Indigenous spiritualities

Cult groups are introduced early in *The X-Files* case load, appearing for the first time in the season one episode 'Gender Bender' (S1: E14), which has attracted little interest in existing scholarship on the series. As an episode, it plays a minuscule role in furthering the conspiracy narrative that the series was trying, at that stage, so hard to establish. Instead, it is an early example of what would become the standard 'monster-of-the-week' episode. Limited retrospective discussion of 'Gender Bender' is offered by television critics and online bloggers Zack Handen and Emily Todd VenDerWerff (2019) in their study of every episode in the series, though their assessment focuses explicitly on dissecting the way in which gender is discussed, with a view towards how the theme grates on the modern viewer for its inappropriate take on what it means to be gender fluid. In being preoccupied with that single element, which is of course a popular topic of social discourse in the 2020s, what the analysis fails to consider is how the episode sets up a much longer narrative, specific to how both the investigations and the characters of Mulder and Scully will interact with fringe religious movements or 'cults' throughout the rest of the series. Despite not being recognized as a standout episode, the story does set the tone for religious debate as it presents later in the season and, indeed, subsequent seasons. 'Gender Bender' is the first cult themed narrative, which focuses on a religious group. In this instance, it uses the fictitious group known as The Kindred, which is modelled on the Amish community, as the focal point. The associated X-File case sees Mulder and Scully investigating a series of murders, which are eventually attributed to a single, gender shifting individual. Tracing a suspect back to The Kindred, the agents end up as unlikely guests of the group, with Scully falling under the spell of one of its male members, who seduces her via pheromone manipulation. As she interrogates and is nearly assaulted by this stranger, Mulder finds a 'womb like' cavern under the communal barn, where deceased members are buried in the clay before being restored to life (presumably as a different gender). In a hurried conclusion, the ability to rejuvenate is used to link back to the season's wider interest in extraterrestrials, although this subplot is introduced in the final third of the episode and is not explored in any significant detail. During a brief exchange with the gender-bending killer, Scully is told that the group will not 'leave' without him and thus he has no fear of being caught or punished for his crimes. In a strange twist of fate, this exchange is a vague insinuation of the group's belief that they will be leaving (presumably earth), the narrative seeming to prophesy the larger beliefs of Heaven's Gate, an American NRM which would commit group suicide in 1997 in support of their beliefs about extraterrestrial resurrection. In the final shot of the episode, Mulder and Scully enter a corn field on the outskirts of The Kindred's sprawling farmland. There are crop circles burnt into the corn, again suggesting extraterrestrial involvement, but there is no clear narrative conclusion to the episode, without a diary entry from Scully nor any voice-over from her or Agent Mulder. The idea of the cult is firmly implanted in the mythology of the series as being deviant, in their sexuality as well as their lifestyle, and from here it continues to germinate, developing further close references to real-life events.

Traditionally, Christian concepts appear more explicitly in season one, in both 'Beyond the Sea' (S1: E13), where Scully loses her father at the same time that she and Mulder are investigating the psychic visions of Luther Boggs, and later in 'Miracle Man' (S1: E18), which is focused on faith healing and the practices of a generic tent ministry. Though the religious beliefs of the faithful are rooted deeply in Pentecostal Christianity, the way in which the members and their practices foreshadow a wider discussion on fringe religions and NRMs is evident. Like 'Beyond the Sea', this episode challenges Mulder and Scully's personal ideas on religion. However, here it is Mulder who is entranced by the possibility of Samuel's ability to heal in the fashion of Jesus, whereas the previous episode focused on Scully's difficult relationship with Catholicism, which was transposed alongside the Spiritualism narrative contained in Luther Boggs's psychic visions. Whilst Boggs and his psychic predictions were discredited in the earlier episode, 'Miracle Man' strongly insinuates that Samuel's gift is genuine and that he shares some parallel qualities with Christ. This is made apparent after his murder, when he is seen to rise again from the dead and return to confront his betrayer. Season one's foray into religious debate ultimately concludes by affirming that while fringe religious beliefs are questionable and should be greeted with doubt, if they fall into the realm of a broadly Christian structure they are generally acceptable (if unpalatable). In contrast, beliefs dealing with the so-called supernatural realm of psychic ability are deviant, their adherents inherently dishonest and dangerous.

Season two begins to take more risks in its discussion of religious themes. Overall, religion appears as a central plot device in seven of the twenty-five episodes, all of which appear after episode ten, where the cult theme is picked up again in 'The Red Museum' (S2: E10). This episode adopts the concept of 'walk-ins' as the basis for the beliefs of the group being investigated. Popularized in the 1989 book *Strangers among Us* by journalist Ruth Montgomery, 'walk-ins' are thought to be advanced souls, who take over the body and life of lesser souls (described in 'The Red Museum' as the souls of people who have given up on life, which is not entirely accurate) so that they can achieve a greater purpose (Montgomery 1979: 22–3). The souls of the displaced return to Source until they are prepared to be born again into new bodies. Early in the episode, the leader of the Red Museum is seen receiving prophecy in a similar way as described in Montgomery's book, which is conveyed to the congregation via automatic writing, which is projected from a computer onto a large video screen. While the episode draws from Montgomery's work only briefly, it is a key example of how the series begins to engage popular spiritual texts into its myth building, muddying the waters between fact and fiction. Here, the oversimplification of Montgomery's work furthers the notion that New Age spiritual seekers are reliant upon the voices of disembodied entities.

Indigenous religions appear first in 'Fresh Bones' (S2: E17), which cites Haitian Vodou as its inspiration. It is important to note that this spelling reflects the recognized religion of 'Vodou', as practised in countries like Haiti where it is a state religion, as opposed to 'voodoo' which describes unstructured folklore practice. Here, Mulder and Scully become engaged with the spirit of a deceased child in their investigation of an apparent case of zombification. In this instance, the academic work of cultural anthropologist Wade Davis (specifically his 1988 book *Passage of Darkness* which explores a medical explanation for the so-called zombie phenomena) is used as a centrepiece for Mulder's understanding of the case. While viewers would need to be keenly observant to draw the direct link between Davis's study and Mulder's investigation, the specifics of where Mulder has gathered his information and who the author of this information is are less important than the idea that the series is building its plot from reputable source materials. In this instance, the mysterious events surrounding a Haitian refugee camp provide the setting for a larger discourse on America's relationship with Haiti and its stance on refugees and asylum seekers more broadly. While there are certainly clear points made about the mistreatment of vulnerable people who have found themselves displaced in processing centres, these are ultimately overshadowed by the spectre of Vodou. Regardless of its origin, Vodou is a deeply complex religion, often feared and misunderstood as a form of devil worship, a theme which is also blatantly apparent in the episode. As such, Mulder and Scully miss the opportunity to legitimize a practice that is an intrinsic part of the Haitian identity (alongside Catholicism, Vodou is the primary religion in Haiti) and instead cast the Haitian people as one might more commonly see them in a horror film.

Similarly, the Chaco Chicken Cult described in 'Our Town' (S2: E24) draws on cannibalism and tribal spiritual practices from New Guinea, also depicting Indigenous spiritualities in a difficult light. Whereas Haitian Vodou is commonly preoccupied in onscreen depictions with returning from the dead or instating a living death on otherwise healthy people (McGee 2012), the practices of New Guinea are simplified in this episode to suggest that cannibalism is undertaken in their quest to attain eternal youth. In this case, the antagonist of the episode is eventually revealed as Walter Chaco, a Second-World-War veteran once marooned in New Guinea where he presumably became familiar with the cannibalistic practices of the native population ('Fresh Bones' also used a military general as its antagonist). The episode suggests that the townsfolk have lived as cannibals for several decades and that they sacrifice members of the community who are deemed to be outsiders. Their practice is complicated by the murder of a man suffering from an obscure degenerative disease which, after his flesh is consumed, begins to infect the wider population. As a medical doctor, Scully first becomes suspicious of the community deaths, advising Mulder that unless the disease is passed on through familial lineage it can only be shared through consumption. Using this knowledge, it is once again Mulder who solves the case, while the townsfolk are uniformly described as senseless flesh eaters united by a single, deviant practice.

In both instances, the belief systems of indigenous cultures are parlayed into a larger narrative in which cosmologies and mythologies central to the respective group are viewed with speculation and blame, and the narrative construction shares a very clear message that being complicit with deviant spiritual beliefs is a quick pathway to damnation. As we have seen in the case of Haiti specifically, the perpetuation of stereotypes around Vodou has only further complicated the relationship which the country shares with other nations and cultures (Katz 2013). Considering the continued poverty which Haiti endures, which is exacerbated by natural disasters as much as it is by the influence of the West on the economic market, the fear and disinformation which depictions of Haitian spirituality encourage continue to be disastrous to the relief effort (McGee 2012). Though we can only attribute a single episode of *The X-Files* to this issue, it does play a role in the construction and legacy of a larger and enduringly problematic cultural narrative.

To balance the discussion of indigenous religious beliefs, later episodes 'The Calusari' (S2: E21) and 'Kaddish' (S4: E15) draw on Romanian belief and orthodox Judaism in their construction. Unlike the episodes which appropriate Indigenous spiritualities though, in both instances, the practitioners and, indeed, the victims, are viewed with sympathy. 'The Calusari' ultimately deals with death and grief as it relates to the loss of a child. Although Mulder is present at an exorcism, during which the antagonist spiritual entity of the deceased male child is disconnected from the body of his living twin, Mulder's field notes at the end of the episode focus not on the power or even the place of folklore practice in Romani spiritual tradition, but instead on the power of grief. There is a medicalization of the case, which seeks to remove it from the spiritual roots which had, until that point, underpinned the episode. In contrast, 'Kaddish' draws on the Judaic folklore of the Gollum in its exploration of a grieving woman, who raises the spirit of her slain lover so that he might avenge his own murder. In the final scene of the episode, the lovers are reunited, with the woman destroying the entity she has raised after realizing that she has vilified his memory.

While both episodes are empathetic, their view is problematic because it gives preference to Abrahamic religious traditions (even those which appear on the fringes of orthodoxy) over those of native or Indigenous origin. Whilst practitioners of Vodou are not portrayed in the exact same way as cults, the suggestion that meddling in magic and folk religion is dangerous is implied. Similarly, portraying religions in this way suggests that they are based around make-believe practices. This attitude undervalues the lived experience of original adherents and undermines the larger culture from which the belief systems arose. Thus, the episode plays a destructive role in building an understanding and acceptance of spiritual beliefs which exist outside of the Western status quo and, among non-believers, only instigates further antipathy towards religious groups. The most troubling discussion of NRMs comes in the season four episode 'The Field Where I Died' (S4: E05), which premiered on Fox on 3 November 1994. This falls roughly eighteen months after the end of the siege on the Branch Davidian compound in Waco, Texas, an event clearly used as inspiration for the narrative which underpins the episode.

The Waco siege: Mount Carmel, Texas

On the morning of 28 February 1993, the Bureau of Alcohol, Tobacco, and Firearms (BATF) arrived at Mount Carmel, the rural home of a religious sect and offshoot of the Seventh Day Adventist Church, known as the Branch Davidians. Agents had been investigating the group and its members for several months, though the official pretence for the search warrant they sought to serve that morning related to seizing a weapons cache from the leader of the Davidian Group, David Koresh (real name Vernon Howell). Koresh had been the charismatic leader of the Davidians for several years when he came under scrutiny from the FBI. Initial interest was raised over claims of child abuse within the compound, claims relating specifically to sexual assault of underaged girls whom Koresh sought to make his wives (Wessinger and Doyle 2012: 83–4). Other instances of physical abuse, delivered as punishment for transgression, had also been reported (Thibodeau 1999: 119; Wessinger and Doyle: 70). Although numerous sources exist to support claims of dubious treatment of children, investigators were able to find evidence likely to stand up to prosecution. Knowing that Koresh and the Davidians financed their lifestyle in part through their involvement at legal gun shows, the decision was made to instead execute a search order to investigate the stockpiling of weapons. A detailed account of the lead up to the siege can be found in the academic work of Reavis (1995), Tabor and Gallagher (1995), and Wessinger and Doyle (2012) with each highlighting several flaws in both the investigation and the execution of the search order, even though they differ on the guilt of Davidian members in relation to both the weapons charges and the outcome of the siege. On the morning the search warrant was executed, Koresh and the occupants of the compound were prepared for the arrival of the officers and BATF agents were ill prepared for the response of Koresh and other members of the church, who killed several agents. Thus commenced a stand-off lasting nearly two months, which was brought to an end only when the BATF used military tanks and tear gas to storm the compound. More than seventy members of the church died, including Koresh (from a gunshot wound) and all his children. The latter, along with their mothers and several other members were incinerated alive when they were unable to escape a below-ground bunker (Wessinger and Doyle: 160).

Survivors of the siege have blamed the BATF for causing the fire (Thibodeau: 274–5), however the government maintains that it was in fact the Branch Davidians who set fire to their own compound, and themselves, to avoid capture (Reavis: 272–3). Overwhelmingly, what research and analysis of the situation highlights (regardless of whether it supports or critiques the actions of BATF and governmental authorities) is the fact that a lack of understanding around the motivations of the group and their understanding of apocalyptic theology contributed to the length of the stand-off and the deaths in the fire (Cowan and Bromley 2008: 130).

The 'Field Where I Died' begins with a voice-over from Mulder, who is narrating from Robert Browning's poem, *Paracelsus* (1835):

> At times I almost dream I too have spent a life the sages' way,
> And tread once more familiar paths. Perchance
> I perished in an arrogant self-reliance
> Ages ago; and in that act a prayer
> For one more chance went up so earnest, so
> Instinct with better light let in by death, That life was blotted out –
> not so completely
> But scattered wrecks enough of it remain,
> Dim memories, as now, when once more seems
> The goal in sight again. (21)

The purpose of the poem is to foreshadow the overlying 'supernatural' theme of the episode, which investigates the notion of past lives and returning souls. In this case, Mulder encounters a woman, Melissa (Kristen Cloke), who is the member of a religious cult known as the Church of the Seven Stars. Exhibiting multiple personality disorder, Melissa has also been in contact with the FBI (acting under one of her alternative personalities) to offer them information about the practices of the cult leader, specifically to highlight that he is stockpiling weapons in a series of underground bunkers located on the rural property which the members of the church occupy in a commune style living arrangement. During one of her interrogations, she slips into the persona of a Civil War nurse and, in recognizing Mulder as her previous lover, recounts the story of their lives together during this period, which concludes when he dies in her arms. Mulder, struck by her sincerity and, to a degree, enchanted by the notion that they were in fact lovers, undergoes his own session of deep hypnosis, whereby he recalls the memory of the interaction with Melissa and the identity of that previous life, in which he was Civil War soldier, Solomon Biddle.

Throughout the episode, Mulder uses his encounters with Sarah's Civil War alter ego to try and tempt her away from the hand of cult leader Vernon Ephesian, though he ultimately proves unsuccessful in this mission. At one point in the narrative, Mulder and Scully accompany Melissa to the compound, where she has been living as one of Vernon's wives. During the visit, Melissa recounts instances of violence and abuse which she and other women in the compound have suffered at the hands of Vernon (accounts which mirror those brought against Koresh by several ex-Davidian members). After becoming distressed, one of her multiple personalities emerges, which leads Mulder and Scully to the conclusion that there are guns and a stockpile of military equipment hidden somewhere on the property. Ultimately, there is not enough evidence to hold Vernon on the weapons charges however, and he and the remaining members of the group return to the compound. Though Mulder attempts to access further past life memories to determine where the bunkers might be, he is unable to do so. Scully does manage to locate images of the two people identified in Melissa and Mulder's shared past life vision, and in doing so finds a map of the property which confirms the presence of the hidden Civil War bunkers. Equipped with a search warrant, Mulder and Scully (along with a sizable contingent of FBI agents) rush to the compound, finding that the members of the church have gathered in the barn and, under the guidance of Vernon, have consumed cyanide-laced cordial. Mulder arrives moments after Melissa has succumbed to the poison, and he is unable to save her or any other members of the church.

The mass death of the community does deviate from the events of Waco, which would have been difficult to get past network censors, and which likely also ran the risk of attracting criticism and litigation from the survivors. From a technical perspective, it also seems likely that replicating the real-life events was outside the capacity of the budget for the series. As such, the episode adapts the tragedy of Jonestown in the conclusion of its cult narrative. Although the events of Jonestown had taken place well over a decade prior to the episode airing, the event remained fixed in the psyche of the American populace. Indeed, the term 'drinking the Kool-Aid' continues to be a form of shorthand cultural vernacular which directly references both the deaths at Jonestown and insinuates that the victims were incapable of individual thought.

The problem with the adaptation of the Jonestown tragedy in 'The Field Where I Died' is that it fails to account for the social conditions which precipitated the circumstances which lead people to join these kinds of religious groups. Similarly, in portraying 'cult' members as mentally unstable personalities, incapable of decision-making, detracts from the fact that these are almost exclusively vulnerable people, made more so by the fact that they are ignored and maligned by society. Interestingly, portraying fringe religions in this way bears a strong resemblance to the notion of the zombie as it is understood in traditional Vodou. Waco, like Jonestown, did not happen in a vacuum. Jim Jones and his church Peoples Temple were well known for their abusive and criminal behaviour prior to Jones fleeing America with a large contingent of his congregation (Layton 1998: 97).

'The Field Where I Died', like other television programmes that have dealt with fringe religious groups in their plotlines, adopts elements of both the Jonestown tragedy and Waco, oversimplifying the circumstances of each and attributing the outcome of the events to the cult leader and his followers. This completely discounts the role of the government in negotiations (with the Branch Davidians) and collates that event with Jonestown, which was equally complex, but which was allowed to evolve under very different circumstances. Writers have chosen to stick closely to the governmental narrative which surrounded the outcome of the siege in the events of this episode, a decision which is ultimately at odds with the larger purpose of the series and the narrative of its 'trust no one' myth-arc.

During the stand-off and in the aftermath of the tragedy, there were a multitude of questions asked of the BATF and their approach throughout. Among these was the misunderstanding of the BATF of the Millennialist beliefs of the Branch Davidians and how the militant actions of governmental agencies both played into these and reaffirmed the message which Koresh had preached throughout his time as the group leader (Cowan and Bromley: 132). This is reaffirmed by the fact that most adult members of the church chose not to leave once the siege of the compound had begun, even though they were given several opportunities to do so. How and why these decisions were made can be difficult for audiences to grasp. Indeed, it is still difficult for the public to completely understand, but this does not free television and other forms of visual media from investigating the questions in a way that engages with more difficult aspects of theological belief, whilst also respecting the dignity of the dead. The discussions we have about these groups matters and, as history has demonstrated, failure to understand and to respect these religious beliefs and practices frequently ends in discord and, in extreme circumstances, tragedy.

Season five and beyond: The continuing 'cult' issue

'Signs and Wonders' (S7: E09) and 'Theef' (S7: E14) are two of the later examples of Mulder and Scully encountering fringe religious movements. 'Signs and Wonders' invokes the backdrop of a snake worshipping Christian sect, which Mulder ultimately runs afoul of though Scully remains oddly immune to the folk magic which the episode suggests is at work. By this point in the series, the original tone of enduring governmental distrust had been usurped by a far more comedic approach, and monster-of-the-week episodes became increasingly whimsical in their subject matter. Written by Jeffrey Bell, 'Signs and Wonders' seems to support the idea that scepticism and a certain level of intolerance around spiritual belief and practice can be a good thing. This concept is demonstrated in the antagonist of the episode, who not only escapes arrest by Mulder and Scully but moves on to continue his ministry in another part of the country. In the final shot of the episode, the pastor is seen to eat a mouse, suggesting that he has begun to take on qualities of the snakes which he has used to do his bidding. Again, this throws back to the idea of shape-shifting and totemism which are frequent motifs in the discussion of native spiritualities and are often misunderstood and oversimplified.

The later episode, 'Theef', revisits the idea of folklore and folk magic in its discussion of Appalachian spiritualities and the tenuous relationship which they have with American voodoo (itself a derivative of Haitian Vodou). In many ways, this episode offers a parallel to the discussion of 'Fresh Bones', although at this point in the series, Scully has undergone a pronounced turnaround in her relationship to religious ideologies. Rather than being dismissive of the beliefs of the antagonist, she contemplates how much they differ from her own ideas about modern medicine and its use to treat the dying. The crux of the episode relates to the death of a young woman who Scully suspects has been administered painkillers to hasten her demise after it becomes apparent that she cannot be saved from injuries sustained during a bus crash. In the moment, this is seen as something of a mercy death, though it is not viewed as such by the family of the woman, who are also aware that she has not only died but has also been buried in an unmarked grave. Upon learning of his daughter's death, her father, an Appalachian shaman, is offended that he was denied the right to heal his child and thus seeks vengeance on the doctors responsible for her murder. Speaking from the perspective of a medical doctor, Scully contemplates if her own actions would have differed had she found herself as the treating physician of this woman. This is a stark turnaround from her attitude in 'Fresh Bones', where she is unable to believe that Haitian Vodou is responsible for the apparent death of Private Jack McAlpin. What the episode does not build upon however is the suggestion that the practices under discussion are a valid form of belief and ritual. Scully may be encountering the start of a character arc which will see her drastically change the way she engages with the supernatural and metaphysical aspects of her career (a journey which is amplified after Mulder's abduction and her pregnancy at the end of the season); the series at large is unable to move away from the temptation to engage with nuanced and realistic discussions of religious ideologies which exist on the fringes of cultural acceptability.

Conclusion

In the two decades since the conclusion of the original series, social ideas about religion and spirituality have shifted dramatically. This has been the result of a range of sociological factors, including the changing narratives around the place and purpose of organized religion in an increasingly secular world. Still, there lingers an enduring fascination with ideas and practices that are related to NRMs and religion in general. For instance, at the time of writing in 2022 there are two films in production which look at the Jonestown story and the impact of the mass suicides on history. One of these features Leonardo DiCaprio in the role of Jim Jones. Similarly, Waco has been the focus of ongoing discussion and speculation. It has been used as a storyline in television series such as *Criminal Minds* (CBS, 2005–20) and has also been the subject of its own television mini-series, *Waco* (2018). Unlike other accounts, *Criminal Minds* was based on the survivor account of David Thibodeau and gives a more sympathetic view of the Davidians whilst also acknowledging fractions and illegalities within the group. The claim that 'religion is on the decline' in Western culture is a sentiment often used to evoke outrage from the faithful and praise from the non-believer and yet, whilst there may have been a downturn in membership to organized religion and well-established faith communities in many parts of the world, America maintains a strong relationship with Christian worship. In contrast, spiritual exploration and engagement with varying forms of New Age belief continue to be popular. This suggests that rather than religion being on the decline, people are instead seeking new avenues through which to practice and engage with spirituality. For this reason, it is essential to consider the role which television series like *The X-Files* have played in establishing a cultural narrative which preferences select forms of spiritual belief above others. Revisiting religiously themed episodes, only some of which have been touched upon herein, allows us an opportunity to interrogate how ideas to which we prescribe have been informed by disinformation and sensationalism that appear, ubiquitously, every day.

References

Browning, R. (1904), *Paracelsus*. London: Aldine House.
Cowan, D. E., and D. G. Bromley (2008), *Cults and New Religious Movements: A Brief History*, Blackwell: Oxford.
Criminal Minds 'Minimal Loss' (2008), [TV Programme] CBS, 8 October 21:00.
Davis, W. (1988), *Passage of Darkness: The Ethnobiology of the Haitian Zombie*. Chapel Hill: University of North Carolina Press.
Handlen, Z., and E. T. VanDerWerff (2019), *Monsters of the Week: The Complete Critical Companion to The X-Files*. New York: Abrams Press.

Katz, J. M. (2013), *The Big Truck That Went By: How the World Came to Save Haiti and Left Behind a Disaster*, New York: St Martin's Press.

Layton, D. (1998), *Seductive Poison: A Jonestown Survivor's Story of Life and Death in the Peoples Temple*. Toronto: Anchor Books.

McGee, A. M. (2012), 'Haitian Vodou and Voodoo: Imagined Religion and Popular Culture', *Studies in Religion/Sciences Religieuses*, 41 (2), 231–56.

Montgomery, R. (1979), *Strangers among Us*, Toronto: Random House.

Reavis, D. J. (1995), *The Ashes of Waco: An Investigation*, New York: Syracuse University Press.

Tabor, J., and E. Gallagher (1995), *Why Waco? Cults and the Battle for Religious Freedom in America*. Berkeley: University of California Press.

Thibodeau, D. (1999), *A Place Called Waco: A Survivor's Story*. New York: Public Affairs.

Waco (2018), [TV mini-series] Dir. John Erick Dowdle and Dennie Gordon, USA: The Weinstein Company.

Wessinger, C., and C. Doyle (2012), *A Journey to Waco: Autobiography of a Branch Davidian*. Maryland: Rowman and Littlefield.

8

The end of history?: Contesting the legacy of the 1960s and 1970s in *The X-Files*

Gregory Frame

In its representation of the US system of politics and government as fundamentally corrupt, manipulated and controlled by shadowy forces far beyond any semblance of democratic accountability, *The X-Files* can be viewed as the progeny of the breakdown of trust in authority that occurred as a result of the political events of the 1960s and 1970s. In its often *noir*-ish visual style and inconclusive narratives, *The X-Files* took obvious inspiration from the conspiracy thrillers of the 1970s such as *Klute* (1971), *The Parallax View* (1974), *The Conversation* (1974), *Three Days of the Condor* (1975) and *All the President's Men* (1976), which were responses to the political trauma and scandal of the period. Series creator Chris Carter cited the Watergate scandal (1972–4) as 'the most formative event' of his youth (quoted in Graham 1996: 57). *The X-Files* largely rejected the prevailing optimism and triumphalism of the immediate post-Cold War period in which it enjoyed its greatest popularity. The series challenged Francis Fukuyama's bold claim that, with the triumph of capitalist democracy over totalitarian communism, history was at an end, and liberal, capitalist democracy was the last, best form of government to which the rest of the world would now progress (1989: 3–18; 1992). As a 'postmodern series par excellence', *The X-Files* remained 'incredulous toward ... a teleological or progressive model of history' (Geller 2016: 23). While the series attracted criticism in its later seasons for the convoluted nature of the overarching conspiracy narrative, it nevertheless retained a fairly coherent critique of the post-Second-World-War history of the United States as 'one huge exercise in militarism' (Cantor 2001: 114). This chapter will focus particularly on the way these critiques function in relation to its version of events between the assassination of President John F. Kennedy in November 1963 and the final confirmation of the US defeat in the war in Vietnam in 1975 – widely understood as the nation's 'traumatic decade' – and the way these events are incorporated into its wider 'myth-arc' of government concealment of the existence of aliens. The traumatic events of the 1960s and 1970s were, according to *The X-Files*, part of the military-industrial complex's ruthless attempts to prevent communist forces from threatening their power, with the FBI itself a core part of the establishment's efforts to conceal the truth and maintain control (Malach 1996: 65). *The X-Files* therefore suggests that the political upheaval of the 1960s and 1970s was purposely driven by the same sinister forces with which its heroes, FBI special agents Fox Mulder and Dana Scully, did battle every week.

Throughout the series' eleven seasons, *The X-Files* poses a substantive challenge to what Trevor McCrisken and Andrew Pepper describe as the 'benign metanarrative' of US history, instead offering a paranoid revisionism of the nation's post-Second-World-War global hegemony (2005: 188). In its portrayal of the assassinations of John F. Kennedy and Martin Luther King Jr., the war in Vietnam and the Watergate scandal, often understood as among the events which precipitated the US loss of innocence, *The X-Files* questions the nation's self-image as a superpower on the side of peace, prosperity and democracy. In their relentless pursuit of 'the truth', Mulder and Scully sought not only to prove the existence of aliens, but also to resurrect the repressed and forgotten aspects of the relatively recent past. From President Gerald Ford's insistence on taking office on 9 August 1974 after Nixon's resignation that 'our long national nightmare is over', to President Ronald Reagan's re-evaluation of the war in Vietnam as 'a noble cause' and President Bill Clinton's invocation of Elvis Presley and John F. Kennedy as emblematic of the idealism of the early 1960s (rather than the nightmare which followed), it seemed the period between 1963 and 1975 was a time that the US leaders were determined to forget.

The X-Files forces a confrontation with these traumatic events as part of its wider intention to question the motives and actions of those in power. The patriarchal establishment in *The X-Files*, embodied by the old, grey-haired white men who run 'The Syndicate', led by the arch-villain of the series, Cigarette Smoking Man (or CSM), tell themselves that concealment of 'the truth' is in the best interests of the people, for to reveal the alien plot to colonize Earth would cause widespread panic and social breakdown (Malach 1996: 73). This patronizing 'father-knows-best' attitude is rejected by *The X-Files* from the very outset through the figure of Mulder, who positions the concealment of the alien colonization alongside the other outrages perpetrated and repressed by these shadowy forces in the name of maintaining order: 'the Kennedy assassination, MIAs, radiation experiments on terminal patients, Watergate, Iran-Contra, Roswell, the Tuskegee experiments ... where will it end?' Alison Graham suggests that in his determination to dig beneath the official version of events, Mulder 'becomes the custodian of America's secret postwar history ... the living 'memory bank' of officially denied images ... What he shelters in his psyche is a nightmare – a 'long national nightmare', to be precise' (1996: 58). In making clear reference to Ford's attempt to erase Watergate from the national psyche when taking office, Graham reinforces the argument of this chapter that the events of the 1960s and 1970s are pivotal to the series' overall perspective on US history. In its determination to remember rather than repress, therefore, *The X-Files* is more aligned with Robin Wood's suggestion that 'the true subject of the horror genre is the struggle for recognition of all that our civilization *re*presses or *op*presses: its re-emergence dramatized, as in our nightmares, as an object of horror, a matter of terror' (2018: 80). The applicability of Wood's argument is manifest from the very first scenes of *The X-Files*, where we discover Mulder's office is in the basement of the FBI building ('Nothing down here but the FBI's most unwanted!' Mulder exclaims), investigating cases about which the rest of the bureau does not want to know. The remainder of this chapter will demonstrate how *The X-Files* represented the events of the traumatic decade for the United States as part of its wider suggestion that the nation's post-war history, contrary to conventional wisdom, has been consistently subject to denial, cover-up, manipulation and subversion by powerful forces existing outside the nation's democratic mechanisms.

The Kennedy assassination

In its suggestion that the assassination of John F. Kennedy was not perpetrated by a 'lone gunman' – the communist sympathizer and social misfit Lee Harvey Oswald – *The X-Files* conforms to widespread doubt about the official version of events that have characterized popular understanding since at least the 1970s (Knight 2015: 166). *The X-Files* premiered just two years after Oliver Stone's hugely successful and controversial *JFK* (1991), which suggested the 'progressive and reform-minded' president was murdered by 'a right-wing conspiracy' that led to the 'debacle in Vietnam ... and the rise to power of Nixon' (Marcus 2004: 104). The series adopted a similar perspective on the assassination, positing it as the root of many of the nation's contemporary ills and symbolic of the overwhelming power of the military-industrial complex and national security apparatus that had grown exponentially in the early years of the Cold War. The show's dismissal of the official explanation that Kennedy was killed by Oswald alone is embodied in the recurring characters of The Lone Gunmen, a trio of quirky computer hackers who believe conspiratorial forces govern most aspects of life in the United States (with their nominal leader, John Fitzgerald Byers, born on 22 November 1963). The trio are representative of *The X-Files'* conflation of the apparent establishment plot to kill JFK and the broader conspiracy with which the show deals: they operate as 'committed countercultural governmental watchdogs deeply critical of the United States' covert operations and the failure of real systems of justice' (Geller 2016: 75).

However, the importance of Kennedy's assassination to *The X-Files'* overarching conspiracy narrative goes beyond this. We learn of its position in relation to the series' historical perspective in 'Musings of a Cigarette Smoking Man' (S4: E07), where it is revealed that the CSM, the series' most prominent villain, was responsible for orchestrating and executing the assassination, acting on a directive from within the military to murder Kennedy for the Bay of Pigs disaster in 1961 and the perception that he wanted to prevent all-out war in Vietnam. *The X-Files* reinforces the tendency to present the assassination as the moment that it all started to go wrong for the United States, an abrupt change of course that led to violence and social breakdown: further political assassinations, the rise to power of Nixon and the Watergate scandal, and the catastrophe in Vietnam. This counterfactual has persisted in popular culture, from Stone's *JFK* to Stephen King's popular novel *11/22/63* (2011). *The X-Files* reinforces this notion: CSM is also responsible for the assassination of Martin Luther King, Jr. who, in espousing similar leftist, pacifist ideals, is deemed a threat to the military establishment's interests in its battle against communism. CSM is shown to be the arch-manipulator of US history, responsible for rigging Olympic ice hockey matches, Oscar nominations and the Superbowl, as well as orchestrating the Anita Hill hearings and the Rodney King trial. As confirmed by CSM himself at the conclusion of the episode, as he and Deep Throat (Jerry Hardin) contemplate the destruction of an extraterrestrial, history is determined by these 'unknown men, standing in the shadows', but that their names 'can never grace any pages of record. No monument will ever bear [their] image.' *The X-Files* therefore posits CSM as the individual, determining factor in the events of the 'traumatic decade' of the United States.

The mythological counterfactual about Kennedy in which *The X-Files* indulges has been largely debunked by historians who have agreed that the fallen president was a cautious pragmatist, a reluctant spokesperson for civil rights and social justice, as well as a liar who misled the press about his health and his achievements, as well as his numerous extra-marital affairs. That such perspectives have gained very little traction in the wider memorialization of Kennedy is unsurprising not only because of the careful management of his image by his family, but the compelling nature of the historical narrative for which his murder appears to have been the catalyst, 'the event that began the slide of 1960s idealism into national tragedy' (Marcus 2004: 164–5). In order for his death to possess the grand significance with which it has been understood, it needs to have been perpetrated by forces much greater than someone as inconsequential as Oswald. This is because, according to Alice George, 'Americans are disinclined to accept an explanation that suggests randomness or the capacity of relatively insignificant individuals to alter history.' (2012: 169). A leader as important as Kennedy needs to have been felled by a force of equal power: in *The X-Files*, this is the CSM who, by the end of the series' run in 2018, had been confirmed as the malevolent overlord pulling the strings of the overarching conspiracy. In 'My Struggle III' (S11: E01), further confirmation that CSM was responsible for Kennedy's murder is offered, with footage of the fateful day in Dallas met with voice-over narration that CSM has 'had a privileged seat at the centers of power, held the reins of that power, making sacrifices few are capable of, of which even fewer are willing'. It is therefore crucial to *The X-Files*' mytho-historical perspective that CSM is guilty of JFK's death, as it weaves the conspiracy theories about the assassination into the show's broader narrative: Kennedy was murdered by the same shadowy forces, operating far beyond democratic accountability or the rule of law, facilitating the alien colonization of Earth.

CSM's responsibility for Kennedy's death is interesting given that it is established that baby Mulder's first word was 'JFK'. As I have argued elsewhere, a succession of politicians who came after sought to construct themselves as the sons who might fulfil the promise of the idealized, deceased father figure in the form of Kennedy (Frame 2012). Therefore, the fact that the precocious Mulder's first word is 'JFK' and not the more common 'dada' is instructive: Kennedy's death at the hand of shadowy conspiratorial forces represents both the origin of his personal mistrust of the establishment and the wider historical trauma that the assassination precipitated. His motivation in uncovering the truth, therefore, is to return the nation to the ideals for which Kennedy – his symbolic father, if not his real one – died. This notion is only further reinforced by the much later revelation that CSM is in fact Mulder's biological father. If, as Graham contends, *The X-Files* invites us to view Mulder as the 'custodian of America's secret postwar history' (1996: 58), of which JFK's assassination is a crucial part, then in this instance the show clearly reinforces the belief that Kennedy's death was the turning point. The death of the ideal, symbolic father in the form of JFK at the hands of the evil, real one in CSM suggests the historical trajectory of the United States has been subverted by conspiratorial elements far beyond the comprehension of ordinary citizens.

However, imbuing individuals like CSM with these enormous levels of power and control betrays the show's very simplistic attitude towards history.

As Douglas Kellner suggests, *The X-Files* is guilty of 'reducing history to the production of cartoon-like conspiratorial figures' (2002: 226). It is not my intention here to chastise *The X-Files* for lacking a sufficiently rigorous historicist perspective, but to explain it: positing CSM as the villain who set in motion the traumatic historical events of the 1960s and 1970s reinforces the popular desire to believe that history is not a series of random, traumatic events but instead has a coherent pattern, even if it is dystopian. Kennedy's death at the hands of CSM, and CSM's central role in the conspiracy to facilitate the alien colonization of Earth, demonstrates the extent to which *The X-Files* invests the historical trajectory of the United States with a grand, cosmic significance. Don DeLillo suggested Oliver Stone's *JFK* revealed 'the nostalgia for a master plan, the conspiracy which explains everything' (quoted in Knight 2015: 171). I contend that *The X-Files* does so on an even grander scale, placing JFK's assassination as part of a conspiracy of intergalactic proportions.

The Watergate scandal

A decade after the Watergate break-in, the *Los Angeles Times* suggested that the American people appeared determined to allow 'the gravest Constitutional crisis since the Civil War' to fade from memory, and to 'allow those guilty of wrongdoing to gain a measure of rehabilitation' (quoted in Schudson 1993: 61). *The X-Files*, however, showed no inclination to go along with this collective amnesia, making numerous references to the Watergate scandal throughout the series' life: Mulder's governmental source is nicknamed 'Deep Throat', named after FBI special agent Mark Felt who acted as informant to *Washington Post* journalists Bob Woodward and Carl Bernstein during their investigations into the cover-up. It is revealed in the series' final season that Deep Throat's real name is Ronald Pakula, a clear reference to filmmaker Alan J. Pakula, whose 'paranoia trilogy' of conspiracy thrillers *Klute, The Parallax View* and *All the President's Men* is an obvious point of inspiration for the style and tone of *The X-Files*. Section Chief Blevins, the man responsible for recruiting Scully to The X-Files and, later, of giving her cancer, is played by Charles Cioffi, the oily, Nixon-like Peter Cable in *Klute*. *The X-Files* makes several other important, knowing references to Watergate-era media. Deep Throat's quotation – 'Keep your friends close, and your enemies closer' – references *The Godfather Part II* (1974), the second instalment of Francis Ford Coppola's family saga examining the immorality, violence and corruption in American capitalism. The film was released in December 1974, a matter of months following Nixon's resignation. Mulder rips up his apartment looking for surveillance devices, much like Harry Caul (Gene Hackman) in Coppola's *The Conversation* (1974). Multiple attempts are made on Mulder's life in his search for the truth, much like Joe Turner

(Robert Redford) in *Three Days of the Condor*. As Graham notes, 'if there is a ghost animating the machinery of *The X-Files*, it is most likely Richard Nixon, the icon of paranoia whose career virtually defined the golden age of American conspiracy theory. Quoting lavishly from Watergate-era films, the series makes no secret of the inspiration it draws from Nixon's political demise' (1996: 58–9).

To further reinforce this point, a screensaver mocking Nixon is featured on The Lone Gunmen's desktop computer.

However, *The X-Files* makes more than clever intertextual references to the Watergate scandal: as with the Kennedy assassination and the war in Vietnam, it implicates the events of 1972–4 within its larger 'myth-arc', positing the corruption of US democracy by the Nixon administration as part of the show's broader examination of the shadowy forces manipulating the trajectory of the nation's history. Specifically, in the opening episode of the show's second season, 'Little Green Men' (S2: E01), Watergate is linked to the abduction by aliens of Mulder's younger sister, Samantha, on the night of 27 November 1973, the day it was discovered following a congressional subpoena that a taped conversation between Nixon and his chief of staff, H. R. Haldeman, was missing eighteen minutes. The wider plot of the episode sees Mulder travel to Puerto Rico, where he uncovers a radio signal potentially confirming the existence of extraterrestrial intelligence. Mulder believes the printouts and tapes at the facility to be the proof for which he has longed, but all the evidence is destroyed and erased. Crucially, the episode draws an equivalence between this particular cover-up and the missing eighteen minutes of taped conversation between Nixon and Haldeman: discussion of this is on the television as the young Fox and Samantha argue over what to watch during the flashback sequence. Given that Mulder is only able to recall these memories of his sister's abduction thanks to deep regression hypnosis, it could be argued that *The X-Files* constructs the Watergate scandal itself as a repressed memory: while Americans might have been determined to move on, and perhaps forget, the implications of Watergate, *The X-Files* wants to bring these memories to the surface. Indeed, the absence of eighteen minutes from the Watergate tapes is akin to the experience of 'lost time', an aspect of the alien abduction experience (discussed by David Clarke in Chapter 6 of this volume) with which the show contends throughout (it happens to Mulder and Scully in the show's pilot episode, for example). This sense that traumatic histories, or awkward historical facts, can be willed away by forces beyond your control speaks to the series' wider sense that the governmental authorities look to deny, obscure and erase the truth. Indeed, this is a theme *The X-Files* shares with *JFK*, which Robert Burgoyne suggests reflects explicitly upon 'time and its vulnerability to manipulation [which] serves to create a sense of discontinuity and loss' (quoted in Gruner 2016: 141). In *The X-Files*, this discontinuity and loss is equated with the continued inability to hold powerful forces accountable for their actions: evidence of all wrongdoing is covered up, destroyed or erased.

While *The X-Files* suggests JFK's assassination as one potential origin for Mulder's mistrust of the government, this is even more apparent in the case of Watergate. 'Little Green Men' begins with The X-Files unit shut down, so Mulder and Scully meet in clandestine fashion in the underground parking garage of the Watergate Hotel. The intertextual references here seem obvious, recalling both Woodward and Bernstein's meetings with Deep Throat in *All the President's Men* as well as the hotel being the site of the infamous break-in at the Democratic National Committee headquarters in June 1972. The Watergate Hotel sign in the garage introduces the flashback to the night of 27 November 1973 (Kubek 1996: 189). In keeping with the notion that Mulder is our conduit into a version of US history that has been repressed by secret forces of malign intention, here 'what Mulder recovers is both the memory of erasure (Nixon's) and the erasure of memory (his own)' (Graham 1996: 58). As it is revealed later, Samantha was taken as part of the deal made between The Syndicate and the aliens: the fact that this occurs simultaneously with one of the greatest crises to date in US democracy suggests *The X-Files* sees the forces behind both conspiracies to manipulate and subvert the trajectory of US history for the benefit of a powerful elite as one and the same. Though Ford suggested the 'national nightmare' was over after Nixon's resignation, *The X-Files*' equation of Mulder's trauma with that of the nation suggests it is an experience that cannot, or should not, be so easily forgotten.

The war in Vietnam

The X-Files returns persistently to the war in Vietnam as a site of trauma throughout the series' eleven seasons. As Kellner points out, 'The Vietnam War is obviously an unhealed wound for Chris Carter's generation that keeps festering and generating tales to capture its hideousness and horrors' (2002: 216). In this regard, *The X-Files* presents a challenge to the rhetoric of the political establishment, which sought to redefine the war in the American consciousness as a 'noble cause' and incorporate its veterans into the nation's self-image as a force for good in its conflicts overseas (quoted in Bates 2011: 32). In its determination to remember the crimes of Vietnam, *The X-Files* rather conforms to the suggestion put forward by psychiatrist Robert Jay Lifton that it was not only the people who committed the atrocities in Vietnam who were guilty, but American society as a whole had become immersed in evil, so that 'we are responsible for one long, criminal act of behavior in our project in Vietnam' (quoted in Hagopian 2009: 59). In *The X-Files*, the deeds of the past haunt the present, reinforcing Wood's argument that the horror genre drags everything society represses back to the surface in the form of nightmares: the return in *The X-Files* of Vietnam veterans from beyond the grave, or possessive of supernatural powers, determined to take revenge against those who wronged them (more often than not, military and governmental authorities) is a consistent theme in these episodes. In adopting Lifton's position, therefore, *The X-Files* resists the 'morally vacuous [discourse of] 'healing' [that] emerged as a solution to both veterans' and society's wounds', instead positioning Vietnam veterans 'as the symptom carriers for a society that refuses to recognize unpleasant facts about the past' (Hagopian 2009: 77–8). Through key stand-alone episodes, as well as the recurring character of Assistant Director (and Vietnam veteran) Walter Skinner, *The X-Files* positions the war in Vietnam as part of the broader conspiracies and establishment corruption with which the show deals.

In 'Sleepless' (S2: E04), Mulder and Scully investigate mysterious deaths perpetrated by a Vietnam veteran, Augustus Cole (Tony Todd), one of the victims of a military experiment that eradicated soldiers' need to sleep in order to dull feelings of fear and to heighten aggression. The experiment was a catastrophic failure, as it precipitated a psychotic breakdown in the soldiers and led them to commit heinous atrocities, calling to mind the visceral horror of the My Lai massacre in 1968 which 'came to stand for all the wrongs that Americans perpetrated in Vietnam' (Hagopian 2009: 51). An unforeseen side effect of the treatment, Cole is able to force his victims – the doctors who experimented on him, or his fellow soldiers – to relive their nightmares and atrocities as real occurrences, becoming a walking trigger for symptoms of post-traumatic stress disorder. It is not an accident that Tony Todd plays Cole, given his role in *Candyman* (1992) as the son of a slave lynched for the crime of falling in love with a white woman, returning from the dead to exact his revenge. In positioning crimes committed in the execution of the war in Vietnam as comparative with the horrors of slavery and racism, *The X-Files* challenges the benign self-image of the United States, suggesting the nation was forged in, and maintained by, acts of appalling violence. 'Unrequited' (S4: E16) uses The Vietnam Veterans Memorial in Washington, DC, as a means through which to engage with the continued impact of the conflict on the United States. What initially appears to be the ghost of a Vietnam veteran returning to avenge the deaths of his comrades turns out to be a forgotten (presumed dead) POW, Nathaniel Teager, who has developed the ability to hide in plain sight, effectively placing himself in the 'blind spot' of human vision in order to kill his victims. Teager's ability to appear and disappear at will causes the eyes of those who see him to bleed, suggesting that the residues of the conflict remain unresolved sites of trauma. The episode concludes with Skinner gazing plaintively at Teager's name on the memorial, thereby acknowledging their common experience as veterans of a conflict which remains a site of unresolved trauma for the United States (for further analysis of this episode, see Frame 2017: 195–7).

Indeed, it is through the figure of Skinner that *The X-Files* seeks to establish the war in Vietnam as part of the broader conspiracy 'myth-arc' and suggests that the forces guilty of the disgraceful conduct and mismanagement of the conflict are part of the wider corruption and malfeasance of the US government. Skinner's veteran status is established in 'One Breath' (S2: E08), where he explains how he enlisted voluntarily in Vietnam because he 'believed it was the right thing to do', suggesting a confidence in the righteousness of the cause to stop communism and a belief in the nation's exceptionalism. That ended three weeks into his tour, when he killed a ten-year-old Vietnamese boy who had walked into their camp covered in grenades, precipitating not just a loss of faith in his country, but everything. We learn later that Skinner signed up to fight in 1969, *after* it was widely agreed that the war was unwinnable. As Raya Morag argues, 'Most Hollywood films refer to the pre-1968 period (before the Tet offensive – preceding the American acknowledgment of the certainty of defeat)', perhaps as a means to elicit sympathy for the veterans depicted who can be reasonably characterized as innocent and naïve at that point in the war (2006: 191). That *The X-Files* opts for a different trajectory for Skinner is emblematic of its attitude to US history: in emphasizing the nation's appalling conduct in Vietnam alongside critiques of slavery and, beforehand, the genocide of the First Nation Americans (in a cluster of episodes bridging the show's second and third seasons), *The X-Files* suggests there was *never* a time the United States could be meaningfully described as 'innocent'.

Until then presented as an establishment figure looking to hinder Mulder and Scully's search for the truth about extraterrestrials, 'Avatar' (S3: E21) represents *The X-Files*' gradual development of Skinner's character into a sceptic towards the authorities for whom he works in part due to the trauma he has endured in Vietnam. In this episode, Skinner contends with the end of his marriage. Drowning his sorrows at a bar, he meets a woman with whom he sleeps, but later wakes up next to her corpse. The prime suspect in her murder, he is pursued by an old woman in a red coat, who we are led to believe is the one responsible. Later, we learn Skinner had previously encountered the old woman in Vietnam, who watched over him during the near-death experience he explained in 'One Breath'. He had initially considered her one of many hallucinations he experienced during the war brought on by drug use, but her return prompts him to consider her larger significance. Mulder suggests she could be a succubus, a supernatural figure in folklore who preys on the souls of vulnerable men. 'Avatar' therefore remains consistent with the show's other Vietnam-related episodes, where memory of the conflict that had been repressed – either by the authorities in the cases of soldiers experimented upon or, in the case of Skinner, by the veterans themselves – erupt violently into the present, demanding to be confronted, and avenged or resolved. The spectre of the old woman in the red coat materializes throughout the episode: when Skinner answers the door to his estranged wife, she is wearing it. The imagery clearly references *Don't Look Now* (1973), in which grieving father John Baxter (Donald Sutherland) pursues a diminutive woman in a red coat through the wintry streets of Venice in the belief that it is his dead daughter, who drowned in a coat of the same colour. *The X-Files* employs the red coat to draw on similar themes of trauma, grief and loss of innocence: where Baxter fails to rescue a child, Skinner is forced to kill one on duty in Vietnam. An equivalence is drawn therefore between the trauma he suffered in Vietnam and the angst caused by the end of his marriage: indeed, it reinforces the tendency to portray Vietnam veterans as unable due to their experiences 'to conform to the heteronormative mythical model' as fathers, husbands or brothers (Morag 2006: 190).

Skinner's personal and professional failures are further reiterated in the series' final season in an episode entitled 'Kitten' (S11: E06), in which it is revealed that Skinner and his fellow soldier John 'Kitten' James (Haley Joel Osment) were part of a government experiment with a gas that makes those exposed to it see their worst nightmares, becoming more violent and aggressive as a result. Investigating Skinner's disappearance, Mulder and Scully look for clues in his apartment, Scully noting its sparse furnishing and complete lack of personal items, reinforcing the sense that the trajectory of his life – divorced, childless with a stagnant career – has been irrevocably affected by his experiences in Vietnam. Refusing the Reaganite revisionism of the Vietnam veteran as an 'avenging angel of a reborn American patriotism, assertiveness, and toughness' (Marcus 2004: 97), Skinner's mental vulnerability and emotional reticence result from the unresolved trauma of his experiences in the conflict. However, forced to confront memories he has worked so hard to repress, Skinner begins to entertain some of the 'extreme possibilities' to which Mulder (and later Scully) is open, and becomes an ally in their fight against the forces manipulating the nation's history to their own malevolent ends.

Conclusion

In its portrayals of the Kennedy assassination, the Watergate scandal and the war in Vietnam, *The X-Files* resisted the political attempts through the 1980s and 1990s to redefine the meanings of these events within the overall narrative of US history. Indeed, *The X-Files* appears to suggest Ronald Reagan's project to 'Make America Great Again' was contingent upon what Noam Chomsky described as 'organized forgetting' (quoted in Graham 1996: 58) of the recent past. The series' portrayal of a cabal of powerful old white men desperately trying to conceal and repress the truth about the nation's past misdeeds is resonant of the vociferous contemporary arguments about how we remember, memorialize and work through problematic aspects of our history. Therefore, in its demand that we remember key moments in US history in their ugly reality, *The X-Files* was remarkably prescient. The people in charge of our governments and institutions now are largely unwilling to confront the realities of the past – colonialism, slavery, misogyny – because to do so could precipitate an institutional and structural overhaul that may undermine their power and legitimacy. In order to combat this danger, any critical attitude towards conventional historical wisdom is dismissed as unpatriotic, elitist and characterized pejoratively. Though assigning responsibility for events of grand historical significance to malevolent individuals can be seen as naïve, it is notable that *The X-Files* offered alternative, revisionist perspectives on US history at a time when a conservative consensus about the past was broadly hegemonic. *The X-Files'* suggestion that the trajectory of US history has been subverted, corrupted and altered by men of overwhelming power and malign intention chimes with contemporary arguments about the past, and how command of the narrative of the past will ultimately determine how we fight the future.

References

All the President's Men (1976), [Film] Dir. Alan J. Pakula, USA: Warner Bros.
Bates, T. G. (2011), *The Reagan Rhetoric: History and Memory in 1980s America*, Dekalb: Northern Illinois University Press.
Candyman (1992), [Film] Dir. Bernard Rose, USA/UK: Propaganda Films/ PolyGram.
Cantor, P. (2001), 'This Is Not Your Father's FBI: *The X-Files* and the Delegitimation of the Nation-State', *The Independent Review*, 6 (1): 113–23.
The Conversation (1974), [Film] Dir. Francis Ford Coppola, USA: Paramount.
Don't Look Now (1973), [Film] Dir. Nicolas Roeg, UK/Italy: Casey Productions/ Eldorado Films.
Frame, G. (2012), 'Seeing Obama, Projecting Kennedy: The Presence of JFK in Images of Barack Obama', *Comparative American Studies*, 10 (2–3): 163–76.
Frame, G. (2017), '"The Lincoln Memorial Was Too Crowded": Interpreting the United States' Memorial Landscape through Film and Television', *Journal of Popular Film and Television*, 45 (4): 190–201.
Fukuyama, F. (1989), 'The End of History?', *National Review*, 16: 3–18.
Fukuyama, F. (1992), *The End of History and The Last Man*, New York: Free Press.
Geller, T. (2016), *The X-Files*, Detroit, MI: Wayne State University Press.
George, A. (2012), *The Assassination of John F. Kennedy: Political Trauma and American Memory*, London: Taylor and Francis.
The Godfather Part II (1974), [Film] Dir. Francis Ford Coppola, USA: Paramount.
Graham, A. (1996), '"Are You Now or Have You Ever Been?": Conspiracy Theory and *The X-Files*', in D. Lavery, A. Hague and M. Cartwright (eds),

'Deny All Knowledge': Reading The X-Files, 52–62, Syracuse, NY: Syracuse University Press.
Gruner, O. (2016), *Screening the Sixties: Hollywood Cinema and the Politics of Memory*, London: Palgrave Macmillan.
Hagopian, P. (2009), *The Vietnam War in American Memory: Veterans, Memorials and the Politics of Healing*, Amherst: University of Massachusetts Press.
JFK (1991), [Film] Dir. Oliver Stone, USA: Warner Bros.
Kellner, D. (2002), 'The X-Files and Conspiracy: A Diagnostic Critique', in P. Knight (ed.), *Conspiracy Nation: The Politics of Paranoia in Postwar America*, 205–32, New York: New York University Press.
King, S. (2011), *11/22/63*, New York: Scribner.
Klute (1971), [Film] Dir. Alan J. Pakula, USA: Warner Bros.
Knight, P. (2015), 'The Kennedy Assassination and Postmodern Paranoia', in A. Hoborek (ed.), *The Cambridge Companion to John F. Kennedy*, 164–77, Cambridge: Cambridge University Press.
Kubek, E. (1996), '"You Only Expose Your Father": The Imaginary, Voyeurism, and the Symbolic Order in *The X-Files*', in D. Lavery, A. Hague and M. Cartwright (eds), '*Deny All Knowledge': Reading The X-Files*, 168–204, Syracuse: Syracuse University Press.
Malach, M. (1996), '"I Want to Believe ... in the FBI": The Special Agent and *The X-Files*', in D. Lavery, A. Hague and M. Cartwright (eds), '*Deny All Knowledge': Reading The X-Files*, 63–76, Syracuse, NY: Syracuse University Press.
Marcus, D. (2004), *Happy Days and Wonder Years: The Fifties and Sixties in Contemporary Cultural Politics*, New Brunswick, NJ: Rutgers University Press.
McCrisken, T., and A. Pepper (2005), *American History and Contemporary Hollywood Film*, Edinburgh: Edinburgh University Press.
Morag, R. (2006), 'Defeated Masculinity: Post-Traumatic Cinema in the Aftermath of the Vietnam War', *The Communication Review* 9: 189–219.
The Parallax View (1974), [Film] Dir. Alan J. Pakula, USA: Paramount.
Schudson, M. (1993), *Watergate in American Memory: How We Remember, Forget, and Reconstruct the Past*, New York: Basic Books.
Three Days of the Condor (1975), [Film] Dir. Sidney Pollack, USA: Paramount.
Wood, R. (2018), 'Return of the Repressed', in B. Keith Grant (ed.), *Robin Wood on the Horror Film: Collected Essays and Reviews*, 57–62, Detroit, MI: Wayne State University Press.

9

'You believe what you want to believe – that's what everybody does now': *The X-Files*, fake news and the rise of QAnon

Bethan Jones

The X-Files has always been concerned with The Truth: the nature of it; the search for it; the belief in it. Indeed, the truth is the reason for Mulder's, and by extension Scully's, work. In his efforts to find out what really happened to his sister, Samantha, Mulder discovers the existence of a global conspiracy to colonize the earth. Knowing the risks Mulder poses to the project, Scully is sent to debunk his ideas and fundamentally discredit him, preventing anyone from believing the truth. Of course, it does not quite work out that way. Over the course of nine series and one feature film, our intrepid FBI agents tackle assassins, Nazi war criminals, alien bounty hunters and a shadowy cabal of men at the highest reaches of government, ultimately revealing that the final alien invasion of earth will take place on 22 December 2012.

By the end of the original run in 2002, however, critics felt that the series had lost its way. A combination of falling ratings, the loss of David Duchovny for most of the final two seasons and the September 11 terrorist attacks meant that there was no place for a show preoccupied with an extraterrestrial threat and a government that couldn't save its people. As Andrew Stuttaford (2002) wrote: '*The X-Files* is a product of a time that has passed. It is a relic of the Clinton years as dated as a dot-com share certificate, a stained blue dress or Kato Kaelin's reminiscences.' Fans did not necessarily agree and campaigned for a follow-up dealing with the threat of colonization. A second feature film, *The X-Files: I Want to Believe*, premiered in 2008 but this was treated as a stand-alone, similar to the series' 'monster-of-the-week' episodes and garnered disappointing reviews from fans and critics. Eventually an 'event' series, comprising six episodes, was announced in 2015 but, given the changes to technology, television production and viewing, and politics since the end of season nine, fans and critics were concerned that a modern-day *X-Files* simply would not work.

This chapter examines the revival seasons in relation to the shifting political, social and economic contexts which began in the late 2000s and continued through the 2010s. The financial crash of 2008, the election of Barack Obama and the rise of conspiracy theories surrounding his presidency, the emergence of streaming sites like Netflix and the 2016 announcement that Donald Trump would become president of the United States of America meant that *The X-Files* returned to a fundamentally different landscape. I assess how these cultural shifts were used diegetically while drawing on data collected from questionnaires completed by viewers and the larger media discourse to examine how fans understand the show in its current cultural context. I begin, however, by looking back at the original series and how its cultural context paved the way for its approach for season ten.

'Who would have thought we'd look back with nostalgia and say that was a simpler time?': The sociopolitical history of *The X-Files*

The X-Files' focus on aliens and the paranormal was a large part of its success and a testament to its understanding of the cultural moment. In the introduction to the first scholarly book on the series, *Deny All Knowledge: Reading* The X-Files, academics David Lavery, Angela Hague and Marla Cartwright point out that the years prior to *The X-Files* airing, as well as the early years of the show itself, saw fascination with UFOs and alien abductions (as Chapter 6 in this volume outlines) ranging from tabloid stories to syndicated television series like *Unsolved Mysteries* and *Believe It or Not* (Rapping 1995). But if the focus on the paranormal was indicative of the cultural moment of the early 1990s, its underlying themes of distrust and paranoia dated back to earlier cultural events in the United States. Media studies professor Allison Graham, discussing Watergate, argues that Chris Carter 'not only revisited the moment but established it as the central crisis of *The X-Files*, television's fin de siècle compendium of conspiracy theories' (1996: 56). As highlighted by Gregory Frame in Chapter 8 in this volume, Carter himself notes the impact Watergate had on him: 'I always liken myself to a child of Watergate ... and that's where I developed my kind of distrust of the government' (quoted in Mooney 2017: 16). Despite its occurrence over twenty years before the 'Pilot' episode (S1: E01) aired, Watergate reverberated through the first nine seasons in Deep Throat, Mulder's first informant who Graham refers to as 'a 1990s version of Woodward's informant' (1996: 58); in a flashback to the night of Samantha's abduction; in the name of the hotel in 'Little Green Men' (S2: E01). But Watergate wasn't the only influence on the show. Indeed, Charles Taylor argues that it is almost impossible to understand *The X-Files* without taking into account the political, cultural and economic context of its time, writing 'what links up the show to the zeitgeist is that Mulder and Scully are working to get out from under the most enduring legacy of the Regan/Bush era: the way government proclaims ... that the truth is irrelevant' (1994: 9).

Research I carried out with fans of the series after the revival was announced in 2015, and after season ten aired in 2016, demonstrated that these viewers were not only aware of the political and cultural contexts in which the series was located, but the importance that had led to the success of the series itself. Respondent 201649 noted the way *The X-Files* has infiltrated the cultural lexicon, writing 'The cultural context of conspiracy theories has changed since the beginning of *X-Files*. Nowadays, every pseudoscience documentary uses similar soundtrack and narrative', while respondent 2015142 felt that the series' themes of conspiracy, love, mystery and drama were perfect for the current atmosphere: an unsure time, politically, socially, economically and technologically. Indeed, many of those who responded to my questionnaires explicitly referred to the paranoia, conspiracy theories and politics of the original series and wanted to see how they would be treated in the current climate:

> times have changed since the show went off the air in 2002 – I'd like to see how Chris Carter and the other writers do a 21st century *X-Files* after all that has gone on with post 9/11 counterterrorism, Wikileaks and Edward Snowden, technology advances, social media, and more. What do people fear now? What is the tension between paranoia and skepticism in modern society? How much trust is there of government and other institutions? (Respondent 2015709)

Respondent 2015709 raises a series of questions that demonstrate how much had changed in the years between 2002 and 2015 and what climate *The X-Files* was returning to. The beginning of season nine in November 2001 coincided with the end of the Clinton presidency, the election of George W. Bush, the September 11 terrorist attacks and the invasion of

Afghanistan. If the origin of *The X-Files* was in events that shook Americans then, its (original) ending was doubly so: the period immediately after 9/11 was marked by anthrax and sniper attacks in Washington, DC, events which were reported almost hysterically by the media and which fed into a discourse of fear that ultimately led to a renewed trust in the government. Although audience figures had already begun to decline, there was a marked drop-off between the first and second episodes of season nine and a 30 per cent drop in viewing figures compared to season eight (Kessenich 2002). Academics Enrica Picarelli and M. Carmen Gomez-Galisteo suggest that 9/11 sounded the death knell for the show, writing 'In the aftermath of 9/11, the "Trust No One" of *The X-Files* became too subversive and out of touch with the public need to trust the government to keep them safe from future attacks' (2013: 83). The American public thus turned away from shows that asked them to question their government, but the years following 9/11 brought their own issues, including the War on Terror, the invasion of Iraq and increasing use of surveillance programmes that allowed the US government to track and monitor billions of phone calls made by its citizens. The late 2010s were also defined by the financial crash of 2008, which led to increasing political instability, economic austerity and a further polarization between the left and the right across the globe – topics that seemed pertinent to the series' concerns.

News about the possibility of another season of *The X-Files* began circulating in 2014, when Carter confirmed that he had been talking to Fox about the series returning (Adalian 2014). A Nerdist interview with Gillian Anderson in January 2015 called for fans to tweet their support for a revival, and in March of the same year Patrick Munn reported that *The X-Files* would return as a short-order event series. Although some viewers were not sure if the revival would be able to adapt to a new landscape – respondent 2015630, for example, wrote 'I'm sceptical about the possibility of a successful revival of anything whose heyday was 20 years ago' – many others felt that the themes originally dealt with were just as relevant in the mid-2010s. Respondent 201554 wrote 'I think this is the perfect political climate for this revival to occur. The subject of the show is relevant now in ways that it might not necessarily have been since the release of *I Want to Believe*' while respondent 2015795 focused on the role of surveillance: 'if the post 9/11 aggressively patriotic environment in the US dealt a serious blow to a paranoid government questioning series, now, in a time of government spying, and a new wave of disenchantment with the government and authority, the show is more relevant than ever'.

Indeed, in an interview with *The Guardian*, Carter highlighted the use of surveillance as a key concern for the revival series, saying 'We're trying to be honest with the changes dealing with digital technology: the capability of spying. Clearly we're being spied on in the US – or at least spying on you – and there seems to be no shame in it' (quoted in Dredge 2015). Media studies scholar Kathleen Loock, in her introduction to the *Television & New Media* special issue on American TV Series Revivals, writes that 'the main challenge lies in creating a comeback that is consistent with the show's past but also manages to meaningfully ground the series revival in the present' (2018: 303) and critics and fans felt that the revival series would be suited for a contemporary moment in which trust in the government, scientists and other authority figures was at an all-time low. Respondent 2016112 wrote

> I wanted to see what shape *The X-Files* would take in 2016, after so many years of absence from the cultural landscape, and after exerting so much influence on existing television content. I wondered how its conspiracy-laden narrative would reconcile with the post-90s governmental paranoia that has provided a fertile ground for profoundly damaging real-world conspiracy theories to flourish (anti-vaxxing, birtherism, 9–11 trutherism, gamergate, the rise of neoreactionaries, and the online flourishing of white supremacist communities on 4chan, reddit, and the daily stormer).

Similarly, respondent 2015721 felt that 'the show still has so much it could do: i.e., there's so many stories that could fit so well in our current society (they could explore the NSA spying, WikiLeaks, drones, or so much more)'. Reflecting key issues of American cultural consciousness had always been one of *The X-Files'* strengths, and it is therefore no surprise that the headlines of the early to mid-2010s provided fertile ground for a revived series. Indeed, as Mark Lawson (2016) notes, 'the new series specifically positions itself in a new era of governmental paranoia and public scepticism, with lines such as: 'Since 9/11, the country has taken a very dangerous turn in a wrong direction.' The revival seasons of *The X-Files* embraced this cultural shift, with season ten's 'My Struggle' (S10: E01) featuring a conservative 9/11 truther named Tad O'Malley, and season eleven more explicitly referencing Trump in 'The Lost Art of Forehead Sweat' (S11: E04), written by Darin Morgan. I focus on these episodes in the next two sections, exploring the diegetic shift to contemporary politics and reactions to it.

'Your own government lies as a matter of course, as a matter of policy': Updating *The X-Files* for the modern era

Season ten comprised six episodes, bookended by the conspiracy-focused 'My Struggle' and 'My Struggle II' (S10: E06), with four monster-of-the-week episodes in between. The season opens with a voice-over from Mulder, providing the viewer with a brief introduction to the X-Files and a potted history of UFO sightings before ending with the question 'are we being lied to?'. Following the opening credits comes a flashback to a UFO crash in Roswell in 1947, before throwing us into the 2010s and an older Scully, preparing for surgery. If this brief introduction situates the viewer in the present day, footage of a Jimmy Kimmel interview with Barack Obama and Mulder calling an Uber makes it clear we are in the here and now. This is cemented when we discover the reason for Mulder and Scully meeting in Washington, DC: online talk show host Tad O'Malley believes that a global conspiracy of men has been developing alien technology in order to take over the world, using the idea of an alien invasion as a smoke screen. O'Malley is positioned as a right-wing conspiracy theorist, his online talk show titled *The Truth Squad* focusing on a range of fringe topics. When we first see him, a video of the burning World Trade Center is playing behind him as he argues that 9/11 was a 'false flag' operation and the mainstream liberal media lie to Americans about life, liberty and the right to bear arms. Although not explicitly named as such in the episode, O'Malley can be identified as a 'truther' both in the sense that he is a believer of conspiracy theories in general and is a member of the '9/11 truth movement', which emerged following 9/11 and believes that individuals within the US government may have been responsible for, or complicit in, the attacks. As the episode progresses, we discover he is suspicious of drones, that he believes to be employed by anonymous individuals, recording conversations; the use of 'tools like the Patriot Act' to 'distract, enrage, and enslave American citizens at home' and 'a government that taps your phone, collects your data and monitors your whereabouts – with impunity'.

Mulder likens O'Malley to Bill O'Reilly, and indeed the parallels with real-life conspiracy theorists like Alex Jones and Glenn Beck were noted by both fans and critics. Respondent 2016597 wrote 'After watching the trailer I was even more excited because they had incorporated modern conspiracy theories into the storyline (mass surveillance, false flags alluding to 9/11 conspiracy)' while respondent 2016269 referred to real-life conspiracy theorists by name, writing 'I particularly enjoyed the first episode where many of my favorite conspiracy theories were discussed. I loved the Alex Jones character.'

Although the nature of the series' central conspiracy theory had changed, the inclusion of topics such as surveillance, governments' misuse of power and methods of social control meant that season ten was very much situated in the politics of the time. Respondent 2016531 felt as though the revival really brought the show into the current day:

> *The X-Files* was always a 90s show and focused on stuff relating to that Era (like the Internet was going to become intelligent and kill us all) so I didn't know how well they would update that. Well I was very pleasantly surprised that not only did the episodes have a 2016 feel but they also focused on social issues of the day, something that the older episodes

tended to skirt around. I appreciated the show not just trying to recapture its glory days (although there was some of that too) but really trying to also say something important about our society while still keeping within the expectations of the genre.

The media in the mid-2010s was awash with a range of controversial topics, with many news networks affording an equal amount of airtime to respondents on either side of the debate. Issues being discussed during 2014 and 2015 included an increasing awareness of ISIS, a militant Islamic group designated a terrorist organization by the United Nations, in the United States, following airstrikes in Syria; the shootings of Michael Brown, Eric Garner and Walter Scott by police officers and the subsequent protests; terrorist attacks in France and other European countries and mass shootings in the United States, including the Charleston church shooting which was rooted in white supremacy and led to a re-evaluation of the display of the Confederate flag. Many of these topics were heavily partisan and led to increasing friction between political parties and communities in the United States. The use of a clearly right-wing internet pundit as an ally to Mulder was thus subject to much debate.

Reviewing 'My Struggle' for *Inverse*, Rowan Kaiser writes that *The X-Files* deliberately 'picking sides' in the political debate is dangerous territory and argues that on the rare occasions that it did, 'it always made that more about the specificity of the episode than a general belief that someone's conspiracy theories were right or wrong' (Kaiser 2016). Yet, both 'My Struggle' and 'My Struggle II' prove O'Malley to be right, leaving – as Kaiser notes – 'the vast majority of this 10th season of *The X-Files* to ask "Wait, why is Mulder on Glenn Beck's side?"' (Kaiser 2016). Carter, in an interview with *Entertainment Weekly*, argues that the revival season is not embracing right-wing theories, saying 'I don't see Alex Jones as right-wing, I see him as libertarian ... [and O'Malley is] a character who casts *everything* in doubt.' He further says 'I don't think Mulder and Scully adopt any political position so much as a new approach in their search for the truth. While I think their politics are balanced, I think the turn they take is toward a more heretical political position' (quoted in Hibberd 2016). However, some fans clearly felt that there was a political agenda to season ten; respondent 201649 only watched the first episode, saying they became disgruntled after viewing it because of what they perceived as its current ideological standpoint and respondent 2016112 also said they found it 'curious to see that the first and last episodes touched on right-wing tea partier rhetoric, without really doing much to challenge it, beyond a wry hint of distaste'.

Although developed, written and produced between 2014 and 2015, season ten aired in 2016, six months after Donald Trump launched his presidential campaign. Season ten touched on some of the issues that had become apparent in the years prior to this, even though mainstream discourse around fake news and the rise of conspiracy movements like QAnon had yet to really come into the spotlight. As Ben Lindbergh writes in *The Ringer* the season 'nodded in the direction of recent political trends [but] Tad O'Malley was a fringy figure conceived before "fake news" became a buzzword and a conspiracy theorist became president' (2018). Season eleven, premiering in 2018, emerged into a political climate where multiple versions of the truth were out there, and conspiracy theories were wilder than even Mulder could have imagined.

'We're now living in a post-cover-up, post-conspiracy age': *The X-Files* in the Trump era

While season ten comprised six episodes, season eleven returned with ten. Eight of these were stand-alone episodes, while the series opener and finale continued the mythology from season ten. While season ten, written before Trump took office, dealt with some of the political and social changes that had occurred since 2002, season eleven was firmly situated in the era of post-truth and fake news. Lindbergh argues that while season ten's Tad O'Malley was conceived before 'fake news' became a buzzword, 'Season 11 ... is steeped in 2017, when once-disreputable and easily dismissed movements monopolized mainstream attention and staged a cultural (and Constitutional) coup' (Lindbergh 2018). Indeed, Carter notes the political changes and the way the show deals with them in an interview with *Bustle*, saying:

> So much has changed politically since 1993 ... radical changes to 2001, radical changes through the Obama years, and even more radical change with President Trump. So *The X-Files* has gotten to deal with a lot of political realities, and I'll always think it's given the show a lot of its life. I can tell you there's not an episode that deals directly with the political realities ... The political realities are part of the way we think about the show. But we're not responding to the political reality the way [shows like *American Horror Story: Cult*] are, where they're taking it head on. (quoted in Thomas 2018)

The political realities are, instead, referred to at various points throughout the season, such as in the opening montage, where we see footage of Trump's inauguration, Black Lives Matter protestors, Russian president Vladimir Putin and robed Ku Klux Klan members beneath a voice-over provided by the Cigarette Smoking Man. 'This' (S11: E02) shows Skinner refused assistance from the executive branch of the FBI because 'the bureau's not in good standing with the White House', and 'Plus One' (S11: E03) again reflects the real world conflict between Trump and the FBI, Mulder telling Scully that the world is going to hell, 'the president working to bring down the FBI along with it': the continued threat posed by a shadow government to democracy around the globe. The latter in particular parallels the QAnon movement, a far-right conspiracy theory that emerged in late 2017. QAnon began with a post by a user called 'Q' on the website 4Chan, claiming to be a high-ranking US government official with access to classified government information. Among the many accusations made in a variety of posts were that a 'deep state' cabal, which included Hollywood actors, government officials and politicians, were involved in child sex trafficking, and they were working against Trump during his time in office. Although initially posted to 4Chan, QAnon rapidly spread across the internet, becoming more visible across the United States and global media landscapes and entering mainstream political discourse. Support for Trump was a key part of the movement, with Trump amplifying QAnon posts on Twitter and refusing to denounce the group. The movement saw conspiracy theories enter mainstream discourse in a way they hadn't before, and buzzwords like 'fake news' and 'post-truth' became part of an everyday lexicon, epitomized in 'The Lost Art of Forehead Sweat' (S11: E04).

Written by Darin Morgan, the episode introduces us to Reggie Something, a conspiracy theorist and apparent former FBI agent who worked with Mulder and Scully on the X-Files. Reggie claims that 'they' are trying to erase him from society and, when questioned by Mulder, reveals that 'they' are actually Dr Thaddeus They, a scientist responsible for manipulating people's memories. In an interview with *Entertainment Weekly*, Morgan stated that Trump was one inspiration for the series, saying: 'The initial thing was trying to find some sort of Trump thing. I wanted to write something about it because [the show's] whole premise is "The Truth Is Out There", and now your fictional characters work for someone for whom the truth is a bit fuzzy' (quoted in Coggan 2018a).

The episode uses the Mandela Effect, the misremembering of facts by multiple people, as a vehicle to consider what truth means in the current climate. Reggie argues that 'They want you to think all conspiracies are nutty so that you ignore the ones that are true', while the following exchange between Mulder and Dr They highlights the shifting nature of belief in both the show and wider society:

Dr They   Your time has passed.
Mulder   Okay. So, what is or what was my time?
Dr They   Well, it's a time when people of power thought that they could keep their secrets secret, and were willing to do anything to keep it that way. Those days are passed. Gone. We're now living in a post-cover-up, post-conspiracy age …

Mulder	As long as the truth gets out.
Dr They	They don't really care whether the truth gets out. Because the public no longer knows what's meant by the truth.
Mulder	What do you mean?
Dr They	No one can tell the difference anymore ... between what's real and what's fake.
Mulder	There's still objective truth, objective reality.

For Dr They and, increasingly, the world beyond *The X-Files*, objective truth is difficult to find. Dr They creates and circulates 'phony fake news' – that is, real facts presented in a way that assures no one will believe it – on an online platform and tells Mulder how easy it is to manipulate people: rather than controlling people's minds, 'All you need is some people to think it's possible, and then you've sown the seeds of uncertainty. All you really need is a laptop.' The spread of fake news and disinformation throughout the course of the Trump presidential campaign, as well as the rise of QAnon, demonstrates just how easy that is.

There are several more explicit references to Trump during this episode however. Not only does Dr They tell Mulder that 'our current president once said something truly profound. He said, nobody knows for sure', but the retelling of Reggie, Mulder and Scully's final case draws directly from a presidential announcement speech Trump gave in June 2015. In the episode, Mulder, Scully and Reggie meet an alien representative of the Intergalactic Union of Sentient Beings from All Known Universes and Beyond. The alien tells them that they are barring humans from exploring the galaxy by

> building a wall. It will be a beautiful, albeit invisible, electromagnetic wall, that will sub-atomically incinerate any probes you attempt to send beyond your solar system. ... We can't allow your kind to infiltrate the rest of the cosmos. You're not sending us your best people. You're bringing drugs, you're bringing crime, you're bringing rapists. And some, I assume, are good people. But we have no choice, believe me.

The wall of course refers to the wall Trump announced he would build across the southern border to prevent Mexicans from entering the United States and the cost of which would be paid for by Mexico. Morgan notes he never hesitated to inject too much of the political climate into the episode saying, 'I thought, people who support Trump or who support the wall, what would they think if an alien came down and flipped it on them? How would they regard it?' (quoted in Coggan 2018b). He argues that using the contemporary political climate allowed him to make a comment about perspectives on truth and lies in a way that wouldn't turn people off, yet the episode divided fans. Respondent 2018114, responding to a questionnaire I released post-season eleven, wrote 'The best part of season 11 was [Chris

Carter] taking on the current state of affairs – fake governments, fake news, the brainwashing of the media, the role of technology' while Respondent 2018679 disagreed, saying 'much of what worked in the original now feels dated and [Carter's] vision of the series was oftentimes stretching to make itself feel relevant and politically engaged with its too obvious digs at the Trump administration and fake news'.

The X-Files, while heavily influenced by cultural events in the United States and steeped in the paranoia that that was prevalent in popular discourse, rarely commented directly on contemporary politics in its original run. While the show may have been anti-government, it did not specify *which* government, leaving viewers to make up their own minds as to which political party the series referred to. Dealing with concepts like fake news, misinformation and truther conspiracy theories in the revival seasons was par for the course for the show, but the explicit references to Trump shifted the series' political commentary from general to specific and highlighted, perhaps more than any other season, the way the revival seasons took on meaning in the late 2010s.

Conclusion

Media studies scholar Dan Hassler-Forest (in his article on TV revivals) argues that the one characteristic returning media texts like *The X-Files* have in common 'is that they are also and irreducibly cultural texts that take on meaning in a historically specific social, political and economic context' (2020: 177). Much academic analysis has identified how *The X-Files* drew on important historical events and the prevailing mood of the contemporary period in its original nine seasons, and in this chapter I have set out to examine how the show functions as a product of its time through the revival seasons. I would argue that the revival was broadly successful in ensuring *The X-Files'* relevance to the contemporary period, including references to conspiracy movements introduced following the show's ending in 2002, increasing use of government surveillance and the proliferation of fake news and disinformation. Respondent 2018420 felt the revival seasons reflected the current moment, writing 'I always thought of the X Files in retrospective as an (incidental?) instrument to getting people to become paranoid of their government, which is an instrument of the real powers to manipulate democracies. I feel now they owned this conception and started focusing the enemy in the post-truth, I felt this change was particularly interesting.'

And indeed, many other viewers – fans and critics – felt the same way. However, the fact that the show managed to reflect the contemporary mood did not make the revival seasons a success. Reviews were mixed among both fans and critics, with viewing figures decreasing as the seasons continued, for a variety of reasons – particularly Carter's treatment of Scully. In this regard, some fans felt that not every aspect of contemporary politics, culture or society were accurately reflected. Respondent 201828 focused on the storyline involving William's conception, writing: 'yet again we have medical rape. It's getting old. That might have been acceptable in the 90's, but it's 2018 and women are sick of those stories. CC, who seems to understand the times we're living in (Trump, deep state, Dr. They!) missed the #metoo movement completely.'

Several other fans highlighted the #MeToo movement, a social media movement highlighting the prevalence of sexual harassment, particularly in Hollywood, which became viral after sexual-abuse allegations were made against Harvey Weinstein in 2017. They argued that Carter had failed to engage with discussions taking place around sexual harassment, gender equality and the depiction of women in the media. Felix Brinker argues that a revival is 'not simply a continuation of a television narrative that has ceased to unfold, but an attempt to reboot the larger cultural mobilizations that clustered around it in the past' (2018: 328). While *The X-Files* has built its mythology around UFO conspiracies, it has also been lauded for its depiction of Scully as a strong female character. The revival's inability to engage with contemporary debates around gender whilst successfully reflecting technological and political changes suggests that fans may have been right to worry about its continued relevance to the modern day.

References

Adalian, J. (2014), 'Chris Carter on *Area 51*, Playing Softball with Brandon Tartikoff, and the TV Musical in His Closet', *Vulture*, 24 July. Available online: https://www.vulture.com/2014/07/chris-carter-amazon-after-x-files-chat.html (accessed 19 December 2021).

Brinker, F. (2018), 'Conspiracy, Procedure, Continuity: Reopening *The X-Files*', *Television & New Media*, 19 (4): 328–44.

Coggan, D. (2018a), '*X-Files* Writer Darin Morgan Teases *Twilight Zone*-Inspired Episode', *Entertainment Weekly*, 3 January. Available online: https://ew.com/tv/2018/01/24/x-files-darin-morgan-lost-art-of-forehead-sweat/ (accessed 19 December 2021).

Coggan, D. (2018b), '*X-Files* Writer Breaks Down His Trump-Inspired Episode "about Truth and Lying"', *Entertainment Weekly*, 24 January. Available online: https://ew.com/tv/2018/01/24/x-files-writer-darin-morgan-trump-inspired-episode/ (accessed 9 November 2022).

Dredge, S. (2015), '*X-Files* Revival Inspired by Surveillance Revelations, Says Show's Creator', *The Guardian*, 6 October. Available online: https://www.theguardian.com/tv-and-radio/2015/oct/06/return-of-the-x-files-inspired-by-nsa-surveillance-revelations (accessed 4 December 2021).

Graham, A. (1996), '"Are You Now or Have You Ever Been?" Conspiracy Theory and *The X-Files*', in D. Lavery, A. Hague and M. Cartwright (eds), *Deny All Knowledge: Reading The X-Files*, 52–62, Syracuse, NY: Syracuse University Press.

Hassler-Forest, D. (2020), '"When You Get There, You Will already Be There": *Stranger Things, Twin Peaks* and the Nostalgia Industry', *Science Fiction Film and Television* 13 (2): 175–97.

Hibberd, J. (2016), 'Fox's "X-Files" Revival Has Controversial New Theories', *Entertainment Weekly*, 11 January. Available online: https://ew.com/article/2016/01/11/x-files-revival-conspiracy/ (accessed 21 November 2021).

Lavery, D., A. Hague and M. Cartwright (eds) (1996), *Deny All Knowledge: Reading The X-Files*, New York: Syracuse University Press.

Kaiser, R. (2016), 'What's Going On with "The X-Files" Glenn Beck Wannabe Tad O'Malley?', *Inverse*, 25 January. Available online: https://www.inverse.com/article/10560-what-s-going-on-with-the-x-files-glenn-beck-wannabe-tad-o-malley (accessed 21 November 2021).

Kessenich, T. (2002), *Examinations: An Unauthorized Look at Seasons 6–9 of The X-Files, Featuring the Reviews of Unbound 1*, Bloomington, IN: Trafford Publishing.

Lawson, M. (2016), '"Your Government Lies": Why the X-Files Revival Is Just Right for Our Climate of Extreme Scepticism', *The Guardian*, 9 February. Available online: https://www.theguardian.com/tv-and-radio/tvandradioblog/2016/feb/09/your-government-lies-why-the-x-files-revival-is-just-right-for-our-climate-of-extreme-scepticism (accessed 18 November 2021).

Loock, K. (2018), 'American TV Series Revivals: Introduction', *Television & New Media*, 19 (4): 299–309.

Lindbergh, B. (2018), '"The X-Files" in the Post-Conspiracy Age of Trump', *The Ringer*, 3 January. Available online: https://www.theringer.com/tv/2018/1/3/16843804/x-files-season-11-age-of-trump (accessed 18 November 2021).

Mooney, D. (2017), *Opening the X-Files: A Critical History of the Original Series*, Jefferson, NC: McFarland.

Picarelli, E., and M. Gomez-Galisteo (2013), 'Be Fearful: *The X-Files*' Post-9/11 Legacy', *Science Fiction Film & Television*, 6 (1): 71–85.

Rapping, E. (1995), 'The X-Files', *Progressive*, 59 (1): 34–6.

Stuttaford, A. (2002), 'The Ex-Files: Mulder and Scully's Exit', *National Review Online*, 17 May. Available online: https://www.andrewstuttaford.com/archive/2002/05/17/the-ex-files-mulder-and-scully%E2%80%99s-exit (accessed 21 December 2021).

Taylor, C. (1994), 'Truth Decay: Sleuths after Reagan', *Millennium Pop* 1.1 Available online: https://timrileyauthor.files.wordpress.com/2012/02/mpopi194.pdf (accessed 2 January 2022).

Thomas, L. M. (2018), '"The X-Files" Is Going to Give Donald Trump the Government Conspiracy Treatment', *Bustle*, 3 January. Available online: https://www.bustle.com/p/trump-references-in-the-x-files-season-11-emphasize-the-shows-obsession-with-government-conspiracies-7764495 (accessed 2 December 2021).

PART THREE

The X-Philes: Fandom and paratextual narratives

Diane A. Rodgers

The notion of 'cults' as examined in Chapter 7 of this volume refers specifically to the religious devotion of groups following a particular figure or path of belief. However, the term 'cult' is often also applied to fanatical commitment to pop culture artefacts, often film or television series with a small but devoted following. *The X-Files* is frequently discussed in the context of cult television, with its own followers dubbed 'X-Philes', to whose responses and affection for the series are referred throughout this section. The status of *The X-Files*, however, despite maintaining a cult sensibility, has a long history of acknowledgement within mainstream media (in examples discussed in our introduction), allowing the series extended cultural influence. The dedication of X-Philes and its 'rabid' fans (such as 'shippers' discussed in Chapter 14 of this volume) help bring a transmedia dimension to *The X-Files*, allowing the narrative to spill beyond the confines of the medium of television (and film adaptations) into various aspects of the lives of fans and extending the experience of *The X-Files* into books, comics and video games.

Briac Picart Hellec's chapter opens this section by examining another significant example of cult television, *Twin Peaks*, in terms of its connections with *The X-Files*, as two sides of the same coin. Picart Hellec looks at the series' common characteristics and how each expanded their narrative into other media in ways that fundamentally shaped the televisual landscape. Will Lorenzo also looks at the notion of cult television and considers *The X-Files* alongside its spin-off series *Millennium*: in particular how some episodes blend elements of science fiction and horror with Christmas-themed aesthetics and motifs.

Iris Haist's discussion of *The X-Files* moves beyond the format of television to its comic-book adaptations. Haist explores how these stories not only adapt existing storylines, but also fill in narrative gaps and extend the narrative universe of *The X-Files*, considering their relationship to the setting (or moving) the boundaries of the series' canon. Janelle Vermaak-Griessel and Natalie Le Clue's discussion examines X-Files fandom through the lens of social media which sees fans contemplating the 'scariest' and 'best' *X-Files* episodes of all time. Vermaak-Griessel and Le Clue's examination evidences fan memory of the series and its lasting impact in terms of the role *The X-Files* continues to play in some people's everyday lives.

Marissa Spada's discussion looks beyond the more generic (typically male) *X-Files* fandom to focus on 'shippers': fans of the series, typically female, who were invested in the notion of a simmering romance between Mulder and Scully. Spada explores how discourses distinguishing between 'rabid' or 'hysterical' shippers and 'intellishippers' (those seen as expressing more 'rational' and eloquent fandom) signal masculinized readings of *The X-Files* and enhanced discriminatory gendered lines amongst the fans themselves.

The final chapter in this section by Ivan Girina and Andra Ivănescu considers the relationship between *The X-Files* and the world of video games by examining the depiction of virtual realities within episodes of the series. The focus moves beyond the series itself, however, as Girina and Ivănescu examine video game adaptations of *The X-Files* (of which there are several, released between 1997 and 2018), with particular focus on *The X-Files Game* of 1998. This chapter aptly brings the section to a close with discussion of *The X-Files* as an example of transmedia storytelling, exploring the relationship between the series and its video game adaptations as an integral part of the cultural phenomenon.

This section illustrates the breadth of the wider universe of *The X-Files*, reaching far beyond the confines of television (and even film) to a huge variety of different mediums spanning all three decades since the series' inception. We see, therefore, in these chapters, how the dedication, commitment and enthusiasm shown by fans of *The X-Files* for the series in all its incarnations helps not only fuel the creation of material surrounding the main series itself, but also how the devotion of 'X-Philes' and 'shippers' helps to define the series as being truly 'cult' in every sense of the word.

10

To escape a legacy: The influence of *Twin Peaks* on *The X-Files*

Briac Picart Hellec

In the 1990s, a popular network television series depicted the investigations of FBI agents confronted with evidence of the paranormal and helped bring profound changes to the way American television is conceived and consumed. This description could obviously refer to *The X-Files*. However, it could also apply to an earlier series, *Twin Peaks*, which was created by screenwriter Mark Frost and filmmaker David Lynch and which aired on ABC from 1990 to 1991. The series dealt with FBI agent Dale Cooper's (Kyle MacLachlan) investigation into the murder of a high-school girl named Laura Palmer (Sheryl Lee) in Twin Peaks, Washington, a charming town that eventually revealed a dark underbelly. Though it began as an offbeat crime drama, *Twin Peaks* progressively incorporated more fantastical elements until the mystery's solution (Laura was killed by her father, who was possessed by an evil spirit) signalled a definite shift in the narrative towards the supernatural. The series was cancelled after its second season leaving its narrative unresolved. It was followed by a 1992 prequel film, *Fire Walk with Me*, and, eventually, a revival season on Showtime in 2017, *Twin Peaks: The Return*. *Twin Peaks* is credited with developing serialized mysteries, showcasing a sophisticated formal approach and allowing weirdness and unease to seep into the allegedly sanitized space of network television.

These characteristics evoke *The X-Files*, which began airing only two years after *Twin Peaks*' final episode, and critics quickly pointed out the similarities between the two series (Wolcott 1994). Indeed, looking at *The X-Files* as an intertextual palimpsest reveals that *Twin Peaks* is deeply ingrained in its underwriting: *Twin Peaks* is as significant an influence on Chris Carter's creation as films like *Close Encounters of the Third Kind* (1977), *Silence of the Lambs* (1991) or the series *Kolchak: The Night Stalker* (1974–1975). Two contradicting tendencies determine the relation between the two texts as *The X-Files* claims *Twin Peaks*' heritage while simultaneously distancing itself from it. Therefore, understanding the legacy of *The X-Files* necessarily implies understanding how the series engages with the legacy of *Twin Peaks*, which is what this chapter seeks to explore. The chapter first examines how *The X-Files* emulates *Twin Peaks* and borrows from the earlier series, before considering how *The X-Files* successfully recontextualizes specific characteristics of *Twin Peaks* and the motivation behind that process.

Emulating *Twin Peaks*

Though the extent of the series' influence is still under debate, film and television scholar Andreas Halskov considers *Twin Peaks* to be a 'game changer' in American television (Halskov 2015: 15). Even before *Twin Peaks* began airing, the press predicted the series would be a turning point:

> '*Twin Peaks*, the series that will change TV.' – *Connoisseur Magazine*
>
> 'Something of a miracle. The most hauntingly original work ever done for American TV.' – *Time Magazine*
>
> '*Twin Peaks* will change television history.' – *Los Angeles Daily News*
>
> 'Unprecedented. *Twin Peaks* easily out-dazzles all the new network shows. This you gotta see.' – Tom Shales, *The Washington Post* (quoted in Olson 2011: 270)

This reputation stemmed partly from David Lynch's then unexpected involvement in a television series. Indeed, from the angst-ridden surrealism of *Eraserhead* (1977), the deceptive classicism of *The Elephant Man* (1980) or the solemn science fiction of *Dune* (1984) to the disturbing eroticism of the neo-noir thriller *Blue Velvet* (1986), Lynch's filmography up to that point hardly suggested his distinctive style could merge with the demands of network television. Yet, with its oneiric atmosphere, its offbeat characters and its 1950s Americana-inspired imagery, *Twin Peaks* felt of a piece with the rest of his oeuvre. Thus, as it undoubtedly bore Lynch's mark, the series benefited from the legitimating effect of his auteur aura (Newman and

Levine 2012: 51). Furthermore, *Twin Peaks* displays features such as its intense use of serialized storytelling and its willingness to disorient viewers (both of which will be discussed more extensively later) that contribute to its reputation as an innovative work. Thus, 'emulating *Twin Peaks*, even in a minor way, may allow a new text to stake a claim for quality, art, surrealism, complexity, or "weirdness"' (Jowett 2016: 220). In the case of *The X-Files*, such an emulation can also be considered strategic: since *Twin Peaks* had been recently cancelled, a ready-made audience was available for a new series that shared some of its characteristics.

The X-Files' emulation of *Twin Peaks* is especially noticeable when studying the series' form. *Twin Peaks* is formally ambitious: its stylized and deliberate direction showcases experimental scenes such as those in the famous Red Room (Olson 2011: 300), its editing broke pacing conventions in television (Halskov 2015: 73–6), while its soundtrack combined Angelo Badalamenti's ever-present score with distinctive sound design to produce an idiosyncratic atmosphere. Lorna Jowett detects a formal continuity between *Twin Peaks* and *The X-Files*: 'Like *Twin Peaks*, [*The X-Files*] prefers a slow pace, smooth camerawork, and measured editing to evoke its sense of strange events or beings glimpsed within an apparently mundane world' (2013: 26). However, in its early episodes, *The X-Files* remains relatively tame in its visual approach. Afterwards, the series progressively turns more daring, in episodes like 'Triangle', (S6: E03) though it never becomes as formally adventurous as *Twin Peaks*.

Most importantly, the opening scene from *The X-Files*' pilot episode ('Pilot' S1: E01) replicates the conclusion of the *Twin Peaks* episode 'Dispute between Brothers' (S2: E10), which depicts the abduction of Major Briggs (Don S. Davis) by an undefined force in front of a powerless Dale Cooper. The scene contains *The X-Files*' visual template in a nutshell with its dark woods, its bursts of blinding light from which emerges a threatening backlit figure and a foreboding synthesizer score by Angelo Badalamenti that anticipates composer Mark Snow's work on *The X-Files*. Other moments of *The X-Files*' pilot contain visual echoes of the pilot of *Twin Peaks*: for instance, both feature the discovery of a young woman's corpse in the wild and a shot that calls attention to a welcome sign when the protagonists arrive in town.

Furthermore, both series share a proclivity for scenes taking place at night in the forests of the Pacific Northwest. This similar choice of scenery can be attributed to the proximity between their filming locations as *The X-Files* was filmed in the Vancouver area and the *Twin Peaks* pilot in the vicinity of Seattle. However, after its pilot was completed, *Twin Peaks* was filmed in California for the rest of its run. Nevertheless, footage filmed on location for the pilot is used as transitions between scenes to preserve the coherence of the series' general aesthetic. *The X-Files* also relocated to California from its sixth season onwards, a decision which marked a departure from the aesthetics of the first seasons and, thus, from *Twin Peaks*.

The connection between the two series extends to casting choices. Indeed, *The X-Files* features several actors who had held significant roles on *Twin Peaks* such as Michael Horse (*The X-Files* S1: E19), Don S. Davis (*The X-Files* S1: E13), Michael J. Anderson (*The X-Files* S2: E20), Kenneth Welsh (*The X-Files* S3: E11) or Richard Beymer (*The X-Files* S4: E06) with Horse, Davis and Welsh being cast in parts similar to the characters they played on *Twin Peaks*. These numerous casting overlaps have led to arguments that *The X-Files* was 'courting' *Twin Peaks* fans (Reeves, Rodgers and Epstein 1996: 32). It is true that in *The X-Files*, casting is sometimes used reflectively to reference the series' inspirations. For instance, Arthur Dales, Mulder's predecessor at the X-Files, is portrayed by Darren McGavin, an actor primarily known for playing the title role in *Kolchak: The Night Stalker*. Similarly, the fact that Don Davis, who had played Major Briggs in *Twin Peaks*, was cast as Dana Scully's father can be interpreted as a nod to the lineage between the two series with *Twin Peaks* being both diegetically and metatextually a parent of *The X-Files*. However, the most famous example of such intertextual casting is *The X-Files*' co-lead, David Duchovny. Duchovny had guest starred in three episodes of *Twin Peaks*' second season as DEA agent Denise Bryson, his most famous performance before Fox Mulder. Though it was probably not the main factor when choosing Duchovny, casting an actor associated with *Twin Peaks* in a central part of a new series was sure to invoke the memory of *Twin Peaks*.

As an eccentric but brilliant FBI agent, Mulder is analogous to Cooper (Wilcox and Williams 1996: 104). Both are attuned to the powers of intuition, willing to consider irrational postulates and highly efficient at their job (Malach 1996: 71). Mulder's debt to Cooper is overtly referenced in the heavily metatextual episode 'Jose Chung's From Outer Space' (S3: E20) when Mulder is shown gorging on vast quantities of sweet potato pie, reminiscent of Cooper's voracious appetite for cherry pies.

However, though both Cooper and Mulder are FBI agents, their rapport with their hierarchy differs. In *Twin Peaks*, the bureau is depicted as a positive institution. Cooper is supported by his superior Gordon Cole (played by Lynch himself), who is equally open to supernatural explanations, and Albert Rosenfield (Miguel Ferrer), who is shown to be as much of a stalwart as Cooper. In a departure from the narrative trope which pits local and federal authority against each other, Sheriff Truman welcomes the FBI's involvement in the investigation. Conversely, in *The X-Files*, the FBI is depicted as unreliable since it is under the sway of the nefarious Syndicate as signified by the Cigarette Smoking Man's insidious presence in the J. Edgar Hoover Building. Though the status of Mulder's superior is ambiguous at first, Walter Skinner is eventually shown to be a trustworthy ally. However, even this beacon of hope can be taken away, as happens when Skinner is temporarily replaced by the authoritarian bureaucrat Alvin Kersh. Furthermore, most of the agents who play an important part in the series, such as Jeffrey Spender (Chris Owens) or Diana Fowley (Mimi Rogers), are also connected to the conspiracy.

As these conflicting depictions of the FBI demonstrate, *The X-Files* does not simply replicate *Twin Peaks*. Indeed, the series' second mode of engagement with *Twin Peaks*' legacy consists in selecting specific traits and recontextualizing them. The contrastive storytelling formulas of the two series are the crux of this process.

Serializing mystery

Twin Peaks is highly serialized. The series prioritizes aperture over closure. While most primetime dramas rely on a combination of episodic and serial storytelling (Newman 2006: 20), episodes of *Twin Peaks* lack formal unity since they rarely feature self-contained storylines. As such, episodes tend to blur together. The macro level – the series – prevails over the micro-level of narration – the episode: in other words, one watches *Twin Peaks* the series rather than an episode of *Twin Peaks*. This intense serialization extends to the series' treatment of mysteries. By mystery, I refer to narrative elements which create curiosity. Raphaël Baroni defines curiosity as an emotional response to a narrative based on a diagnosis of the narrative situation (by contrast, suspense relies on a prognosis of the narrative situation) (2007: 254).

Mysteries have long been an essential narrative device in American television writing, especially genre fiction. For instance, in a science-fiction series like *Star Trek* (1966–9), the crew of the *USS Enterprise* must sometimes investigate seemingly impossible phenomena or explore unknown planets. Similarly, every episode of *The Twilight Zone* (1959–64) focuses on a mysterious situation, a missing context, which baffles both the characters and the audience. However, in both of these examples, mysteries are confined to a single episode. *The Fugitive* (1963–7) is a turning point in that regard. The series focuses on the quest to prove his innocence by physician Richard Kimble (David Janssen) who has been wrongfully accused of his wife's murder. The exact circumstances of the murder constitute a mystery that stretches over several seasons. However, this mystery is not reinforced during the series through red herrings or the gathering of clues: its only real progress occurs during the series finale, during which it is resolved. Instead, the murder of Helen Kimble justifies the series' narrative formula as it forces the hero to flee across the United States. The first instance of a truly major serialized mystery was in *Dallas* (1978–91). The third season finale of the series ends on a cliffhanger: J. R. Ewing (Larry Hagman) is shot by an unseen assailant. During the summer that followed, the mystery of the shooter's identity generated an unprecedented media phenomenon (Thompson 1997: 34). The answer was eventually given in the fourth episode of the following season. *Dallas* thus transformed the pause between seasons into an opportunity to speculate on future narrative developments and try to guess the solution to an enigma before the series offers it. *Dallas* proved that serialized mysteries could increase the implication of television viewers in a series, a discovery on which *Twin Peaks* expanded. However, while the mystery in *Dallas* lasted only for a handful of episodes, the entire narrative formula of *Twin Peaks* revolves around mysteries.

Twin Peaks spearheaded long-form mystery storylines by asking 'Who killed Laura Palmer?', a question which initiates and propels its narrative. The serialization of mysteries endures and expands the story beyond the murder plotline as the supernatural mythos develops. Because of their scope and complexity, the mysteries of *Twin Peaks* stirred the curiosity of viewers in an unprecedented manner. This demanding form of storytelling hence elicited a new participatory form of viewing.

Aided by home video cassette recorders (VCRs), viewers were able to rewatch and analyse the series, poring over every detail hidden in its frames to decipher its clues and produce theories. Discoveries were then shared with the fandom hivemind on the *alt.tv.twin-peaks* Usenet forums (Jenkins 2013: 77), a reaction which surprised Mark Frost:

> I remember about halfway through the airing of the first season, someone came in and dumped on my desk maybe 500 pages of internet chatter about the show – and this was at a point where the internet was only just emerging as something people used for basic communication. But here were these entire forums dedicated to exploring just one aspect of plotting, something that had taken maybe 15 minutes to think up. (quoted in Sharad 2017)

However, as media and cultural studies scholar Henry Jenkins argues, *Twin Peaks* seems specifically designed to arouse such behaviour:

> The space between episodes gave ample time for audience speculations while the core narrative moved forward at a breakneck pace, continually opening up new enigmas while closing down others … The narrative abounded with cryptic messages, codes, and chess problems, riddles and conundrums, dreams, visions, clues, secret passages, and locked boxes, shadowy figures peering through dark windows, and secondary narratives appearing in the televised soap (*Invitation to Love*) that forms a backdrop to the first season's action. All of these details invited the viewer's participation as a minimal condition for comprehending the narrative and even closer consideration if one had any hopes of solving the compelling narrative hook, 'Who killed Laura Palmer'. (1996: 54–5)

Such reception is an early instance of the model of engagement that film and media scholar Jason Mittell defines as forensic fandom, which occurs when series 'convert many viewers into amateur narratologists, noting patterns and violations of convention chronicling chronologies, and highlighting both inconsistencies and continuities across episodes and even series' (2015: 52).

Delaying answers

The intense reaction *Twin Peaks* generated proved to be the source of its downfall. After the first season's finale failed to reveal the identity of Laura's murderer, critics and parts of the audience began to express frustration (Olson 2011: 299). In the face of declining ratings and the growing discontent of viewers who had grown impatient for a solution to the mystery, ABC asked Frost and Lynch to reveal the identity of Laura's murderer earlier than they wanted to. Frustrated by this development, both creators' involvement in the series decreased during the second season (Dukes 2014: 257–9). This situation is often deemed to be the source of both the season's allegedly unfocused storytelling and the series cancellation. Therefore, the intense focus of *Twin Peaks* on a serialized mystery story arc complicated the handling of its audience's patience while making the postponing of answers more challenging to sustain.

In contrast with *Twin Peaks*' macro-oriented narration, *The X-Files*' narrative approach relies on episodic storytelling. Episodes of the series are divided into two categories. The first episode category is the 'myth-arc' and develops the series' mythology. The myth-arc functions as a continuation of *Twin Peaks*' experiment with complex serialized mysteries as it relies on an interrelated set of questions: what happened to Samantha Mulder? What is the exact plan of the Colonists? What is the purpose of the black oil? What are the true intentions of the Syndicate? The list grows longer as the series progresses. The second episode category are monster-of-the-week episodes, which focus on self-contained cases investigated by Scully and Mulder.

However, this division of episodes should not be misconstrued as an opposition between episodic and serialized storytelling. Indeed, episodes of the myth-arc often have strong formal unity since they focus on specific events. In contrast, monster-of-the-week episodes present serialized characteristics when they allow for character development – the evolving romance between Scully and Mulder – or recurring perpetrators – such as Eugene Victor Tooms (Doug Hutchison) or Robert Patrick Modell (Robert Wisden). Nonetheless, the myth-arc does offer a higher level of interconnectedness between episodes. By charting the progress of its protagonists' quest for truth, the myth-arc generates an extensive network of sometimes conflicting information on the series' mythology. To achieve even a partial understanding of the mythology, viewers must therefore connect clues dispersed across every myth-arc episode.

The mythology of *The X-Files* inspired similar online behaviour as *Twin Peaks*: fans of *The X-Files*, known as 'X-Philes', tried to decipher the series' clues and shared their theories on its dedicated forum, *alt.tv.x-files* (Sigiliano and Borges 2019: 14). The fandoms of the two series overlapped, as demonstrated by numerous issues devoted to *The X-Files* by the *Twin Peaks* fanzine *Wrapped in Plastic*. Furthermore, fans wrote fan fiction crossovers that they shared on the internet and even hoped for an official crossover episode, developing connections between the two series (Reeves, Rodgers and Epstein 1996: 32).

Thus, *The X-Files* opposes *Twin Peaks*' serialization with narrative compartmentalization: long-form mysteries are relegated to a specific type of episode. This approach is beneficial to the myth-arc's sustainability. Since ongoing mysteries are not the focus of every episode, writers can rely on monster-of-the-week episodes to modulate the mythology's narrative momentum and delay answers. Consequently, the mystery surrounding Samantha Mulder's fate is introduced in the pilot and only resolved in the seventh season, while *Twin Peaks* provides an answer to the Laura Palmer mystery in its fourteenth episode.

Disorienting viewers

This narrative compartmentalization also affects the recontextualization of another aspect of *Twin Peaks*: its weirdness. The series' reputation for weirdness does not simply result from its quirky characters or peculiar plot but stems from the fact that watching *Twin Peaks* can be an unsettling experience. Indeed, while previous network series were usually designed to be accessible by privileging clarity (in terms of plotting, visual style, or adherence to generic conventions), *Twin Peaks* exhibits a willingness to disorient viewers, as exemplified by its generic hybridity. Indeed, *Twin Peaks* borrows elements from various genres such as crime fiction, soap operas or horror. Therefore, the rules by which the narrative abides are unclear. For instance, its murder mystery is given a destabilizing supernatural solution. *Twin Peaks* also exhibits tonal fluidity: comedic scenes can give way to bouts of violence, while a harrowing passage can be qualified by offbeat humour.

Consequently, viewers of *Twin Peaks* are often left in a state of unease, uncertain of the emotional response that is expected of them. This disorienting effect is exacerbated by Lynch's penchant for formal experimentation in the episodes he directed. Lynch, whose creative process involves intuition, often improvised on the series set. Such improvisations posed a challenge for Mark Frost and other writers who had to find ways to incorporate them into the plot while preserving general narrative coherence (Thorne 2016: 219). As a result, episodes directed by Lynch often stand in contrast with the rest of the series and signal a shift in the direction of its plot. Therefore,

Twin Peaks can sometimes feel as if it is caught between two conflicting impulses as it wavers between relatively straightforward storytelling and avant-garde cinema territory. Consequently, the series has been accused of lacking substance: 'Like a Rorschach test, viewers found all kinds of meaning in *Twin Peaks*, but in the end it turned out to be just a blotch of ink – postmodern bluster, ultimately signifying nothing' (Thompson 1997: 159). In 1994, critic James Wolcott favourably compared *The X-Files* to *Twin Peaks* on this issue: 'David Lynch wrecked the trance of *Twin Peaks* when he abandoned all interest in even a quaint semblance of normality and began to strobe the screen in a fit of expressionism ... *The X-Files* doesn't make the mistake of elevating its sensibility at the expense of its subjects' (Wolcott 1994).

The X-Files' narrative structure channels *Twin Peaks'* weirdness into a less disorienting result. Since it entails variation on fixed constants (story world, characters or episode construction), the expectation that episodes must be even marginally different from one another is built into the conventions of episodic storytelling: Lieutenant Columbo (Peter Falk) cannot investigate the same murder every week. *The X-Files* heightens this approach by broadening the range of such variations. Like *Twin Peaks*, *The X-Files* alternates between different genres and tones, but these changes operate at the episodic level. For instance, comedic episodes are explicitly coded as such (most notably by Mark Snow's musical score), while a myth-arc episode will not suddenly veer into one of screenwriter Darin Morgan's self-referential satires. Shifts in generic identity and tonality are made less confusing since they are self-contained. This approach facilitates formal experimentation as the series visual language can vary wildly in the James Whale-inspired 'The Post-Modern Prometheus' (S5: E05) or in 'Triangle', which relies on single takes and split screens, without repercussions on subsequent episodes.

In *The X-Files*, managing the viewers' reaction to weirdness is also facilitated by the presence of a sceptic figure, Dana Scully (and, later, John Doggett), which *Twin Peaks* lacks. Strangeness is an integral part of life in Twin Peaks and often goes unquestioned: when Dale Cooper asks 'Who is the lady with the log?' he receives the simple reply 'We call her the Log Lady.' Sheriff Truman is Cooper's straight man, the Doctor Watson to his Sherlock Holmes, who invariably goes along with Cooper's outlandish methods. Even the cynical Albert Rosenfield eventually stops mocking Cooper's visions when presented with evidence of the existence of otherworldly entities. Like the other characters, viewers are expected to go along with Cooper's idiosyncrasies and the inherent strangeness of the world of Twin Peaks. Conversely, in *The X-Files*, by doubting Mulder's hypotheses and offering rational explanations, Scully acts as the audience proxy. Though the series always confirms the existence of the paranormal, Scully's scepticism stresses that such occurrences are not considered normal within the storyworld.

Therefore, *The X-Files* stages epistemic doubt to ease the suspension of disbelief.

The two series thus generate a different set of expectations. Because of its fluid storytelling structure, *Twin Peaks* lacks narrative boundaries that could mark shifts in genre, tonality or form, and as a result, the series exhibits an unpredictable quality. Meanwhile, *The X-Files'* narrative structure relies on noticeable variations; the series teaches its audience to expect the unexpected, making the latter more formulaic. *The X-Files* thereby filters *Twin Peaks'* storytelling innovations and its most destabilizing features via narrative compartmentalization, grounding them in a new context, a process that results in a more controlled and eventually less bewildering narrative.

Conclusion

Damon Lindelof, the showrunner of *Lost* (2004–10), recounts that during the conception of the series, then ABC chairman Lloyd Braun warily warned *Lost*'s co-creator J. J. Abrams: 'We can't have another *Twin Peaks* on our hands' (Hibberd 2019). Indeed, after its cancellation, *Twin Peaks* was perceived as a cautionary tale for television producers: its weirdness and reliance on serialized mystery had alienated viewers and should therefore be avoided.

Arguably, those series in the 1990s that drew most inspiration from *Twin Peaks* would aim to avoid direct comparison by selecting some of its specific traits and discarding others. For instance, *Wild Palms* (ABC, 1993) is as eccentric and esoteric as *Twin Peaks*, but it is a miniseries with a definitive endpoint for its storylines. *Picket Fences* (CBS, 1992–6) borrows its quirky atmosphere and small-town setting from *Twin Peaks* but does not feature serialized mysteries. While *The X-Files* followed this approach, it was the first series to not only claim *Twin Peaks'* most innovative characteristics but to achieve significant success by doing so.

In many ways, *Twin Peaks* prepared the ground for *The X-Files*. It demonstrated that American television could welcome more outwardly artful, intricate and unsettling narratives. However, it failed to prove that such experiments could be sustainable, something that *The X-Files* achieved by opting for a more rigidly constructed narrative formula than *Twin Peaks*. In this sense, the relation between the two series echoes the *tessera*, the second revisionary ratio examined by humanities scholar Harold Bloom in *The Anxiety of Influence*:

> I take the word not from mosaic-making, where it is still used, but from the ancient mystery cults, where it meant a token of recognition, the fragment say of a small pot which with the other fragments would re-constitute the vessel. A poet antithetically 'completes' his precursor

by so reading the parent-poem as to retain its terms but to mean them in another sense, as though the precursor had failed to go far enough. (Bloom 1973: 14)

To further emulate Bloom, we could consider *The X-Files* a deliberate 'mistranslation' of its precursor (Bloom 1973: 71). The series uses fragments of *Twin Peaks* to give it another shape, retroactively completing its predecessor, realizing its allegedly unfulfilled possibilities. Through this transformative process, *The X-Files* manages to escape the overwhelming legacy of *Twin Peaks*.

Both series stick to their respective approach as they expand their narrative into other media. *Twin Peaks* remains serialized, with each of its extensions participating in the formation of a continuous narrative ensemble: *Fire Walk with Me* is a prequel to the original series, while *The Return* continues Dale Cooper's story twenty-five years after the end of the second season. On the other hand, *The X-Files* dedicates each cinematic transposition to one side of its dual formula: *Fight the Future* continues the myth-arc while *I Want to Believe* operates as a monster-of-the-week story. Though shorter, the two revival seasons also follow the narrative strategy of the original series.

Regarding these latter seasons, the approach of *The X-Files* is, therefore, quite creatively conservative. The revival seems to be designed to adhere as closely as possible to the template the series had established in the 1990s: its heroes have aged, its mythology is updated to acknowledge the contemporary sociopolitical context but *The X-Files* remain *The X-Files* and the seasons do not achieve any major formal or structural surprises.

Twin Peaks: The Return opts for a strikingly different approach: it displays a sterner but more radical form and strikingly opaque storytelling. *The Return* subverts the nostalgic expectations of revivals by withholding iconic elements from the original series, metatextually addressing its relevance, and picking apart the audience's perception of the original series (Picart Hellec 2021). Thus, despite its title, *The Return* withholds a return to the original *Twin Peaks*. Therefore, while *Twin Peaks* found a way to develop into something new by questioning its past, *The X-Files* was eventually unable to escape its own legacy.

References

Baroni, R. (2007), *La Tension Narrative*, Paris: Seuil.
Bloom, H. (1973), *The Anxiety of Influence: A Theory of Poetry*, Oxford: Oxford University Press.
Blue Velvet (1986), [Film] Dir. David Lynch, USA: De Laurentiis Entertainment Group.

Close Encounters of the Third Kind (1977), [Film] Dir. Steven Spielberg, USA: Columbia Pictures.
Columbo (1968–78), [TV Series] NBC.
Dallas (1978–91), [TV Series] CBS.
'Dispute between Brothers', *Twin Peaks* (1990), [TV Programme], ABC, 8 December, 22:00.
Dukes, B. (2013), *Reflections, An Oral History of Twin Peaks*, Nashville, TN: Short/Tall Press.
Dune (1984), [Film] Dir. David Lynch, USA: Dino De Laurentiis Corporation.
Eraserhead (1977), [Film] Dir. David Lynch, USA: Libra Films.
The Elephant Man (1980), [Film] Dir. David Lynch, USA: Brooksfilms.
The Fugitive (1963–7), [TV Series] ABC.
Halskov, A. (2015), *TV Peaks*, Odense: University Press of Southern Denmark.
Hibberd J. (2019), 'Damon Lindelof Reveals His 7 Biggest Pop Culture Influences', *Entertainment Weekly*, 12 September. Available online: https://ew.com/tv/2019/09/12/damon-lindelof-influences/ (accessed 3 May 2022).
'A House Divided', *Dallas* (1980), [TV Programme], CBS, 21 March, 21:00.
Jenkins, H. ([1993] 2013), *Textual Poachers*, New York: Routledge.
Jenkins, H. (1996), '"Do You Enjoy Making the Rest of Us Feel Stupid?": alt.tv.twinpeaks, the Trickster Author, and Viewer Mastery', in D. Lavery (ed.), *Full of Secrets: Critical Approaches to Twin Peaks*, 51–70, Detroit, MI: Wayne State University Press.
Jowett, L. (2013), '"Mulder, Have You Noticed that We're on Television?": "X-Cops", Style and Innovation', *Science Fiction Film and Television*, 6 (1): 23–38.
Jowett, L. (2016), 'Nightmare in Red? *Twin Peaks* Parody, Homage, Intertextuality, and Mashup', in C. Spooner and J. A. Weinstock (eds), *Return to Twin Peaks: New Approaches to Materiality, Theory, and Genre on Television*, 211–29, New York: Palgrave Macmillan.
Kolchak: The Night Stalker (1974–5), [TV Series] ABC.
Levine, E., and M. Z. Newman (2012), *Legitimating Television: Media Convergence and Cultural Status*, New York: Routledge.
Lost (2004–10), [TV Series] ABC.
Malach, M. (1996), 'I Want to Believe … in the FBI: The Special Agent and *The X-Files*' in D. Lavery, A. Hague and M. Cartwright (eds), *'Deny All Knowledge': Reading The X-Files*, 63–77, Syracuse, NY: Syracuse University Press.
Mittell, J. (2015), *Complex TV*, New York: New York University Press.
Newman, M. Z. (2006), 'From Beats to Arcs: Toward a Poetics of Television Narrative', *The Velvet Light Trap*, 58: 16–28.
Olson, G. (2011), *David Lynch, Beautiful Dark*, Lanham, MD: The Scarecrow Press.
Picart Hellec, B. (2021), '"Brings Back Some Memories": Textual and Metatextual Experiences of Nostalgia in *Twin Peaks: The Return*', *US Studies Online*, 17 June. Available online: https://usso.uk/brings-back-some-memories-textual-and-metatextual-experiences-of-nostalgia-in-twin-peaks-the-return/ (accessed 3 May 2022).
Picket Fences (1992–6), [TV Series] CBS.

Reeves, J. L., M. C. Rodgers and M. Epstein (1996), 'Rewriting Popularity: The Cult Files', in D. Lavery, A. Hague and M. Cartwright (eds), *'Deny All Knowledge': Reading The X-Files*, 22–36, Syracuse, NY: Syracuse University Press.

Sharhad, C. (2017), 'Who killed *Twin Peaks?*', *Little White Lies*, 22 February. Available online: https://lwlies.com/articles/twin-peaks-making-of-cast-and-crew/ (accessed 3 May 2022).

Sigiliano, D., and G. Borges (2019), 'Transmedia Literacy: Analyzing the Impact of *The X-Files* Transmedia Strategies', *Palabra Clave*, 22 (2): 1–25.

The Silence of the Lambs (1991), [Film] Dir. Jonathan Demme, USA: Strong Heart Productions.

Star Trek (1966–9), [TV Series] NBC.

Thompson, R. J. (1996), *Television's Second Golden Age*, New York: Continuum International Publishing Group.

Thorne, J. (2016), *The Essential Wrapped in Plastic: Pathways to Twin Peaks*, self-published.

The Twilight Zone (1959–64), [TV Series] CBS.

Twin Peaks (1990–1), [TV Series] ABC.

Twin Peaks: Fire Walk with Me (1992), [Film] Dir. David Lynch, France: Ciby 2000.

Twin Peaks: The Return (2017), [TV Series] Showtime.

Wilcox, R., and J. P. Williams (1996), '"What Do You Think?" *The X-Files*, Liminality, and Gender Pleasure', in D. Lavery, A. Hague and M. Cartwright (eds), *'Deny All Knowledge': Reading The X-Files*, 99–120, Syracuse, NY: Syracuse University Press.

Wild Palms (1993), [TV Series] ABC.

Wolcott, J. (1994), 'X-Factor', *The New Yorker*, 11 April. Available online: https://www.newyorker.com/magazine/1994/04/18/x-factor (accessed 3 May 2022).

11

A very scary X-Mas: An examination of the Christmas episodes of *The X-Files* and *Millennium*

William J. Lorenzo

The Christmas episodes of any television series fall into a genre unto themselves. This genre often supersedes the specific genre of each television series in question, as it presents a unique lens for storytelling that only happens at most once each television season. But successful Christmas episodes will merge genres with the series' genre in order to facilitate an episode which is often a powerful entry into the series' canon. With a close examination of the two Christmas episodes of *The X-Files* and the two Christmas episodes of its spin-off series *Millennium* (1996–9), it is clear that these four episodes are pre-eminent entries into both series' canon, as well as into the annals of Christmas television. Both series were able to successfully accomplish the amalgamation of Christmas-themed genre signifiers with those of both science fiction and horror and, on top of this, *Millennium* was even able to incorporate elements of the gangster genre into one of their episodes. These festive episodes are some of the most significant episodes of the series, as they all aid in developing the main characters' story arcs, albeit in very different ways. By closely examining each of these four episodes, we can inspect elements of the Christmas genre (religion, holiday, optimism, love, cheerfulness, family, etc.) and analyse their interaction with elements of sci-fi, horror and gangster dramas. Examination of this atypical and at times anomalous amalgamation of genres in four of the most unique episodes of these two series will illustrate what makes them such compelling entries into *The X-Files* canon.

The four Christmas episodes

The first two Christmas-themed episodes of *The X-Files* and *Millennium* aired in December 1997, and the second two in December 1998. *The X-Files* episode 'Christmas Carol' (S5: E06) was the series' first foray into Christmas television, airing 7 December 1997. This episode was the first of a two-part arc that heavily focused on the overall mythology of the series. 'Christmas Carol' takes place during the days leading up to Christmas, when Dana Scully travels back home to celebrate with her family. She receives a phone call seemingly from her deceased sister Melissa (Melinda McGraw), which leads her to investigate a case involving the alleged suicide of a nearby woman. Over the course of the episode, Scully discovers that the woman and her husband were murdered and their deaths staged as two suicides by a pharmaceutical company intent on continuing their experiments on the couple's young daughter, who Scully believes to be Melissa's biological child. Scully unsuccessfully attempts to adopt the young girl, Emily Sim (Lauren Diewold), but she finds out during the final moments of the episode that Emily was born biologically from one of Scully's own ovum, forcibly extracted in a previous episode.

The continuation of this episode, 'Emily' (S5: E07), which takes place around New Year, focuses on the young girl and delves much deeper into the series' overall myth-arc. Both episodes aired prior to the series' midseason break, yet it was specifically 'Christmas Carol' which focused on the Christmas holiday. The filming of the episode featured multiple quirks and conundrums. First and foremost, the entire episode was written for another character, but was rewritten by writers Vince Gilligan, John Shiban and Frank Spotnitz in order to feature Scully as the biological mother of Emily. This was done in part to aid in the overall direction of the fifth season of the series, which the entire creative team knew would become the lead-in for the feature film *The X-Files: Fight the Future* (1998). Second, David Duchovny was unable to film in early October 1997, when this episode was filmed, due to the fact that he was on a promotional junket for his film *Playing God* (1997). This relegated Mulder to a split-second appearance at the opposing end of a phone call, wearing a Christmas nightcap. At the time, the young actress who was cast to play the role of Emily Sim was deathly afraid of hospitals. The filming of 'Christmas Carol' was complete, yet when the character is hospitalized during the following episode, the production was unable to calm the actress down in order to film her scenes in 'Emily'. She was subsequently recast (replaced with Lauren Diewold, who was familiar to production staff from an earlier appearance in *Millennium*), and all of her scenes for 'Christmas Carol' were reshot, many of which had to use Gillian Anderson's double. Also, after many unsuccessful attempts to cast an actress to play a teenage Scully for flashback sequences, series producer Bob Goodwin eventually convinced Gillian Anderson to get her own younger sister, Zoë Anderson, to play the part. These flashback sequences were part of an earlier attempt by the writing trio to make a Christmas adaptation of *Scrooge* (1951, starring Alastair Sim), a prominent British adaptation of Charles Dickens's classic *A Christmas Carol* (1843). This story lent *The X-Files* episode its title, and the Sim family their name, whilst sending three 'ghosts' to Scully in the form of three flashbacks. Though there may have been many difficulties in filming the episode, the final version presents an interesting (if fairly unconventional) Christmas television episode for analysis.

Less than two weeks after that episode's airing, *Millennium* aired its first Christmas episode, 'Midnight of the Century' (S2: E10) on 19 December 1997. This episode takes place on Christmas Eve 1997, with short flashbacks to Christmas 1946. The episode is centred on the relationships between both Frank Black (Lance Henriksen) and his daughter Jordan (Brittany Tiplady), and Frank Black and his father Henry (Darren McGavin). Frank and Jordan both experience visions of angels during this episode, similar to the visions had by Frank's mother Linda (Cheryl McNamara), referenced in the flashbacks to 1946. Through these angelic visions, Frank is able to strengthen his relationships with both his father and his daughter prior to Midnight Mass on Christmas Day.

Episode writers Erin Maher and Kay Reindl originally also wanted to write a version of Dickens's *A Christmas Carol*. They wanted to make it scarier, so their original adaptation called for 'the three ghosts [to be] serial killers of the past, present, and future' (Vitaris 1998: 20). The flashbacks in the proposed episode were similar to the flashback scenes from that season's Halloween episode, 'The Curse of Frank Black' (S2: E06). A rewrite changed the focus of the Christmas episode to Frank's family. There was an early futile attempt at casting Johnny Cash as Henry Black, but Darren McGavin eventually was cast in the role, well known for both his roles as Mr Parker in *A Christmas Story* (1983) and as the lead from the television series *Kolchak: The Night Stalker* (1974–5). Chris Carter has credited *Kolchak: The Night Stalker* as one of his influences in creating *The X-Files* (and *The X-Files* writer/producer Frank Spotnitz even attempted an unsuccessful reboot of the series in 2005). After successfully producing two Christmas episodes in 1997, both *The X-Files* and *Millennium* would film two new festive episodes the following year.

Chris Carter wrote and directed the sixth season episode of *The X-Files*, 'How the Ghosts Stole Christmas' (S6: E06), which aired on 13 December

1998. The episode takes place on Christmas Eve and features Mulder and Scully touring a sinister mansion haunted by the ghosts of a couple, Maurice (Ed Asner) and Lyda (Lily Tomlin). In response to Fox's request for a less-expensive episode of the series, this episode used only the single set of the haunted house and the four aforementioned characters. The episode did, however, feature many unique special effects for the series. The most memorable are the see-through bullet holes in the head and abdomen of the two ghosts, designed in part by special effects editor Bill Millar using orange fluorescent cloths and ultraviolet light. In addition, special set constructs, precise camerawork and green screens allowed for the endless hauntings in the one room of the mansion. The episode also used life casts of Mulder and Scully, which were scaled down and carved into mummified corpses of the two characters, which would be entombed underneath the floorboards. A closing sequence also features Mulder watching Alastair Sim in *Scrooge* on television, before sharing a light-hearted and sentimental closing scene with Scully.

The last of the four Christmas episodes, *Millennium*'s 'Omertà' (S3: E09), aired less than a week after 'How the Ghosts Stole Christmas', on 18 December 1998. Penned by Michael Perry, this episode features Frank Black taking his daughter on a Christmas getaway to Vermont during the days leading up to Christmas 1998. Frank and the local police encounter a formerly deceased mafia hitman, who was brought back to life through the healing powers of two women who live in the woods. After the hitman, Eddie 'Scarpino' Giannini (Jon Polito) is discovered, he aims to protect the two women from the mob, with the help of Frank and Agent Hollis (Klea Scott). Perry's original script featured creatures instead of the two women living in the woods, but the 'spiritual, ethereal quality' of the episode was influenced by writer/producer Chip Johannessen (Perry in 'Endgame: The Making of Millennium Season 3'). Johannessen is also partly responsible for the casting of Jon Polito, who makes a memorable guest appearance.

Additionally, all four of these Christmas episodes incorporate elements of humour into an already complex generic mix. But *The X-Files* and *Millennium* productions were not unfamiliar with injecting comedy into the narrative, such as with *Millennium*'s episode 'Jose Chung's Doomsday Defense' (S2: E09), a quasi-sequel to *The X-Files*' 'Jose Chung's From Outer Space' (S3: E20). The episodes with Jose Chung (Charles Nelson Reilly) were written by Darin Morgan, who also wrote quintessential darkly comedic *X-Files* episode, 'Clyde Bruckman's Final Repose' (S3: E04), for which Morgan and actor Peter Boyle each won an Emmy. So it is clear that both *The X-Files* and *Millennium* are proficient in the amalgamation of genres and genre signifiers, as clearly evidenced in all four Christmas episodes. Each of these is unique in their depiction of the Christmas season and the message that each episode sends to the viewer at this specific time of year. Examining the symbols, tropes and elements of each of these episodes will illuminate how they effectively combine the genres of science fiction, horror and Christmas on television in their own unique ways.

The sounds of Christmas

Music plays an important role in *The X-Files* and *Millennium*. The music in these four Christmas episodes merits examination due to its part in establishing the overall theme and mood of each episode, which is not necessarily the usual atmosphere for either show. Mark Snow scored for all these episodes, as well as the main themes for both series. 'Omertà' writer Michael Perry, in discussing the music of his episode, noted that 'when you're making a *Millennium* episode, the very last thing you do is go over to Mark Snow's house, [where] you go through the episode and he plays you the musical cues' (Perry in 'Endgame: The Making of Millennium Season 3'). Snow's music connects these Christmas episodes in distinct and unique ways.

According to Snow, 'Omertà' is a 'different kind of [*Millennium*] episode. There was a sweetness to it, but couched in the *Millennium* subplot' (Snow in 'Endgame: The Making of Millennium Season 3'). Feeling that the sweetness of this particular episode (which displayed the relationships between Frank, his daughter and the deceased Catherine, along with a parallel display of Scarpino's affection towards the two mystical women) needed to be over-exaggerated, he used the sounds of solo sopranos singing high notes. These angelic sounds from their arias play as a leitmotif over shots including the two healers, Lhasa and Rose. Perry credited Snow's score for the elevation of the entire episode with regards to theme and composition. Though the mobsters in the episode sing 'Silver Bells' multiple times, that song's accompanying music is never played, leaving Snow's operatic score uninterrupted. The music highlights the virtuous innocence of Lhasa and Rose and their impact on the people they come into contact with and heal.

Snow's score for 'How the Ghosts Stole Christmas' is similarly distinctive and, even, downright bizarre in terms of Christmas television. The score works well because, much like the episode itself, it plays as a Halloween 'haunted house' episode. Darkly creepy organs and haunting harpsichords do not exactly scream Christmas yet, for nearly the entire episode, the viewer hears an exceedingly eerie collection of music. Since this episode, however, is a Christmas story with a thematic message for the viewer, Snow successfully transitions his music to a completely different type of score within the final few minutes of the episode, using a haunted record player to bridge the two components of his score. The haunting pangs of the organ and harpsichord play until the needle drops, when Bing Crosby's 'Have Yourself a Merry Little Christmas' takes over. Crosby's somewhat gloomy drawl marries the cheerful Christmas song with the dreary music that the audience has heard for the majority of the episode thus far. As soon as the song comes to a close, Mulder and Scully escape the house, and an entirely new and upbeat score takes over. This delivers an optimistic ending to an otherwise cynical episode, which touches upon the overall Christmas message of family, closeness and love that the ghosts are somewhat indirectly relaying to the viewer.

Like his score for 'How the Ghosts Stole Christmas', Snow's music for 'Christmas Carol' was similarly eerie but, contrarily, begins with more cheerful, happy music. Playing when Scully is celebrating a Christmas visit with her family, these lighter musical motifs repeat during happy, family Christmas moments and flashbacks throughout the episode. But, aside from these moments, Snow's music devolves into another dreary, sorrowful score that accentuates Scully's disheartened mood throughout the episode. This type of score is extended into the follow-up episode, 'Emily', and reuses that music for melancholic scenes in *Millennium*'s 'Midnight of the Century'. Both 'Emily' and 'Midnight of the Century' aired only five days apart, yet Snow slightly altered and repurposed the music from 'Emily' for his score of *Millennium*'s Christmas story. The music was arranged differently, so that the sorrowful undertones of the music were upended by a new piece of music, which used strings and a chorus to evoke a very different tone. The new direction the music takes in this episode is exceedingly angelic in sound and quality, which adds to the angelic theme of 'Midnight of the Century'. During scenes involving Linda Black and her angel drawings, Tchaikovsky's 'Arabian Dance' segment from 'The Nutcracker Suite' is used as a leitmotif. The musical score of each episode, with the addition of new instruments and different orchestration, enhances the other motifs displayed throughout each of these four episodes by marrying the extradiegetic music with the thematic imagery and narrative tone contained within each of these Christmas stories.

Christmas time

Time and temporality are broad thematic ideas underpinning all four Christmas episodes, but the strongest presence of the notion can be found in *Millennium*'s 'Midnight of the Century'. The title of the episode alone suggests multiple literal and metaphoric delineations of time. The series itself continually focuses on the end of the twentieth century, and this specific episode places importance on 12:00 midnight in the form of the Midnight Mass, in which context the climax of the episode takes place. It has multiple metaphorical interpretations – it is a harkening to the angelic revelations that the members of the Black family perceive, and in the overarching myth-arc of the series, it undoubtedly refers to the onset of the apocalypse, drawing imagery from the Doomsday Clock, ticking ever closer towards midnight. From the very opening of the episode, the viewer can hear the sound of a ticking clock, seconds before any image appears on the screen. The first image that appears is the large swinging pendulum of a grandfather clock. The initial supernatural element of this episode occurs when Frank receives (in the present day, Christmas Eve 1997) a letter that he and his mother sealed in an envelope on Christmas Eve 1946. As that letter arrives through his mail slot, all of the clocks in his house begin to clang and chime. We are shown images of a digital alarm clock and an analogue mantel clock, though we can hear the sounds of several more clocks and bells coming from elsewhere in the house.

Early in the episode, Frank attends a Christmas party at Peter's house, where Peter (Terry O'Quinn) delivers a soliloquy on the subject of time. He tells Frank and Lara (Kristen Cloke) that 'something about this time of year always makes me consider time – wouldn't it be wonderful if in life you could pick the speed at which you experience time ... I'd like to know how much time I have left', before raising a glass to the midnight of the century. And it becomes clear throughout the rest of the episode that the characters who experience angelic visions can all see events displaced from linear time. Jordan can see and interact with her grandmother, who predeceased her by over fifty years. Linda not only saw a vision of her brother dying at the Normandy landings on the night before D-Day, but she also had a vision of her own death before she died. Frank also has a vision of an angel, who urges him to unwittingly visit his father. At the very end of the episode, Frank realizes that his father is dying, and questions why it took so long for the two of them to reunite. All the references to time and temporality in this episode refer to the amount of time we each have with our loved ones, and that turns out to be a recurring premise in all four of these Christmas episodes.

An angel of the Lord appeared to them

Religion is an ever-present thematic component of the *Millennium* mythos, particularly so in the Christmas episodes. Depictions of angels appear throughout the entirety of 'Midnight of the Century'. In addition to their traditional placement atop Christmas trees, as Advent wreath centrepieces in churches and window displays, angels also appear as visions to four of the characters in the episode, one of whom appears on screen to Frank in a church courtyard. He tells Frank that 'fetches' (souls of those fated to die in the coming year) walk through churchyards on Christmas Eve. He further explains that these fetches will march into church at midnight, and that those who can see angels will also be able to see the fetches, before declaring that 'it is, after all, the midnight of the century'. The angel then disappears before a large statue of the Virgin Mary.

This meeting between Frank and the angel was foreshadowed prior to this scene, in part by the time that flashed on the alarm clock at the start of the episode, 9:21. In the Bible, the archangel Gabriel appears to the prophet Daniel in order to explain the visions that Daniel is having, similar to the appearance of this angel before Frank Black. Daniel 9:21 states 'while I was still in prayer, Gabriel, the man I had seen in the earlier vision, came to me', which in the case of 'Midnight of the Century' is an allusion to the angel's appearance before Frank. In the Book of Daniel, Gabriel then goes on to prophesize the crucifixion of Christ, before foretelling the seven-year period of tribulation before the end of times. The angels in *Millennium* bring analogous types of messages to the characters who can see them, able to warn of their own impending death, or that of a loved one. And, similar to Daniel's final message from Gabriel, the angel also alludes to the coming millennium, which is a suggestion of the apocalypse within the series' mythos.

While religious elements do not appear in nearly as many episodes of *The X-Files* as *Millennium*, the episode 'Christmas Carol' is a notable exception. From the very first moment of this episode, we can see that there will be religious undertones throughout – the first frame of the episode shows a Nativity scene at the Scully residence. There is an empty manger yet, within seconds, Scully's very pregnant sister-in-law places the figure of the Baby Jesus in the manger. That Nativity scene can also be seen in the two Christmastime flashback sequences, as well as a further, full-screen display of the Nativity just prior to Scully's decision to contact an adoption agent and attempt to adopt Emily. Mulder can also be seen interacting with the same Nativity in the following episode, 'Emily'. At the conclusion of that episode, the viewer is shown a close-up of a stained-glass window depicting the Virgin Mary swaddling the Baby Jesus. These images throughout are clearly displayed as an allusion to the Virgin Birth, as the episode itself features some seemingly miraculous births, particularly that of Emily.

A family Christmas

Christmas is traditionally a time of family and togetherness, and this notion is prevalent throughout each of these four Christmas episodes. In 'Midnight of the Century', the viewer gets an insight into Frank Black's family. The flashback scenes depict a young Frank and his mother Linda. Linda appears to Jordan off-screen in order to deliver her a message in the form of an illustration of an angel (the same angel she drew with Frank fifty-one years prior). In keeping with the religious overtones of this episode, this act can be seen as *Millennium*'s version of a Marian apparition. Instead of the Virgin Mary appearing, the deceased mother of Frank Black appears before Jordan, which sets off a chain of events that allows Frank to reconnect with his father, before it is too late. Peter's soliloquy on time alludes to the notion that one may not have enough time with family throughout their life.

Frank's angel tells Frank not to 'put off until tomorrow what should be done today'. When he discusses the impending appearance of the fetches, he tells Frank that 'there's no telling whose face you might see'. As the church bells chime midnight, Frank and Jordan see Henry marching towards the church doors. While temporality and religion play a major role in this episode, 'Midnight of the Century' is a Christmas episode about family, and the time people tend to share with family members.

Millennium's 'Omertà' is also primarily about family and keeping close the ones we love. From the first instance of Jordan's realization of the miraculous healing/resurrection of Eddie, she attempts to convince Lhasa and Rose to bring her mother back to life. Eddie outwardly 'adopts' Lhasa and Rose into his own family, after he is healed. Eddie is resurrected, both literally in the sense that Lhasa and Rose heal his wounds and bring him back to life, and metaphorically in the sense that he now spends his time protecting the two women, as opposed to his previous life of crime. After Frank and Emma help Eddie, Lhasa and Rose flee, Jordan is left with the realization that the women will never have the opportunity to heal her mother. Frank attempts to comfort Jordan about their mutual desire to be with Catherine at Christmastime, and she responds by saying 'we can think about her and it's kind of like she is'. The viewer is repeatedly shown a Currier and Ives-esque (popular printers in the United States during the mid- to late nineteenth century) image of a cabin in snowy woods, which turns out to be where Eddie, Lhasa and Rose escape so they could spend their Christmas together. The reason this image appears throughout 'Omertà' is to remind the viewer that the quintessential Christmastime is being around family, near or far, living or dead.

The X-Files episode 'How the Ghosts Stole Christmas' also deals with the idea of Christmas being a holiday for family and togetherness. Throughout Scully and Mulder's interactions with both Maurice and Lyda, they are both repeatedly told that they are lonely. This idea of loneliness is ultimately how the ghosts are able to convince Mulder and Scully that each one shoot the other. Once they figure out the deception, Mulder and Scully run out of the house, leaving the ghosts alone for the few remaining moments of Christmas Eve. Through the final interaction between Maurice and Lyda before their disappearance, the viewer is shown the power of togetherness, as the ghosts hold hands before a Christmas hearth. The episode ends with Scully joining Mulder, emphasizing the importance of being together with friends and family around Christmastime.

The genre of Christmas

The X-Files' 'Christmas Carol' is essentially an episode that examines the notion of family (particularly motherhood and new children in the family), and does so through a Christmas story, while remaining in the show's typical science fiction genre. This episode is very much a part of the overall series myth-arc, and therefore it is essential that it is truly a science fiction story. Together with its second part, this episode tells the story of Scully coming to terms with the fact that she can no longer have children, as well as finding out that she somehow has a young child, unbeknownst to her. We find out in the second part of the episode that Emily is an alien-human hybrid, born of Scully's ovum, who came to term courtesy of colonist alien bounty hunters and their medical experiments regarding elderly women giving birth. But as tried and true science fiction as the second half of the episode is, 'Christmas Carol' truly combines science fiction elements with Christmas-themed genre signifiers throughout. The notion of a somewhat miraculous birth is present throughout the entire episode. Scully's return home to visit her family also brings a reunion between her and her sister from the great beyond, yet another example of the union of the science fiction and Christmas genres here. This effectively advances Scully's story arc, but it does so in a unique way, through the notion of family togetherness at Christmas.

Millennium's 'Midnight of the Century' is an episode that examines the idea of spending precious time with loved ones. This episode, too, delivers its message through a Christmas story, while maintaining its archetypal science fiction (with some elements of horror) genre. Like 'Christmas Carol', this episode is central to *Millennium*'s mythos, making it vital to remain closely tied to its distinctive genre. And with apparitions of angels, angelic visions and communion with the dead, this episode certainly fits into the science fiction and horror genres. But 'Midnight of the Century' is an episode that truly endeavours to fuse Christmas genre signifiers with its established genre throughout the episode. The episode's message primarily concerns finite life and how we use the time we spend with our family. This concept can be seen reflected in the Christmas presents that are given out throughout the episode. Jordan receives a Giga Pet, a digital toy pet from Catherine's mother, and the gifting itself (Catherine says) is 'the circle of life'. Jordan later receives an angel figurine from Henry (though it can be seen as coming from Linda, as well). This episode makes a point of naming the three store clerks at a local department store selling Christmas presents Balthazar, Caspar and Melchior, the biblical names of the three wise men, further emphasizing the significance of gift-giving throughout the episode. An allusion to the genre mixing of this episode can be seen in Roedecker's (Allan Zinyk) gifts to Frank. Brian gifts Frank two VHS tapes of Christmas horror movies – *Black Christmas* (1974) and *Silent Night, Deadly Night* (1984) – before Frank quips 'whatever happened to *Miracle on 34th Street*?' This addition to the episode adds another element to the combination of genres, in effect giving a nod to the viewer who is currently watching a horror-infused story. The episode drives the story arcs of Frank, Jordan and Lara forward, in relation to the overall story arc of the entire series. It does so successfully, due to the emotional impact of the Christmas story that was introduced to the viewer throughout this episode.

The X-Files' 'How the Ghosts Stole Christmas' is a tale about the dread of loneliness and the closeness of family and friends. This episode truly exists within the series' distinctive horror genre, though the Christmas genre shines through for the episode's climax. It utilizes many of the tropes associated with a typical haunted house horror story, but does so both in the realm of *The X-Files* and on the occasion of Christmas. The opening shot is an unremarkable, eerie, condemned mansion, with a 'No Trespassing' sign posted outside. Mulder and Scully share their distinctive banter as he tries to convince her to investigate the ghost story within the house, and she tries to convince him that ghosts are figments of the imagination. Once inside the manor, the horror elements of this episode are quickly revealed to the viewer – doors swing open and closed by themselves, deafening grandfather clocks chime unexpectedly, footsteps are heard from above, cold winds run through the house, and Mulder and Scully's own decaying bodies are under the floorboards, to name but a few. There is little mention of Christmas beyond the first few moments of the film until nearly halfway through the episode, when slowly, the light-heartedness of an otherwise shocking story begins to shine through and eventually take over, effectively turning 'How the Ghosts Stole Christmas' into a Christmas episode. The episode begins to show its true colours when a comedic moment occurs between Mulder and Maurice, as Maurice tries to psychoanalyse Mulder. The script even seems to nod to the viewer as Maurice proceeds to spew nonsensical critical drivel at Mulder – much akin to the type of psychoanalysis that non-believers would spew at any viewer. Specializing in manias related to the paranormal, Maurice tells Mulder that he, and everyone who believes in what he does, chases 'paramasturbatory illusions that you believe will give your life meaning and significance and which your pathetic social maladjustment makes impossible for you to find elsewhere'. And it is within this moment of light-heartedness that Maurice first brings up the idea of loneliness, which is the driving force behind the Christmas genre signifiers that only begin to appear close to the episode's climax. Realizing that the 'pop psychology approach' only annoys them instead of driving them insane, the ghosts attempt to trick Mulder and Scully into killing each other, using this idea of loneliness. Once Mulder and Scully realize that they are not alone, they are able to escape the mansion and share a happy Christmas evening with each other.

Millennium's 'Omertà' is a remarkable entry into the annals of Christmas television in terms of successfully combining the genres of horror, science fiction, gangster drama and Christmas all in one episode. This combination of genres can be figuratively seen in the 'character' of 'Littlefoot' (depicted as somewhat like Bigfoot), a sort of mythological town mascot in the episode. Eddie is the character mistaken for the creature, whose gangster nickname was 'Scarpino' (Italian for little shoes) due to his small feet. The episode title itself, 'Omertà', is an Italian word (popularized by Mario Puzo) referring to the Mafia code of silence, which Eddie breaks in order to help Lhasa and Rose in the episode. The crime family is referred to as the 'Santo organization' but, similar to Scarpino, this name also has a double meaning within the episode. 'Santo' literally means 'blessed' as an adjective and 'Saint' as a noun. Though obviously not referring to the organization's criminal activities, this name can allude to the conversion of Eddie from a criminal into a selfless protector of his new 'family', Lhasa and Rose, who themselves selflessly heal others.

Early in 'Omertà', the viewer is shown two particularly gruesome deaths in the woods: Eddie is murdered by being repeatedly shot, and a hunter is attacked and torn limb from limb by a wolf. Both these characters are then miraculously healed and resurrected by two women who live in those woods. Although resurrection and redemption may seem closer thematically to Easter rather than Christmas, the episode evolves into the closeness of the characters and the relationships between loved ones, aligning it with the Christmas genre. The structure of the episode navigates all three genres (horror, science fiction and Christmas), whilst sprinkling gangster genre tropes throughout. 'Omertà' clearly borrows some comedic elements of the gangster genre, along with the more obvious dramatic ones. During the final moments of the episode, the viewer is shown Eddie, Rose and Lhasa in their cabin celebrating Christmas together. Since the Christmas genre successfully supplants the other genres of this episode, Eddie verbally breaks the fourth wall in order to wish the viewer a 'Merry Christmas'.

Conclusion

Through in-depth examination of all of the elements of these Christmas episodes of *The X-Files* and *Millennium*, we can see how each introduces Christmas genre signifiers. This inclusion successfully combines the genres of Christmas television, science fiction and horror, the competing aesthetics of which adds an extra layer of complexity. In 'Midnight of the Century', the viewer sees Linda's room filled with dozens of her sketches of the angel who appeared to her in a vision. As these angelic depictions are directly tied into the somewhat supernatural storyline, they serve as just one example of the visual embodiment of the combination of genres. The viewer is shown a myriad of imagery throughout these episodes, some traditionally associated with Christmas, others with science fiction, horror or gangster genres, yet each episode makes sure to depict a combination of these images to visually illustrate this amalgamation. However, each of these episodes takes careful steps to ensure that the Christmas genre shines brighter than any other, effectively allowing the Christmas genre to supersede the science fiction and horror (and gangster) genres. This complexity is what makes these four episodes distinct from other *Millennium* and *X-Files* episodes, as well as other series, unparalleled in *The X-Files* and *Millennium* canons.

References

Black Christmas (1974), [Film] Dir. Bob Clark, Canada: Warner Bros.
A Christmas Story (1983), [Film] Dir. Bob Clark, USA: MGM.
Dixon, B. A. (1998), 'Interview with Mark Snow', *The Millennial Comet*, 2 (5): 3, 18 December.
'Endgame: The Making of Millennium Season 3' (2008), *Millennium: The Complete Collection*, DVD, 20th Century Fox Home Entertainment, 2008.
'José Chung's Doomsday Defense' (1997), *Millennium* [TV Programme] Season 2, Episode 9, 1997.
Kolchak: The Night Stalker (1974–5), [TV Programme].
Meisler, A. (2000), *The End and the Beginning: The Official Guide to The X-Files Vol. 5*, London: HarperCollins.
'Midnight of the Century' (1997), *Millennium* [TV Programme] Season 2, Episode 10.
Miracle on 34th Street (1947), [Film] Dir. George Seaton, USA: 20th Century Fox.
'Omertà' (1998), *Millennium* [TV Programme] Season 3, Episode 9.
Playing God (1997), [Film] Dir. Andy Wilson, USA: Touchstone Pictures.
Scrooge (1951), [Film] Dir. Brian Desmond Hurst, UK: Renown Pictures.
Silent Night, Deadly Night (1984), [Film] Dir. Charles E. Sellier, Jr., USA: Slayride Productions Inc.
'The Truth about Season 5' (2006), *The X-Files: Season 5*, DVD, 20th Century Fox Home Entertainment.
'The Truth about Season 6' (2009), *The X-Files: Season 6*, DVD, 20th Century Fox Home Entertainment.
Vitaris, P. (1998), 'Millennium', *Cinefantastique*, 30 (7–8), October: 18–22.
The X-Files: Fight the Future (1998), [Film] Dir. Rob Bowman, USA: 20th Century Fox.

12

'The Truth is ...' inside the panels!: Comic adaptations of *The X-Files*

Iris Haist

Most of the academic articles written about *The X-Files* focus on the television series that was aired in the United States on the Fox network between 1993 and 2002, and the revival series between 2016 and 2018. These articles cover the specific topics of the television series and disregard the content of the subsequent *The X-Files* comic book stories published by Topps Comics, by the DC imprint WildStorm and most recently by Idea and Design Works (IDW) Publishing, San Diego. However, these comics, like the television series, became very popular in many countries around the world and were translated into many different languages.

This chapter traces the development of the various *The X-Files* comic adaptations and highlights their main thematic points through targeted comparisons with other media. One of the comics' initial purposes was to fill certain narrative gaps in the television show but, over the years, the comics evolved from adaptations of the television episodes, with special twists and 'monster-of-the-week' storylines, to a more complex story arc. This chapter suggests that comics – as a medium – offer the freedom to show aspects that, due to network restrictions, were not present in the television series. Another point addressed herein is the relationship of these comics to canonicity; that is, they established the limits of canon. They determined, from their inception, what did and did not count in a fictional universe, a standard that would change over time.

This essay gives an overview of the principal comic adaptations, from the very first issue to the latest publications. Some of the adaptations will be examined to offer a better understanding of how the comics were constructed, and what additional value they had for the comic market, for readers and for the writers and artists of this kind of graphic literature – always with an eye on the connections and differences between the media used: television, films and comics.

Development of the comic adaptations

After the great acclaim with which the television series was received, several publishing companies, including DC Comics and Marvel Comics, tried to acquire the licence for producing comics based on *The X-Files* (for the comics history of *The X-Files* until 1998 see Osteried 1998: 10–13). In the end, Topps was selected by Chris Carter and his company. The first issues were written in January 1995 by a former series' fan and author Stefan Petrucha, and illustrated by the young artist Charles Adlard. At that time, a year and a half after it was first broadcast, the *The X-Files* television series was in the middle of its second season. The stories featured in the comic were often complex and retained the original 'mysterious' atmosphere of the television series, as well as drawing on the series' distinct use of two different types of episode: 'monster-of-the-week' episodes and 'cliff-hanger' double episodes (Feise 2005: 88). The later episodes are rather 'serial' in both media, which means that an overarching plot exists, and yet there are always shorter, complete story arcs within one or a few episodes – which makes the structure an 'accumulative narration' (Reeves, Rodgers and Epstein 1996: 22–36).

But the comic artwork was surprisingly original and did not fit in with the familiar 'superhero-style' of the big comic publishing companies. Before working on *The X-Files*, Adlard had only been involved once in a large project: the comic series *Mars Attacks* (Brown and Giffen 1994). His panels were colourful, but not as simple and pristine as those used by DC and Marvel. He had his own original style, for which he was initially criticized by *The X-Files* fans, but with time came to be appreciated. The comics were not just products of another aesthetic paradigm, but rather they became a part of *The X-Files*' merchandising machinery along with the novels, games and trading cards. The fans, also known as 'X-Philes', increasingly asked for more merchandising in different forms and media. So, Topps published the stories repeatedly, in albums, comic collections and the *Comic Digest*. The *Comic Digest* consisted of three issues ('Big Foot, Warm Heart', 'Dead to the World' and 'Scape Goats') published at five-month intervals, beginning at the end of 1995, and also appeared in *The X-Files Magazine* – the latter featuring additional material such as a poster in the middle of the magazine, interviews with the actors, fan-letters, an *X-Files* dictionary and news about the TV series (Petrucha 1995–6). There was even a five-page comic short story in the high-circulation *TV Guide* of 15 July 1995. This helped significantly to increase the print run and the success of the comic adaptations. But there was also a demand for comic adaptations that were true to the original television episodes and what the market wants, the market gets (Middaugh 1997: 23).

The very first comic of *The X-Files* franchise published in January 1996 by Topps Comics, rather a strict adaptation of the television episodes, was a comic version of the pilot episode (S1: E01) aired on 10 September 1993 on Fox TV. *The X-Files: Season One* #0, like the following issues, was adapted and scripted by Roy Thomas and (most of them) drawn by the artist John van Fleet. The episodes, which were reproduced as comic versions, were selected from the first season of the television series (S1: E01–4, 6, 8–9, 12–13). This comic series was discontinued after only seven issues, including the pilot episode.

The X-Files: Hero Illustrated Special, written by Stefan Petrucha and drawn by Charles Adlard, was published in 1995. It was followed in 1997 by the graphic novel *Afterflight*, also written by Petrucha, with artwork by skilled artist and *X-Files* fan Jill Thompson with Alexander Saviuk (Petrucha, Thompson and Saviuk 1997), and by the four-issue mini-series *Ground Zero* (Anderson, Purcell and Mahlstedt 1997–8), written by Kevin J. Anderson and illustrated by Gordon Purcell and Larry Mahlstedt – each one accompanying the ongoing television series, filling some missing links or developing conspiracies. While *Afterflight* is a story inspired by the earliest recorded UFO sightings in the United States, *Ground Zero* switches between mysterious events in the present and those in the future, which are – of course – linked to each other. Almost all these storylines were translated into different languages and sold worldwide (the German versions, for example, were edited by Carlson and Ehapa).

The next comic outings for *The X-Files* were not produced until DC imprint WildStorm published a one-shot *The X-Files Special* (2008), timed to coincide with the release of the second movie, *The X-Files: I Want to Believe* (co-authored and co-produced by Frank Spotnitz, with art by Brian Denham). In total, WildStorm published only seven issues before passing the rights on to the San Diego-based publishing house, IDW Comics. From 2014 onwards, this publisher produced a completely new, innovative long-running comic series that picked up where the television series had left off in 2002 (after season nine). The storyline begins after the events of the 2008 film *The X-Files: I Want to Believe*, with two new comic runs entitled *Season Ten* and *Season Eleven*. This is comparable with the successful adaptation of the series *Buffy – The Vampire Slayer*, which continued as *Season Eight* (2007) in comic form after the final television series (season seven) had ended (Haist 2021: 88–91). The fans didn't want to see *Buffy* end, so the creators produced a comic which developed stories previously unseen, a comic book series which was itself extended due to its popularity. In 2016, Fox produced another two television seasons of *The X-Files* mostly ignoring the events of the graphic versions. To complete this ongoing series, IDW released several mini- or midi-series, in which *The X-Files* teamed up with other pop-culture franchises, such as the crossover graphic novel *30 Days of Night/The X-Files* (2010) and others (discussed later in this chapter). This initiative also led to a new series accompanying the last two television seasons of *The X-Files*, aired on Fox between 2016 and 2018 with the older, more sexualized versions of the two beloved main characters.

The beginning, but not the start: The pilot episode

The very beginning of the *The X-Files*' storyline was not the starting point of the comic adaptations. The idea for a new, second type of comic series which features stories from the television episodes without great narrative changes in a graphic based, sequential medium came directly from its fanbase. *The X-Files: Season One* #0, the comic version of the TV pilot from 1993 was not published until 1996, over a year after the first comic adaptation of *The X-Files* by Topps Comics. As is typical of a zero numbered comic, the narrative re-establishes and reintroduces the main characters, the topographic requirements, the aesthetic parameters and the most important topics of the storyline. The publishers undoubtedly waited for the comics to become a financial success before deciding to bring out a zero number – which could be considered an equivalent to the 'origin story' in the superhero genre. It was a graphic novelization of the very first episode: the pilot of the television series. It retells the story by deconstructing on-screen sequences to reconstruct a graphic version composed of various images in serially arranged panels of the same content – thereby making it a re-experience for the readers who had already watched the television series. This transformation makes this special form of comic adaptation a transmedia format in itself.

The style of John Van Fleet's artwork is dynamic and edgy. He uses mostly blacks and browns, with warm but clear colours for emphasis. The use of *chiaroscuro* creates a spooky atmosphere which makes the paranormal phenomena more plausible – staying faithful to the television series and could be compared to the printing technique of woodcuts of the early twentieth century.

The comic adaptation adheres very closely to the template of the television series. Moreover, the individual panels are graphic implementations of selected stills from the original series which can be accurately identified by comparing the two media. Every narrative hint, every allusion and every symbolic image is also shown in the panels of the comics. Short, less significant scenes are not shown in the comic, such as one scene in S1: E01 where Mulder visits Scully at night to ask if she has made progress. However, movement sequences such as the rumbling of a recovered coffin are shortened by only showing the starting point and the ending point – in this particular example, the tearing of a rope and the coffin sliding to a stop (Thomas 1996: 5). All other images of movement or action are the spaces between the panels, which Scott McCloud refers to as 'gutters', and must be supplemented by the reader's imagination (McCloud 1996). With only forty-eight pages per issue of the *The X-Files: Season One* comics, the author and artist have to present the entire story of a (roughly) 48-minute television episode in one issue: one page per minute.

Van Fleet does not just replicate shots from episodes; he simplifies the backgrounds by omitting parked cars or landscapes, extras or furnishings that are irrelevant to the plot to bring the main action more into focus. In addition, Van Fleet usually frames the image sections a little differently: he relies much more on close-ups of people (face, hands, feet) and objects than television does. Sometimes he puts a little bit of a structure in black fringes of night scenes to make the images more artistic. He also changes the images slightly when it comes to clearly identifying certain characters. For example, the 'Cigarette Smoking Man' is invariably shown smoking a cigarette – a highly decorative effect – even though in the television series he is not seen holding one within these exact scenes. On the last two pages of the pilot episode of the comic is for example a particularly curious scene: the Cigarette Smoking Man goes to a secret archive and somehow manages to hold a cigarette while simultaneously holding a box with both hands (Thomas 1996: 47–8). But the smoke enriches the composition and helps to create a more mysterious and dramatic atmosphere – and even reproduces the iconic quality of this special character from the TV series.

Season Ten and *Season Eleven* – TV series versus comic

The San Diego-based publishing house IDW released a two-season reboot called *Season Ten* (a twenty-five-issue comic book series, 2013–15) and *Season Eleven* (an eight-issue comic book series, 2015–16). These came after the events of the 2008 movie *The X-Files: I Want to Believe* and led to the conception of the most recent seasons, aired between 2016 and 2018. The fact that the television creators did not follow most of the events of these two comic seasons resulted in those storylines sometimes being labelled as 'non-canon' in the fan-pages of *The X-Files* (reddit.com, n.d.). Nonetheless, since Chris Carter was involved in the making of the comic series, they were still considered an essential part of the 'Spookyverse' and Carter himself accepted them as part of it in 2013. He explains the differences between the events of the comic version and the television series of season ten and season eleven as follows: 'It's a comic book series, so it's got its own comic book life, and it has its own mythology' (Carter 2013). Therefore, the *Season Ten* and *Season Eleven* comics sit on the borderlines of what counts as *The X-Files* canon.

The *Season Ten* comic series begins with dark-coloured, action-packed sequences of close-ups and cut-outs of dark (unknown but clearly unfriendly) figures, the environment in which they act and of Agent Dana Scully's face and body. Scully flees from mysterious and frightening characters in black capes, the so-called Acrolytes (a hybrid race linked to the persons who were present as Scully gave birth to her son, also in series eight and nine of the TV series). The atmosphere created on the first two pages of the first issue of this story run is close to that of the television series, and thus corresponds perfectly with what viewers were familiar with. The close relationship between the two main characters is even stronger in the two last seasons of the comic book series in comparison with the television series because, instead of being separated for the years in between the film's events and series ten and eleven, in the comic books Scully and Mulder have been living together as 'Mr and Mrs Blake' (Harris 2013). The idea that Scully and Mulder's son may be in danger and that the FBI agents try to find and protect him, however, is formulated in both the comics (S10: #1) and the television seasons ten and eleven (S10: E02 onward). While the television series develops an extreme end-time character, the comics continue to revolve around the lives and aspirations of the main characters, thereby remaining safer in narrative style which is accepted by the long-time fans of the series. Introducing new characters appears to be easier in TV series than in comic books, as Joss Whedon stated in an interview in 2007 about his *Buffy the Vampire Slayer* comic book series. However, he also states, 'Eventually, you have to let go and move on, and let the comic-book world be the comic-book world. I think after time, people will come to accept some of the characters, if we paint them vividly enough' (Lavery and Burkhead 2011: 144). This is arguably why *The X-Files Season Ten* and *Eleven* comics only present well-known, beloved characters, to the extent to which creators must resurrect several deceased persons.

The 'final evil' is perpetrated by the grown-up Gibson Praise, whom we know as a harmless but highly intelligent young boy chess prodigy played by Jeff Gulka (in various *X-Files* television episodes across seasons five, six, eight and nine), who grows up to clone every human being with the help of alien DNA and technology – an idea that was possibly related to the concept of the 'super-soldiers' in the television series (from S8: E20). To provide a degree of continuity in the comics, the most important supporting characters are, of course, the Lone Gunmen, Walter Skinner (who ultimately gets promoted to deputy director in the FBI), and the Cigarette Smoking Man. The latter is portrayed in the comic books as a mysterious but clear-thinking, quasi-evil protagonist, in contrast with the ugly, world-threatening, almost grotesque character shown in the television series. Minor roles are played by Special Agent Monica Reyes, Special Agent John Doggett and Alex Krycek. Another strategy for maintaining familiar narrative structures is Scully and Mulder initially working on closed X-files. This leads the two FBI agents in *Season Ten* comics #6–7 to the trail of the 'Flukemen' (from S2: E02) into the private world and memories of the Cigarette Smoking Man in the homage-comic episode 'More Musings of a Cigarette Smoking Man' (S10: #10, echoing S4: E07), and to Frank Black, a well-known former member of the 'Millennium Group' (S10: #17, after S7: E04). In the comic book's *Season Eleven* (#2–4), Mulder and Scully finally meet the incestuously degenerated 'Peacock Family' (from S4: E02) again.

The impending doomsday scenario of a worldwide epidemic caused by an alien virus was already exhausted in comic form in the crossover midi-series *The X-Files: Conspiracy* (Crilley, Burnham and Brisson 2014), published by IDW in 2014, and therefore does not appear again in these last two seasons and (spoiler alert), whilst in the television series Scully and Mulder manage to find their long-lost son (S11: E05), 'William' does not appear in the comic books after being a little baby.

Artification: JFK disclosure

One comic book sets itself apart from any of *The X-Files* comics due to its design and a semi-realistic drawing style: *The X-Files: JFK Disclosure*, published by IDW, originally as a two-issue mini-series (Tipton 2018). While the author, Denton J. Tipton, works on a well-known conspiracy theory, perhaps the most notorious of all time, artist Menton J. Matthews III (known as 'Menton3' and was the artist of the *Season Ten* comic episode 'More Musings of a Cigarette Smoking Man') creates on the cover of the comic book a completely new and fascinating world between comic art, painting, printing and graphic design. He uses not only traditional drawing, inking and colouring techniques, but also different artistic mediums such as oil, watercolours, silhouette printing and painting, collage-techniques, digitally altered photographs in postproduction and mixed media, which makes this comic book an unusual work of art. In one double-page spread, the artist creates painterly scene in a horizontal format to be read as if a pin-up poster, showing a woman identified as Jayne Mansfield (Tipton 2018: 12–13). Another page features a leaflet-like historic document for the background to create an authentication effect, inferring that this story is based upon the truth – a common technique to suggest credibility which was also an important element for the television series (Edwards 1997: 38). As in many issues such as 'Musings of a Cigarette Smoking Man', Menton3 shifts from colour to black and white, and back again to colour, always with a sharp *chiaroscuro* – setting the scenes in the present of 2017, or in the distant decades of the 1960s and 1970s.

This issue is packed with references to S4: E07 'Musings of a Cigarette Smoking Man', which also reveals some background information about various famous conspiracies. In places, the comic book reuses images from different iconic scenes from episodes of the television series thus becoming not only a work of art per se, but also takes on characteristic functions of a transmedia archive.

The comic story begins with the fictional character Jack Colquitt, who the Cigarette Smoking Man introduces in the television episode as the main character for his novel. In fact, however, the Cigarette Smoking Man talks about events that were part of Colquitt's life. The reader quickly learns that Colquitt is none other than the Cigarette Smoking Man himself, aka Mr Hunt – a name which at the end defines him as what he is: a hitman for the government and for other, even more powerful secret groups. The comic book ends with the Cigarette Smoking Man citing Colquitt's last sentence, which we saw his alter ego write on the last page of his book in the television episode: 'No matter who you are, I can take you out any time … but today's not the day' (Tipton 2018: 24).

The crashed flying saucer in the desert, on the other hand, is an image that was introduced in the first episode of the tenth season of the television series. The artist uses the technique of collage or montage, not only in terms of craftsmanship, but also in terms of content. But Menton3 invents some images, such as the scenes which take place in Las Vegas, which had never been used in a similar way in any of the television episodes (Tipton 2018, Parts 1 and 2).

Although the story may conclude with some new twists, it is not the most innovative storyline but the continuity, and the fact that most 'X-Philes' can easily recognize references to the television series (of which there are far more than those mentioned in this essay), gives way to completely innovative artwork. In this case, the comic adaptation is a chance to introduce *The X-Files* fans, comic book readers and television viewers to a new kind of modern art in the form of a word-image-story-space-collage by Menton3.

Honouring *The X-Files*

How do you measure the success of a person, a phenomenon or, in this case, a television series? One indicator is a reference by an episode of *The*

Simpsons as was the case in 1997 with *The X-Files*: *The Simpsons* S8: E10, which had the unambiguous title of 'The Springfield Files' (*The Simpsons, The Springfield Files* 1997). In it, Homer sights an alien – a topic that brings agents Scully and Mulder to the scene. The episode was aired on 2 January 1997, on Fox, the same channel that aired *The X-Files* which itself was then in its fifth season. This *Simpsons* episode uses some well-known *X-Files* clichés, such as the Cigarette Smoking Man, the 'I Want to Believe' UFO poster in Mulder's office, and the television series' opening sequence's iconic sentence 'The truth is out there.' Of course, the creators of *The Simpsons* make fun of the mystery series to a certain extent, but they also reveal a notable familiarity with the television series. The episode was produced by the former showrunners Al Jean and Mike Reiss, who won an Annie Award for this production (Ayers 2016).

Other examples evidencing *The X-Files*' popularity include the cameo appearance of David Duchovny in a 2010 *South Park* episode (S14: E01) where he learns 'the truth': that the sex addiction the citizens observe in the episode is caused by a 'Wizard Alien'(*South Park, Sexual Healing* 2010) and the emergence of 1997 computer game parody *The X-Fools: The Spoof Is Out There*, bursting with inside references, iconic images and famous Fox Mulder quotes (*The X-Fools* 1997).

Author Amy Chu, and artists Silvia Califano (pencils), Elena Casagrande (inks) and Monica Kubina (colours) were not satisfied with the gender roles of Scully and Mulder in the television series. In 2017, they went one step further in their parallel world comic narrative asking what if, instead of Mulder's sister Samantha being kidnapped by aliens, it was Fox Mulder? (Chu 2017). The answer provided by Chu, Califano and Casagrande is clear: Samantha would have become an FBI agent, searched for her brother and uncovered the government's secrets. The Samantha of their version is self-confident, fun-loving and rather extroverted with a certain coolness and very open about her nerdom, in contrast to the rather idiosyncratic Fox Mulder. While Mulder uses and trusts the three Lone Gunmen, he personally distances himself from them. Samantha, on the other hand, is directly involved with this group through her regular meetings with them to play *Dungeons and Dragons* (often shortened to 'D&D'). Playing this sort of typically nerdy game while also being one of the 'cool guys' is a familiar trope used to represent intelligent outsider characters in examples of indie cinema such as *Mallrats* (1995) and television series such as *Freaks and Geeks* (1999–2000), and *The Big Bang Theory* (2007–19), the latter still being aired when this comic version of a new *X-Files* world was published. Many of the readers of the comic version of *The X-Files* also play D&D, or similar games (*Magic, The Gathering, The Black Eye*), so this characterization of Samantha brings the readers closer to the comic books.

The basic format of *The X-Files* comic can be characterized as a crime-police genre with action elements, a medical thriller, a mystery series with polit-thriller characters, science fiction and horror: *The X-Files* comics are best described as being a highly hybrid genre (Feise 2005: 111). As a result, the concept can be easily integrated into other formats particularly suited to crossover episodes or issues. It was therefore not surprising when, after the crossover *30 Days of Night/The X-Files* (2010), the mini-series *The X-Files: Conspiracy* was published by IDW in 2014 (see, e.g. Handley 2014: 11–17). This newly introduced format is a series containing four crossover issues between *The X-Files* and a colourful mix of other world-famous licensed franchises: *Ghostbusters* (1984), *Teenage Mutant Ninja Turtles* (1984), *Transformers* (1984; film 2007), and *The Crow* (comic 1991/92; film 1994). The author of the overall arc of this series is Paul Crilley, known for his work *Infestation 2: Dungeons and Dragons* (2012). Asked why *The X-Files* was chosen for the main title, Crilley explained in an interview in 2014: 'The storytelling, the chemistry between the main characters, the balance of mythology and one-off episodes, the cinematography ... It all just came together to capture a perfect series that didn't tap into the zeitgeist – it created it' (Handley 2014: 13). The mixture of these pop culture icons from the 1980s and 1990s had to reach a grown-up readership who had been raised watching these television series and movies. A certain nostalgia helped the comic to achieve respectable sales figures, but there was also artistic innovation in the way every crossover was created and drawn as a separate work, whereby each of these comic issues became an individual piece of art.

What is the additional value of the comics?

Further examination of the comic adaptations of *The X-Files* is necessary to understand what the objective of the work is, what the comics hope to convey and what the additional value of these media transformations may be. The first, and perhaps most important, considerations when creating a new medium in the film and publishing business are of course always of a financial nature. The television series had such high ratings and such a loyal fanbase that the release of a comic adaptation had little risk and promised to be a great success. But for future readers, and for the authors and artists, other questions are worth taking into account: how the comics fit into the whole universe of *The X-Files*, what the best style to represent this show was without transforming it into a photo novel and what fresh content would fit in with the existing material to keep the stories interesting.

As discussed earlier, the first comics published by Topps were intended to fill narrative gaps in the television series. The myths of *The X-Files* included entire unknown, otherworldly civilizations and legends with Christian connotations. Since the largest target group were not the actual comic fans, but followers of the television series, it was only logical to introduce another comic series, which retold the stories of the television episodes without major changes. The added value was no longer in new information or material, but in satisfying the desire for the familiar in a new presentation. The *connoisseurs* of the television series recognized the cases which were re-narrated, the places and the protagonists – something outsiders were not necessarily able to do because of the abstract and large-scale artistic style of John Van Fleet's drawings. In some of the darker panels in terms of artwork the motives are barely recognizable for someone who is not familiar with the series. This made *The X-Files: Season One* comics a homage to the fanbase of the television show. Nonetheless, the numerous reissues of the same comics, especially in the first two years of publication in magazines, albums and other collections, were intended exclusively for the market and generating profit. The main beneficiaries in these cases were the comic industry and the publishers. The added value for the readers consisted exclusively in the low prices for the reprinted editions and their accessibility. The new creations of comics in the 2000s and 2010s catered to fans' nostalgic infatuation.

With the advancing age of the actors, this early period now had to make itself felt in a medium that rarely picks up on the progression of time. In comics, as in other literary genres, the main characters appear unchanged for countless years and decades. In the case of *The X-Files*, however, the close connection between the comics and the television series and films prevents this transgression of temporality. Rather than a reboot, *Episode Ten*, and the subsequent comic runs, mini-series and one shots can be better described as a renaissance of *The X-Files* in the field of graphic literature, which brought about a great artistic variation. In *Episode Ten* and *Episode Eleven* alone, ten artists (Andrew Currie, Colin Lorimer, Tom Mandrake, Menton3, Tony Moy, Stuart Sayger, Greg Scott, Matthew Dow Smith, Kevin VanHook and Michael Walsh) contributed their own artistic style, resulting in different stylistic modes of expression and paved the way for the production of further outstanding new comics (such as Tipton's *The X-Files: JFK Disclosure*).

References

Anderson, K. J., G. Purcell and L. Mahlstedt (1997–8), *The X-Files: Ground Zero*, New York City: Topps Comics.
Ayers, M. (2016), 'When Mulder and Scully Went to Springfield: An Oral History of the "Simpsons"'–"X-Files" Crossover', *Wall Street Journal*, 22 January.
The Big Bang Theory (2007–19), [TV programme] CBS, 24 September 2007–16 May 2019.
Brown, L., and K. Giffen (2004), *Mars Attacks,* #1–2, New York City: Topps Comics.
Carter, C. (2013), at San Diego Comic Con, on YouTube. Available online: https://www.youtube.com/watch?v=w3b8379U-vo (accessed 30 January 2022).

Chu, A. (2017), *The X-Files: Deviations. In a World Where Fox Mulder Was Abducted by Aliens*, San Diego: IDW.
Crilley, P. (2012), *Infestation 2: Dungeons and Dragons*, #1–2, San Diego: IDW.
Crilley, P., E. Burnham and E. Brisson (2014), *The X-Files: Conspiracy*, San Diego: IDW.
Edwards, T. (1997), *Entschlüsselt. Ein Streifzug durch das Archiv der Akte X*, München: Wilhelm Heyne Verlag.
Feise, P. (2005), *Science–Sex–Gender in der Fernsehserie Akte X. Analyze eines popkulturellen Paradigmenwechsels*, Berlin: trafo Verlag Dr. Wolfgang Weist.
Freaks and Geeks (1999–2000), [TV programme] NBC, 25 September 1999–17 October 2000.
Ghostbusters (1984), [Film] Dir. Reitman, Ivan, USA: View Columbia-Delphi Productions, Black Rhino, Columbia Pictures.
Groening, M., Ray Richmond and Antonia Coffman, eds. (1997), *The Simpsons: A Complete Guide to Our Favourite Family*, New York: Harper Perennial.
Haist, I. (2021), 'Buffy the Vampire Slayer, Joss and Kitty: The Impact of the Movie and the TV Series on Comics and Vice Versa', in R. Wiebe (ed.), *Polyptych. Adaptation, Television, and Comics*, 85–109, Wilmington: Vernon Press.
Handley, R. (2014), 'IDW Uncovers an X-Files Conspiracy', *Bleeding Cool*, 8: 11–17.
Harris, J. (2013), *The X-Files: Season Ten*, #1: 'Believers, Part 1', San Diego: IDW.
Lavery, D., and C. Burkhead (2011), *Joss Whedon. Conversations*, Jackson: University Press of Mississippi.
Mallrats (1995), [Film] Dir. Kevin Smith, USA: View Askew Productions, Gramercy Pictures & Alphaville Films.
McCloud, S. (1996), *Understanding Comics. The Invisible Art*, chapter 3, 'Blood in the Gutter', New York City: William Morrow Paperbacks.
Middaugh, D. (1997), 'X-Files Season One Finally Debuts', *Wizard*, 72: 23.
Osteried, P. (1998), 'Comics im Zeichen des X', *Hit Comics*, 4: 10–13.
Niles, S., A. Jones and T. Mandrake (2010), *30 Days of Night/The X-Files*, San Diego: IDW.
Petrucha, S., J. Thompson and A. Saviuk (1997), *The X-Files: AfterFlight. A Graphic Novel*, New York City: Topps Comics.
Reeves J. L., M. C. Rodgers and M. Epstein (1996), 'Rewriting Popularity. The Cult Files', in D. Lavery, A. Hague and M. Cartwright, (eds), *Deny All Knowledge. Reading* The X-Files, Syracuse (NY): Syracuse University Press.
The Simpsons, The Springfield Files (1997), [TV programme] FOX, January 12.
South Park, Sexual Healing (2010), [TV programme] Comedy Central, March 17.
Spotnitz, F. (2008), *The X-Files Special*, La Jolla, CA: WildStorm Comics.
Teenage Mutant Ninja Turtles (1984), [comic series)] Mirage Studios.
Thomas, R. (1996), *The X-Files: Season One*, #0, New York City: Topps Comics.
Tipton D. T. (2018), *The X-Files: JFK Disclosure, Part 1*, San Diego: IDW.
Transformers (1984), [programme] Marvel Productions and Sunbow Productions in association with Toei Animation, September 17.
The X-Fools: The Spoof Is Out There (1997), [Game] T. Camin, I. Deitchman, J. P. Manoux, K. Rusk, B. Posehn and P. Oswalt, developed by Parroty Interactive, PC computer game for Windows and Macintosh.

13

'X Files till I DIE': Fan memory from the X-Philes

Natalie Le Clue and Janelle Vermaak-Griessel

In the history of TV lore, *The X-Files* is considered a cult classic. The influence of this series continues to extend well beyond the small screen. As Short writes, the effect of this show 'on the [SF/horror] genre is undeniable ... leaving an indelible mark on later television and rewriting the definition of "cult" television' (2011: 58). Fans of the series, commonly known as X-Philes (The Urban Dictionary 2002), were plunged into nostalgia with the 2016 reboot of the series. Fans were able to share memories of their *X-Files* experiences through comments on social media. This chapter will analyse comment threads made on three selected YouTube videos: *10 Scariest X-Files Episodes of All Time* (2020), a documentary on twenty-five years of the series titled *The X-Files: Implanted Memories* (2019) and *Top 10 X-Files Episodes* (2016). The chapter draws on fan studies and participatory culture in order to understand the manner in which fans reminisce and share their fan memories of *The X-Files* and analyses the comments through discourse analysis. In addition to Garde-Hansen's work on fan memory (2011), scholarly work on life narratives will be utilized as it potentially informs the life choice of becoming and forming part of *The X-Files* fandom and the subsequent sharing of fan memory. The series has had a lasting impact on its fans, and the way in which these fans have incorporated the show into their lives indicates how the small screen and popular culture play an important role in people's everyday lives, through life stages, memories and life narratives.

Literature on fandom

On occasion, the stories that we tell of our lives are infused with experiences and narratives that can only be defined by offering a glimpse into the phenomenon that is fandom. Fandom, defined as a 'form of cultural creativity' (Duffet 2013: 18), is not confined to simply being a fan of a certain object or creation. Instead, it has the potential to extend well beyond this rudimentary understanding to embody genuine impact and to make an authentic contribution to the quality of life: 'the way individual lives unfold is shaped by both internal psychological and external social processes' (Harrington and Bielby 2010).

In an academic field wherein the study of fans and their fandoms are abundant, this chapter endeavours to understand and unpack how substantial the integration of a love for *The X-Files* can be whereby nostalgia and the creation of life memories are some of the driving forces. McAdams and colleagues state, 'A person's life story is an internalized and evolving narrative of the self that selectively reconstructs the past and anticipates the future in such a way as to provide a life with an overall sense of coherence and purpose' (2006: 1372). Through blogs, forums, chatrooms and comment threads, the fans' ability to engage within the context of their chosen fandom has grown exponentially.

The X-Files fans, nicknamed X-Philes (Anon 2016), is an ardent fandom that launched, along with the show, in the late 1990s. The comment threads on YouTube illustrate too that it has been preserved well into the twenty-first century. It is not complicated to understand what may first draw viewers to the show and succeed in holding them in rapt attention, especially those inclined towards speculative fiction, which encompasses the science fiction and horror genres: 'Science fiction and horror tend to attract loyal, engaged fans' (Vermaak 2022: n.p.). *The X-Files* is premised on two characters: Mulder and Scully. Scully is a doctor whose scientific background forms the fundamental basis for her initial sceptical approach to the unexplained and unsolved cases. In contrast, Mulder is convinced and bent on proving that the paranormal is more than just conspiracy theories: 'This believer/sceptic dichotomy frames the relationship between Mulder and Scully as they are forced to negotiate each new twist to the conspiracy … propagated by the Syndicate, a multi-national group of elderly white men in league with the aliens and attempting both to stall and advance colonization through sinister means' (Wooley 2001: 31).

What is crucial to the understanding of fans, fandom and fan culture is the prominent notion that all fans are unique, from different backgrounds and with differing belief systems. Still, they find common ground and the sense of inclusion when engaging with other like-minded fans often via social media. In reference to social networking, Larabie writes that fan engagement 'plays a key role in participatory culture and is regarded as an essential skill to have, [like] a cultural competency' (2011: 68). Through these social media platforms and with these networking skills, fans are enabled and emboldened to form 'groups' and to share their opinions, views and feelings (Watson 2010: 12). What is more, for several decades, fans were mostly considered as passive consumers. In the 1970s and 1980s, screen theory argued that many fans acted as little more than unresponsive receivers (Fagelson 2001: 95). However, the advent of social media perpetuated an explosion of interaction and engagement from fans and audiences alike.

To understand fans and fandom, it is imperative for the subject to be considered through the prism of participatory culture. Of primary importance, writes Henry Jenkins, is the discernment that 'not every member must contribute [to the fandom], but all must believe they are free to contribute and that what they contribute will be appropriately valued' (Jenkins et al. 2009: 6). Furthermore, participatory culture is not restricted or contained within specific social media platforms such as Facebook, Twitter or YouTube. Instead, it is about the practices and the sharing of norms and values, within the various environments, that defines participatory culture (Jenkins and Ito 2016: 184).

To thoughtfully and meticulously compartmentalize the fan responses from the selected YouTube clips, discourse analysis has been employed. This approach is defined by Jørgensen and Phillips as 'a particular way of talking about and understanding the world (or an aspect of the world)' (2002: 1). In addition, Fairclough proffers a 'systematic framework for connecting the micro-analysis of texts with the macro-level discourses circulating within society as a whole by working through the three dimensions of text, discursive practice, and social practice' (Rear 2013). Subsequently, the social media platform YouTube represents not only a type of social order but also an aspect of discourse.

The definition of fans, fandom and fan culture is well covered by a plethora of remarkable scholars, including the previously mentioned Jenkins. In this chapter, the consideration of this phenomenon is expanded and as such allows the opportunity to explore additional perspectives such as fan memory. Garde-Hansen proposes this thoughtful concept as imagining 'the relationship between media and memory is not one of simple connection, as if a piece of string has been secured into a complete circle and now we see the join and understand the relationship. At last, we say, the circle is complete and it has always been going around and around' (2011: vii).

This quote implies an almost potentially infinite loop of fan experience and the subsequent ability to reminisce through familiarity of the encounter with, in this instance, *The X-Files*. Moreover, this can be considered from the perspective of fans transferring or sharing their own fandom experience with different generations. Garde-Hansen, Hoskins and Reading refer to the rediscovering or revitalization of memories through social media (such as YouTube) as 'digital memories' which 'deal with the past's relationship with the present through digital media technology' (2009: 4). By watching the YouTube videos under analysis, fans are able to reignite their memories of their experiences of being or becoming a fan of *The X-Files*.

Analysis and discussion

To ascertain the fans' experience, interpretation and perception of being an X-Phile this chapter has analysed selected comments on the chosen YouTube videos. These three videos were selected as the level of engagement, in terms of viewership (roughly 2.8 million views) and comments (4,224), illustrated the potential to extract meaningful data.

The initial selection of the comments for analysis required that there be some mention, indication or tonal reference to the element of memory and nostalgia. Through analysis of 4,224 comments on all three selected YouTube videos, additional themes were revealed and proven to be relevant to the point of discussion for this chapter. Furthermore, the comments included were selected based on their relation to *The X-Files* fandom. The identification of several themes through the analysis has prompted the subsequent grouping of the comments.

Generational connection

The concept of passing the appreciation of *The X-Files* to younger generations is a clear theme detected in the analysis of the comment threads. One user writes that 'X Files is still my favorite show ever on TV. My son and I watch all the episodes over and over and never get tired of them. We visited Roswell last May searching for Mulder and Scully but never could find them. They were probably at area 51. Actually ET was easier to find in Roswell!' [*sic*] (User 1). This is echoed by another user who underscores the importance of their fandom as a means of encouraging familial connection: 'It was nice to hear Gillian Anderson say how much she appreciates how much "X-Files" meant to some people. When my daughter was growing up, no matter how mad she was at me, we always had the Mulder and Scully to talk about. Thanks' [*sic*] (User 2).

The lure of sharing fandom with the next generation was also evident in the comments analysed. While one fan writes that 'I love watching this show with my parents when I was a kid' [*sic*] (User 3), another remarks that 'my daughter is the same, into big fan, and now we will work on my granddaughter. God bless, happy Friday. 🇨🇦' [sic] (User 4). These comments can be linked to what Vermaak calls 'heirloom fandom' (2022: n.p.). This means that fandom of *The X-Files* is passed on from parents to their children and, even, grandchildren. This not only speaks to the power of fandom but perhaps also expresses an ingrained desire to share an experience characterized by appreciation and pleasure so as to transfer the same positive experience to the next, potential fan.

Yet, it is not only a generational inheritance between parent and child that is observed but also a type of companionship that is formed with *The X-Files* throughout the different phases of some fans' life narratives – a type of companionship that is very much viewed through the prism of nostalgia. The comments speak to 'the possibility that one's fandom might be constructed by significant others and then unconsciously adopted as though it is an inherent component of one' [sic] (Dixon 2013: 339). This is especially notable in comments such as the one from Inferno Satx who writes: 'I love *Game Of Thrones* but I'm 34 and grew up with Mulder & Scully. They will always be my fav faces on television', while others add that '*The X-Files* theme still gives me the chills ' [sic] (User 5). 😨😨😨 These comments point to a lack of 'viewer/fan fatigue' (Harrington and Bielby 2010) and that *The X-Files* has an impact on its fans regardless of their age.

Given the prodigious rate at which series and films are being produced in the early twenty-first century, the question of how well *The X-Files* may have aged also entered the 'discussion' amongst the fans. While some say 'it hasn't aged well. Used to be my favorite show' [sic] (User 6) there are those who disagree and opine that the show has not lost all of its lustre (User 7, User 8) and some who take it even one step further to declare that it has held up 'as one of the best shows of all time' [sic] (User 9). Although these fans are sharing their obviously subjective opinions of a series which they revere, it is interesting to note that despite the plethora of 'new' content available to them, they are still drawn not only to engaging with *The X-Files* fandom but also to relive a part of their life through this engagement. These comments also link with 'fans' accounts of encountering media texts that resonate so powerfully that they transform one's identity, daily activities, and life trajectories' (Harrington and Bielby 2010).

User 10 notes how his perception of the show has changed since watching the show as a '12/13 year-old in 1994' especially considering that he 'understand[s] it more now because [he's] older' [sic]. Similarly, another comment noted that their love for *The X-Files* has endured from the age of thirteen to forty (User 11). This is an especially notable feature of *The X-Files* fandom and indicative too of a fandom that continues to thrive and engage despite the fact that the majority of their veneration for the show is based on decades-old content. *The X-Files* fandom can be theorized as a slow-burner: 'These film fandoms grow slowly over many years and appeal to different parts of successive generations ... The slow-burner fandoms allow for a broad scope and often offer more adult/complex themes' (Vermaak 2022: n.p.).

Existential questions

Throughout the process of the analysis, it became clear that the reading of the data extended beyond the consideration of simply being an X-Phile. It illustrated that the impact of this fandom and this particular group of fans extended and became part of the life of the person and, in some cases, played a role in shaping, at least partly, their life narratives: storytelling can be defined as being 'at the heart of both stability and change in the self' (McLean, Pasupathi and Pals 2007: 262), and the life story can be defined as a 'selective set of autobiographical experiences that, together with interpretations of those events, explain how a person came to be who he or she is and projects a sense of purpose and meaning into the future' (Pasupathi and Mansour 2006: 798).

At its most rudimentary purpose, a television series is intended to offer an hour of entertainment or a bit of escapism for those who seek a break from everyday life. But every so often great television writing, directing and acting transcends this simplistic ambition. From the comments analysed, it is clear that *The X-Files* is such a show. In reference to a specific episode of the series a fan writes, 'I will forever be in love with "The Unnatural" and its perfect balance of typical X-Files themes, horror, comedy and emotions! Plus the heart-wrenching question of what does it really mean to be human' [*sic*] (User 12). As previously stated, the experience and perception may differ from one fan to the other. However, in this example this type of thought-provoking and profound response indicates the potential weight that fandom carries.

There are those too who would proclaim their undying fandom support through grand declarations: 'Many tried to copy it, none got at that level! A pioneer series in this topic, the series who made every pure minded citizen to have second thoughts about everything!' [*sic*] (User 13). Although more effusive in its declaration, this comment nevertheless reinforces the capacity that fandom has to form these existential considerations.

Enduring legacy and reach

Two decades into the twenty-first century, the world of entertainment media is saturated with streaming platforms, underscored by binge-watchers who gorge on content on a daily basis across the globe. Williams writes that 'mediated texts may become a source of comfort and pleasure for fans, working alongside their memories of their own histories and past selves'

(2015: 22). Through this prism it is interesting to note the endurance of *The X-Files* fan base.

A fan reminisces by recalling an earlier period of their life: 'My childhood and young adulthood. Nobody my age (28) fucks with x files but I feel like it changed the world of tv. Underrated to the max. Season 1 is rewatchable a thousand times over man. Light up' [*sic*] (User 14). It is interesting how this fan implies a sense of ownership and protection of their fandom object. In so doing, it illustrates a sort of emotional connection which, feasibly, indicates a significant immersion into the fandom. Another fan, not quite as demonstrative, writes that *The X-Files* 'is one of the best piece of American culture that is contributed to this world ... Even here in Philippines this show is quite popular. I am fan since I was 5 now 33' [*sic*] (User 15). Given the location of this fan, in the Philippines, it underlines the inclusivity and reach of this fandom. It accentuates Jenkins's earlier point too of fans finding a space in which they feel free and able to participate regardless of their perceived differences.

There exists a level of pride too within this fandom: 'The X-Files surpassed being just a TV show & became a MOOD. I still get the same feels I got 25 yrs ago from some of the same episodes, no matter how many times I've seen them. Very much in the vein of The Twilight Zone; Classics never die. Proud to be a Day One X-Phile!👽👾👻'[*sic*] (User 16).

These types of comments prompt debates around how some fandoms endure. Williams puts forward that when, for example, a television show ends 'fans will inevitably react in different ways in order to negotiate the rupture and change in self-identity' (2015: 30). In this case, one such reaction is the maintaining of a 'peripheral fandom' (2015: 29) through online engagement. When analysing the comments, a suggestion, which could begin to explain the endurance of *The X-Files* fandom, is the perceived quality of the television show. The analysis conducted also suggests that, at least in part, the persistence of *The X-Files* fandom also stems from the fans' own nostalgia and subsequent desire to sustain a feeling that reminds them of a period of time which is underscored by pleasing memories which Williams (2015) notes as 'inextricable and ongoing fan engagement [that] helps to maintain connection to both the fan object and to the "self" who was the fan at that time' (2015: 44).

Influence

The study of the comments also revealed some instances in which being part of *The X-Files* fandom has affected the decision that some fans have made about their life journeys: 'I can proudly say that the xfiles made me want to get my job as an FBI agent' [*sic*] (User 17). What is evident in these comments is that the ability for fandom to serve as a paradigm for the fans within it should neither be underestimated nor discounted. From these selected comments it is apparent that, through their perception, being a part of *The X-Files* fandom transcended the boundaries of a television show to impart noteworthy life lessons: 'Scully has always been an inspiration to me. She's confident & headstrong, motivated me to fight all the odds, move on and never to stop ☺ ☺ ☺' [*sic*] (User 18) This extends further to the ability to absorb information and the learning of new skills:

> I was 10 or 11 the first time I saw this show. I probably shouldn't have been watching it, but I did and I loved it. Way back in the early 90s when digital TV wasn't a thing yet, we couldn't get Fox to tune in at our house but a friend of mine could. His mom was taping the episodes and we would borrow the tapes to make our own copies. That's how we watched *The X Files* until we got a satellite and that's probably why I'm such a big proponent of file-sharing as a means of cultural preservation [*sic*]. (User 19)

This experience, as referred to in the quote, highlights the impact that a show like *The X-Files* had on this user's life. This experience of becoming a fan is seen as a transformative moment, a milestone that marks a clear division between the person's life before and after their encounter with the show.

This resonates with the idea of fandom as a part of a person's identity and with the concept of being a fan as a defining characteristic of one's self-concept. When one becomes a fan, it is a defining moment in one's life, and it is a memory that can be cherished and shared with other fans: 'becoming a fan is, for most fans, a milestone in their lives in which "everything changed"; they tend to think of themselves in terms of being a fan and not being a fan' (Cavicchi 1998: 153). The embracing of a fandom and the incorporation of that into one's life and life story is an important aspect of life narratives and can be theorized to affect the fan's self-perception in a significant manner.

Emotional attachment

The visceral reaction that can be evoked from a fan should not be unappreciated. Therein, most likely, lies the forging of a bond that will last a lifetime: 'I just found *The X-Files* on Hulu, and it brought back so many great memories. The stories were so engaging that Mulder and Scully became like family members ... All-in-all, I'm going to have a lot of fun revisiting the old friends again [*sic*]' (User 20).

Through this quote the user describes Mulder and Scull as 'family members', underscoring the emotional connection that fans can develop with the fictional worlds they engage with. This connection can go beyond mere entertainment, as fans often invest a significant amount of time and emotional energy into their favourite shows, thereby creating a type and sense of kinship with the characters and the stories.

So too the essence of camaraderie permeates and characterizes *The X-Files* fandom:

> I remember I went to the cinema to see *Fight the Future* and when the bee stung the whole cinema screamed out 'no!' and everyone turned to each other, even to strangers, laughing with frustration, and as cheesy as it sounds, it felt like you were all part of something. I don't think I've ever experienced that as a cinema audience member sinc [*sic*]. (User 21)

In this quote, the user describes a communal experience of watching *The X-Files* movie, where the audience's emotional reactions to the plot point created a shared bond among the viewers, even with strangers. This suggests that, for some fans, there exists a level of genuine emotional attachment with their fandom and with each other, which exemplifies their connection to *The X-Files* and, possibly, aids in the sustaining of their fan memory. It is important to distinguish too that not all fans experience fandom in the same manner and that any level or connection to fandom is equally valued and valuable.

Finding your place

A notable theme throughout the comment threads of the selected clips is the sense of camaraderie that being an X-Phile has afforded these fans. In a seemingly ever-increasingly divisive society, what the X-Philes fandom illustrates is an all too unfamiliar occurrence of inclusivity and acceptance based solely on the premise of a mutual adoration of a science-fiction television series. A user writes, 'I can still remember going to school the next day after an X-Files episode and the majority of people would have also watched it and talked about it' [*sic*] (User 22). This quote highlights the sense of inclusivity and acceptance that can arise within a fandom, where people from diverse backgrounds can come together based on a shared love of a particular show. What becomes evident through the users/fans comments is the discovery of a type of safe haven which not only offers a sense of community but also presents as a mechanism to revisit and relive the pleasure experienced. User 23's comment highlights the cultural significance of *The X-Files* in the 1990s: 'Back when I was in elementary school it was always the coolest kids got together on Monday mornings to discuss what they saw on the x-files the night before. It's a real bummer they don't have xfiles on Netflix anymore ... feels so nostalgic watching those old episodes' [*sic*]. This quote illustrates the sense of nostalgia that many fans feel when revisiting the show today.

Conclusion

This analysis reveals the intricacy of a relationship between fans and their chosen fandom. It is clear that it extends beyond mere enjoyment of a television series towards something more profound. Not only is the adoration for *The X-Files* encapsulated in the memories and experiences shared by these fans but it also demonstrates how fandom has the ability to permeate throughout a fan's life. It is interesting to discern how these fans have embraced their fandom of *The X-Files* as more than just liking a television show. As User 24 writes, 'It's not just watching the show again and again … It's being an X – Phile' [sic]. This user's comment highlights how fans may embrace their status as X-Philes as a defining aspect of their identity, akin to a cultural or social affiliation. This underscores the significance of fandom as a cultural phenomenon, which can inspire deep emotional attachments and connections among fans. Moreover, it emphasizes the role of popular culture in shaping our identities and experiences, as fans draw meaning and value from their engagement with media texts and the communities that surround them.

As such, the journey of exploring and understanding fans and the manner in which they engage and interpret and nurture their fandom is one that continues to evolve. Through this chapter, and the study of fans of *The X-Files*, it is realized that through participation, connection and dedication to their respective fandoms, an authentic and lasting attachment can be cultivated and maintained. Perhaps it is this very point, the perseverance of the fans, that lends a greater understanding as to why some fandoms, not least of all *The X-Files* fandom, continues to not only welcome new members, but keeps the zeal of being an X-Phile well and truly alive. This is perfectly encapsulated in User 25's words: 'X files till I DIE' [sic].

References

10 Scariest X-Files Episodes of All Time (2020), [YouTube video]. Available online: https://www.youtube.com/watch?v=EFRbef3bsPY&t=2s (accessed 14 November 2020).

Anon. (2016), 'X-Phile', *x-files.fandom.com*. Available online: https://x-files.fandom.com/wiki/X-phile (accessed 1 February 2022).

Cavicchi, D. (1998), *Tramps like Us: Music and Meaning among Springsteen Fans*. New York: Oxford University Press.

Dixon, K. (2013), 'Learning the Game: Football Fandom Culture and the Origins of Practice', *International Review for the Sociology of Sport*, 48 (3): 259–383.

Duffet, M. (2013), *Understanding Fandom: An Introduction to the Study of Media Fan Culture*, New York: Bloomsbury.

Fagelson, W. F. (2001), 'Fighting Films: The Everyday Tactics of World War II Soldiers', *Cinema Journal*, 40 (2): 94–112.
Garde-Hansen, J. (2011), *Media and Memory*, Edinburgh: Edinburgh University Press.
Garde-Hansen, J., A. Hoskins and A. Reading (2009), *Save as... Digital Memories*, London: Palgrave Macmillan.
Harrington, C. L., and D. D. Bielby (2010), 'Autobiographical Reasoning in Long-Term Fandom', *Transformative Works and Cultures* (5): https://doi.org/10.3983/twc.2010.0209 (accessed 9 August 2021).
Jenkins, H., and M. Ito (2016), *Participatory Culture in a Networked Era: A Conversation on Youth, Learning, Commerce, and Politics*, Cambridge, United Kingdom: John Wiley & Sons.
Jenkins, H., R. Purushotma, M. Weigel, C. Clinton and A. J. Robison (2009), *Confronting the Challenges of Participatory Culture: Media Education for the 21st Century*. Cambridge, MA: The MIT Press.
Jørgensen, M. W., and L. J. Phillips (2002), *Discourse Analysis as Theory and Method*, California: Sage.
Larabie, C. (2011), 'Participatory Culture and the Hidden Costs of Sharing', *The McMaster Journal of Communication*, 7 (1): 66–87.
McAdams, D. P., J. J. Bauer, A. R. Sakaeda, N. A. Anyidoho, M. A. Machado, K. Magrino-Failla, K. W. White and J. L. Pals (2006), 'Continuity and Change in the Life Story: A Longitudinal Study of Autobiographical Memories in Emerging Adulthood', *Journal of Personality*, 74 (5): 1371–400, http://dx.doi.org/10.1111/j.1467-6494.2006.00412.x.
McLean, K. C., M. Pasupathi and J. L. Pals (2007), 'Selves Creating Stories Creating Selves: A Process Model of Self-Development', *Personality and Social Psychology Review*, 11 (3): 262–78, http://dx.doi.org/10.1177/1088868307301034.
Pasupathi, M., and E. Mansour (2006), 'Adult Age Differences in Autobiographical Reasoning in Narratives', *Developmental Psychology*, 42 (5): 798–808, http://dx.doi.org/10.1037/0012-1649.42.5.798.
Rear, D. (2013), 'Laclau and Mouffe's Discourse Theory and Fairclough's Critical Discourse Analysis: An Introduction and Comparison', *Academia.edu*. Available online: https://www.academia.edu/2912341/Laclau_and_Mouffe_s_Discourse_Theory_and_Faircloughs_Critical_Discourse_Analysis_An_Introduction_and__Comparison (accessed 9 August 2021).
Top 10 X-Files Episodes (2016), [YouTube video]. Available online: https://www.youtube.com/watch?v=8rhge-os-18&t=1s (accessed 14 November 2020).
Urban Dictionary (2002), 'X-Phile'. Available online: https://www.urbandictionary.com/define.php?term=X-Phile (accessed 19 January 2021).
Vermaak, J. (2022), '"I Named My Daughter Ripley": Fan Gifting and Internal Hierarchies in the Alien Fandom', in B. Kies and M. Connor (eds), *Fandom: The Next Generation*, 112–22, Iowa: University of Iowa Press.
Watson, J. (2010), 'Fandom Squared: Web 2.0 and Fannish Production', *Transformative Works & Cultures* 5 (1): 12.
Williams, R. (2015), *Post-Object Fandom: Television, Identity and Self-Narrative*, London: Bloomsbury.

Wooley, C. A. (2001), 'Visible Fandom: Reading *The X-Files* through X-Philes', *Journal of Film and Video*, 53 (4): 31.

The X-Files: Implanted Memories (Documentary) (2019), [YouTube video]. Available online: https://www.youtube.com/watch?v=V-SA61fWg3c&t=1s (accessed 14 November 2020).

14

Reading into the romance: Gender, genre and the rabid fangirls of *The X-Files*

Marissa Spada

In the late 1990s, an unauthorized biography of *The X-Files* star Gillian Anderson defined the average fan of the series as, 'typically male, 25–34 years old, college educated, residing in northeastern United States, considers self moderate television viewer but is also a *Star Trek* fan, and an Internet user' (Crenshaw 1997: 227). I recall reading this line, as a preteen girl and middle-schooler with limited internet access, bewildered as to how I had so completely and unwittingly defied conventions. But at the excruciating speed of dial-up, on my family's one shared computer, I would come to learn that a then-emerging term, 'shipper', described a different kind of fan of the show that had activated my fascination with perpetually drawn-out love stories. Predominantly women, shippers were fans who insisted on reading into a romance that barely made screen time, turning up the brightness on television monitors to catch almost undetectable glimmers of emotion between Agents Mulder and Scully and unpacking the significance in vibrant, creative and passionate online communities.

This essay proceeds from that fascination, still percolating in me nearly twenty-five years later, as I reflect on the significance and legacy of *The X-Files* shipper subfandom. In the 1990s, proponents of the MSR ('Mulder/Scully Romance') were among the first television audiences to generate an immersive and ever-expanding emotional world online and, in doing so, positioned themselves at the centre of the series' genre and gender politics. This decades-long 'battle of the sexes' was alluded to in 2018, leading up to the series reboot, when showrunner Chris Carter announced that 'shippers were heard', conceding that Mulder and Scully were, indeed, a couple. Of course, not all shippers were women (and not all women were shippers); however, the discursive feminization of this audience is inseparable from their exclusion from official discourse and their marginalization within the larger fandom. These so-called sentimental fans displayed an over-invested and highly emotional attachment to the series, which, for many of their detractors, marred the cerebral science fiction drama with soapy aspirations. As many have observed, *The X-Files* provided a template for twenty-first-century 'quality' television – a label that regularly deals in melodrama, while it disavows the medium's lowbrow, feminized past. In fact, it was the shipper's fervid obsession with the series that most resonates with contemporary audience practices in the age of binge watching and social media. There were few others who watched and re-watched, studying the details with avid, unwavering commitment.

In what follows, I introduce 'the FBI's most unwanted fangirls': the shippers who emerged online in the 1990s, seeking legitimacy within the greater fandom. Various 'shipper wars', subcategorizations and naming practices negotiated the series' genre identity by way of establishing a gendered hierarchy of 'true fans'. Next, I address the fluid nature of television genre, to explore how the 'sentimental fan' interacted with a text that provided plenty of fodder for the shipper imagination, even as it evaded their desires. Lastly, I discuss how that same audience generated their own texts, which reinstated the feminized emotionality that was so often absent from the series' narrative, plot and character development.

The FBI's most unwanted fangirls

In May 1996, a fan by the username of Kristel S. Oxley-Johns submitted the following rallying cry to the usenet group, alt.tv.x-files:

> To date, except in the realm of fanfiction, the 'Relationshippers' have been a pretty quiet, unassuming bunch. We tend to get treated unfairly if we should dare, *gasp* have an opinion, so we keep to ourselves except in forums specifically designed for us. That day is coming to an end. We are loyal, legitimate fans who deserve to have our say, ESPECIALLY in the forums where what we have to say just might be picked up on by TPTB. What we think about the direction the characters of the show should take does not in any way, shape, or form disqualify us from the ranks of the TRUE fans. (Oxley-Johns 1996)

Kristel's post was one of the first strikes in what would become known, within the *X-Files* fandom, as The Great Shipper War. The acronym, TPTB, stands for The Powers That Be – in other words, the series' creators, who, in the ideal scenario, would acknowledge the wishes of these otherwise 'quiet and unassuming' devotees and adapt the narrative trajectory accordingly. This fantasy of dialogic exchange anticipates what media scholar Henry Jenkins later articulated in *Convergence Culture: Where Old and New Media Collide* as the digital age transitioned away from traditional hierarchies of producer/consumer relations. As Jenkins argued, fans, once relegated to 'the invisible margins of popular culture', have moved into 'the center of current thinking about media production and consumption' (Jenkins 2006: 12). For industry, audience participation across multiple platforms produces more active consumers, better data and better revenue. For fans, however, the incentive is that which was voiced by Kristel in 1996: to engage with TPTB, to be seen and heard, and thus play an active role in shaping the series' plotlines and character development.

The fans Kristel called 'relationshippers', identified by their desire to see the series' protagonists become lovers, were plagued by more than their insatiable hunger for romance. In a fandom that was once described as 'typically male', the vast majority of these fans were women. As Suzanne Scott argues, convergence culture has 'cultivated a structured secondariness for female fans'. She contends that, even when the media industries are economically motivated to encourage fan participation, masculinized modes of engagement are generally preferred over feminized ones. 'What has emerged in convergence culture's wake', she states, 'is a gendered politics of participation designed to privilege male fans and their preferred mode of participation'. Scott demonstrates how digital cultures, which have demarginalized fan practices, have paradoxically catalyzed interfandom boundary policing and reinforced misogynistic notions of fannish 'authenticity'. Women are often perceived as fandom interlopers, whose presence threatens to mainstream the subculture and void it of exclusivity (Scott 2019: 5, 7, 93).

We might observe a similar phenomenon of gendered gatekeeping in the pre-Web 2.0 battles of the Great Shipper War. As Kristel claimed, 'relationshippers' were marginalized on the most prominent, and therefore visible, of online forums, forced to defend their status as 'TRUE fans'. Kristel's essay garnered a wave of inflamed comments from fans on both sides of the aisle, including one who expressed an 'uncontrollable [*sic*] urge to do a little cleansing with a nice 2X4, with a couple of nails in it, to a few fans that seem to take some "ideas"' to an extreme' (JackBelow 1996). Later that same month, an aggrieved fan with the username, Tony R. Boies, replied with the quasi-manifesto, 'My Problem with the "Relationshippers", in which they argued simply that the coupling narrative had been done "TO DEATH" – a fair point which nonetheless implies that the relationshipper's tastes are prosaic, uncultured, and unimaginative' (1996). Others sought to expose relationshippers' detractors of their covert biases. As one fan explained: 'what's been insinuated here is that wanting and/or *seeing* the development of a romantic relationship between M&S means that one is immature and somehow emotionally stunted' ('My Problem with the "Relationshippers"' n.d.). Indeed, the anti-relationshippers, who would later become known within the fandom as 'noromos', were defined not for their own aspirations vis-à-vis plot or character development, but rather, by the objects of their distaste: in this case, romance, as well as the fans who longed for it. The noromo's repudiated 'other' was the swooning (or, in fan lingo, 'squeeing'), fangirl, trapped in an inferior state of emotional development, unable to manage her base and unruly desires.

It remains unclear as to which side of The Great Shipper War ultimately claimed victory. Relationshippers, however, would certainly outlast noromos, not only within *The X-Files* fandom, but throughout popular culture at large. The shortened term, 'shipper', is now used widely across media fandoms and while the etymology is contested, the dominant historical narrative locates the word's origins in *X-Files* usenet groups, alt.tv.x-files and alt.tv.x-files.creative, in the mid-1990s. No longer invisible, the shipper is still the fan who yearns to witness the fruition of a romance – usually fictional, but occasionally real world, such as in the case of many celebrity pairings. To ship means to spend one's time daydreaming, imagining the various scenarios by which two (or more) individuals might finally come to realize their undying love for one another. It often means to speculate, visualize and rewrite this would-be relationship into being, engaging in a collective fantasy online, with like-minded others. Today, there are hundreds of ship fandoms, who communicate and congregate virtually on the likes of Tumblr, Reddit and the fanfiction site Archive of Our Own (AO3).

From 1998, up until a server crash in 2003, the main hub for MSR-related content was the fan site, Haven for the FBI's Most Unwanted. The Haven featured spoilers for romance-hungry X-Philes, as well as images and fanfiction – typically of the NC-17 or 'fluff' variety. The Haven, however, was perhaps best known for its notorious community message boards, which still exist today, albeit with less fervour and flame wars. The Haven owed its name to Mulder's very first line of dialogue in S1: E01: 'Sorry. No one here but the FBI's most unwanted'. Unsuspecting that he is about to meet the love of his life, Mulder has assumed an outsider status, tucked away in a spacious private office in the bowels of the FBI's J. Edgar Hoover Building. The Haven's outsider status was equally complex and contradictory. At the height of the site's popularity, it was one of the show's largest online communities and undeniably the home of some of its loudest voices; and yet, its content was, in many ways, 'unwanted' by a dominant minority of fans.

Among the Haven's membership were some of the most 'rabid' of shippers. The Oxford English Dictionary defines 'rabid' as, 'a feeling, passion, disease, etc.: raging, rampant; unbridled, uncontrollable; (also, of an attitude, view, etc.) extreme, fanatical' (OED, 2022). Indeed, within fan cultures, the discourse on 'rabidness' is often entangled at the nexus of feeling, passion and disease. It pathologizes the fan's surfeit of emotion, which is perceived, by those who name it, to have transgressed the limits of proper engagement, even when the text itself has been intentionally constructed to elicit that emotion. Melissa Click, commenting on the gender politics that comprise the popular discourse on the *Twilight* fandom, has argued that Victorian era words, such as, 'rabid', 'fever', 'madness', 'hysteria' and 'obsession' are used to denigrate and dismiss the franchise's largely female fanbase (2009).

Throughout *The X-Files*' run, a pathologizing discourse of rabidness contributed to the subjugation of feminized viewing practices. Even within the shipper community, there were designations and hierarchies, which mocked and renounced these activities as forms of extremism. The term, 'intellishipper', for instance, originated on the series' official site message boards as a means of differentiating the thoughtful, rational-minded shippers from their more erratic counterparts. The intellishipper was defined by the following qualities and behaviours:

1. believes in the furthering of the romantic relationship as a natural, believable extension of the deep bond between Mulder and Scully;
2. is able to articulate the logical reasons for this attitude in a clear, witty and grammatically correct manner, without 'flames' or rudeness;
3. feels that *The X-Files* stories should be more important than the Mulder–Scully relationship and does not expect blatant, mushy romance between the characters;
4. has a sense of humor: intellishippers can laugh at themselves and the show;
5. does not suffer from the delusions, poor netiquette, excessive emotional reactivity and other problematic symptoms of Rabid Shipper Syndrome. (Glossary of X-Files Message Board Terms 2021)

By this definition, the intellishipper was restrained, non-impulsive and articulate – all the better to discuss how and why their two favourite characters should 'get it on'. The intellishipper was not interested in 'blatant' and 'mushy' romance – the kind depicted in Harlequin or Mills and Boon romance novels, or on daytime soaps. By default, therefore, rabid shippers were deemed unintelligent, beholden to a surplus of emotion and too involved with the text to 'laugh at themselves and the show'. Kristina Busse argues that, within fandoms, internal hierarchies, which designate certain fans as more unusual, cringeworthy or 'out there' function to reaffirm feelings of normalcy for the fan whose practices are relatively moderate. She states, 'wherever one is situated in terms of mockable fannish behavior, there is clearly a fannish subgroup even more extreme than one's own, and it is that group that one can feel secure in not being a part of' (Busse 2017: 182). Likewise, the intellishipper subcategory emerged out of shippers' yearning to be authenticated and taken seriously within the larger fandom. By the same token, however, it subordinated and disavowed those suffering from Rabid Shipper Syndrome.

The intellishipper category legitimizes certain fans, at the expense of others; however, we might also venture that the term productively renegotiates gendered audience stereotypes. If we consider, as many do, that *The X-Files* was a forerunner of a contemporary breed of 'quality' television – programmes that have been said to transcend the medium's historically low cultural value – the intellishipper erodes an implicit and highly gendered binary. The term, intellishipper, a portmanteau of 'intelligent' and 'shipper', combines the 'high' taste culture associated with quality drama and the 'low' pathos of melodrama. As Michael Kackman reminds us, melodrama is 'the constitutive force behind much of what we call quality television', which is defined not only by aesthetics, but by what we, as audiences, bring to the text. Much of the discourse on 'quality', however, privileges 'masculine sentimentality and excess' and reembraces the gendered hierarchies that once figured television as a 'bad object' (Kackman 2008). In the common conceptualization of 'quality', feminized viewing practices, such as shipping, are superfluous, if not incompatible. In a sense, therefore, the intellishipper designation problematizes the dichotomies between masculinized and feminized audience practices, distanced aesthetic appreciation and rabid infatuation, cerebral sci fi and soapy excess.

Generic boundaries and the 'sentimental fan'

While various 'shipper wars' were enacted in online forums, the series' generic boundaries were prodded, teased and reaffirmed by the mainstream media. In 1997, *Entertainment Weekly* noted the preponderance of a particularly 'sentimental' group of fans:

> Fan adoration has also spawned some 20 sites by and for 'relationshippers', such as the X-Files Institution for Relationshippers (pages.prodigy.com/KYOUSE/xf-love.htm), where sentimental fans – usually female – share subtle hints of Mulder and Scully's unacknowledged passion. Moreover, at least two dozen fanfic sites – call them the Triple X-Files – devote themselves to the erotic cavortings of Scully and Mulder, Scully and assistant director Walter Skinner, even Mulder and Skinner. (*Entertainment Weekly* 1997)

Although *Entertainment Weekly* assigned the shipper's gender with the aside, 'usually female', the qualifier was hardly necessary given the description provided. The image of the 'sentimental fan', invoked by *Entertainment Weekly*, is unequivocally the archetypal love-starved woman, attracted to romance, angst and the heightened state of emotions associated with the likes of soap operas, romance novels and melodrama.

Melodrama is a fluid and contextual cultural category but in nearly each instance, is characterized by excess: the circuitous plot that poses a challenge to narrative linearity, the aesthetic representation of the repressed or unseen or the over-the-top, drawn-out, ecstatic suffering that implores an embodied response in its audience, typically gendered as feminine. Feminist scholars have argued that the film melodrama of the 1950s was subsumed into television, and as Lynne Joyrich once argued, melodrama is so pervasive on television that 'it is difficult to locate as a separate TV genre' (1996: 47). Likewise, Linda Williams contends that serialized television is inherently melodramatic, noting its rhythms and 'beats' that enable the cumulative development of the diegetic world: 'Time suspended, time resumed, time manipulated are all basic ingredients of the strong emotions generated by melodrama because melodrama, most fundamentally, wants us to care for its protagonists. The more we invest our time in their worlds and their changes, the more we care' (Williams 2018: 177).

By even the most conventional of textual readings, *The X-Files* often veered into melodramatic territory. We might recall the protagonists' proclivity for what one journalist called 'melodramatic gloom and overheated monologues' (Handlen 2013). We might also note its shifting tonal registers, from the dark and moody 'mythology' episodes, vocalizing the postmodern condition with a wailing 'ugly cry' from David Duchovny in a church, hospital or government building, to the self-reflexive comedic stand-alones that playfully deviated from the overarching narrative, often explained away as a strange dream (such as in the episodes, 'Triangle', S6: E03 and 'Dreamland', S6: E04). Finally, there was the greater series 'myth-arc', which chronicled a multigenerational crisis of patrilineality; an emotionally charged crusade of a son who avenges the sins of his father. Meanwhile, the more soapy melodramatic fare of romance, tears and unbridled passion was all but absent. Week after week, the 'sentimental fan' would watch until the words 'Executive Producer Chris Carter' crawled their way across the darkened screen, hoping for a telling shot-reverse-shot, a few lines of dialogue or an exchange that might mean more (if only we were to record the sequence and play it back ad nauseum – which we always did).

As a science fiction drama, *The X-Files* invited a dominant reading that some shippers appeared to not merely oppose but ignore. Consider, for instance, the following breakdown of the pilot episode, on a fan website dedicated solely to the MSR: '(1) Scully runs to Mulder's room wearing only her bra and panties. (2) Scully turns to Mulder for a hug when he tells her they are only mosquito bites. (3) Mulder trusts Scully enough to tell her what happened to his sister, Samantha' ('Nicky's Ultimate X-Files Shippers Page' n.d.). Reading shippers' (often humorous, tongue-in-cheek or self-deprecating) episode guides, reviews and predictions, one might assume that *The X-Files* was all UST ('unresolved sexual tension'). A spoiler for S7: E11 'Closure' summarizes only the most important moments:

> Mulder is angsty in this one. Short-tempered with Scully a few times. On the phone ... in a motel room. But, when it comes to the final moments of Mulder finding out. He can't quite do it. She asks if he wants her to do it alone. He nods. In the entire episode ... in the seven years of this ... that moment spoke volumes about the strength of their relationship. No touching ... nothing overtly shippy. Just a given that Scully would find out for him. ('Closure', n.d.)

While the shipper might have enjoyed the series' monsters, aliens, and government conspiracies, these elements were often secondary to character development.

We thus might articulate yet another 'problem with "relationshippers"': namely, that their very existence troubled the series' genre identity; however, they were not alone in this pursuit. As film and media scholar Jason Mittell has argued, television genres are 'cultural categories', determined not by 'textual essence' but by the manner through which they are created, circulated and consumed (Mittell 2004: 11). By this definition, *The X-Files* was a shapeshifter: a masculine melodrama that took on more feminized characteristics in its reception, promotion and hype.

While romance was typically suppressed or unrealized on screen, mainstream periodicals offered plenty of visual fodder for the shipper imagination. *TV Guide*, for instance, regularly featured images of Gillian Anderson and David Duchovny posed in some variation of a loving (or lusting) embrace. Adopting the aesthetic of grocery store romance novels, these magazine covers depicted a romance between Mulder and Scully that straddled the line between official and unofficial discourse. Media and television scholar Jonathan Gray, building on Gérard Genette's conceptualization of paratexts, has argued that promotional materials, which may appear peripheral to the main product, are, in fact, integral to its functioning: 'they create texts, they manage them, and they fill them with many of the meanings that we associate with them' (Gray 2010: 6). While these covers feature a couple that are not quite Anderson and Duchovny – nor are they quite Mulder and Scully – they nonetheless condition the viewer's experience of the show, injecting angst and eroticism into the otherwise platonic pairing. Furthermore, these images were easily recycled, edited and converted into fan art – texts which, in their construction and consumption, kept the fan engaged with the series; their desires were free to reimagine its contours.

Fluff, smut and feminist rage

Online, shippers generated a variety of fantexts, including *manip*s, in which promotional photographs or stills were digitally altered and recontextualized. In the style of the late-1990s photo editing software, Mulder and Scully could consummate their canonically platonic relationship or move to the suburbs in a haze of gauzy pastel hues. Digital effects – blurred edges, fadeouts and transposition – were particularly suited to the shipper dream world aesthetic. Fan sites boasted repositories of screen stills, featuring 'favorite shippy moments' that might be used as creative inspiration. Perhaps unsurprisingly, however, these photo mashups often resulted in failed, awkward and campy visualizations of shipper desire. Their amateur constructions often broke the illusion they sought to achieve, forcing fans to, as the intellishipper credo stated, 'laugh at themselves'. One's tolerance for cringe was, in many ways, a barometer of rabidness.

The most common form of shipper texts were stories that expanded upon the series' canon, otherwise known as fanfiction, or fic. At one time, in fact, the *X-Files* fanfiction site Gossamer was the largest archive of stories dedicated to a single fandom on the web. Often melodramatic in both form and content, fanfiction settles in the gaps and fissures, with its most common themes being angst, 'fluff' (a pleasant, light-hearted romp) and smut (graphic sex). For readers and writers alike, these stories facilitate an embodied interaction with the source text. As English and film studies professor Francesca Coppa has argued, fanfiction belongs to dramatic, rather than literary, storytelling traditions – it 'directs bodies in space even when it's not overtly written in theatrical form. Readers come to fan fiction with extratextual knowledge, mostly of characters' bodies and voices.' She adds, 'We know who these characters are because we know the actors who play them, and we bring our memories of their physicality to the text, so the reader is precharged, preeroticized' (2014: 228–9). The most popular *X-Files* fics were typically written in character, included light references to specific episodes and rated NC-17. The body was thus featured heavily in these stories, and descriptions of the characters' physicality – the markings on their skin, the colour of Scully's hair and the size of Mulder's engorged member – included a mix of that which could be easily confirmed by the canon (her hair was indeed red), as well as speculations, which over time, developed into inter-fandom tropes (yes, it was always the same size).

Much like melodrama, both the creation and consumption of fanfiction requires putting oneself in the mind and body of one, or both, of the characters, and these practices are often ascribed low cultural value. Coppa critiques humorist Lore Sjöberg's parody of inter-fandom dynamics and stereotyping, 'Geek Hierarchy' (published in 2002 on his now defunct website), arguing that the low-ranking placement of 'Erotic Fanfic Writers

Who Put *Themselves* in the Story' is revealing of the gendered power structures in media fandoms, which often relegate the most embodied and feminized of fan activities to its lowest rungs. She writes, 'As we descend, we move further away from "text" and more toward "body"' and, at least on the media fandom side of the diagram, toward the female body (because fan writers are likely to be women)' (2014: 225). While most authors did not put themselves, literally, into the story, the process of writing, reading and rereading is an all-consuming experience that allows the fan to stay present in the story world for hours, weeks or even months.

Although often waved off as a 'guilty pleasure', fanfiction did more than resolve the painfully unresolved UST. It also restored the woman's perspective where it was lacking and offered a means of exploring emotions that were largely absent on screen. One of the most infamous and controversial of *The X-Files* fan texts was RivkaT and MustangScully's novel-length fic, *Iolokus*. The first of its chapters was released online in 1998, following the two-part arc, 'Christmas Carol' (S5: E06) and 'Emily' (S5: E07), which revealed that, due to Scully's reproductive cells having been harvested during her abduction three years prior, she was now the biological mother of a young child, who ultimately dies from an incurable illness. In the series, Scully is forced to process her grief in little to no screen time, moving on from this highly traumatic event by the next episode, investigating the latest monster-of-the-week as if nothing of significance had recently transpired. Indeed, throughout much of *The X-Files*' eleven seasons, Scully's harrowing experiences with motherhood, abduction and medical rape were largely elided by the overarching paternal melodrama. In *Iolokus*, however, Scully feels and acts on anger, pleasure and sorrow in ways that were often dismissed by *The X-Files* creators and the all-male writing team. *Iolokus*, according to one of its authors, was 'written in a white-hot fire of specifically feminist rage at what "Chris Carter" (standing in for the entire TV apparatus) had done to Scully' (Rivkat 2006). That which was unrepresented on screen, disavowed by 'the entire TV apparatus', surfaces in a tortuous narrative which, over the course of its many installments, oscillates between violent revenge-drama, graphic sexual encounters and, in the case of its holiday-themed epilogue, a saccharine portrait of family bliss.

These texts possessed an all-encompassing emotionality that allowed *The X-Files* to remain present in the fan's psychic space, in between episodes and seasons, and long after the series had gone off the air. By the final two seasons, the series' writers began to take notice, as many fans commented, with plotlines and dialogue beginning to resemble fanfiction more than fanfiction itself. Most emblematically, in 'Trust No 1' (S9: E06), Scully reads aloud a letter to her infant son: 'Chance meeting your perfect other, your perfect opposite – your protector and endangerer. Chance embarking with this other on the greatest of journeys – a search for truths fugitive and imponderable.' A montage of past season moments between Mulder and

Scully fills the screen – recycled and recontextualized, much like fan art. 'For the truest truths', Scully's letter explains, 'are what hold us together, or keep us painfully, desperately apart'. We might read this angsty soliloquy as representative of an organic and inevitable narrative development; however, it also stands to reason that 'shipping' was the only form of audience engagement that had not significantly waned, as ratings dropped, and the series drew to a close.

Conclusion: 'Shippers were heard'

By the end of *The X-Files*' original run, it appeared the 'sentimental fan' had finally received her due. 'Alone' (S8: E19) even named a character after a popular erotic fanfiction writer, Leyla Harrison, who had recently passed away. In many ways, this character is an affectionate tribute to Harrison, and a celebratory portrayal of the show's female fan base – Leyla is sweet, smart and excited to work on *The X-Files*. At the same time, however, the episode lightly parodies the fangirl's obsessive, indeed rabid, preoccupation with the series. Leyla has voraciously read through all of Mulder and Scully's case files and, in the final scene, as she excitedly questions Mulder and Scully from her hospital bed, the two agents, whom we might interpret as stand-ins for the show's producers and creative team, look upon her, bemused and incredulous. Even as the series came to embrace its soapy, melodramatic, angst-riddled romance of the ages, the 'sentimental fan' still needed to laugh at herself.

Nevertheless, her legacy is more than an origin story for one of the first internet ship fandoms – more than the usenet groups, the Haven, Gossamer or the half a dozen *TV Guide* and *US Weekly* covers that are framed on the wall above me as I write. We might observe, in the various 'shipper wars', a reckoning with gendered audience stereotypes and, in the clash between 'rabids' and 'intellishippers', a struggle for legitimacy within masculinized fan cultures vis-à-vis the emerging tradition of quality television. It was not, however, shippers working alone, who troubled the series' genre identity; it was in its promotion, hype and melodramatic form that the series elicited its fans' emotional investment, even as feminized viewing practices were largely excluded and marginalized. Indeed, the shippers' love–hate relationship with the series (and with Carter, who, in contemporary memes and blog posts, is typically assigned the role of the sadistic antagonist) might itself be likened to a toxic and prolonged love affair, as their desires were often teased but rarely validated. But if the lingering online presence of Mulder and Scully's romance and their 'somewhat resolved' sexual tension is any indication, shippers have more than earned their status as 'TRUE fans', offering irrefutable proof that a series can live in their collectively constructed world, just as much as it exists on screen.

References

Boies, T. R. (1996, May 29), alt.tv.x-files [online forum comment]. Available online: https://archive.fo/TmEr4 (accessed 2 January 2022).

Busse, K. (2017), 'Geek Hierarchies, Boundary Policing, and the Gendering of the Good Fan', in K. Busse (ed.), *Framing Fan Fiction: Literary and Social Practices in Fan Fiction Communities*, 177–96, Iowa City: University of Iowa Press.

'Cataloguing the "X-Files' (1997), *Entertainment Weekly*, 7 November. Available online: https://ew.com/article/1997/11/07/cataloging-x-files-websites/ (accessed 12 January 2022).

Click, M. (2009), '"Rabid," "Obsessed," and "Frenzied": Understanding Twilight Fangirls and the Gendered Politics of Fandom', *Flow*. Available online: http://www.flowjournal.org/2009/12/rabid-obsessed-and-frenzied-understanding-twilight-fangirls-and-the-gendered-politics-of-fandom-melissa-click-university-of-missouri (accessed 30 August 2022).

'Closure' (2000), The Haven for the FBI's Most Unwanted, [blog post] Available online: http://web.archive.org/web/20000526104813/http://idealists.simplenet.com/hftfbismu/711new.html (accessed 12 January 2022).

Coppa, F. (2014), 'Writing Bodies in Space: Media Fan Fiction as Theatrical Performance', in K. Hellekson and K. Busse (eds), *The Fanfiction Studies Reader*, 218–37, Iowa City: University of Iowa Press.

Crenshaw, N. (1997), *Scully X-Posed: The Unauthorized Biography of Gillian Anderson*, Rocklin, CA: Prima Publishing.

'Glossary of X-Files Message Board Terms' (2021, 7 December). Available online: http://web.archive.org/web/20011207001523/www.geocities.com/kpcatalia/philes.html (accessed 12 January 2022).

Gray, J. (2010), *Show Sold Separately: Promos, Spoilers, and Other Media Paratexts*, New York: New York University Press.

Handlen, Z. (2013), 'The X-Files/Millennium: "Within"/ "Without"', *The AV Club*, 5 October, Available online: https://www.avclub.com/the-x-files-millennium-within-without-1798178205 (accessed 12 January 2022).

JackBelow (1996, 14 May), alt.tv.x-files [online forum comment]. Available online: https://groups.google.com/g/alt.tv.x-files (accessed 2 January 2022).

Jenkins, H. (2006), *Convergence Culture: Where Old and New Media Collide*, New York: New York University Press.

Joyrich, L. (1996), *Re-viewing Reception: Television, Gender, and Postmodern Culture*, Bloomington: Indiana University Press.

Kackman, M. (2008), 'Quality Television, Melodrama, and Cultural Complexity', *Flow*, 31 October. Available online: https://www.flowjournal.org/2008/10/quality-television-melodrama-and-cultural-complexity%C2%A0michael-kackman%C2%A0%C2%A0university-of-texas-austin%C2%A0%C2%A0/ (accessed 12 January 2022).

Mittell, J. (2004), *Genre and Television: From Cop Shows to Cartoons in American Culture*, New York: Routledge.

'My Problem with the "Relationshippers"' (n.d.) *Fanlore* [wiki]; [https://fanlore.org/wiki/My_problem_with_the_%22relationshippers%22 (accessed 2 January 2022).

'Nicky's Ultimate X-Files Shippers Page' (n.d.). Available online: https://members.tripod.com/nicola_scully/ (accessed 12 January 2022).

Oxley-Johns, K. S. (1996, 13 May), alt.tv.x-files [online forum comment]. Available online: http://groups.google.com/g/alt.tv.xfiles (accessed 2 January 2022).

'Rabid' (2022), *OED Online*. Available online: http//www.oed.com (accessed 2 January 2022).

Rivkat, 'I Should Be Grading' (2006, May 18), [blog post]. Available online: https://rivkat.livejournal.com/128585.html (accessed 12 January 2022).

Scott, S. (2019), *Fake Geek Girls: Fandom, Gender, and the Convergence Culture Industry*, New York: New York University Press.

Williams, L. (2018), 'World and Time: Serial Television Melodrama in America', in C. Gledhill and L. Williams (eds), *Melodrama Unbound: Across History, Media, and National Cultures*, 205–17, New York: Columbia University Press.

15

'The real is out there': Digital games and cyberculture at the threshold of virtual reality in *The X-Files*

Ivan Girina and Andra Ivănescu

In this chapter, we address *The X-Files*' liminal representation and remediation of virtual worlds, looking closely at the series' relationship with digital games. Indeed, a large part of the series' appeal was credited to its genre hybridity (Lavery, Hague and Cartwright 1996), its approach to gender (Willcox and Williams 1996) and its liminal status in relation to American television programming (Reeves, Rodgers and Epstein 1996). Retrospectively, locating itself as a television programme on the cusp on the twenty-first century, *The X-Files*' border status becomes visible through its themes, its aesthetics and its engagement with audiences: as a television series on the verge of pervasive digital culture; in terms of its post-Cold War but pre-9/11 politics and simultaneously paranoid and open-minded navigation of changing technological and sociopolitical domains. The second half of the 1990s was characterized by anxieties about the new millennium, which materializes through a complex relationship with technology in light of the impending 'digital turn', of which video games are an integral part. The turn of the century thus foreshadowed the apocalyptic end of analogue media, and of culture with it, which surfaced in public discourses through the doom of information technology brought about by the 'Y2K problem' also known as 'millennium bug'. In this context, the liminality of *The X-Files* emerges through its ambiguous relationship with digital technologies that entangle bodies (social and physical ones) and consciousness, politics and identity, information and knowledge, undoing Cartesian subject/object dichotomies that are destabilized in both posthuman discourses (Hayles 2004: 314) as well as postmodern approaches (Stephanson and Jameson 1989: 7).

This chapter particularly looks at video games and virtual worlds as a salient nexus wherein these domains coalesce via *The X-Files*' depiction and remediation of games and virtuality in 'Kill Switch' (S5: E11) and 'First Person Shooter' (S7: E13), as well as *The X-Files Game* (HyperBole Studios 1998). Together with the game, these episodes display not only *The X-Files*' awareness of cyberspace and cyber-culture, but also its liminal position as 'cybertext' (Aarseth 1997) in itself, via its game adaptation and its relationship with fandom. Such cyber-discourses allow the post-human question to emerge prominently across the episodes: firstly, 'Kill Switch' depicts the Frankensteinian fantasy of a techno-body assemblage realized in the merging of organic and inorganic life within an experimental AI that can absorb human consciousness into cyberspace; secondly, in 'First Person Shooter' the 'ghost in the machine' trope defies fantasies of mastery in digital environments as a gaming AI gone rogue kills the players, stripping them of agency over the cybertext and subverting its structure of power. At the same time, *The X-Files* is *remediated* across multiple platforms, participating in the postmodern intertextual and increasingly self-referential explosion that characterizes media culture of the 1990s. In fact, around the same time of release of these episodes, media scholars Jay David Bolter and Richard Grusin's influential concept of *Remediation* (2003) traces a 'genealogy' of new media through the 'refashioning' of older technologies and vice versa, establishing a growing network of aesthetic relationships with each other. *The X-Files Game* promises to provide the user with power over its text, allowing control over the characters and plots, delivering the medium specific pleasure of 'agency' (Murray 2017: 123). The introduction of interactivity, particularly the agency of the player to make choices within the game, poses questions of canon and authenticity and furthers existing audience manipulation practices over the text. In turn, such practices introduce questions of authorship that echo with the series' preoccupation around the liminality of knowledge (articulated in categories such as known/unknown and truth/conspiracy), which are here translated in the tension between the real and the virtual.

The concept of liminality was initially proposed in 1967 by anthropologist Victor Turner, who used it to describe the transition between states within social rituals. The concept was later adopted to signal the similarly unstable character of psychological, social and cultural boundaries within digital media, and its porous material and immaterial borders. Margo Buchanan-Oliver and Angela Cruz notice how ideas of liminality largely inform cyberpunk cultural production and post-human theories contesting human/ non-human dichotomies:

> Liminality refers to a hybrid condition characterised by ambiguity, indeterminacy, contradiction, incoherence, and blurring of boundaries. Within popular culture, the genre of science fiction sees classic literary texts (e.g., Gibson's (1984) 'Neuromancer', Asimov's (1967) 'I, Robot', Huxley's (1955) 'Brave New World') and popular films (e.g., 'The Terminator', 'Blade Runner', and 'The Matrix') representing a liminal vision of human–machine interactions alongside their psychological and socio-cultural repercussions. (2011: 287)

In what follows, we analyse *The X-Files* through its liminal position within digital culture drawing three axes of investigation: (1) the series' ambivalent representation of the *cyberspace* and cyberpunk culture, as well as its own nature as a *cybertext* in the game; (2) the tension between gender and technology and the post-human representations of the *cyborg* and the *hacker* and (3) the oscillation between *immediacy* (the desire for proximity to the virtual worlds) and *hypermediacy* (the foregrounding of interfaces and technology mediating the virtual experience), both in the episodes and the game. We argue that these three trajectories of enquiry emphasize how the liminal remediation of the virtual in *The X-Files* fits within its aesthetics of epistemological crisis and the series' critique of power relationships between authority and knowledge, ultimately questioning the very notion of the 'real'.

Cyberspace and cybertext

The blurred boundaries between digital and physical environments and the dangers of human–machine relationships are explored in the two episodes of *The X-Files* examined here. These are expressed in thematic tensions between reality and virtuality: physical spaces and cyberspace; human consciousness and Artificial Intelligence (AI); and control over technology and being controlled by technology. In 'Kill Switch', a former game developer helps Mulder and Scully survive crossing paths with a rogue AI and enter an oppressive virtual world. In 'First Person Shooter', the protagonists find themselves at the site of a crime that centres around a video game and enter another virtual reality to stop a series of murders perpetrated by an in-game character. The anxieties expressed here shift focus from science fiction conspiracy theories about otherworldly alien threats that constitute the generic makeup of the series to cyberpunk paranoid relationships with virtual worlds. In *Deny All Knowledge*, editors David Lavery, Angela Hague and Marla Cartwright underline this generic liminality, whereby *The*

X-Files' 'has experimented – televisually, narratologically, semiotically – with the medium in innovative ways' (1996: 3). For the authors, the series' aesthetic of knowledge denial – which infiltrates the episodes' plots with social paranoia, suspicion of authority and the unattainability of 'truth' – is foregrounded in the opening credits by the use of UFO stock imagery described as having a 'hazy, imprecise, even dreamy quality that underscores its possible unreliability' (1996: 7). Allison Graham adds that if '*The X-Files* is overtly indebted to 1970s conspiracy films, however, it owes its soul to the science fiction films of the 1950s', further noting that while 'the splicing of the two genres might seem genetically impossible, for their politics are hardly compatible ... one is undoubtedly the progenitor of the other' (1996: 59). 'Kill Switch' and 'First Person Shooter' draw on these ideas, but move them into a different domain, shifting from a physical reality wherein government agencies impede knowledge and exert a form of collective control, to virtual realities where individual agency remains an unfulfilled promise. Here the meaning of 'agency' as the possibility of 'deputizing' action (the agency representing a subject) or 'taking' it (a subject exerting agency) brings forth the tension between the virtual and the real (Girina and Jung 2019: 6). The commentary underlying these episodes is no less political, but its themes and broader concerns draw on a cyberpunk tradition of which the respective screenplay writers – William Gibson and Tom Maddox – are pre-eminent members.

The cyberpunk aesthetic is not immediately evident in the two episodes – there are no bodily augmentations, the 'high tech' and 'low life' do not merge in busy neon-lit streets, and the megacorporations are not the main antagonists. After all, despite some of the futuristic technology, the episodes are not set in the near future. Nevertheless, spectres of the future to come are clear. The role of corporations is not as explicit and important as it is in this genre (Csicsery-Ronay 1988: 275), but their presence informs much of what occurs in the two episodes. Mulder describes Gelman, the creator of the AI in 'Kill Switch', as a 'folk hero' for his technical prowess but also for disappearing 'on the eve of the deal that was supposed to set him up as another Bill Gates' and thus rejecting the corporate world. At the same time, in 'First Person Shooter' the Lone Gunmen are defensive of their contribution as consultants on the game, with Frohike underlining that they are not 'major profit participants' in the corporation. Emergent corporatism and surveillance culture are constructed through the remediation of satellite and CCTV camera footage in 'Kill Switch', also signalled in 'First Person Shooter' through the bureaucratic jargon of intellectual properties, non-disclosure agreements and investors' accountability, making evident the rejection of any utopian vision of cyber-socialism.

The visual aesthetic of the genre is similarly present, but not as pronounced as in films of the era and shows an evolving visual interpretation of post-humanism. 'Kill Switch' draws on the tradition of cyberspace through its discourses of surveillance culture and the focus on the materiality of the apparatus: masks, cables, the physical integration of body and machine as expressed both in literary cyberpunk like *Neuromancer* (Gibson 1984) as well as in films such as *Nirvana* (1997), *Johnny Mnemonic* (1995) and *The Matrix* (1999). Instead, 'First Person Shooter' channels the aesthetic of the cybertext characteristic of video games, in which the digital world has been co-opted by the companies that commodify it for the gamer as consumer: the gritty chrome materiality of cyberspace becomes the sleek polished monochrome of virtual reality. What remains unchanged from the broader cyberpunk tradition, however, is the post-humanist exploration of the liminality between human and machine, and its relationship to artificial intelligence. Csicsery-Ronay argues that this 'rich thesaurus of metaphors linking the organic and the electronic' is one of the main characteristics of the genre (1988: 274). This becomes central to both episodes, wherein the two AI entities are complex loci of identification and ontological consideration, but also to the game, which implicitly configures a techno-human assemblage between cybertext and player.

The centrality of cyber-culture in discourses around gaming is evidenced by the metaphoric language of the *cybertext* and the *holodeck*, which in 1997 are proposed respectively by game scholars Espen Aarseth and Janet Murray to describe emerging digital textual forms, particularly those of digital games as medium characterized by 'interactivity'. While the concept of cybertext points at the materiality of these textual forms (both on semiotic and physical levels) and their presence in the world, the holodeck captures ideas of virtuality and seamless transition across spaces focusing on the users' movement towards or within the digital world. If Aarseth emphasizes the ontology of cybertexts not as 'texts', but rather as 'textual machines' (1997: 22), then Murray argues that the holodeck experience is defined by the qualities of *immersion* within the virtual world and the *agency* afforded to the user. Describing the productive tensions surrounding digital media in the 1990s, Murray states that 'one of our main activities, as creators and audience, involves testing the boundaries of the *liminal* world' (2017: 102–3, emphasis added).

Scholars have acknowledged *The X-Files*' impact on internet culture as contributing to the rise of 'cyberliteracy' (Trainor 2004). Here, audience 'literacy' is not constrained by the 'authority' of the text or by its 'originality' as source of cultural value, making *The X-Files* a primary object of early online fandom (Chin 2013; Clerc 1996; Howell 2000; Wooley 2001). In this sense, cybertextuality is one of the threads weaving the relationship between *The X-Files* and digital games, as the 'original text' of the episode is only a virtual instantiation among the many made possible by the cybertextual machine, that of the show itself which is manipulated by the fans. In *Cybertext*, Aarseth argues for a semiotic break in *ergodic* textual forms (from the I Ching to crosswords and video games) which require non-trivial efforts in order to be traversed (1997: 1). Aarseth's theory addresses those textual objects requiring user interaction to be performed, echoing the crisis of authority and authoriality in postmodern culture. *The X-Files* is symptomatic of such onto-epistemological instability that characterizes trends in contemporary philosophy, from the rejection of human/non-human divides in Donna Haraway's post-humanist 'Cyborg Manifesto' (2016), to the undoing of subject/object ontological hierarchies in Ian Bogost's proposition of an *Alien Phenomenology* (2012), in which the 'alien' becomes an epistemological metaphor for the 'real' nature of objects or, rather, their unattainability.

The X-Files Game further pushes the liminality of the cybertext through its interactivity and the (illusion of) agency, which offers control not only over the virtual world of the game but also over *The X-Files* narration. In line with the interactive movie genre (Wolf 2008: 85), the game uses pre-recorded video featuring many characters from the series and numerous 'Easter eggs' referencing popular episodes, allowing the player to: talk to Scully and rescue Mulder, pick up Morley cigarette butts and conduct interrogations, find Jose Chung's *From Outer Space* and consult the Lone Gunmen. At the same time, the defining low interactivity of the genre (Perron 2008) limits the actions of the player as well as the virtual world's responses to these actions: while there are different ways in which characters can respond, and a variety of ways in which the player can fail (e.g. by getting the player-character Agent Willmore dismissed, or through the death of Mulder), the game presents a particularly linear and relatively short 'Seven Days' plot. Due to its technical and design constraints, the promise of agency is never truly fulfilled by the game, mirroring the two episodes in which virtual worlds are viewed through the lens of cyberpunk. On the one hand, 'Kill Switch' demystifies the promise of social agency embedded in digital technology and embodied by the AI's virtual utopia. On the other hand, 'First Person Shooter' reflects the aesthetic pleasure of agency in ludic virtual environments and its nature as illusory (Girina and Jung 2019), fractured by the uncanny AI claiming the players' lives. Ultimately, like the game, the episodes critically engage with the relationship between human and non-human agency – the female NPC (non-player character) known as Maytreya (a variation of the Buddhist avatar Maitreya) in 'First Person Shooter' and the unnamed AI in 'Kill Switch'. As Maytreya declares while executing her first victim, 'This is my game.'

Cyborgs and hackers

According to Csicsery-Ronay, cyberpunk is 'allied with video games' as 'the vanguard white male art of the age' (1988: 267). The male-dominated discourses of both episodes under consideration are evident, but ultimately provide domains of transgression, also expressed through women's relationships with digital technologies throughout *The X-Files*.

The technological and the digital are seen as domains of authority, both governmental and alien. While alien technology is presented as incredibly advanced and able to disrupt the 'biological' and the 'technical', government information technology is part of a system of bureaucratic control, best exemplified through Scully's reports to her superiors early in the series. As Lisa Parks notes, 'Scully's law enforcement power is constructed more through her connection to information technologies than through her resilience to violence. Rather than being a cop on the go like Mulder, Scully is a cyborg detective who works at the computer interface' (1996: 128).

Parks's remarks echo Donna Haraway's conceptualization of the cyborg as an entity that is not only post-human but also belonging to a 'postgender world' of feminist possibility and radical change. Scully's liminal position as feminist cyborg, empowered by the integration with technology, grants her the higher ground of science and knowledge across the early seasons of the show, which is echoed by the two female characters in the episodes who rebel not only against patriarchal systems but the very physical world to which they belong. In contrast, Mulder's office is often represented as low-tech and wilfully analogue: filing cabinets and yellowed folders in disorganized piles, the famous 'I Want to Believe' poster, a pin-board full of notes and images. This position of masculinity as analogue is also reflected in *The X-Files Game*, where the only prominent female character, police officer Mary Astadourian, compliments Agent Willmore's use of a mobile phone saying 'I love a man who's good with technology.' This assertion of technologies – and particularly digital technologies – as non-readily masculine speaks to a time of digital transition but also of tensions between traditional views of masculinity and geek masculinities, which are so pervasive today. The Lone Gunmen occupy this liminal position, in that they publish their eponymous zine in analogue form, while they still have profound connections with the hacking counterculture. Brendan Keogh highlights how the figure of the 'hacker' emerges across computer and gaming culture recuperating forms of masculinity through its assertion of power over technology (2018: 176). In contrast with Haraway's feminist cyborg, in which bodies and technologies are merged without hierarchies, the hacker asserts masculine power through technological mastery.

At the same time, both episodes present this mastery as precarious. While men are credited with creating the AI in 'Kill Switch' and the game in 'First Person Shooter', reflecting an increasingly corporate vision of geek masculinity mediated in both cases by the Lone Gunmen, both programmer Donald Gelman and the designer Ivan Martinez are ultimately victims of their own hubris. The two men overestimate their control over the virtual worlds and their agency over their creations. Instead, it is the two female developers who, like cyber-goth heroines, mediate between the physical world and the virtual world. For Csicsery-Ronay, 'cyberpunk is fundamentally ambivalent about the breakdown of the distinctions between human and machine, between personal consciousness and machine consciousness' (1988: 275). This post-humanist view is reflected in both episodes as the rogue AIs do not just play 'monster-of-the-week' but exist as extensions of the two women. In 'Kill Switch,' Invisigoth justifies the murderous actions of the AI and desires to merge her own consciousness with it, whereas in 'First Person Shooter', Maytreya is created by Phoebe and exists as an embodiment of her desires and her frustration. Both cyborgs reflect the attitudes of their creators, responding to the gendered attitudes of society. The unnamed AI in 'Kill Switch' is ambiguous in terms of gender: it uses a male voice to lure members of the criminal underworld to murder its creator, but it is implicitly framed as female when Gelman whispers 'You won't feel a thing' as he inserts a CD containing a virus disguised as a romantic song (The Platter's 'Twilight Time'). Maytreya, however, is explicitly gendered from the beginning. Even before she appears on screen, her presence is signalled through the sound of her heels clicking on the floor. Her physical appearance, sexualized through the iconography of bondage, is modelled after an exotic dancer named Jade Blue Afterglow, herself object of the male gaze of both police officers and Mulder in a later scene.

The gendering of the AI in 'First Person Shooter' can be read as a commentary on sexualized video game female characters, whose positions as 'sexy, strong, and secondary' persist to this day. Their degree of sexualization is often directly correlated with their in-game capability, drawing on long-standing femme-fatale archetypes (Lynch et al. 2016: 15). The nurses that appear in the virtual world created by the AI in 'Kill Switch' also play with these tropes. The blonde, heavily made-up women that care for, seduce and ultimately try to manipulate Mulder and initiate a 'cat fight' with a digital Scully play into stereotypical sexual fantasies. These fantasies are either suggested to pertain to Mulder himself, or to the AI's perception of normative heterosexual desire. While the under-representation (Cassell and Jenkins 1998; Williams et al. 2009) and misrepresentation (Dietz 1998; Lynch et al. 2016; Phillips 2021) of women in video games have been studied extensively in the field of game studies, it is important to note that these characters are often sites of identification for both women and queer players (Kennedy 2002; Macallum-Stewart 2014; Shaw 2014). Similarly, the AIs act as sites of possibility for the two female characters who best understand them: Invisigoth and Phoebe. Their relationships with the virtual world and the AI are explicitly framed in contrast with the physical world, which they find inadequate or insufficient. Through cyberpunk-mirrored shades, they find their monstrosity reflected in each other and, like Scully, they are both monsters and cyborgs. However, while Scully 'structures a hermeneutic relationship within the feminine that positions the female scientist as confronting a feminized monstrosity located ultimately within her own body' (Parks 1996: 133), Invisigoth and Phoebe move beyond the female (human) body to actualize their cyborg selves in virtual worlds.

These complex gendered discourses are mirrored throughout the series, particularly in the relationship between Mulder and Scully. Wilcox and Williams note that, 'on its most basic level, the program appears to advocate an ideology in which Mulder and Scully are free to invert traditional male/female characterizations ... The two characters are presented as gender-liminal, moving back and forth across the border of traditionally accepted gender patterns' (1996: 99).

Scully's alignment with science and Mulder's with intuition are essential to their gendered representation, as is their partnership. Mulder is occasionally rescued by Scully – as happens in both episodes discussed here – somewhat addressing the 'damsel in distress' trope also widely used in video games. At the same time, throughout the series it is Mulder's view that is privileged, as 'ironically, their frequent sex role reversals result in Scully's investigative gaze being disempowered'. This is because 'time and again, Mulder sees evidence of the supernatural that Scully, by the structure of the episode, is disallowed from seeing' (Wilcox and Williams 1996: 99).

The audience alignment with Mulder's (metaphorical) male point of view is taken even further in *The X-files Game*, where the player's (literal) viewpoint is framed through FBI Special Agent Craig Willmore's first-person perspective. Moreover, the game's 'UberVariables' system also reflects Mulder's world view. The system entails monitoring the player's dialogue choices and the attitude they represent in terms of 'demeanour towards certain characters in the game' as well as the player-character's 'psychological state' (Barba 1998: 20). The three variables are, paranoia (that follows 'the ultimate X-Maxim "Trust No One"'), loss (that focuses on Willmore's fatherhood and divorce), and the x-track (that focuses on the player-character's 'willingness to believe in the supernatural'). While the latter is described in the manual as an option whereby 'your Willmore' can be aligned with either 'a Mulder-esque true believer' or 'a Scully-like sceptic' it soon becomes clear that the viewpoint and belief system mirrored in the game are those of Mulder, through his own paranoia, the loss of his sister Samantha and his propensity for the paranormal. Not only is Scully's mode of scientific enquiry ultimately unavailable to the player, but a closer alignment with Mulder's traits will reveal more game content, such as disclosing that they are being followed or divulging more of the plot (drawing on the series' myth-arc).

Remediating virtual worlds through interfaces: Immediacy and hypermediacy

The opening scene of 'First Person Shooter' displays the complex relationship that film and television establish with digital media, and particularly the representation of virtual environments and technologies. The shots convey what Bolter and Grusin call a desire for 'transparent immediacy' (2000: 21) that characterizes the experience of digital interfaces. This is the desire to bring the mediated object close to the audience, without filters, according to a mimetic drive for which the virtual world becomes perceptually indistinguishable from the physical one. As the camera frames a group of three men 'gearing up' inside an elevator, a display counts down to 'level 1' informing the audience of its descending trajectory, actualizing Murray's influential metaphor of 'immersion' as a distinctive trait of digital environments (2017: 98). The descent to lower levels materializes the lowering of awareness and the transition from the physical to a 'deeper' psychological reality. In the passage through the elevator, the interface 'erases itself, so that the user is no longer aware of confronting a medium, but instead stands in an immediate relationship to the contents of that medium'. There is no formal signalling in the transition between the physical and the digital world, prompting the spectator to experience the virtual reality as seamless and sustaining the effect of an '"interfaceless" interface' (Bolter and Grusin 2000: 23–4).

The military tropes represented in the scene recall those of the first person shooter, which have become signifiers of the genre in the iconography of digital games at the cinema. In this sense, the scene seems to anticipate and inform both in style and tone sequences in films such as *The Edge of Tomorrow* (2014), which similarly introduce the arrival of the protagonist to the battlefield by displaying the military troop getting ready on an aircraft carrier. The iconography of militarization, in fact, exceeds the boundaries of the first-person-shooter genre to embrace the industrial formation of gaming as a whole through what scholars have termed the 'military-entertainment complex', signalling the confluence of competitive neoliberal market and warfare aesthetics within the production of digital entertainment industries (Dyer-Whiteford and de Peuter 2009).

The camera cuts to the players' vitals displayed on a computer screen: heart rate, blood pressure and respiration quantify the psychology and physiology of the virtual experience in the attempt to control and contain its liminality, showcasing its monitoring via scientific apparatus. Such aestheticization of game user experience (GUX) is flipped in *The X-Files Game*, which uses UberVariables as part of the game mechanics to convey the illusion of human-like psychological states simulated by the machine and performed through its digital actors. Nevertheless, while 'First Person Shooter' displays the user vitals as signifier of the gameplay 'realism', *The X-Files Game* hides UberVariables behind dialogue trees (dialogue options designed to affect subsequent events) to naturalize the game mechanics, fostering the mimetic immersion in the diegesis of the series. Both the episode and the game 'simulate' the tension between knowable (GUX and UberVariables) and unknowable (the psychological experience of the players in the episode and the liveness of the characters in the game) that informs the conflict between rationality and irrationality through the entire series. In 'First Person Shooter', post-production effects are used to mark the transition from the 'virtual' to the 'real' in the form of audiovisual noise that interrupts the camera's state of immersion. The death of the first player is followed by an acute whistling sound and a visual flickering, as the photographic image is fragmented into a mosaic of colourful prisms fading to white, conveying the interruption of the data flow through a visual 'death' by overexposure. Similarly, Mulder's realization of being trapped inside the 'Kill Switch' simulation is revealed by the camera through the 'glitching' of Scully's virtual clone and the flickering between her photographic image and her digital polygonal model. In the episodes, the camera is an integral part of the interface, what game scholar Michael Nitsche terms the 'performing camera' of contemporary 3D games (2008: 112): a liminal entity providing the audience with access to the virtual world and information about the experience of the characters within it. The oscillation between visibility and invisibility of the interface in the episodes also reflects game design's preoccupation with the immediacy of access to the virtual world via a 'transparent' camera interface, negotiated against the functionality of overlay buttons and menus that provide clear affordances to the user but might impact the immersive aesthetic experience (Jørgensen 2013).

Moreover, a tension between the immateriality and materiality of digital worlds traverses the two episodes. On the one hand, 'Kill Switch' foregrounds the materiality of its hardware apparatus, appealing to tropes of cyberpunk culture that connect human and technological bodies. On the other hand, the gaming environment in 'First Person Shooter' underlines the immateriality of its software using of low-fi special effects and simple editing techniques like explosions and jump cuts that emphasize the ontology of disappearing digital assets. Nevertheless, the experience of the 'virtual' here is not only represented as exclusively 'digital', but instead through photographic artifice also appeals to a liminal 'cinema of attractions' between analogue effects and digital technologies (Strauven 2006). In fact, the episode does not forsake photographic indexicality which instead grounds the materiality of the gameworld, remediated in the iconography of older weaponry such as the Flintlock gun and the katana used by the rogue AI Maitreya.

The investment in material discourses and its conflicting relationship with the digital is also central to the aesthetic of *The X-Files Game* both on visual and mechanical levels. The generic liminality of the game is testified by its hybrid status as an 'interactive movie' and 'point-and-click adventure': the former defined by the use of pre-rendered full motion video sequences and dialogue trees, while the latter is characterized through its concatenated puzzles and investigation systems. The material discourse of the game is twofold: firstly, the indexical remediation through 'live action' footage grounds it within the same space inhabited by Scully and Mulder in the show;

secondly, its epistemological scientism is conveyed through game mechanics that require the player to find, analyse and use material evidence. These two dimensions (the visual and the ludic ones) are not always compatible, creating a paradoxical hyperreal but uncanny experience, leading to 'pixel hunting' moments during which the identification of objects within the environment is hindered by the density of the visual interface in the attempt to achieve photographic immediacy. For example, on 'Day One' the player must investigate a warehouse where Mulder and Scully were last seen, to retrieve evidence in the form of a bullet embedded in a wooden post. Here the goal is obstructed by the complexity of navigating photorealistic 'adjacent spaces displayed one at the time' (Wolf 1997: 16) with a 2D interface, and the difficulty of identifying the silhouette of objects within the dense and shadowy mise en scène.

At the same time, the hypermediation of computer technologies in the game via mobile and desktop devices aids the player navigation of the virtual world on several levels. For instance, Agent Willmore's PDA (Personal Digital Assistant) allows the player to move between locations, read emails to gather information and keep track of progress through pre-written notes that become available on the device. Computers found in the diegetic space also allow the player to search databases checking licence plates or matching fingerprints, expanding the narrative of the game by referencing *The X-Files* universe through files and articles. Hence, the computers and PDA offer more expansive and functional exploration than that available in the representational space of the diegesis, creating a tension between the photorealistic but limited cyberspace framed by the camera and the expanded digital cybertext accessed through these devices. Indeed, the game embodies the postmodern transition from linear narratives to 'database narratives' (Manovich 2002: 199): the story emerges from the recombinatory quality of the information, which is enabled by the remediation of *The X-Files* from text to cybertext. Nevertheless, the cybertextual logic is not always coherently attached to in-game technology, occasionally recuperating the linear aesthetic of non-digital media forms by linking narrative and ludic progression. For example, a predetermined cut scene is triggered on 'Day Five', whereby the Lone Gunmen share GPS data containing information on the location of Mulder via a videocall on a diegetic computer, establishing a mise-en-abyme of an interface within the interface. Here, the game progress is not achieved through the player's interaction with the database cybertext, but through the narrative exposition delivered by the Lone Gunmen as *deus ex machina*, providing essential information that ultimately leads to the rescue of Mulder and the game's climax.

While genre-busting action and even horror moments occur throughout the game, and particularly on 'Day Six' when Agent Willmore needs to collaborate with Scully to rescue (once again) Mulder, the game's tendency to draw on much of the series' aesthetics ultimately leads to conservative moments of narrative linearity and the remediation of the filmic interface that strips the digital cybertext of its defining interactivity.

Conclusion

The representation and remediation of the digital space encapsulates *The X-Files*' liminality between utopian promises of unlimited knowledge and cyberpunk information disillusionment, enacting the search not only for what is 'true' but also for what is 'real'. The liminality of virtual spaces in the episodes is reflected on an aesthetic level by the collapsing borders between the material/physical world and the immaterial/digital one, and on a thematic level by the merging of synthetic life and organic death. While the AI of 'First Person Shooter' comes alive within the digital gamespace killing players 'for real', that of 'Kill Switch' extends its reach beyond the boundaries of the cyberspace deploying satellite military technology to eliminate any human threats. The latter also provides Invisigoth with the gift of immortality by merging her consciousness with that of the machine. Conversely, while Agents Willmore and Mulder can be killed in *The X-Files Game*, 'death' is only temporary as the player can use the save/load game feature to bring them back, allowing for different choices, different actions and an altogether different instantiation of the ludic cybertext. Here, the lines of life and death can be crossed more than once, short-circuited by the blurring of the digital material/immaterial boundaries.

In 'First Person Shooter', the two game designers reject the material nature of the crime scene, condescendingly addressing Mulder and Scully to explain the 'virtual' nature of the gameplay experience as 'intensely real, but harmless'. Designer Ivan Martinez proudly describes the technological apparatus of the game: 'Stun suit. See, it's rigged with paint for wounds and kill shots. It's total bleeding-edge technology.' Responding to Scully's sarcastic inspection of the bleeding body, he continues:

Ivan: He's dead. I got it.
Mulder: Who was he playing against?
Ivan: Against the game. You waste the cyberthugs before they waste you. It's all about body count. But they're computer-generated images running on a projector. It all happens in the game space.
Phoebe: It's a total digital environment. Nothing's real. It's all virtual.

The techno-ludic language employed by the designers emphasizes the immaterial nature of the experience in the 'gamespace'. At the same time, the metaphor of the 'bleeding-edge' technology encapsulates the unease surrounding the sealed character of the virtual experience, foreshadowing its potential to violently interfere in the real world. Beyond media panics attached to the idea of in-game violence translating into violent behaviours outside of the game (Faltin 2015), the metaphor suggests more profound societal anxieties around the nature of these worlds as not truly separate but, rather, liminal.

The 'game space' is used by the designer as a ludic jargon and shorthand to signal the separateness of the 'virtual' world from the 'real' one, reminiscent of theories of play that locate it within a sealed 'magic circle'. Nevertheless, as pointed out by scholars in game studies, such edges are never impenetrable and do not fully separate it from the real world (Consalvo 2009). Indeed, as argued by media philosopher McKenzie Wark (2009), the 'gamespace' is not a fearful projection of the anxiety surrounding the real-world conditions, but instead describes our relationship with the material conditions of living within late capitalism, particularly under the influence of neoliberal and military rhetoric:

> Whether gamespace is more real or not than some other world is not the question. That even in its unreality it may have real effects on other worlds is. Games are not representations of this world. They are more like allegories of a world made over as gamespace. They encode the abstract principles upon which decisions about the realness of this or that world are decided. (Wark 2009: 14)

Wark's theorization of the gamespace as 'allegorithm' reifies the allegory of gaming through the pervasive algorithmic materiality of contemporary information technology, deconstructing the dichotomy between the 'virtual' and the 'real' and highlighting instead the complex relationship between the planes of 'virtual reality' and 'physical reality' which are now entangled in a computerized socio-economic network (2009: 42). *The X-Files* embodies the epistemological crisis that in the 1990s merges postmodern concerns around 'the lack of truth' with cyberpunk anxieties towards 'the real'. The true liminality of *The X-Files* then is its resilience in the belief that there is still a truth to be found in the virtual world of hyperreality. To paraphrase *The X-Files*' notorious tagline: 'The real is out there.'

References

Aarseth, E. J. (1997), *Cybertext: Perspectives on Ergodic Literature*, Baltimore, MD: JHU Press.
Barba, R. (1998), *The X-Files: Prima's Official Strategy Guide*, Rocklin, CA: Prima.
Bogost, I. (2012), *Alien Phenomenology, or, What It's Like to Be a Thing*, Minneapolis: University of Minnesota Press.

Bolter, J. D., and R. Grusin (2000), *Remediation: Understanding New Media*, Cambridge, MA: The MIT Press.

Buchanan-Oliver, M., and A. Cruz (2011), 'Discourses of Technology Consumption: Ambivalence, Fear, and Liminality', in R. Ahluwalia, T. L. Chartrand and R. K. Ratner (eds), *NA – Advances in Consumer Research*, 287–91, Duluth, MN: Association for Consumer Research.

Cassell, J., and H. Jenkins (1998), *From Barbie to Mortal Kombat: Gender and Video Games*, Cambridge, MA: The MIT Press.

Chin, B. (2013), 'The Fan–Media Producer Collaboration: How Fan Relationships Are Managed in a Post-Series X-Files Fandom', *Science Fiction Film and Television*, 6 (1): 87–99.

Clerc, S. J. (1996), 'DDEB, GATB, MPPB and Ratboy: *The X-Files*' Media Fandom: Online and Off', in D. Lavery, A. Hague and M. Cartwright (eds), *Deny All Knowledge: Reading The X-Files*, 36–51, London: Faber and Faber.

Consalvo, M. (2009), 'There Is No Magic Circle', *Games and Culture*, 4 (4): 408–17.

Csicsery-Ronay, I. (1988), 'Cyberpunk and Neuromanticism,', *Mississippi Review*, 16 (2 and 3): 266–78.

Dietz, T. L. (1998). 'An Examination of Violence and Gender Role Portrayals in Video Games: Implications for Gender Socialization and Aggressive Behavior', *Sex Roles*, 38 (5 and 6): 425–42.

Dyer-Whiteford, N., and G. De Peuter (2009), *Games of Empire: Global Capitalism and Video Games*, Minneapolis: University of Minnesota Press.

The Edge of Tomorrow (2014) [Film], Dir. Doug Lima, USA: Warner Bros.

Faltin, K. (2015), 'Analysing Game Controversies: A Historical Approach to Moral Panics and Digital Games', in T. Mortensen, J. Linderoth and A. M. L. Brown (eds), *The Dark Side of Gameplay*, 15–32, London: Routledge.

Gibson, W. (1984), *Neuromancer*, New York: Ace.

Girina, I., and B. Jung (2019), 'Would You Kindly? The Interdisciplinary Trajectories of Video Game Agency', *G/A/M/E Games as Art, Media, Entertainment*, 8 (1): 5–28.

Graham, A. (1996), '"Are You Now or Have You Ever Been?" Conspiracy Theory and *The X-Files*', in D. Lavery, A. Hague and M. Cartwright (eds), *Deny All Knowledge: Reading* The X-Files, 52–62, London: Faber & Faber.

Haraway, D. J. ([1984] 2016), *A Cyborg Manifesto*, Minneapolis: University of Minnesota Press.

Haraway, D. J. (2016), *Manifestly Haraway*, Minneapolis: University of Minnesota Press.

Hayles, N. K. (2004), 'Refiguring the Posthuman', *Comparative Literature Studies*, 41 (3), 311–16.

Howell, A. (2000), 'The X-Files, X-Philes and X-Philia: Internet Fandom as a Site of Convergence', *Media International Australia*, 97 (1): 137–49.

Johnny Mnemonic (1995), [Film] Dir. Robert Longo, USA: Tristar Pictures.

Jorgensen, K. (2013), *Gameworld Interfaces*, Cambridge, MA: The MIT Press.

Kennedy, H. W. (2002), 'Lara Croft: Feminist Icon or Cyberbimbo? On the Limits of Textual Analysis', *Game Studies*, 2 (2). Available online: http://www.gamestudies.org/0202/kennedy/ (accessed 11 February 2023).

Keogh, B. (2018), *A Play of Bodies: How We Perceive Videogames*, Cambridge, MA: The MIT Press.

Lavery, D., A. Hague and M. Cartwright (eds) (1996), *Deny All Knowledge: Reading* The X-Files, Syracuse, NY: Syracuse University Press.

Lavery, D., A. Hague and M. Cartwright (1996), 'Introduction: Generation X – *The X-Files* and The Cultural Moment', in D. Lavery, A. Hague and M. Cartwright (eds), *Deny All Knowledge: Reading* The X-Files, 1–21, London: Faber & Faber.

Lynch, T., J. E. Tompkins, I. I. van Driel and N. Fritz (2016), 'Sexy, Strong, and Secondary: A Content Analysis of Female Characters in Video Games across 31 Years', *Journal of Communication*, 66 (4): 564–84.

MacCallum-Stewart, E. (2014), '"Take That, Bitches!" Refiguring Lara Croft in Feminist Game Narratives', *Game Studies*, 14 (2). Available online: http://gamestudies.org/1402/articles/maccallumstewart (accessed 11 February 2023).

Manovich, L. (2002), *The Language of New Media*, Cambridge, MA: The MIT Press.

The Matrix (1999), [Film] Dir. The Wachowskis, USA: Warner Bros.

Murray, J. H. (2017 [1997]), *Hamlet on the Holodeck, Updated Edition: The Future of Narrative in Cyberspace*, Cambridge, MA: The MIT Press.

Nirvana (1997), [Film] Dir. Gabriele Salvatores, Italy: Dimension Films.

Nitsche, M. (2008), *Video Game Spaces: Image, Play, and Structure in 3D Worlds*, Cambridge, MA: The MIT Press.

Parks, L. (1996), 'Special Agent or Monstrosity? Finding the Feminine in *The X-Files*', in D. Lavery, A. Hague and M. Cartwright (eds), *Deny All Knowledge: Reading The X-Files*, 121–34, London: Faber & Faber.

Perron, B. (2008), 'Genre Profile: Interactive Movies', in M. J. P. Wolf (ed.), *The Video Game Explosion: A History from PONG to PlayStation and beyond*, 127–33, Westport, CT: Greenwood-Heinemann Publishing.

Phillips, A. (2021), *Gamer Trouble: Feminist Confrontations in Digital Culture*, New York: New York University Press.

Reeves, J. L., M. C. Rodgers and M. Epstein (1996), 'Rewriting Popularity', in D. Lavery, A. Hague and M. Cartwright (eds), *Deny All Knowledge: Reading The X-Files*, 22–35, London: Faber & Faber.

Shaw, A. (2014), *Gaming at the Edge: Sexuality and Gender at the Margins of Gamer Culture*, Minneapolis: University of Minnesota Press.

Stephanson, A., and F. Jameson (1989), 'Regarding Postmodernism – A Conversation with Fredric Jameson', *Social Text*, 17 (autumn): 3–30.

Strauven, W. (2006), *The Cinema of Attractions Reloaded*, Amsterdam: Amsterdam University Press.

Trainor, J. S. (2004), 'Critical Cyberliteracy: Reading and Writing *The X-Files*', in J. Mahiri (ed.), *What They Don't Learn in School: Literacy in the Lives of Urban Youth*, 123–38, New York: Peter Lang.

Turner, V. (1967), *The Forest of Symbols: Aspects of Ndembu Ritual*, Ithaca, NY: Cornell University Press.

Wark, M. (2009), *Gamer Theory*, Cambridge, MA: Harvard University Press.

Williams, D., N. Martin, M. Consalvo and J. D. Ivory (2009), 'The Virtual Census: Representations of Gender, Race and Age in Video Games', *New Media & Society*, 11 (5): 815–34.

Wilcox, R., and J. P. Williams (1996), '"What Do You Think?" *The X-Files*, Liminality, and Gender Pleasure', in D. Lavery, A. Hague and M. Cartwright (eds), *Deny All Knowledge: Reading The X-Files*, 99–120, London: Faber & Faber.

Wolf, M. J. (1997), 'Inventing Space: Toward a Taxonomy of On- and Off-screen Space in Video Games', *Film Quarterly*, 51 (1): 11–23.

Wolf, M. J. (2001), *The Medium of the Video Game*, Austin: University of Texas Press.

Wolf, M. J. (2008), 'Genre Profile: Adventure Games', in M. J. Wolf (ed.), *The Video Game Explosion: A History from Pong to Playstation and Beyond*, 81–8, Westport, CT: Greenwood Press.

Wooley, C. A. (2001), 'Visible Fandom: Reading *The X-Files* through X-Philes', *Journal of Film and Video*, 53 (4): 29–53.

The X-Files Game (1998), [video game] Dir. Greg Roach, USA: HyperBole Studios.

PART FOUR

Intersectional legacies: Identity and representation

James Fenwick

David Duchovny and Gillian Anderson were transformed into not only major celebrities as a result of their roles as Fox Mulder and Dana Scully on *The X-Files*, but also iconic, sexualized pop culture objects of desire. Gender and sexuality are central to *The X-Files*, with the human body – in particular, the female body – subjected to probing, assault, rape and objectification. Similarly, questions of race and racial identity are core to the series' myth-arc, not least through the repeated discussion of alien hybrids and alien colonization, immediately invoking discourse on imperialism and the Western legacy of slavery and colonialism. Elspeth Kydd has discussed how identity in *The X-Files* centralizes a 'white norm' (2001/2002: 73).

Whilst Gillian Anderson as Dana Scully has been celebrated as a feminist icon, *The X-Files* has a much more problematic legacy in terms of identity and representation. The series premiered just a few years after Kimberlé Crenshaw introduced the idea of intersectionality. Crenshaw argued for a new analytical framework in which gender, racial and sexual identities are not mutually exclusive, but rather that an individual's social, political and cultural identities contribute to both discrimination and privilege (Crenshaw 1989). *The X-Files*, however, centres whiteness and white superiority with people of colour marginalized and even demonized. As such, the contributors to this section reflect upon the problematic legacy of *The X-Files* with regard to identity and representation.

In Chapter 16, Lzz Johnk and Gabrielle Miller focus on the representation of racialized disability, specifically of Black veterans in the episode 'Sleepless' (S2: E04). Whilst Johnk and Miller argue that *The X-Files* does attempt to challenge hegemonic, Western imperialist narratives through Mulder and Scully's quest to thwart the plans for colonization by the Syndicate, the series undermines its efforts by drawing on ableist and racist tropes. Johnk and Miller offer a counter analysis of Black veterans in the episode in a bid to reframe the central character's (Augustus Cole) radical potential.

In Chapter 17, Erin Siodmak focuses on the representation of violence against women in the series, and in particular the recurrent use of the 'rape-by-deception' troupe. Siodmak argues that whilst Scully was a defining feminist character, she existed within a television series that remained entrenched in misogynistic portrayals of women. Siodmak analyses the persistent violence perpetrated on women in the series to argue that a key legacy of *The X-Files* was its normalization of such gendered representational violence.

In Chapter 18, Klára Feikusová focuses on the male body, specifically on Fox Mulder as a gay icon. Feikusová argues that Mulder is an outsider figure within society that embodies queerness as defined by Queer Theory. Throughout the series, Mulder displays a feminized character that leads various antagonists to possess his body in a bid to 'unqueer' him. As such, Mulder represents a figure that is against the heteronormative, patriarchal, masculine society and must be repressed at all costs.

In Chapter 19, Andrew Sydlik returns the focus to representations of disability, but across the series as a whole. Sydlik argues that *The X-Files* has a problematic legacy of reinforcing ableist troupes, demonstrating this by applying a Disability Studies analytical framework to the series' monster-of-the-week episodes. Sydlik argues that the series is about challenging structures of power within society, but one overlooked structure of power is ableism. Therefore, Sydlik brings to the fore this particular structure and representation to demonstrate how *The X-Files* consistently explores identities of difference.

In Chapter 20, Jolene Mendel focuses on Scully as a feminist icon, but specifically on the character's lasting legacy on the study of science, technology, engineering and maths (STEM) in the United States. Scully's place in scientific laboratories, her role as the logical and reasoning presence in her partnership with Mulder and her representation of medical science have made her an icon to subsequent generations of women seeking to enter the profession. Mendel focuses on a recent report, 'The Scully Effect', to understand the continuing legacy of Dana Scully on STEM subjects and the way in which the series undermines Scully's feminist iconography through misogynistic representations, building on the work of Siodmak in this collection.

Together, the chapters in this section present a critical re-evaluation of identity and representation in *The X-Files* to understand and challenge its much broader intersectional legacy on cultural and television history.

References

Crenshaw, K. (1989), 'Demarginalizing the Intersection of Race and Sex: A Black Feminist Critique of Antidiscrimination Doctrine, Feminist Theory and Antiracist Politics', *The University of Chicago Legal Forum*, 1989 (1): 139–67.

Kydd, E. (2001/2002), 'Differences: *The X-Files*, Race and the White Norm', *Journal of Film and Video*, 53 (4): 72–82.

16

A reparative reading of mad/ disabled Black veterans in 'Sleepless'

Lzz Johnk and Gabrielle Miller

A forerunner to much current science fiction and conspiracy-themed media storytelling, *The X-Files* continues to exert a powerful influence on popular culture thirty years after its debut. Part of the series' enduring appeal is its critical commentary on the abuses of hegemonic authority, which often takes the forms of shadowy organizations (for example, the Syndicate) or the US government itself. This chapter focuses on the monster-of-the-week episode 'Sleepless' (S2: E04), in which Agent Fox Mulder investigates the case of Augustus Cole (Tony Todd), a Black war veteran who appears to have telepathic abilities. As the case unfolds, Cole is revealed to have been part of a Marine recon unit that was experimented upon by the US government during the American War in Vietnam. The experiments are an effort to transform Cole and the others into more efficient soldiers – namely, by performing a type of lobotomy that induces permanent insomnia. Though the experiment succeeds in rendering the soldiers unable to sleep, the unintended consequence of this is that they are ultimately disabled. Some two decades after the end of the war, the veterans – unable to rest or process their traumatic experiences through sleep and dreams – live pleasureless, peaceless lives. Their tortured reality represents in literal form the perception of the American War in Vietnam as a waking nightmare disturbing the American Dream and its attendant order. Cole is also maddened/disabled by the traumas of war and military experimentation. Unlike his peers, he was institutionalized sometime after returning to the United States and his pathologization continued at the hands of new psy scientists. After escaping psychiatric incarceration, Cole begins hunting down and killing his former comrades and the psy scientists in charge of the sleep elimination experiments.

By exploring themes of anti-imperialism, 'Sleepless' contributes to the ongoing critique of US hegemony in *The X-Files*. However, this critical commentary is undermined by the use of sanist/ableist and racist tropes, which recur in both the episode and the series. The Mad/disabled Black character of Augustus Cole serves as a vessel to explore themes of war, complicity and institutionalized anti-Blackness within the United States and abroad. We assert that Cole's Mad/disabled Blackness represents a form of narrative prosthesis that is used to forward both the plot and the subcurrent of anti-Imperialist critique that nevertheless fails to interrogate pathologization and scientific experimentation as anti-Black and sanist/ableist (Mitchell and Snyder 2000). As frequently happens in monster-of-the-week episodes, Cole meets a fatal end – perhaps the just consequences of his actions, as the story leads us to believe Cole would say. We offer a reparative reading of 'Sleepless' that attempts to reframe the radical potential of Augustus Cole's non-white subjectivity as a connective thread between Madness/disability and Blackness.[1] Feminist scholar Eve Sedgwick encourages the epistemological practice of reparative reading against what she theorizes as paranoid readings (2002). Whereas a paranoid reading prompts readers to take an interrogative stance to interpreting a text, a reparative one is 'additive and accretive', seeking to understand and repair rather than tear down. We also theorize this 'non-white subjectivity' (a term we borrow from bell hooks and James Cone) as intervening upon US colonialism in the Americas and American imperialism abroad.

The following section charts the connections between racialized ableism, Atlantic slavery and Eurowestern imperial conquest around the globe. Foregrounding our analysis within histories of anti-Blackness allows us to situate Augustus Cole in the conditions of white supremacy that have continually denied disabled Black soldiers and veterans access to life chances (for example, access to social and economic resources). Later in the text, we trace genealogies of Black exclusion from institutionality and social subjecthood back to Atlantic slavery. In doing so, we demonstrate how the radical potential of 'Sleepless' is embodied by Mad/disabled Black veterans against the backdrop of globalized white supremacy. Our verb tense regarding systemic and structural anti-Blackness shifts between past

---

[1]We generally refer to Madness and disability as Madness/disability (or Mad/disabled), joined with a slash mark, to indicate the interconnectedness of these social locations.

and present. Working from the understanding that anti-Black systems and structures originating from Atlantic slavery directly and materially impact Black people today, we sometimes use the past tense to discuss how anti-Blackness was operating during specific historical moments.

Because Atlantic slavery involved rupture from land and culture, there is no neat delineation for describing when enslaved Indigenous Africans 'became Black', particularly because US Blackness was constructed through the race-crafting processes of Atlantic slavery. However, it is important to not collapse categories of belonging; therefore, we do not use 'African' and 'Black' interchangeably in order to highlight the complexities behind Black people's relationships to land, kin and culture during and after Atlantic slavery.

Racialized disability and the American War in Vietnam

The military experiences of Black men in the American War in Vietnam were remarkably different from those of enlisted white men. According to statistics, 'eligible Black men were drafted at twice the rate of qualified white men' (Graham 2003: 17). Conscription and the various economic and social appeals of enlistment concealed how the US government targeted Black men for soldiering, particularly by exploiting their limited opportunities (for example, access to employment), framing military enlistment as an alluring promise. Enlistment propaganda touted chances to become skilled labourers, which was particularly appealing for Black men who faced legacies of institutional barriers and economic injustice as a direct result of systemic anti-Blackness (Graham 2003: 17). Enlisted Black soldiers were disproportionately assigned frontline combat roles and low-status positions (Chow and Bates 2020). This subjected them to a greater likelihood of being injured or killed in Vietnam. Their experiences demonstrate the ways that the effects of war are disabling.

Prior to the American War in Vietnam, the Servicemen's Readjustment Act of 1944, more popularly known as the GI Bill, was created to better reintegrate the Second-World-War veterans into American society. The bill provided them with social and economic benefits such as 'low-cost mortgages, high school or vocational education, payments for tuition and living expenses for those electing to attend college, and low-interest loans for entrepreneurial veterans wanting to start a business' (Smithsonian Institute 2015). However, Black veterans were denied many of the GI Bill's benefits, demonstrating how Black people remain materially constrained by the strategic maldistribution of resources away from their communities.

Furthermore, social and economic campaigns, such as *The Moynihan Report* of 1965, strategically linked US military efforts with cultivating an upstanding able-bodyminded[2] Black manhood – a manhood that was increasingly considered ineffectual, particularly in the context of hegemonic expectations around male providership (Graham 2003; Spillers 1987). Since hegemonic conceptualizations of manhood are grounded in white heteronormativity in the United States (for example, economic stability, wealth accumulation and leadership), enlistment was enticing because it advertised an honourable masculinity, encouraging Black men 'into the military with the "manhood hustle"' (Graham 2003: 15). This kind of military propaganda operated through prisms of anti-Black logics that served to continually question the integrity of Black masculinity, always casting it as outside the bounds of acceptable and intelligible manhood.

The Moynihan Report, created by Senator Daniel Patrick Moynihan, attempted to attribute the economic downfall of the Black American family to the supposed matriarchal Black family structure (Spillers 1987). For Moynihan and many other white Americans, the heterosexual nuclear family was the 'basic social unit of American life' (Moynihan 1965: 5). Black Studies scholars have critically outlined how *The Moynihan Report* frames Blackness as deviant from the social norm of whiteness, a pathologization of Blackness that renders it unviable. This pathologization was directly connected to eurowestern Enlightenment science, wherein Blackness and notions of animality were linked. As such, *The Moynihan Report* (re) produced stereotypes and controlling images about Black men and women that framed Black kinship as structurally incapacitated while also misnaming and misattributing Black struggle to matriarchal power, reinforcing the notion of a failing Black masculinity (Collins 2000; Spillers 1987).[3] This served to continually obfuscate the ways in which conditions of possibility for Black people under US empire can be directly traced to the Atlantic slavery and its ensuing afterlife (Hartman 2007). Coined by Black Studies scholar-activist Saidiya Hartman, 'the afterlife of slavery' describes the

---

[2]We thread together 'compulsory able-bodymindedness' from what Disability Studies scholars Robert McRuer and Alison Kafer theorize as 'compulsory able-bodiedness' (Kafer 2003; McGruer 2006) and what Mad Studies scholar Margaret Price theorizes as 'compulsory able-mindedness' (2013).

[3]In *Black Feminist Thought*, Black feminist scholar-activist Patricia Hill Collins discusses the historical and cultural impact of controlling images of Black women that continue to constrain Black women's lives (1990). Controlling images, such as the mammy, the sapphire and the domineering Black woman, can be traced to the roles and conditions of Atlantic slavery, in which Black women were subject to various forms of psycho-sexual and physical domination. In addition to controlling images of Black men that originate from Atlantic slavery, Black scholar-activists have theorized that the nexus of Blackness and womanness create particular controlling images, owing to the relationships between reproduction, motherhood and patriarchal whiteness (Jackson 2020).

ways in which Atlantic slavery continues to produce 'skewed life chances, limited access to health and education, premature death, incarceration, and impoverishment' for Black people (Hartman 2007: 6).

The Atlantic slave trade involved the kidnapping and transportation of Indigenous Africans to various parts of the colonized Americas. At the same time, genocidal projects of assimilation, dislocation and extermination were concurrently securing US settler colonial expansion and domination of Native lands and peoples (Mignolo 2011; Wynter 2006).

Enslaved Africans' violent rupture from culture, tradition and land intergenerationally and violently restructured forms of Black kinship and belonging in the United States (Patterson 1982). Kinlessness and landlessness strategically situated enslaved Africans' unbelonging within US social and economic spheres. In this way, enslaved Black men and women were denied various social and institutional privileges and opportunities (Wilderson III and Cooper 2020). Black Studies scholar-activist Jared Sexton uses the term 'borrowed institutionality' to describe Black people 'attempting to be in ways that we can never be' (Wilderson III and Cooper 2020). This term names how forms of institutionality, including gender and sexuality, secure the kinds of material privileges that naturalize white supremacy and abstract Black life. For instance, many slaves were banned from legal marriage (Holden 2018); denied rights to parent their own children (Spillers 1987); prohibited from publicly practising Indigenous religious beliefs and forbidden to read and write (Walker 1983). These measures attempted to prevent slaves from accessing institutional and material benefits that provide social intelligibility, agency and subjecthood under US empire. These were also the rubrics by which compulsory able-bodymindedness would come to determine who is disabled and, by extension, who can participate as a citizen-subject in American society. Transnational Feminist Disability Studies scholar Nirmala Erevelles writes that it was 'precisely at the historical moment when one class of human beings was transformed into cargo to be transported to the New World that [B]lack bodies become disabled and disabled bodies become [B]lack' (Erevelles 2011: 40). In other words, we cannot understand disability in what is presently called America without accounting for the Middle Passage and chattel slavery.

Subjecthood and personhood were also directly informed by the race-making project of Atlantic slavery in tandem with the sanist/ableist Enlightenment period. Darwinian philosophies and scientific empiricism sutured Blackness with biological inferiority, thereby justifying the 'racial calculus and political arithmetic' that subjugated Black lives (Hartman 2007: 6). In her discussion about the Black family and *The Moynihan Report*, Tiffany Lethabo King outlines how

> in Darwin's seminal Enlightenment tome, Black families (specifically Australian Aborigine and African families) were placed on the bottom of

the evolutionary continuum as a primitive form of family. The scientific category of the family was applied to Black and 'Aborigine' populations in order to mark out a space of subhumanity or an outside to the normal, European family. *The Moynihan Report* (1965) sets up a similar comparative schema in that family is imposed upon Black households in order to mark a racial-biological and now cultural space on an evolutionary continuum. (King 2018: 71–2)

Scientific empiricism sustained a human/non-human hierarchy that linked humanness to whiteness and non-humanness to Blackness (Wynter 2006). Eurowestern science and medicine crafted and naturalized the bounds of normative whiteness, racializing the colonial sex/gender binary wherein whiteness was a precondition for intelligible gender and moral sexuality (Somerville 2000). This denial from the realm of the social produced a 'different cultural text' for Black Americans, one that marked Black men and women as outside the realm of humanity (Spillers 1987). 'Being human' is not only socially constructed but also sutured to philosophies of gendered racialization that maintain relationships of domination and subordination. In this way, *The Moynihan Report* weaponized and pathologized Black kinship, while also naturalizing white patriarchy as the precondition for 'humanness' (King 2018).

Quite literally pointing to African bodyminds as axioms of biological inferiority and non-humaness, eurowestern medical and scientific experimentation functioned to ground biological hierarchies in a presupposed material 'Truth' (Mignolo 2011). Born in 1789, Khoikhoi woman Sara 'Saartjie' Baartman was sold into slavery by Dutch colonizers, only to later be exhibited in freak shows in London. According to historical accounts, 'For two shillings, people entered 225 Piccadilly and watched Sara Baartman walk onto a stage, sing a song, and turn around. The spectators could even poke her with their walking sticks ... [T]he showman was Hendrik Cesars, a man from Cape Town. He displayed Baartman as 'the Hottentot Venus', a marvel of nature, if a freakish one' (Scully and Crais 2008: 301).

Baartman's body parts, particularly her buttocks, were ogled as 'monstrous' and 'freakish', not only evidence of Africans' biological inferiority but also proof of their deviation from a sexual and gendered 'normalcy' being outlined against whiteness. Within white supremacist logics, Baartman's body was corporeal evidence of African people's non-humanness or animality as she was quite literally marketed as 'the "link" between ape and human in nature's great hierarchy' (Qureshi 2004: 234). After Baartman's premature death at 26 in 1815, her body was posthumously kept for scientific study before being displayed in European museums for nearly two centuries. In fact, 'her brain, skeleton and sexual organs remained on display in a Paris Museum until 1974. Her remains weren't repatriated and buried until 2002' (Parkinson 2016). Baartman's 'story' demonstrates how the psychic-sexual terrors of anti-Blackness texture all aspects of social and cultural life while also illuminating how Blackness informed emerging scientific and medical doctrines around disability and disfigurement. Hartman questions how storytelling functions for Black women, particularly stories that become entombed in history (2008). This is precisely because Black women's stories from Atlantic slavery are not told from first-hand accounts; rather, they show up as violent retellings in ledgers, manuscripts, letters and so on by enslavers and others with social and economic power. Unable to read and write in English, Sara Baartman is largely remembered by her captivity and posthumous experimentation, narratives written from her enslavers' perspectives.

The history of medical and scientific experimentation on Black people highlights the disabling effects of the Atlantic slave trade, as well as how disability is sutured to anti-Blackness as social text (Pickens 2019). Under a eugenicist white supremacist politics of cure, disability as a category of difference has been violently cast as inferior, pathologized and requiring strategic eradication (Clare 1999). According to historian Stefanie Hunt-Kennedy, 'The legal disablement of the enslaved, coupled with the legally sanctioned disfiguring and disabling of enslaved bodies, made slavery a preeminent site of disability ... Emerging notions of race in the seventeenth century fostered and validated such violence against African bodies as the limits of "worthy" humanity were set against or defined by the backdrop of English capitalism' (Hunt-Kennedy 2020: 38).

Many of the same words used to describe African bodyminds, such as 'monstrous' in the case of Sara Baartman, were also used to describe disabled and disfigured people as distinctly deviant from the sanist/ableist construction of a 'normal' bodymind (Hunt-Kennedy 2020: 38).

After inventing various gynaecological tools and procedures still used in medicine today, J. Marion Sims is often cited as the father of gynaecology. To achieve his success, Sims medically experimented on three enslaved Black women – Anarcha, Betsey and Lucy – without anaesthesia or their consent (Kuppers et al. 2008). At the time, it was predominantly believed that Black men and women felt less pain, which supposedly justified brutal treatment and disablement for the advancement of eurowestern medical science. At the intersections of disability and anti-Blackness, these three women's bodyminds were cast as outside the bounds of humanity. The disabling effects of Atlantic slavery and its afterlife were intertwined with scientific and medical racism. This reproduced conceptions of normativity that propagated the violent fiction of able-bodyminded heteropatriarchal whiteness, as well as Black people's disposability and fungibility (Hartman 1997). Conjured from the thought-work of Black Studies scholars such as Spillers and Hartman, fungibility 'capture[s] the violent expansiveness of the Black body in the New World' (Zellars 2018), referring to how the Black bodymind, including its parts, was and is considered always already dispensable under US capitalism.

In 1938, the 'Tuskegee Study of Untreated Syphilis in the Negro Male' was a government-sponsored medical and scientific study that sought to research the impact of untreated syphilis infection in Black men. A majority of the men involved in the study were poor and illiterate Black sharecroppers from the rural American South. According to historical documentation surrounding the study,

> Researchers had not informed the men of the actual name of the study … its purpose, and potential consequences of the treatment or non-treatment that they would receive during the study. The men never knew of the debilitating and life threatening consequences of the treatments they were to receive, the impact on their wives, girlfriends, and children they may have conceived once involved in the research. (Tuskegee University 2021)

Furthermore, after penicillin was discovered as treatment for syphilis in 1947, the Black men who unknowingly participated in the study did not receive the treatment. This historical example of Black disabled men's disposability makes salient the eugenicist logic inherent in the strategic maldistribution of death and injury in the United States.

In their modern shape and form, anti-Blackness and ableism are historically and culturally inextricable. Since Atlantic slavery, racialized ableism and its violent material legacies have continued to shape white supremacist projects around the globe. Global capitalism (beginning with Atlantic slavery) and eurowestern military conquest exported these particular anti-Black ableist logics. Although forms of violence and oppression around what we now call 'race' and 'disability' existed prior to eurowestern conquest and occupation, imperialism transported and gelled a particular form of globalized anti-Blackness inextricable from Atlantic slavery and disability. While playing out differently across space and time, many significant roots of global anti-Blackness can specifically be traced to eurowestern white supremacist ideologies. American/eurowestern involvement in war and military conquest around the globe has been instrumental in transporting and (re)circulating anti-Blackness, including the American War in Vietnam (Man 2018). Understanding the connections between gendered anti-Blackness and American imperial domination is integral for conceptualizing the connections between disabled Black soldiers and veterans and the intense neglect, impoverishment and violence many servicemen experienced upon their return to the United States. Many veterans also returned with physical and mental disabilities acquired during service. Because of their fungible and disposable status, Black veterans were 'presented with menial job opportunities, denied support by Veterans Affairs, and received little empathy from their own communities' (Chow and Bates 2020). As a result, they experienced compounding and cumulative challenges, especially the physically and mentally disabled veterans struggling to find work and reliable, safe access to healthcare.

The histories and legacies surrounding racialized ableism and its attendant violence continue to structure conditions of possibility for Black disabled veterans. *The X-Files*' episode 'Sleepless' demonstrates these connections through Augustus Cole's experience as a mad/disabled Black veteran who experiences the intersections of anti-Blackness and sanism/ableism, particularly because of medical experiments carried out by the US military during the American War in Vietnam. The following analysis offers a reparative reading of racialized disability and the interconnected histories of American imperialism, pathologization and Atlantic slavery in 'Sleepless'.

Angry ghosts: Racialized disability and the spectres of American imperialism

In the very first scene of 'Sleepless', we see Dr Saul Grissom awaken during the night to his apartment filling with smoke. He rushes to the front door and finds the hallway burning. After calling 911 (the emergency services), the man unsuccessfully attempts to extinguish the fire. Coughing from the smoke, he falls to the floor. When the firefighters arrive, they find Grissom dead, but see no evidence of a fire. The doctor's death is brought to the attention of Agent Mulder, who learns that Grissom was a sleep scientist. Agent Scully discovers during her autopsy that Grissom's body has no burns anywhere, yet his cause of death is smoke inhalation. When Mulder makes the connection that Grissom is Augustus Cole's doctor and experimenter, he theorizes that Cole used Grissom's mind against him, making him believe that there was indeed a fire and causing him to suffocate.

Mulder's theory turns out to be right, of course; at some point following the lobotomy and military experiments, Cole develops telepathic abilities so powerful that he can change the way others perceive reality. Mulder's speculation that Cole has 'built a bridge between the dream world and the waking world' further frames him as having extraordinary mental and psychic abilities. The audience is tempted to understand Cole as hyper-abled because of these psychic powers. He seems to be what Disability Studies scholars Alison Kafer and Eli Clare call a 'supercrip', an ableist archetype of disabled people in which they 'must accomplish incredibly difficult, and therefore inspiring, tasks to be worthy of nondisabled attention' (Kafer 2013: 90). And yet Cole is paradoxical: his status as a psychiatrized and medicalized Black veteran marks him as disabled, while the same processes that maddened/disabled him – joining the military, being experimented upon by the state, committing atrocities in Vietnam, being institutionalized – also gave him his superhuman powers. He is the only member of his Marine reconnaissance unit for whom the experiments result in psychic abilities; moreover, the others are essentially disabled both by their perpetual wakefulness and unaddressed trauma associated with the American War in Vietnam.

After dispatching Grissom, Cole visits his comrade Wittig, whom he finds living alone in a dreary-looking apartment building. Wittig is watching TV, still unable to sleep. His skin is sallow, and his eyes are rimmed with red. At first, Wittig seems happy to see 'Preacher', calling Cole by his nickname. Wittig also seems exhausted by his plight. Endlessly haunted by images of their unit's victims, Wittig lives a waking nightmare, mirroring the ways that the American War in Vietnam remains a spectre in the US imaginary (Gustaffson 2009). When Cole expresses that they must all pay for their deeds, Wittig seems ready to face the past. Suddenly sensing they are not alone, Wittig turns to face what appears to be his victims: Vietnamese women, elders and small children, covered in blood. Some of them have burns, severed limbs and other wounds, thereby recalling historical memories of American war crimes in Vietnam, perhaps the most notorious being the Mỹ Lai massacre. On the morning of 16 March 1968, American soldiers from Charlie Company raped, maimed and murdered as many as 504 villagers over the course of four hours (Hersh 1972). Several soldiers later stated that when they arrived in the village, they were greeted by friendly villagers who waved to them. Despite finding no Viet Cong and only a few arms, the Americans quickly began rounding up and executing villagers and burning their houses to the ground. In the episode, the psychic projections of Cole and Wittig's victims bear similar wounds as were inflicted on the victims in Mỹ Lai.

Cole's psychic apparitions seemingly gesture towards the angry ghosts left in the wake of American imperialist atrocities in Vietnam, Afghanistan and Haiti, among other places in which the United States was stalemated by insurgent and guerrilla forces (Alexis 2015). Nevertheless, the episode's story unfolds primarily from an American point of view; the 'ghosts' are silent, reinforcing Orientalist projections of Asians as voiceless, invisible, at times even subjectless. Anthropologist Mai Lan Gustaffson argues that the American War in Vietnam is not just a spectre of US history, but continues to haunt Vietnamese people, as well – some of them being literally haunted by loved ones who died in the war (Gustaffson 2009).

A reparative reading of this story asks us to notice the ways that the abject positions of Blackness and Asianness are brought into intimate relation through the character of Cole. He seeks revenge not only for himself and his fellow experiment victims but also for those he has harmed in service of American imperialism. Cole seems ready to sacrifice himself in service of this mission. Further, Cole's use of his powers to access other people's minds and make them experience situations that are not 'real' enacts resistance against American and eurowestern assertions of a singular 'Truth' and reality. The episode aired more than two decades after the end of the war, at a time when the question of who had really 'won' continued to wear on the whitestream American psyche. Throughout 'Sleepless', the audience is invited to question what is real, including who the real villain in this story is. Mulder characterizes Cole as an 'avenging angel', suggesting that the US military and government are just as guilty as the soldiers they created who perpetrated war crimes.

Although 'Sleepless' intentionally troubles a black-and-white view of good and evil, we are encouraged to perceive Cole as a maniacal force incapable of sound judgement who must be stopped. As the victim of military experimentation, Cole's traumatized embodiment and psychic abilities are the unfortunate outcome of racist imperialist US hegemony. Yet, Cole's mad/disabled Blackness also marks him as a monstrosity under hegemonic logics and structures. His monstrosity manifests as a literal marking in the form of a large lobotomy scar on the back of his neck. This use of racialized madness/disability as a narrative metaphor and plot device exemplifies one manifestation of narrative prosthesis, a framework for theorizing the reliance upon sanist/ableist tropes and themes in film, literature and other media (Mitchell and Snyder 2000). In his discussion of narrative prosthesis, Mitch Ploskonka explains that 'disability primarily serves to enhance the characterization of the able-bodied. Physical or mental disability metaphorically mirrors thematic or personality abnormality and degeneration. The presence of disability signals that something is amiss and needs to be fixed' (2000: 281). 'Sleepless' reifies sanist/ableist anti-Blackness by dooming Cole to die the fate of a 'monster'. Kidnapping the second of his experimenters, Dr Girardi, Cole takes him to an abandoned building. Laying out scalpels on a table next to his Bible, Cole says, 'We all have to pay for what we did over there.' The doctor attempts to deflect blame by retorting that Cole and the other Marines volunteered. Cole summons a psychic manifestation of the doctor's other victims, who pick up the scalpels and walk menacingly towards the screaming doctor. While the subtext of the episode is that violent American imperialism is the 'real monster', it is the mad/disabled Black veteran carrying out a mission of retributive justice who acts as Agent Mulder's nemesis. Most pressingly, Cole's death is the result of state killing, implying that perhaps he is as guilty as the state which forced him into the violent circumstances of the American War in Vietnam and deserves to be punished by the state.

As a form of narrative prosthesis, Augustus Cole's monstrous mad/disabled Blackness works to forward the story's plot. Further, Cole's strange, extrahuman relationship with the angry ghosts of his waking nightmares – the victims of his unit's violence – serves to carry an anti-imperialist critique. However, as we have shown, the episode's critique fails to connect American imperialism abroad to sanist/ableist anti-Blackness within the United States. Although his mission of retribution succeeds, Cole can only find peace in death, which turns out to be a violent one at the hands of the state. At the end of the episode, Mulder encounters Cole several stories up in the abandoned building, apparently considering suicide. Mulder emphatically begins to question Cole about the experiments, but Cole replies only that he is exhausted, having not slept in twenty-four years. Viewers are left with the impression that he has spent even more than a lifetime contemplating the ghosts of his unit's Vietnamese victims, as well as histories and ongoing legacies of medical experimentation on Black bodyminds. Acting as a literal agent of the state, Krycek catches up with Mulder and shoots Cole after mistaking (or 'mistaking', we could say, given repeat instances of white cops 'mistaking' ordinary objects for weapons in the hands of Black people) Cole's Bible for a gun. The scene is framed as suicide by the cops; Cole apparently uses his psychic powers one last time to convince Krycek that he is pointing a gun at Mulder. Though alluding to anti-Black police violence, the episode leaves the specifically anti-Black nature of his death unanalysed. In fact, Mulder tells Krycek that he 'did the right thing' by shooting Cole. In the end, Mulder simply moves on from the case, seemingly more fazed by losing the evidence he needed to prove the existence of a larger government conspiracy than by witnessing Cole's death at the hands of state agents. It is worth noting that in the very last scene of 'Sleepless', the audience learns that Krycek is a mole working for Mulder's enemies who has been sent to sabotage him.

A generous reading might interpret Cole's death as a self-conscious critique of state killings of Black people, and analysing 'Sleepless' in isolation might confirm this. However, this episode reinforces a general tendency of *The X-Files* to treat Black characters as disposable, especially those who are overtly pathologized as mad/disabled. Recuperating the critical potential of this episode necessitates attending to the ways that conditions of sanist/ableist anti-Blackness spring from interconnected histories of Atlantic slavery, American imperialism, militarism and pathologization.

Conclusion

In this chapter, we have argued for reframing the radical potential of 'non-white subjectivities' – in this case embodied by a mad/disabled Black veteran – by resuturing histories of Atlantic slavery and the pathologization of Blackness to those of American imperialism in Vietnam in *The X-Files*' episode, 'Sleepless'. While the episode's engagement with non-white subjectivities may not redeem its reliance on sanist/ableist or racist tropes – specifically, mad/disabled Blackness as narrative prosthesis – to forward its story, 'Sleepless' is still instructive for critically examining these interconnected transnational histories. In particular, we learn how sanist/ableist anti-Blackness is at work within the bounds of the United States and at the sites of American imperialism, including the American War in Vietnam.

Numerous episodes of *The X-Files* utilize forms of narrative prosthesis when representing disability on screen, including 'Humbug' (S2: E20) and 'The Walk' (S3: E07). Additionally, there are episodes where representations of Blackness (re)produce tropes and controlling images of Black people, such as 'Fresh Bones' (S2: E15) and 'Teliko' (S4: E03). Critically and historically situating anti-Blackness and sanism/ableism allows the potential for a reparative reading of other *X-Files* episodes that draw on stereotypes and tropes to forward narrative. Doing so reminds us to be attentive to hidden stories and truths that may resist hegemonic narratives. Generating reparative readings of these and other unexamined and uninterrogated representations of madness/disability and anti-Blackness can help determine if and how such representations hold radical potential. Such reparative readings also elucidate the extent of *The X-Files'* continuing influence in popular culture and collective imagination.

References

Alexis, Y. (2015), 'Mwen Pas Connait as Resistance: Haitians' Silence against a Violent State', *Journal of Haitian Studies*, 21 (2): 269–88, Special Issue on the US Occupation of Haiti, 1915–34.
Chow, A. R., and J. Bates (2020), 'As Da 5 Bloods Hits Netflix, Black Vietnam Veterans Recall the Real Injustices They Faced during and after the War'. Available online: https://time.com/5852476/da-5-bloods-black-vietnam-veterans/ (accessed 20 October 2020).
Clare, E. (1999), *Exile and Pride*, 1st edn, Boston, MA: South End Press.
Collins, P. H. (2000), *Black Feminist Thought: Knowledge, Consciousness, and the Politics of Empowerment*, 2nd edn, New York: Routledge.
Erevelles, N. (2011), *Disability and Difference in Global Contexts*, New York: Palgrave Macmillan.
Graham, H. (2003), *Brothers' Vietnam War: Black Power, Manhood, and the Military Experience*, 1st edn, Gainsville: University Press of Florida.
Gustaffson, M. L. (2009), *War and Shadows: The Haunting of Vietnam*, Ithaca, NY: Cornell University Press.
Hartman, S. (1997), *Scenes of Subjection: Terror, Slavery, and Self-Making in Nineteenth Century America*, New York: Oxford University Press.
Hartman, S. (2007), *Lose Your Mother: A Journey along the Atlantic Slave Route*, New York: Macmillan.
Hartman, S. (2008), 'Venus in Two Acts', *Small Ax*, 12 (2): 1–14.
Hersch, S. (1972), 'The Massacre at My Lai', *The New Yorker*. Available online: https://www.newyorker.com/magazine/1972/01/22/coverup (accessed 25 October 2020).
Holden, V. (2018), 'Slave and Free Black Marriage in the Nineteenth Century', *Black Perspectives*. Available online: https://www.aaihs.org/

slave-and-free-black-marriage-in-the-nineteenth-century/ (accessed 22 October 2020).

hooks, b. (2014), *Black Looks: Race and Representation*, New York: Taylor and Francis.

Jackson, Z. I. (2020), *Becoming Human: Matter and Meaning in an Antiblack World*, Durham, NC: Duke University Press.

Hunt-Kennedy, S. (2020), *Between Fitness and Death: Disability and Slavery in the Caribbean*, Champaign: University of Illinois Press.

Kafer, A. (2013), *Feminist, Queer, Crip*, Bloomington: Indiana University Press.

King, T. L. (2018), 'Black "Feminisms" and Pessimism: Abolishing Moynihan's Negro Family', *Theory & Event*, 21 (1): 67–87.

Kuppers, P., A. Gonzalez, C. Sandahl, T. Giraud and A. Meredith Cox (2008), 'The Anarcha Project: Anarcha Anti-Archive', *Liminalities: A Journal of Performance Studies*, 4 (2). Available online: http://liminalities.net/4-2/anarcha/ (accessed 8 August 2021).

Man, S. (2018), *Soldiering through Empire: Race and the Making of the Decolonizing Pacific*, Oakland: University of California Press.

McGruer, R. (2006), *Crip Theory: Cultural Signs of Queerness and Disability*, New York: New York University Press.

Mignolo, W. (2011), *The Darker Side of Modernity: Global Futures, Decolonial Options*, Durham, NC: Duke University Press.

Mitchell, D. T., and S. L. Snyder (2000), *Narrative Prosthesis: Disability and the Dependencies of Discourse*, Ann Arbor: University of Michigan Press.

Moynihan, P. (1965), 'The Negro Family: The Case for National Action'. Available online: https://web.stanford.edu/~mrosenfe/Moynihan%27s%20The%20Negro%20Family.pdf (accessed 18 September 2020).

Parkinson, J. (2016), 'The Significance of Sarah Baartman'. Available online: https://www.bbc.com/news/magazine-35240987 (accessed 25 October 2020).

Patterson, O. (1982), *Slavery and Social Death*, Cambridge, MA: Harvard University Press.

Pickens, T. A. (2019), *Black Madness:Mad Blackness*, Durham, NC: Duke University Press.

Price, M. (2013), 'Bodymind Problem and the Possibilities of Pain', *Hypatia*, 30 (1): 268–84.

Qureshi, S. (2004), 'Displaying Sara Baartman, the "Hottentot Venus"', *History of Science*, 42 (2): 233–57.

Scully, P., and C. Crais (2008), 'Race and Erasure: Sara Baartman and Hendrik Cesars in Cape Town and London', *Journal of British Studies*, 47 (2): 301–23.

Sedgwick, E. (2002), *Touching Feeling: Affect, Pedagogy, Performativity*, Durham, NC: Duke University Press.

Smithsonian Institute (2015), 'After the War: Blacks and the GI Bill'. Available online: https://americanexperience.si.edu/wp-content/uploads/2015/02/After-the-War-Blacks-and-the-GI-Bill.pdf (accessed 19 October 2020).

Somerville, S. (2000), *Queering the Color Line: Race and the Invention of Homosexuality in American Culture*, Durham, NC: Duke University Press.

Spillers, H. (1987), 'Mama's Baby, Papa's Maybe: An American Grammar Book', *Diacretics*, 17 (2): 64–81.

Tuskegee University (2021), 'About the USPHS Syphilis Study'. Available online: https://www.tuskegee.edu/about-us/centers-of-excellence/bioethics-center/about-the-usphs-syphilis-study (accessed 22 October 2020).

Walker, A. (1983), *In Search of Our Mothers' Gardens*, San Diego, CA: Harcourt Brace Jovanovich.

Wilderson III, F. B., and C. M. Cooper (2020), 'Interviews on Critical Race and Trans/Queer Approaches to Filmmaking: Incommensurabilities – The Limits of Redress, Intramural Indemnity, and Extramural Auditorship', *Performance Matters*, 6 (1): 68–85.

Wynter, S. (2006), 'On How We Mistook the Map for the Territory, and Re-imprisoned Ourselves in Our Unbearable Wrongness of Being of Désêtre: Black Studies Toward the Human Project', in L. R. Gordon and J. A. Gordon (eds), *A Companion to African-American Studies*, 107–18, Hoboken, NJ: Wiley.

Zellers, R. (2018), 'Transness as a Category for Possibility', *Black Perspectives*. Available online: https://www.aaihs.org/transness-as-a-category-for-possibility/ (accessed 30 September 2020).

17

'I'm a medical doctor, and a scientist': Powerful women, angry men and representational violence in *The X-Files*

Erin Siodmak

When *The X-Files* debuted in 1993, Gillian Anderson's portrayal of FBI Agent Dana Scully quickly became iconic in a decade of final girl heroism, corporate pop-feminism – in the form of 'Girl Power', the Lilith Fair and *Sex and the City* (HBO, 1998–2004) – and a media culture that frequently made entertainment of publicly shaming and discrediting women who spoke out, held power or otherwise posed a threat to powerful men (see Lewinsky 2018; Doyle and Jones 2006). Yet *The X-Files* often reflected this treatment of women by the media, culture and politics of the 1990s. It is therefore surprising how little scholarly attention has been paid to the use of deception, intoxication and abduction of women that can be found at the centre of many of the series' episodes. Notably absent from critical analysis of the series is the use of a 'rape-by-deception' trope, a plot device deployed more than once for comedic effect.[1] The comedic episodes that employ a rape-by-deception trope have gone so far as to excuse the violation by suggesting that a mother's

---

[1] Scholar Theresa Geller (2016) addresses these concerns in a critical analysis of several of the episodes covered in this chapter in her book, *The X-Files*. However, I generally find that television and media critics have been more attentive to these themes.

love for the resulting child trumps the fact of the assault. Following the broadcast of the 'revival' seasons of the series in 2016 and 2018 (seasons ten and eleven), however, reviewers did highlight the troubling use of Scully (see Bowman 2018; Imhoff 2018; Pantozzi 2018). As much as the character of Scully challenged existing tropes and broke the 'woman as sidekick' mould, she nevertheless exists within a series that remained committed to entrenched ideas about women and the correlative gender/ed tropes. *The X-Files* has often reproduced and reinforced images of violence against, and inequitable treatment of, women and, at the same time, been applauded for creating one of the most iconic woman characters of the decade.[2] This chapter continues the critical re-evaluation of *The X-Files* through an examination of its use of women's victimization in ways that normalize or leave unexamined multiple forms of gendered representational violence.

In what follows, I examine and interrogate the use of and violence against women characters in *The X-Files* through an analysis of tropes and the character of Dana Scully. Doing so will demonstrate how she and other women characters are repeatedly undermined and victimized throughout the series' eleven season run. At the same time, there is a necessary distinction to be made between the plot – the events of the stand-alone 'monster-of-the-week' episodes and the core of the mythology and conspiracy narrative (the myth-arc) – and the experience and *feeling* attached to the character, despite storylines that regularly reproduce rape culture tropes and imagery. So, while the character of Scully is repeatedly used as a womb, a body in the service of men (and the series' writers), Scully cannot and should not be equated with the violence and trauma of plot alone. To do so is to deny Scully all agency and autonomy, ignore the affective power of the character and dismiss the importance of the character for the generations of viewers, writers and characters she inspired.

The X-Files and the 1990s

The success of *The X-Files* stems in part from its ability to tap into evolving norms of distrust of government and institutions that had been simmering since at least the 1970s economic recession, gas crisis and Watergate scandal (for more on the distrust of government and the political contexts of the series, see Chapter 9 in this collection). The series' central protagonists, Dana Scully and Fox Mulder, and their beloved on-screen partnership also led to the creation of the verb 'to ship' in the vernacular of online fandom.[3]

---

[2] And, arguably, in television history.
[3] To 'ship' a couple on a television series is to hope that they end up together romantically. There were fierce Mulder–Scully 'shippers' but also plenty of fans who wanted the relationship to remain platonic and professional.

Dana Scully became the quintessential 1990s post-feminist liberated white woman. Scully is a medical doctor (and scientist) turned FBI agent more devoted to her job than to her personal life; she is smart, armed and single. Scully is sexy and serious, whether dressed in an early season ill-fitting pantsuit or the more tailored pencil skirts and suits of later seasons. Scully, a rational thinker and sceptic, is assigned to the X-Files in order to monitor and report on the work of Agent Fox Mulder. Though she remains the reasoned sceptic to Mulder's disciple of the paranormal, as Mulder's partner, Scully is driven to fight authority, chase the real bad guys and punish abuses of power. The intelligent, driven, complex and more fully realized women characters seen on television since Scully – Annalise Keating (*How to Get Away with Murder*), Peggy Olson (*Mad Men*), Alicia Florrick (*The Good Wife*), Olivia Pope (*Scandal*), Jessica Jones (*Jessica Jones*), Elizabeth Jennings (*The Americans*), Eve Polastri (*Killing Eve*) – while arguably holding greater influence over more recent generations, exist in the cultural wake Scully made. Gillian Anderson's portrayal of Scully opened up new possibilities for women on television but the character's influence also extended beyond popular culture. Perhaps the character's most notable contribution is in what has been termed the 'Scully Effect', a measure of the number of women in science, technology, engineering and mathematics (STEM) who were encouraged by Scully's role on the series to enter these fields (see Chapter 20 in this collection for a specific discussion of the 'Scully Effect').

The X-Files also reflected the norms of its time regarding race, gender, class and citizenship through its storytelling as well as in the early-season treatment of Gillian Anderson. As influential and iconic as the character of Scully was and continues to be, Anderson was positioned monetarily and physically second to David Duchovny. For the first three seasons, Anderson was paid less than Duchovny: in 2016, during negotiations for the reboot (season ten), she was offered half of what Duchovny was to be paid (Grinberg 2016). When the series began its run, Anderson was told to stand behind Duchovny on screen, positioning her as a sidekick more than a co-lead (Leon 2016). So, despite the influence and importance of the series in television and science fiction history, *The X-Files* was not without its failures, which include its use and portrayal of women characters, its casual racism, xenophobia and stereotype-laden depictions of Black, Asian and Indigenous cultures, as well as of people with disabilities. After re-evaluation and reappraisal by fans, scholars and critics, several episodes, including 'Roland' (S1: E23) and 'Audrey Pauley' (S9: E11) have lost or are likely to lose favour with contemporary viewers for their insensitive, infantilizing and demonizing depictions of people with disabilities. Episodes that rely on racial and cultural stereotypes to shock, evoke danger or advance the story of the series' white protagonists, such as 'Fresh Bones' (S2: E15), 'Hell Money' (S3: E19), 'Teliko' (S4: E03) and 'The Unnatural' (S6: E19), face a similar fate. While the latter issues are not the focus of this chapter, the happy multiculturalism and appropriation that typified the era (see Melamed 2001) coincide and share much with the watered-down feminism of 1990s mainstream media culture and the ongoing representational violence done to women characters in service of a plot or to advance a man's story.

The narrative misogyny of *The X-Files*

The X-Files is heavily premised on the abduction of girls and women. Two key storylines exemplify this: the abduction of Mulder's sister, Samantha, and, later, in season two, the abduction of Scully. Scully is placed at the centre of the myth-arc episodes and is made a victim in numerous 'monster-of-the-week' episodes. Scully is threatened with or is the victim of violence or abduction (see episodes 'Squeeze' (S1: E03), 'Duane Barry' (S2: E05), 'Ascension' (S2: E06), 'Irresistible' (S2: E13), 'Unruhe' (S4: E04), 'Never Again' (S4: E13), 'Tithonus' (S6: E10), 'Milagro' (S6: E18) and 'Orison' (S7: E07)) and is drugged or subjected to tests and procedures to which she did not consent (see 'Gender Bender' (S1: E14), 'Three of a Kind' (S6: E20), 'En Ami' (S7: E15), 'Roadrunners' (S8: E04), 'Per Manum' (S8: E13)). Rape-by-deception is established as a trope in the context of more than one of the series' comedic episodes; and, in the final season, Scully's son, William, is revealed to be the result of medical rape committed by the Cigarette Smoking Man ('En Ami'), a member of an extra-governmental Syndicate at the centre of the series' myth-arc. The narrative and representational violence of *The X-Files* robs women characters of their agency; these tropes are worth tracing if we seek to understand and continue to challenge rape culture and normalized forms of violence and disempowerment. However, I also argue that to identify such concerns is not incompatible with a recognition of Scully's status as a feminist icon. Indeed, to dismiss the series and the character of Scully is to ignore the work Gillian Anderson did to make Scully more than the plot, irreducible to the traumas the writers heaped upon the character.

It is beyond the scope of this chapter to address all the instances in which women in *The X-Files*, including Scully, are used in ways that deny their autonomy and agency and exploit forms of gendered violence in order to tell a story. The remainder of this chapter, therefore, focuses on two central ideas: first, the regular deployment in the series' storytelling of violation and loss of autonomy and the centrality of women's bodies as and in relation to technologies of reproduction; and, second, the character of Scully as a recuperable feminist icon via a 'structure of feeling' (Jameson 1991) wherein something new emerges out of (and despite) existing hegemonic narratives or interpretive frames, resulting in an altered affective and cultural landscape. I address the first point through an analysis of several episodes that use rape or rape-by-deception as an introduction to the way *The X-Files* deploys sexual and gendered violence and tropes. I then trace the exploitation of Scully's body within the series' myth-arc episodes. The chapter concludes by addressing how Scully as a character exists at the liminal nexus of a structure of feeling where tropes of violence exist alongside and, through an experience of, to borrow from José Muñoz (1999), disidentification, recede behind a more feminist and nuanced character. It is from this nexus and disidentification that new cultural possibilities emerge.

Gendered violence as plot

Several monster-of-the-week episodes use the violation of women's bodily autonomy centrally in their story arcs. The most overt use of sexual violence occurs in the season two episode, 'Excelsis Dei' (S2: E11). Michelle Charters (Teryl Rothery), a nurse at an elderly care facility, is sexually assaulted by a ghost seeking revenge for the mistreatment experienced at the hands of the staff and doctors while a patient at the facility. Little concern or empathy is shown Michelle except by Scully, and even that is brief; Scully's incredulity grows as she listens to Michelle's account of the attack. Michelle pushes back, insisting that she isn't 'some kind of shrinking violet who would repress the memory of a rapist's face'. The episode quickly shifts its focus away from the assault to the paranormal explanation for the ghosts' presence, leaving Michelle without support or resolution, sidelining the seriousness of sexual assault while assuming the impossibility of justice. Michelle, too, participates in the construction of a victim hierarchy by positioning herself as credible, *not* a 'shrinking violet' who suppresses the experience of assault. The multiple forms of victim/survivor experience, including memory loss, and ways that a survivor's credibility is undermined or that cases go unresolved, are left unexamined by the end of the episode.

'The Post-Modern Prometheus' (S5: E05) takes inspiration from James Whale's 1931 film *Frankenstein*. The story also draws upon the sympathy for the monster found in Mary Shelley's novel *Frankenstein; or, The Modern Prometheus* (1818), but trades violent revenge for non-consensual pregnancy. The episode is experimental, framed as a comic book story, shot in black and white and comedic in tone. The story opens in a small town. A whimsical circus music-like theme accompanies the viewer as Shaineh Berkowitz's (Pattie Tierce) house is covered over with fumigation tarps; inside, a 'monster' burns something on the stove, filling the house with fumes and smoke. The music changes when the intruder puts on Cher's 'The Sun Ain't Gonna Shine Anymore' inside the house. Shaineh glimpses the 'monster' outside her living room before she is rendered unconscious and, she later learns, impregnated (this occurs offscreen). Eighteen years earlier, Shaineh had a similar experience that resulted in the birth of her son, Izzy (Stewart Gale). Shaineh writes to Mulder – after seeing him on *The Jerry*

Springer Show (1991–2018) – to ask him to investigate. After a mob-led pursuit, the agents and townspeople learn from the 'monster', Mutato (Chris Owens), that he was created by Dr Pollidori (John O'Hurley), a power-hungry man who believes his work will eventually earn him a Nobel prize. Pollidori's father raised Mutato and later attempted to create a mate for him but failed, instead populating the town with human-appearing animal–human offspring. Mutato impregnated Shaineh (as well as Dr Pollidori's wife) in his continued effort to produce a companion for himself. Mutato's story elicits compassion from the townspeople who decide that Mutato is not in fact a monster; and though he committed medical rape when he drugged and impregnated women without their consent, the agents bring him to see Cher, his favourite artist. Shaineh and Mrs. Pollidori (Miriam Smith) appear on *The Jerry Springer Show* with their Mutato-like babies. Jerry asks if these babies are hard to love. Shaineh's response, 'What's not to love?' reaffirms that a mother's love trumps all, including home invasion, lack of consent and forced insemination.

In 'Small Potatoes' (S4: E20), Eddie Van Blundht (Darin Morgan), a janitor at the local hospital, has sex with and impregnates five different women. Due to a genetic abnormality that allows him to alter his appearance to look like anyone, the women believe they are having sex with their husbands or, in one case, Luke Skywalker (the central character of the *Star Wars* trilogy). Four of the women are married and want children; the other, Amanda, was Eddie's high-school girlfriend, currently single, and not trying to get pregnant. When Scully and Mulder question Van Blundht, he asks, hypothetically speaking, that if these women wanted children and their husbands were not capable, and in the end everyone's happy, where is the crime? Mulder, unable to come up with a theory, turns to Scully for help. Scully, finding it unlikely that these were cases of consensual sex, suggests that the 'date rape drug' Rohypnol might have been used, something Mulder sheepishly admits he had not considered. Later, Eddie locks Mulder in the hospital basement and assumes his appearance. Back in Washington, DC, Scully and 'Mulder' discuss the case report with Assistant Director Skinner. Van Blundht evaded capture but Scully confirms that he was indeed a rapist and that he has been entered into the national sex offender database. That night, 'Mulder' shows up unannounced at Scully's apartment with a bottle of wine. 'Mulder' questions why he and Scully never really talk; he asks, 'Well, what's stopping us?' This is a 'Mulder' who listens, asks questions and is not consumed by his personal quest and need for an elusive truth. As he moves to kiss Scully, the real Mulder bursts into the apartment. Later, Mulder visits Eddie in prison. Eddie says that he was born a loser, but Mulder is one by choice, and advises Mulder to get out and live more, to appreciate what he has. Scully reminds Mulder that he is not a loser. 'Yeah', he says, 'but I'm not Eddie Van Blundht either, am I'?

'Small Potatoes' is an episode that, through Eddie, offers Scully and Mulder some lessons: Scully should acknowledge that she desires the intimacy and personal connections that are missing from her life; and Mulder needs to remember that there is more to life than his egomaniacal quest for the truth and appreciate what is right in front of him. That Scully, the sceptical doctor and scientist, does not notice anything amiss is difficult to believe and threatens the logical integrity of the character. But the use of a rape-by-deception story to tease an audience with romance or to teach characters some life lessons does not stand out as a particularly surprising example of the representational violence done to women, for which reason it begs scrutiny. 'Small Potatoes' intentionally denies the monstrousness of the week's villain for comedic purposes and undermines the integrity of Scully's character. Scully's vulnerability and desire for connection are exploited by Eddie, a man who only Scully acknowledges and labels as a rapist with any conviction. But within the broader cultural and entertainment context and vernacular, Scully's ability to look past or ignore the glaringly obvious signs that she is not in fact sitting on her couch with Mulder follows cultural gendered tropes and logics of the time. The scene and Scully are legible because the audience can see that Scully, no matter how dedicated to her career she may be, is almost always ready to let it all fall away for love and connection. She's just waiting for the right guy.

'You're a medical doctor?': Scully undermined, abducted and used

The character of Dana Scully is at once a feminist icon, a touchstone in the history of women television characters and a character perniciously exploited and abused by the series' writers. 'Small Potatoes' is an example of a monster-of-the-week episode that exploits both the audience and the character of Scully for the sake of humour. More significant, however, is Scully's role in the series myth-arc. In its service, Scully suffers repeated violence and physical and emotional trauma. In this way, Scully has much in common with the 'final girl' trope of the horror film genre. The 'final girl' is a term devised by Carol Clover and that entered the popular lexicon of the 1990s (Clover 1992). The final girl is the character that survives, but she is brutalized and witness to brutality, including seeing her friends and family die. She fights and survives though because she is smart, strong, boyish and not driven by sex or romance; she lives with the knowledge that she is always in peril. The final girl represents a shift in women's roles in horror from passive victim to traumatized survivor who fights for her life and, often, to kill the monster, but she is not necessarily feminist. She serves the monster's story, or a moral or cautionary tale, and fulfils the need in horror to show how threatening the evil is, what it can and will do.

Scully, too, is smart, fights the bad guys to save Mulder and is motivated by things she values more than sex.[4] She is repeatedly abducted by the series' 'monsters': she is twice kidnapped by Donnie Pfaster (Nick Chinlund), a death fetishist ('Irresistible' and 'Orison'); nearly lobotomized by a man who wants to free her from the 'howlers' he believes are tormenting her ('Unruhe'); comes close to dying in a furnace after a date ('Never Again') and survives a cult that wants her to be the next host for a slug-like creature they believe is the second coming of Christ ('Roadrunners'). Scully survives because she does not let normative standards of femininity and heterosexual, cisgender womanhood define her. The final girl is Scully's predecessor, from whom she inherits the role as reasoning survivor and fighter who sees what others don't or won't, who assimilates new information without giving herself over to the irrational. But Scully, more than the final girl, comes to be defined by her body and used as a tool for reproduction. The series' fixation on reproduction and pregnancy mines the depths of cruelty and representational violence. A summary of the myth-arc events that most directly impact Scully follows to demonstrate how the non-consensual use of women's bodies – including the body of a lead character – is central to and goes unexamined in many of the series' plotlines and thus narratively undermines a character who remains a milestone figure in the history of popular culture.

Scully: Significant events

Scully begins a career at the FBI as a means to distinguish herself beyond the field of medicine. On the orders of powerful men in the FBI, Scully is assigned to work on the X-Files, a fringe unit devoted to the investigation of the paranormal. Scully is specifically ordered to spy on and debunk the work of another agent who works in the X-Files unit, Fox Mulder. Mulder is driven by a need to uncover the truth about his sister, Samantha, who was abducted from their home as a child. The cases that Mulder and Scully investigate draw them into the conspiracy orchestrated by the Syndicate. Since 1947, the men of the Syndicate have worked to hide proof of the existence of extraterrestrials and the inevitable colonization with which humanity is threatened. In exchange for their survival, the Syndicate members decide to aid the colonists in preparation for the takeover. Humanity will die once exposed to an alien virus, so the Syndicate works to create alien–human

---

[4] In accordance with another horror trope, sex=death, the few times Scully expresses desire or is in a sexual situation almost all lead her to danger.

hybrids who will survive but be enslaved by the colonists. At the same time, the Syndicate secretly works to develop a vaccine against the alien virus that would give humanity a chance to survive and fight the alien colonists. Integral to their project are reproductive technologies for the use of cloning and hybridization. Women are abducted not only so their ova can be harvested and used in the creation of the hybrids to be enslaved ('Nisei' (S3: E09), 'Memento Mori' (S4: E14)) or to carry the test foetuses to term ('Emily' (S5: E07)), but also in their attempts to create hybrids resistant to the virus. Women, including Scully, are made both victim and sacrificial hero.

Over the course of the series, Scully is made the centre of the myth-arc. Though both of the agents' lives are repeatedly threatened, Mulder enters into these dangerous situations as a direct result of his personal quest for the truth; Scully, by contrast, is subjected to violence as and because she is a woman, and specifically through acts of structural, reproductive violence which begin when she is abducted and experimented on as part of the Syndicate's project ('Duane Barry' and 'Ascension'). As a result, she is left infertile, her eggs extracted to be used in the creation of alien–human hybrids. Scully is twice abducted or nearly killed by an alien bounty hunter sent to protect the colonization project ('End Game' (S2: E17), 'Without' (S8: E02)); in 'End Game', the bounty hunter appears as Mulder. The effect is to watch 'Mulder' assault and nearly kill Scully. The Syndicate's assassins make an attempt on her life because she wants 'something they don't – justice', but they mistakenly kill her sister, Melissa (Melinda McGraw), instead ('The Blessing Way' (S3: E01)). In addition to infertility, Scully develops cancer after removing a chip that was implanted in her neck during her abduction ('Memento Mori')[5] and survives only because the Cigarette Smoking Man needs her for his own plans ('Redux II' (S5: E02)).[6] Despite her inability to conceive, Scully discovers that she is the biological mother of Emily, a child created by scientists using Scully's harvested ova ('Christmas Carol' (S5: E06)). Shortly after, Emily dies while in Scully's care; maybe, Mulder tells her, Emily was 'not meant to be' ('Emily'). When the Syndicate's project begins to fall apart, Scully is almost immolated by alien rebels who, in an attempt to stop colonization, target previous test subjects/abductees ('The Red and the Black' (S5: E14)). Ignoring Assistant Director Skinner's warnings, Mulder and Scully continue searching for details about and proof of the Syndicate's conspiracy (*The X-Files: Fight the Future* (1998)). Scully is stung by a bee carrying a version of a virus that initiates gestation of an alien foetus in a human host. Mulder cures her using a vaccine given to him by a

---

[5] It is in this episode that Mulder finds out Scully's ova have been taken from her. He does not tell her but she learns sometime after her diagnosis.
[6] The Cigarette Smoking Man hopes to manipulate Mulder into working for him. Scully's death would only increase Mulder's dedication to finding and exposing the truth.

defiant member of the Syndicate and rescues her from an alien ship buried under the ice in Antarctica.

Finally acting on her desire to have children, Scully sees a doctor who uses the stolen ova recovered by Mulder,[7] but Scully's attempts to conceive using IVF, with Mulder as the donor, appear to fail ('Per Manum'). Not long after Mulder and Scully's relationship turns romantic, Mulder is abducted (by aliens) and Scully learns that she is pregnant ('Requiem' (S7: E22)) and believes Mulder is the father. Mulder is later found and believed to be dead ('This Is Not Happening' (S8: E14)), leaving Scully devastated and alone. Scully attends Mulder's funeral but does not accept his death. She later exhumes his body based on evidence that he may still be alive and is subsequently able to save him ('Deadalive' (S8: E15)).[8] Scully gives birth to their son, William, while surrounded and threatened by alien soldiers, and without Mulder ('Existence' (S8: E21)). After a brief reunion, Mulder goes into hiding based on threats to his life and William's. However, despite Mulder's absence, William is kidnapped and found ('Providence' (S9: E10)),[9] and survives an attempt on his life ('Provenance' (S9: E09)). In order to protect William, Scully gives him up for adoption ('William' (S9: E16)). Mulder returns and he and Scully are united as he awaits trial after being framed for murder ('The Truth' (S9: E19–20)). Mulder is sentenced to death and Scully again confronts the possible loss of her partner. The series' original run concludes with Scully and Mulder going into hiding, not knowing what has become of William.

The 'My Struggle' episodes that bookend the revival seasons (seasons ten and eleven) are a continuation of the emotional and physical violence to which Scully has been subjected and do additional narrative injustice to the character. In 'My Struggle III' (S11: E01), Scully is hospitalized with seizures caused by visions she is experiencing, visions she shares with her son, William. She leaves the hospital to begin a search for William but suffers a car accident due to the visions and is hospitalized again, where she is almost killed by a man who tries to strangle her to death. In the same episode, the Cigarette Smoking Man tells Skinner that he, not Mulder, is the father of Scully's son. He drugged and impregnated Scully, an act of medical rape, with a super-soldier-like embryo to create a human–alien hybrid ('En Ami'). Scully is again reduced to a body, a test tube in an experiment to which she did not consent, by a man who claims to care for her. The Cigarette Smoking

---

[7]In a 'Per Manum' (S8: E13) flashback, Mulder tells Scully that he found her ova and had them tested but that they weren't viable. He found the ova in a lab while searching for a cure for Scully's Cancer ('Memento Mori' (S4: E14)).

[8]During the abduction, Mulder underwent a process to turn him into a super soldier, an alien replacement working to ensure that plans for colonization continue.

[9]William has strange abilities due to alien DNA. It is not clear at this point why William is different.

Man tells this to Skinner; Scully will not find out until the season (and series) finale when Skinner tells Scully the truth about William ('My Struggle IV' (S11: E10)). Scully and Mulder each search for William but, before they reach him, William is shot in the head by the Cigarette Smoking Man who is then shot and killed by Mulder. Scully finds Mulder mourning the loss of William. He asks her what he is if not a father. Scully tells him the truth about William: he was an experiment that 'wasn't meant to be', echoing what Mulder said to Scully about Emily. Scully appears largely unaffected by William's death,[10] as if learning of his parentage negates the connection she and Mulder share because of William.

This revelation rewrites the past, taking from Scully her choice, and from both characters their consensual partnership and connection as William's parents. The Cigarette Smoking Man-as-William's-father revelation thus turns Scully into a victim of assault, a 'twist' used by the writers as a plot device, a source of drama, in service of a narrative for which they have, since 1993, mined and exploited a wide array of means for women to be tortured, killed, assaulted or otherwise suffer physical and emotional trauma. These tropes were already problematic in the 1990s, but by 2018 they are near intolerable. In the #MeToo era, the negative responses from critics and fans are signs of a culture less willing to ignore and more able to see the problem with a narrative built on reproductive violence. The ignorance Chris Carter demonstrated when he denied that this was rape was hard to read as anything but more of the passive/aggressive misogyny found throughout the series.[11] 'My Struggle IV' ends with Scully comforting Mulder over the loss of a son he showed little interest in finding and asserting that he *is* a father: Scully pulls his hand to her stomach, revealing that she is (impossibly) pregnant. Scully's story ends by reminding us that she is, in the end, her womb; and, to complete her subsumption into proper, disciplined, heterosexual womanhood, she takes care of Mulder's feelings instead of her own and reminds us that the only child worth having is the one they create together. In *The X-Files*, where children are experiments and women are vessels, it is tempting to understand this moment as a radical refusal by Scully of all that has been done her. But, with the fate of the humanity-destroying virus unknown, Scully's desire for a child and her pregnancy are as cruelly optimistic as it gets (see Berlant 2011). In a world with no future, a child

---

[10] This is not shown, but it is possible that, because of her psychic connection with William, Scully knows that he is still alive but believes that he is safer if believed to be dead.
[11] That the Cigarette Smoking Man says he's the father makes it clear that he did this to Scully and sees himself as intimately connected to her. Fans were angry about Carter's treatment of Scully in season eleven's 'My Struggle' episodes, many calling out the use of medical rape and Scully's uncharacteristic apathy over the death of William; even Gillian Anderson shared her disappointment.

holds not promise or hope but instead reminds us of inevitable destruction and death (see Edelman 2004).

Conclusion: I want to believe in Scully

Fear-mongering technoscientific nightmare, metaphor for the horrors of colonization or the xenophobic fears of immigration, beacon of liberal multiculturalism, feminist recasting of gender roles, a cynical use of representation that abuses the other even while making otherness central, one of the most influential series ever made, a love story: *The X-Files* could be all of these things in a decade that was saturated with pop culture feminism, public takedowns of women as entertainment, a culture war, a sex war, 'super-predators' and tough-on-crime politics, chatroom panic, digital economies, new technologies of warfare, censorship and parental advisory labels and, perhaps most significantly, increasingly diffused and enmeshed relations of power via neoliberal governmentality wherein consolidated and transnational micro-networks of power displaced the fiction of the bounded nation state. The Syndicate is a group of nameless men who represent no one and no nation and thus are beholden to no law. One thing that *The X-Files* makes clear through the atrocities committed by the Syndicate is that the assumption of legal or constitutionally guaranteed rights of bodily autonomy and integrity, or of privacy, have never been self-evident. The passage of the Patriot Act following the attacks of 11 September 2001 eroded the right to privacy, but to highlight it as a universal or radical shift is symptomatic of a cultural amnesia that erases the histories of queer, Black, indigenous and immigrant populations, of people of colour and of women. The series' writers engage with these histories, but the line between critical representation and exploitative reproduction is hard to discern and often crossed. The series, on occasion and in flawed ways, addresses and names discriminatory practices, policies, ideologies and outcomes tied to racism, xenophobia and political/economic marginalization.[12] By contrast, when it comes to violent appropriation of women's bodies that function as the foundation of the myth-arc, wherein the Syndicate scientists are using

---

[12]Some examples include: 'Fresh Bones' (S2: E15), 'The Blessing Way' (S3: E1), 'Teso Dos Bichos' (S3: E18), 'Hell Money' (S3: E19), 'Teliko' (S4: E3), 'El Mundo Gira' (S4: E11), 'Drive' (S6: E2), 'The Unnatural' (S6: E19), 'Release' (S9: E17), 'Badlaa' (S8: E10), 'The Gift' (S8: E11) and 'Babylon' (S10: E5). In some cases, audience sympathies are directed towards the 'other' as victim; in others, the writers take a revenge of the oppressed approach. Episodes that garner sympathy often feel patronizing and/or fetishizing, while the vengeance episodes, despite trying to teach a 'you reap what you sow' lesson, are nevertheless muddled by the 'monster' status of the character. See 'Badlaa' for a particularly salient example. 'Babylon' is also a notoriously tone-deaf episode.

women to create the alien–human hybrids that the alien colonists require, no feminist analysis or critique exists to name the gendered and structural nature of this violence.

Dana Scully, however, emerges from the morass as one of the most influential women characters of the 1990s. Despite scriptwriting that repeatedly undermined and made her second to Mulder, Anderson and Duchovny developed a dynamic depiction of equality and mutual respect. Scully kept it together while Mulder was over-emotional, his judgement clouded by his obsessive search for his sister and the truth. She eye rolled his quirks and most absurd theories, and she mocked his masculinity and bravado. Mulder respected Scully's intellect, valued her work as a scientist and offered her the safety to be vulnerable without judgement. In a series that did so much gender-specific violence to one of its leads, the dynamic created by the actors, and making it believable, was no small feat. Through and around the character of Scully there exists a structure of feeling indicative of a change in the portrayal and reception of women characters that makes it possible to see and *feel* characters differently, causing a kind of code- or trope-slippage. These characters are still most often written by men and exist within the dominant cultural frames of their time, but culture is constituted by structures of feeling and affective landscapes by which it is possible to describe how cultural and social norms change. Through what José Muñoz (1999) has called 'disidentification', queer people and people of colour negotiate the exclusionary and normative ideological codes embedded in, for example, popular culture in order to creatively read themselves into, rework or appropriate such codes or images. I am extending Muñoz's theory to subjects who may find themselves visible in popular media but must read themselves in, through and against misogynistic, violent or victim tropes around gender. It is in this way that Dana Scully could become a feminist icon in the 1990s despite the victim role she was regularly made to play and accounts for how, from a vantage point three decades later, we more easily identify the misogyny inherent within the series.

It is because of characters like Scully that we come to develop a new frame of reference and from which new characters and codes that challenge normativity are created. For example, much has been made by fans and critics of Scully's missing desk. While it is easy (and important) to read Scully's lack of a desk as a sign of an unequal partnership and sexist writing that treated her as a sidekick, I always viewed the basement office as undesirable, as a recurring joke. The joke is almost never at Scully's expense because we, too, roll our eyes at a sexist cop or Mulder's quips and fits. Mulder only has that office and the X-Files, and it is from there that he pursues his quest for the truth;[13] Scully is a doctor and a scientist, who takes her fight to the laboratory

---

[13]Mulder doesn't have much outside of the X-Files. Scully may not have a desk, but Mulder doesn't have a bed. He goes between his couch in his apartment, where he sleeps or watches

or morgue. She is not passive: Scully calls Mulder out for always taking the lead, not treating her as an equal, and because she does not have a desk (see, for example, 'Syzygy' (S3: E13), 'Never Again' and 'All Things' (S7: E17)). But a desk and her name on the door would reveal her total acceptance of the X-Files and her assignment, whereas her outsider position proves to be useful and strategic: her effectiveness as an investigator, and how she can continue to be taken seriously despite her association with Mulder, are due in part to the distance she maintains. Scully, too, wants answers and, more importantly, justice. A desk and her name on the door would jeopardize her ability to find and deliver either. Though it is years before Mulder recognizes that Scully makes her own choices, and for him to hear her when she says that it is not all about him, Scully commits to the X-Files, a commitment in part fomented by the part she comes to play in the Syndicate's conspiracy. Scully – just as much as, if not more than, Mulder – has stakes in the game. For Mulder, his quest to expose the Syndicate is personal; for Scully, a government conspiracy is political, a failure of the institutions to which she and much of her family have dedicated and lost their lives. Mulder wants the truth; Scully wants answers ('Paper Clip' (S3: E02)). The tension in the structure of feeling that exists between Scully's role in the series' conspiracy plot and Scully as a character is due in large part to Gillian Anderson's choices for the character. Scully's eye rolling, along with Mulder's tone of self-deprecating humour, are just two of the affective and interactional tools used by the actors to establish equality and complicate the power dynamic between the characters. The actors provide viewers – and future creators – a starting point from which to disidentify with the writers' choices; thus exists the potential to read and rewrite Scully, and realize new characters and stories in the future.

The X-Files may or may not fade into obscurity – dependent in a significant way on the streaming ecosystem and economy – but contemporary creators and show runners, directors and writers continue to cite it as an influence. As long as that iterative intertextuality exists, its influence and importance remain through genre television's repetition and revision of tropes and stories. In the media of the 1990s, women who challenged men or defied social norms were regularly demonized and mistreated, or had the violence committed by or against them turned into spectacle or cautionary tale.[14] It is within and because of this context that Dana Scully – mistreated and used by powerful men – was an icon whose influence continues. These women of the 1990s, real and fictional, exist beyond the narratives and events that

---

porn and old science fiction movies, and his office, where he watches porn and reviews slides of crop circles and UFO sightings.

[14] Some examples (in no particular order): Anita Hill, Lorena Bobbitt, Amy Fischer, Aileen Wournos, Tonya Harding, Pam Smart, Jon Benet Ramsey, Nicole Brown Simpson, Princess Diana and Monika Lewinsky, to name a few.

brought them attention and, often, notoriety. The story each told, or told in their name, must be recognized amid the swirl of competing misogynistic narratives proffered by the media in the form of entertainment or takedowns. Scully, likewise, cannot be reduced to the writing or plot of *The X-Files*. Recounting the myth-arc and conspiracy events of the series makes Scully little more than a womb, but the *feeling* affixed to Scully is not bound by the punishments and plot service the character faced. Without this distinction, Scully-as-icon is lost to the audience, thus repeating the representational violence done by writing that, in service to the structures of feeling through which we create something new, must be tossed aside.

References

Berlant, L. G. (2011), *Cruel Optimism*, Durham, NC: Duke University Press.

Bowman, S. (2018), 'Gillian Anderson's Response To "The X-Files" Season Finale Is Seriously All Of Us Right Now', *Bustle*, 24 March. Available online: https://www.bustle.com/p/gillian-andersons-response-to-the-x-files-season-finale-is-a-reminder-that-shes-always-got-scullys-back-8596058 (accessed 9 January 2023).

Clover, C. J. (1992), *Men, Women, and Chain Saws: Gender in the Modern Horror Film*, Princeton, NJ: Princeton University Press.

Doyle, J., and A. Jones (2006), 'Introduction: New Feminist Theories of Visual Culture', *Signs*, 31 (3): 607–15. Available online: https://www.jstor.org/stable/10.1086/499288 (accessed 9 January 2023).

Edelman, L. (2004), *No Future: Queer Theory and the Death Drive*, Durham, NC: Duke University Press.

Frankenstein (1931), [Film] Dir. James Whale, USA: Universal Pictures.

Geller, T. L. (2016), *The X-files*, Detroit: Wayne State University Press.

Grinberg, E. (2016), 'Gillian Anderson: I Was Offered Less Pay for "X-Files" Reboot', *CNN.com*, 24 January 24. Available online: https://www.cnn.com/2016/01/23/entertainment/gillian-anderson-pay-gap-X-Files-feat/index.html (accessed 9 January 2023).

Imhoff, A. (2018), 'The Rape Culture Is Out There in *The X-Files* Season 11 Premiere, and Fans Are Angry', *The Mary Sue*, 4 January. Available online: https://www.themarysue.com/x-files-season-11-premiere/ (accessed 9 January 2023).

Jameson, F. (1991), *Postmodernism, or, The Cultural Logic of Late Capitalism*, Durham, NC: Duke University Press.

Jerry Springer (1991–2018), [TV Programme] NBCUniversal.

Leon, M. (2016), 'Gillian Anderson: I Was Offered Half Duchovny's Pay for "The X-Files" Revival', *The Daily Beast*, 22 January. Available online: https://www.thedailybeast.com/gillian-anderson-i-was-offered-half-duchovnys-pay-for-the-x-files-revival (accessed 9 January 2023).

Lewinsky, M., (2018), '"Who Gets to Live in Victimville?": Why I Participated in a New Docuseries on The Clinton Affair', *Vanity Fair*, 13 November. Available

online: https://www.vanityfair.com/news/2018/11/the-clinton-affair-documentary-monica-lewinsky (accessed 9 January 2023).
Melamed, J. (2001), *Represent and Destroy: Rationalizing Violence in the New Racial Capitalism*, Minneapolis: University of Minnesota Press.
Muñoz, J. E. (1999), *Disidentifications: Queers of Color and the Performance of Politics*, Minneapolis: University of Minnesota Press.
Pantozzi, J. (2018), '*The X-Files* Finale Was So Horrible I Completely Understand Why Gillian Anderson Isn't Coming Back', *Gizmodo*, 22 March. Available online: https://gizmodo.com/the-x-files-finale-was-so-horrible-i-completely-underst-1823987599 (accessed 9 January 2023).
Sex and the City (1998–2004), [TV programme] HBO.
Shelley, M., (1818), *Frankenstein: Or, the Modern Prometheus*, London: Lackington, Hughes, Harding, Mavor & Jones.
The X-Files: Fight the Future (1998), [Film] Dir. Rob Bowman, USA: 20th Century Fox.

18

Invasion of body snatchers: Fox Mulder's queerness, monstrosity and status quo

Klára Feikusová

When Dana Scully, and the audience with her, first encounters Fox Mulder, he introduces himself as the 'FBI's most unwanted' ('Pilot' S1: E01), thereby immediately presenting himself as an outcast and troublemaker. Mulder is a curious hero because he challenges, instead of upholding, the law and status quo. In the narrative of *The X-Files*, Scully is 'normal' and Mulder is marked as the Other. Even though he is able-bodied, white, middle-class and heterosexual, he resists the patriarchal system, which is represented by the FBI, law and government. In this chapter, I argue that Mulder's voluntary outsider status, opposition to authority and feminization can be read as queer, as well as monstrous. I specifically investigate how Mulder's queerness is challenged in those episodes that feature the concept of shapeshifting: 'Small Potatoes' (S4: E20), 'Dreamland' (S6: E04) and 'Dreamland II' (S6: E05). The antagonists in these episodes – Eddie van Blundht and Morris Fletcher, respectively – take over Mulder's body and life and try to 'unqueer' and thus repress him.

Mulder's duality and liminality

Fox Mulder holds all the privileges that Western culture champions: he is a white, able-bodied cisgender and heterosexual male from a middle-class family, who has obtained a prestigious University of Oxford education. He is also good-looking and physically strong. At the beginning of his FBI career, he was considered a brilliant profiler and agent. When his former colleagues and supervisors from the Violent Crime Unit seek his advice, they exhibit both admiration and jealousy for his talents and consider them lost working in the X-Files unit ('Ghost in the Machine' (S1: E07), 'Young at Heart'(S1: E16), 'Grotesque' (S3: E14)). Thanks to his social capital, Mulder has access to highly sensitive and confidential information and powerful connections: Mulder's legal father, Bill Mulder (Mulder's biological father is revealed to be the Cigarette Smoking Man), worked for the US State Department, and Mulder also has a friend in the US Senate who is a patron of his work. All these privileges allow him to work in the X-Files, even though the unit is viewed as ridiculous and undesirable by many in Washington, DC.

According to *The X-Files* scholar Michele Malach, the FBI usually represents normalcy and Mulder's tall, lanky, black-coated figure seemingly presents him as an 'old-school' FBI agent (1996: 64, 70). On the outside, Mulder seems as normal and normative as can be, which is evident when other characters encounter him for the first time. For example, in 'Humbug', an episode taking place in a town formed by, and of, sideshow performers, numerous people consider him abnormal in his normality. When Mulder and Scully are checking into a motel, Mulder unwittingly offends the owner, Mr Nutt (Michael J. Anderson), because he assumes he has also performed in the sideshows as he has a shortened stature. Mr Nutt rejects the idea and retaliates by pointing out Mulder's stereotypical looks:

Mr Nutt	Just because it's human nature to make instantaneous judgements of others based solely on their physical appearances? Why, I've done the same thing to you, for example. I've taken in your all-American features, your dour demeanour, your unimaginative necktie design, and concluded that you work for the government … an FBI agent. But you see the tragedy here? I have mistakenly reduced you to a stereotype, a caricature, instead of regarding you as a specific, unique individual.
Mulder	But I am an FBI agent.

The exchange asserts that Mulder physically does indeed adhere to the traditional image of the FBI (male) agent. Later in the episode, performer Dr Blockhead laments a loss of uniqueness with possible genetic engineering. While talking to Scully, Blockhead claims the following: 'Twenty-first-century genetic engineering will not only eliminate the Siamese twins and the alligator-skin people, but you're gonna be hard-pressed to find a slight overbite, or a not-so-high cheekbone. You see, I've seen the future, and the future looks just like him! [points to Mulder] Imagine, going through your life looking like that.' The irony and joke of this scene are emphasized by Dr Blockhead's disgusted look and a following shot of Mulder standing with his hands on his hips and his chin held high. In 'Jose Chung's 'From Outer Space' (S3: E20), a paranoid UFO enthusiast, Blaine, describes Mulder, mistaking him for a man in black, as 'the tall, lanky one, his face was so blank and expressionless. He didn't even seem human. I think he was a mandroid.' These meta-narrative and sarcastic accounts exhibit Mulder's supposed normativity, not only as an FBI agent but also as a privileged white male.

While Mulder gives the impression of a stereotypical FBI agent, his attitudes and beliefs are not traditionally associated with the FBI. Through his pursuit of the paranormal and government conspiracies, Mulder turns away from masculinized science and logic and 'resist[s] assimilation into patriarchy and demonstrate[s] independent thinking' (Badley 2000: 68). This puts him on a path of feminization since, as film scholar Barbara Creed argues, 'proper masculinity embodies phallic power and asserts masculine qualities of power, rationality, ascendancy, and control' (2005: xvi). Mulder's methods are unusual and considered feminine: he relies on his instinct and intuition, seeking advice from astrologers ('Syzygy' (S3: E13)), seers or mediums ('Clyde Bruckman's Final Repose' (S3: E04), 'Oubliette' (S3: E08), 'Closure' (S7: E11)) and voodoo practitioners ('Fresh Bones' (S2: E15), 'Theef' (S7: E14)). Television Studies scholars Rhonda Wilcox and J. P. Williams draw on Carol J. Clover's argument that 'the conflict between White Science and Black Magic is a deeply gendered one, constitutive of a conflict between male and female ... "masculine" and "feminine"' (1992 98), thereby connecting Mulder with magic (Wilcox and Williams 1996: 107). Not only are Mulder's methods associated with the feminine, but they also manifest a connection between his body and mind, as Malach argues: 'Mulder especially subverts the boundaries that separate mind and body, so important for traditionally defined law enforcement officials ... Mulder relies on his hunches; psychic evidence is as important to him as the physical kind, and he relies heavily on the dreams and visions of others' (Malach 1996: 71). Therefore, Mulder has his feet in two worlds – a real, physical one (as an FBI agent) and a spiritual one (as a believer seeking the Truth).

At the same time, Mulder is athletic, physically strong and can be aggressive when angry ('Ascension' (S2: E06), 'One Breath' (S2: E08), 'Zero Sum' (S4: E21)). Some of his hobbies, like sport – he favours baseball and basketball – and even pornography, are traditionally associated with masculinity. So, while his body represents masculinity, his mind is feminized, making him 'gender-liminal, moving back and forth across the border of traditionally accepted gender patterns' (Wilcox and Williams 1996: 99). This gender liminality makes him a 'New Man' open to solutions not accepted by rational, linear, Western patriarchy (Wilcox and Williams

1996: 104). He represents a liminal figure, who 'inhabits the threshold between opposing realities' (Thompson 2017: 181), merges and subverts masculine and feminine and later also becomes liminal when infected by the black oil ('Tunguska' (S4: E08), 'Terma' (S4: E09), 'The Sixth Extinction II: Amor Fati' (S7: E02)) and an alien virus ('Deadalive' (S8: E15)), putting him on the verge of becoming a human–alien hybrid.

A hero against the status quo

In horror, crime fiction and conspiracy thrillers – those genres central to the narrative of *The X-Files* – there is usually a violation of the status quo that the hero tries to remedy (for example, by destroying a monster, catching the criminals, preventing the conspirators from overtaking or infiltrating the government/country). Whether the threat is posed by monsters or conspiring villains, it has usually come from the outside. In the story world of *The X-Files*, the threats are already present and always have been: there are demons, mythical creatures, mutants, alien–human hybrids and more living among humans, while the government is filled with and manipulated by the 'men in black' who hide these threats from the ordinary citizen. Therefore, this alternative dystopian present-day world has already been twisted and subverted. The conspiracy that Mulder seeks to uncover has started long before he was born. In consequence, Mulder, as the protagonist of the series, does not safeguard 'the status quo of American culture' (Dorsey 2002: 450), but disrupts it through his attempts to expose the US government and its conspiracies. As Communication and Cultural Studies theoretician, Leroy G. Dorsey asserts, Mulder represents a 'tricksterish "anti-hero"', who tries to uproot the foundations of the community he is supposed to protect (Dorsey 2002: 451, 459). So, while Mulder 'resembles the traditional mythic hero; good-looking, respected, accomplished, dedicated, and fearless' (Dorsey 2002: 460), he is a postmodern anti-hero who often breaks rules (and the law), has selfish reasons for his quest (the abduction of his sister, Samantha) and can push past ethical boundaries (for example, his vengeful and violent behaviour in 'One Breath' or 'Paper Hearts' (S4: E10)). But most importantly, Mulder threatens the status quo that is already corrupted but presents normalcy to unsuspecting citizens. This is evident when Mulder confronts the Cigarette Smoking Man in 'One Breath':

Cigarette Smoking Man	I'm in the game because I believe what I'm doing is right.
Mulder	Right? Who are you to say what's right?
Cigarette Smoking Man	Who are you? If people were to know of the things that I know, it would all fall apart.

So, both Mulder and the status quo are ambiguous, complicating the narrative of the horror and conspiracy genre in The X-Files. The institutions that usually represent what is normal and good (the law enforcement, government, authorities in general) are untrustworthy and villainous, most prominently represented by the Syndicate and the Cigarette Smoking Man, Mulder's personal enemy. These are the myth-arc's main antagonists and the series overall, but even the monsters-of-the-week serve as their proxy – or victims. As X-Files scholar Theresa Geller argues, monster-of-the-week episodes 'frequently construct narratives that introduce unexpected others as suspects, only to turn this suspicion back on to the system that categorizes others as monstrous' (2016: 28). Monsters-of-the-week aside, the ultimate villains are mainly older, white men who control everything and everyone, revealing the series' 'denunciation of patriarchy' (Kubek 1996: 182). This is especially the case with the Syndicate, which represents the patriarchy since the 'group of older white men seems the embodiment of "the Man", the stereotypically faceless, nameless, rich, and powerful men responsible for running the state' (Malin 2005: 126). In the series' message of 'distrust toward established authority, representing institutions of government and the established order as highly flawed, even complicit in the worst crimes and evil imaginable' (Kellner 1999: 169), it implies that patriarchy is an untrustworthy institution as well.

Queer reading of Fox Mulder

Mulder's liminality, his status as an outcast and Other and his rebellion against patriarchal villains can be read as queer. Queer theory lacks definition, but this lack indicates the nature of the theory; it can't be defined, otherwise it ceases to be queer. Queer and Feminist theory scholars Hannah McCann and Whitney Monaghan argue that, the persistently repeated idea of queer theory as "indefinable" works as its own form of definition. The insistence on indefinability hints at queer theory as a lens that emphasizes the slipperiness of meaning and the transgression of categories and boundaries' (McCann and Monaghan 2020: 1–2). For the purposes of this chapter, I am drawing upon the work of Harry Benshoff and Darren Elliott-Smith on queer horror cinema. Benshoff and Elliott-Smith provide the theories that create an intersection between horror studies and queer theory, which offers an ideal theoretical framework for this chapter. Benshoff sees queer as going beyond 'categories based on the concepts of normative heterosexuality and traditional gender roles to encompass a more inclusive, amorphous, and ambiguous contra-heterosexuality (thus there are those individuals who self-identify as "straight queers")' (1997: 5). Benshoff also influences Elliott-Smith's definition of queer theory that 'seeks to investigate, and therefore trouble, the ways in which the structures of heteronormativity pervade culture' (2016: 4). The Benshoff notion of 'straight queers' is especially important to my reading of Mulder. While queer usually relates to non-straight identity and sexuality, it can apply to heterosexual people and practices too, since normative, institutionalized heterosexuality affects and regulates people who are both inside and outside of it (Jackson 2006: 105). Therefore, queer does not only have to be about non-straight sexuality but instead can be about everything that defies heteronormativity and the patriarchal.

While Mulder is heterosexual and cisgender, he defies norms. His feminization and feminine methods make the most obvious departure from masculine expectations. Although Mulder has had relationships with women in the past (Phoebe Green and Diana Fowley), the relationships did not work out and his relationship with Scully is platonic for a long time; even after becoming romantically involved, they do not behave as a normative couple. While actor David Duchovny, who portrays Mulder in the series, is not a subject of this chapter, it should be noted that his persona is also often interpreted through queer reading. Many male gays growing up in the 1990s revered Mulder and Duchovny as they represented a scopophiliac object of desire for them; Duchovny is well aware and welcoming of this following (Milton 2020; Voss 2008). Duchovny's and Mulder's status as a sex symbol is not only reserved for gay males, as evidenced by the famous red speedos scene ('Duane Barry' (S02: E06)) which was intended for the female audience. However, when Duchovny appeared as himself on the comedy series *The Larry Sanders Show* (HBO, 1992–8), it was implied that he was gay or bisexual and there was also mention of his male gay fanbase ('The Bump' (S04: E04) and 'Everybody loves Larry' (S05: E01)). Duchovny is also aware of the fan factions and fan arts pairing Mulder and Alex Krycek (Voss 2008). Queer reading fans have established numerous 'fanons' (fan canons) about Mulder being either bisexual, transgender or other (Earp 2020).

In the episode 'Arcadia' (S6: E15), Mulder and Scully go undercover as a married couple in a gated community that has a dark underbelly, not dissimilar to *The Stepford Wives* (1975). When in the presence of their neighbours, Mulder and Scully embrace each other and call each other pet names – with notable sarcasm – but jump away from each other once they are alone, in a 'No romo' fashion. 'No romo' is a term used by, or referring to, fans that did not support the romantic pairing of Scully and Mulder. In line with playing the traditional couple, Mulder jokingly demands that Scully makes him a sandwich, but only gets a latex glove thrown in his face. During his investigation of the community, Mulder enjoys disrupting their rules (for example, he places an aesthetically unpleasing plastic flamingo on the front lawn) which agitates his neighbours. Here, Mulder mocks the notion of suburban, middle-class normativity and tradition.

When Mulder shows interest in other women ('Syzygy', 'The War of Coprophages' (S3: E12), '3', (S2: E07)), it goes unfulfilled or ends badly. His lack of romantic life or interest in it, is summed up by Scully in 'Rain King' (S5: E10) after he informs her that he is to give dating advice to another male character: 'Mulder, when was the last time you went on a date?' Other women often find him attractive, but he is shown or described as obsessed with his work ('Jersey Devil' (S1: E05)). David Duchovny himself stated that 'Mulder thinks about UFOs the way other men think about sex' (Badley 2000: 75), something that is also implied in the series when Jose Chung's voice-over, in 'Jose Chung's From Outer Space', comments that '[Mulder's] quest into the unknown has so warped his psyche, one shudders to think how he receives pleasures from life.' Chung's voice-over accompanies the shot of bare-chested Mulder lying in a bed and watching Bigfoot footage. In 'How the Ghosts Stole Christmas' (S6: E06), the ghost Maurice attempts to psychoanalyze Mulder: 'you're a lonely man. A lonely man chasing paramasturbatory illusions that you believe will give your life meaning and significance, which your pathetic social maladjustment makes impossible for you to find elsewhere. You probably consider yourself ... passionate, serious, misunderstood. Am I right?' Mulder never seems to go on dates or have sex, but instead watches lots of pornography. All of this enhances his 'loser' status as well as shows him as failing at heterosexuality/heteronormativity; he simply chooses to chase UFOs and aliens instead of women. This failure is also perceived by other characters that cannot understand how he can be only a friend to Scully ('Rain King', 'Small Potatoes').

Mulder, despite his social and cultural capital (his education, middle-class origin, social status and connections), talent, success in the FBI's Violent Crime Unit and physical attractiveness, chooses to queer himself by rejecting societal expectations. According to McCann and Monaghan, to 'undertake "queering" is to deploy queer as a verb, to challenge and resist expectations or norms' (2020: 3). McCann argues elsewhere that queering can be employed beyond sexuality and involve, for example, a social life, as she considers a queering of femininity a way to '"make strange" the natural order of gender' (McCann 2018: 7–8). By queering himself, Mulder becomes an outsider, he is moved down to the basement office of the FBI's J. Edgar Hoover Building and ridiculed by his peers. But none of this appears to bother Mulder. Media Studies scholar Brenton Malin argues that 'given this marginalized status, it is easy to read Mulder as a critique of traditional gender roles' (2005: 124). Most of Mulder's peers are men, especially those who perceive him as a failure or disappointment. Since Mulder likes to tease people, especially law enforcement, he often uses his 'Spooky' reputation by explicitly talking about the paranormal ('Squeeze' (S1: E03), 'Soft Light' (S2: E23), 'Quagmire' (S3: E22)), deliberately alienating those around him. Fellow FBI agents do not understand why Mulder gave up his career and status, perceiving it as a 'fall from grace' ('Young at Heart'). This is thematized in 'Grotesque' (S3: E14), an episode in which Mulder encounters his former boss, Bill Paterson. When Paterson tells Mulder he is disappointed in him, Mulder retorts: 'I wouldn't want to disappoint you by not disappointing you.' Mulder's disregard for rules and lack of interest in the normative FBI cases or methods places him outside of institutional order. His obsession in his work and quest for the Truth, combined with indifference to heteronormative life, places him outside the societal order.

Traditional family life does not interest Mulder, as is evident in episodes like 'Dreamland' and 'Home' (S4: E02). In 'Dreamland', his disinterest is parodied when he switches bodies with Morris Fletcher and must pretend to be him for a time being. Mulder is confronted with Morris's disgruntled family; his wife yells at him and children scoff and profess hate for him. The episode starts with a question posed by Scully: asking why she and Mulder 'just keep driving' (that is, chasing monsters and conspiracies), while other people get married, have kids and dogs – in other words, live a 'normal' life. Mulder insists their life is normal and while playing house with Morris's family, his belief is confirmed. It is a glimpse into the life he would hate to have. His own broken family might explain his lack of interest but more importantly, patriarchal family values are shown as 'the biggest lie of all' in the series (Badley 2000: 66). Curiously, in 'The Sixth Extinction II: Amor Fati' (S7: E02), Mulder has a vision of the Cigarette Smoking Man providing him with a new identity and life, giving him a home in the suburbs with his former love interest Diana Fowley. In this scenario, the Cigarette Smoking Man invites Mulder and Fowley to his house next door for dinner in a neighbourly manner and, soon, Mulder is marrying Fowley, having kids with her and getting older. The implication is that this vision has been forced on Mulder by the Cigarette Smoking Man given it comes after he injects Mulder with a drug. It may even reflect the Cigarette Smoking Man's desires for Mulder's future: that Mulder abandon his quest and live a normal life. In the vision, Mulder has no control: it is a montage in which he marries, has children and grows old, but it leaves him confused. Moreover, the Cigarette Smoking Man is a good friend to Mulder throughout the vision, making it even more obvious it is something he, not Mulder, wants. Since the Syndicate, represented by the Cigarette Smoking Man, stands for patriarchy, this vision indicates what the patriarchal and heteronormative society would want Mulder to be.

'Monsters, I'm your boy'

Aside from his outsider status and alignment with femininity, Mulder is liminal due to his proximity to the monstrous. As his nickname 'Spooky' indicates, he works with monsters, he works in the shadows: he is a 'monster boy' ('Folie à deux' (S5: E19)). Not only does Mulder seek out the monsters, but he also often sympathizes with them ('Jersey Devil', 'Shapes'; (S1: E19), 'Kaddish' (S4: E15), 'The Post-Modern Prometheus' (S5: E05)).

While the monsters who Mulder investigates endanger him, he does not seek to destroy them (although sometimes he must), as the traditional horror hero would, but rather he wants to study and understand them. At times, Mulder comes close to being monstrous himself, for example when he is suspected of being responsible for a series of murders in 'Grotesque', threatened by zombification in 'Folie à deux', or when he is in danger of becoming a human–alien hybrid. In 'Tunguska' and 'Terma', Mulder is infected by the black oil, which later leads to an unknown sickness ('Biogenesis', 'The Sixth Extinction', 'The Sixth Extinction II'), leaving the Cigarette Smoking Man to conclude that Mulder is becoming a human–alien hybrid. In the episode 'Deadalive', Mulder is both dead and alive, both human and alien, because of an alien virus that he survives, remaining human. Mulder's origins also equate him with monsters because of his family background. Badley calls the Mulders an '"anti-family" (a nest of conspiracy, betrayal, abduction, and uncertainty concerning parentage and identity, gender and species)' (2000: 71), which makes their initial image of a traditional, nuclear, middle-class family ironic. But it is a lie; Bill Mulder is revealed not to even be Mulder's biological father, while he gave up his daughter for the sake of the government conspiracy. Mulder's actual father, the Cigarette Smoking Man, personifies all evil and corruption in the series, thereby making Mulder the descendant of a human monster. Therefore, Mulder is bound to monsters by blood. These liminal positions between the human and alien, dead or alive, as well as his family, bring Mulder close to monstrous. And while he never becomes a monster, the monstrous always lurks within him.

According to Barbara Creed, the classical male monster is associated with what she terms 'the primal uncanny' – woman, the animal and death (2005: xii). Since these three areas constitute the Other, it means a male monster doesn't adhere to proper masculinity: masculinity is therefore a fragile concept, highlighting the patriarchal contradictions (Creed 2005: xvii). But most importantly the male monster threatens the symbolic order and 'problematize[s] the belief that civilization represents progress' (Creed 2005: xix). Mulder can be linked to all three others: woman, through his feminization, and Samantha as his 'bleeding wound' (Wilcox and Williams 1996: 108); animal, because of his forename (Fox) and his closeness to nature, again through feminine traits as the woman is closer to nature (Creed 2005: 15) and death, through his work in which he deals with death and dead bodies on a daily basis and through his liminal existence (for example, in 'Deadalive'). In the story world of *The X-Files*, where roles are subverted, the protagonist is aligned with the monstrous and the symbolic order represents the corrupted government (Kubek 1996: 170). But this is in an agreement with the notion that the status quo has already been disrupted. Therefore, it makes sense that the monstrous anti-hero should challenge it. In the horror genre overall, it is not unusual for the monsters to be sympathetic. Both Creed and Robin Wood argue that it is so because the monster represents a rebellion against the society that tries to repress it (Creed 2005: 15; Wood 2018: 84–5). Monsters are often read as queer precisely because they stand outside patriarchal and heterocentric order (Benshoff 1997: 12). Queerness 'disrupts narrative equilibrium and sets in motion a questioning of the status quo' (5), just like the monster does in the horror fiction and just as Mulder does.

Freaks and geeks and shape-shifters

Episodes that are about shape-shifting – 'Small Potatoes', 'Dreamland' and 'Dreamland II' – show how Mulder is perceived by others, since the antagonists try to impersonate him. Self-image and reputation are the main theme in 'Small Potatoes', as summed up by Mulder: 'Maybe it's other people's reactions to us that make us who we are.' In Mulder's case, he is a 'Spooky' UFOlogist, a brilliant FBI-profiler, a 'ticking time bomb' ('Jose Chung's From Outer Space') and a stereotype of an FBI agent ('Humbug'). Eddie in 'Small Potatoes' and Morris in 'Dreamland' are both attracted by Mulder's symbolic capital as well as his good looks, which they wish to have, but they are put off by his interests and hobbies.

The bodysnatching that occurs in these episodes is significant because the body frequently acts as a 'sight/site of horror' that serves to address differences (Grant 2015: 8–9), as does Mulder's in this case. Taking over Mulder's body is also a queer act. As Elliott-Smith claims, 'cinematic masculinity is conventionally impenetrable in a physical and sexual sense, as opposed to the patriarchal view of the feminine subject as penetrable' (2016: 7). In *The X-Files*, there are monsters who penetrate male bodies specifically, for example in 'Jersey Devil', 'Teliko' (S4: E03), 'Tooms' (S1: E21), 'Badlaa' (S8: E10) and 'Grotesque'. Mulder is threatened by them sometimes, depending on Scully to save him ('Jersey Devil', 'Teliko', 'Folie à deux'). According to film scholar Peter Hutchings, 'male victims in horror are themselves usually marked as "unmanly", sometimes childish ... but most often as feminine' (1993: 90). Therefore, Mulder's body is penetrable (also by Eddie and Morris), which feminizes and queers him even further. But while the bodysnatching is the queer action, the way these shape-shifters use it is not.

Since 'Small Potatoes' and 'Dreamland' fall into the narrative form of the monster of the week, Eddie and Morris can be considered monsters. Although they represent rather humorous figures, since these episodes are comedic, they can also be dangerous. Eddie uses his shape-shifting ability to take over the identities of men to rape their wives, attacks a policeman and hides his father's dead body so he can collect his security checks. Also, he attacks Mulder and locks him in a hospital basement to impersonate him. As for Morris, he is a 'man in black', part of the secret agenda within the government that Mulder fights against. With his smoking and dark suits, Morris is likened to the Cigarette Smoking Man. But ultimately, they are 'shapeshifting losers' (Geller 2016: 89), ridiculous and ridiculed.

Eddie is an unattractive janitor and nerd, presented as a failure. His looks are judged by others; women look at him with disgust and when questioning his parentage to five different babies, Scully says dryly: 'On behalf of all the women in the world, I seriously doubt this has anything to do with consensual sex.' While the first time Eddie shape-shifts into Mulder, he does so to extract himself from a difficult situation, later he does it specifically to steal Mulder's identity, motivated by his symbolic capital and physical stature (he no longer wants to be a 'loser' and so wants to adopt Mulder's attractiveness). Just before he attacks Mulder, Eddie observes: 'you're a damn good-looking man', a phrase that he repeats later when looking at his new image in the mirror. However, Eddie soon finds that Mulder is far from suave; he looks incredulously at the 'I want to believe' poster in Mulder's office and scoffs at his lack of social life. After Eddie is arrested and put in prison, Mulder visits him and Eddie informs him that 'I was born a loser, but you're one by choice.' Eddie's shock at Mulder's status not only simulates the reactions of Mulder's peers but also demonstrates how Mulder's appearance contradicts his personality.

Although Morris can be considered successful at his job, in which he is (mainly) respected, his private life is quite the opposite. His wife and kids voice their irritation with him (although these interactions are only shown after the body-swapping and Mulder only worsens the situation with his cluelessness) and Morris himself considers them a burden. Both his job and family became tiresome, so he regards the body-swapping as a chance to start over. Morris's motivations for wanting to take over Mulder's life are therefore a little different from Eddie's, but social capital, attractive job and physique certainly still play a role as well, since Morris is eager to keep Mulder's body. His own looks are reflected by Scully when she tells Mulder, in Morris's body and after finding out that the body swap might be permanent: 'I'd kiss you if you weren't so damn ugly.' Just like Eddie, Morris sees Mulder as a loser. His voice-over at the beginning of 'Dreamland II' sums him up:

> he pretty much led a normal life. … Now, Fox buckled down and worked his butt off. Graduated at top of his class at Oxford, then top of his class at the FBI academy. None of that hard work made up for his sister though. It was just a way of putting her out of his mind. Finally, the way I figure it, he went out of his mind, and he's been that way ever since. Fox Mulder pissed away a brilliant career, lost the respect of his supervisors and friends, and now lives his life shaking his fist at the sky and muttering about conspiracies to anyone who'll listen.

Even though Morris swapped his body with Mulder by accident, he readily takes over his identity, calling it 'a gift from heaven', because he can get away from his old frustrating life and enjoy his position (he bullies a motel owner into giving him a free room) and good looks to seduce women. He actively tries to save Mulder's career by sucking up to his supervisor, betraying Scully and an informant – eradicating his quest for the truth in the process – and even remodels Mulder's apartment to look more normal (he buys a bed). One of the first things he tries to do as Mulder is seduce Scully, just as Eddie does. But unlike the first case, Scully gets suspicious quickly and calls him out as an imposter. Just as getting Mulder's career back on track or buying a bed implicates an attempt to normalize Mulder, so too does the attempt at seducing Scully.

Just like other male characters, Eddie and Morris think it is not normal that Mulder does not try to have sex with Scully and tries to remedy his heterosexuality and masculinity through such an attempt. While Eddie plays a more sensitive Mulder to impress and seduce Scully, he also makes him more heteronormative (he takes an initiative by visiting Scully with wine and tries to kiss her). On the other hand, macho Morris acts so chauvinistically it makes Scully gape and stare. He smacks her bottom, patronizes her and flirts with a secretary. For Eddie and Morris, Scully represents an object to gaze at. This disturbs the egalitarian relationship between Mulder and her in which 'their looks acknowledge each other as subjects rather than fetishizing or denying the other person' (Wilcox and Williams 1996: 120). Such a relationship diverges from the expectations that society has, which is evident in the numerous encounters in which Mulder and Scully are mistaken for a couple ('Red Museum' (S2: E10), 'Small Potatoes', 'Rain King'). Through their hyper-heterosexual behaviour, Eddie and Morris reveal the masculine traits of Mulder's body. With Mulder's feminized mind gone, there is only his traditionally masculine body left. Even though, in both cases, Mulder's body remains monstrous and liminal in duality by two people sharing one body, his other liminal aspects (femininity, queerness, resistance to status quo) are diminished. Mulder's body may now represent normalcy, at least partially.

In the subversive logic of *The X-Files*, by trying to repress and destroy monstrous Mulder and bringing back the status quo, Eddie and Morris act as the heroes in the classic horror film. But although Mulder is the anti-hero and monstrous, Eddie and Morris are the villains here. Their attempt to push Mulder back into the status quo and symbolic order is repressing and serves to ruin the protagonists' quest – especially Morris, as a former man in black, who tries to eradicate Mulder's 'Spooky' career and all uncovered secrets with it. Therefore, unqueering and normalizing Mulder would be destructive to the narrative. Mulder must stand outside the status quo because he fights against it. In *The X-Files*, to be normative means being either ignorant or conforming.

References

Badley, L. (2000), 'Scully Hits the Glass Ceiling: Postmodernism, Postfeminism, Posthumanism, and *The X-Files*', in E. R. Helford (ed.), *Fantasy Girls: Gender in the New Universe of Science Fiction and Fantasy Television*, 61–90, Lanham, MD: Rowman & Littlefield.

Benshoff, H. M. (1997), *Monsters in the Closet: Homosexuality and the Horror Film*, Manchester: Manchester University Press.

Clover, C. J. (1992), *Men, Women and Chain Saws: Gender in the Modern Horror Film*, Princeton, NJ: Princeton University Press.

Creed B. (2005), *Phallic Panic: Film, Horror and the Primal Uncanny*, Carlton: Melbourne University Press.

Dorsey L. G. (2002), 'Re-reading the X-files: The Trickster in Contemporary Conspiracy Myth', *Western Journal of Communications*, 66 (4): 448–68.

Earp, J. (2020), 'Happy Bi Visibility Day to Mulder and Scully, My Preferred Bisexual Gateway Drugs', *Junkee*, 23 September, Available online: https://junkee.com/mulder-scully-bisexual-icons-x-files/272029 (accessed 29 July 2022).

Elliott-Smith, D. (2016), *Queer Horror Film and Television: Sexuality and Masculinity at the Margins*, London: I.B. Tauris.

Geller, T. L. (2016), *The X-Files*, Detroit, MI: Wayne State University Press.

Grant B. K. (ed.) (2015), *The Dread of Difference: Gender and the Horror Film*, 2nd edn, Austin: University of Texas Press.

Hutchings, P. (1993), 'Masculinity and the Horror Film', in P. Kirkham and J. Thurmin (eds), *You Tarzan: Masculinity, Movies and Men*, 84–94, London: Lawrence & Wishart.

Jackson, S. (2006), 'Gender, Sexuality and Heterosexuality: The Complexity (and Limits) of Heteronormativity', *Feminist Theory*, 7 (1): 105–21.

Kellner, D. (1999), 'The X-Files and the Aesthetics and Politics of Postmodern Pop', *The Journal of Aesthetics and Art Criticism*, 57 (2): 161–75.

Kubek, E. (1996), '"You Only Expose Your Father": The Imaginary, Voyeurism, and the Symbolic Order in *The X-Files*', in D. Lavery, A. Hague and M. Cartwright (eds), *Denny All Knowledge: Reading* The X-Files, 168–204, New York: Syracuse University Press.

Malach, M. (1996), '"I Want to Believe … in the FBI": The Special Agent and *The X-Files*', in D. Lavery, A. Hague and M. Cartwright (eds), *Denny All Knowledge: Reading the X-Files*, 63–76, New York: Syracuse University Press.

Malin, B. J. (2005), *American Masculinity under Clinton: Popular Media and the Nineties "Crisis of Masculinity"*, New York: Peter Lang.

McCann, H. (2018), *Queering Femininity: Sexuality, Feminism, and the Politics of Presentation*, London: Routledge.

McCann, H., and W. Monaghan (2020), *Queer Theory Now: From Foundations to Futures*, London: Red Globe Press.

Milton J. (2020), 'Men Share Celebs Who First Made Them Realise They Were Gay – And It's a Blast from the Past', *Pink News*, 3 April. Available online: https://www.pinknews.co.uk/2020/04/03/twitter-gay-queer-awakening-celebrities-chris-evans-jake-gyllenhaal-david-duchovny-coming-out/?fbc lid=IwAR0MWSUVC_uRsA2YQuw2Mui_sh39jr64vBuh60I9l0eQh9oEZy3g KLwqhZ4 (accessed 29 July 2022).

The Stepford Wives (1975), [Film] Dir. Bryan Forbes, USA: Columbia Pictures.

The Larry Sanders Show (1992–8), [TV Series] Creators Dennis Klein, Gary Shandling, USA: HBO.

Thompson, J. M. (2017), 'The Madness of Sneaky Fox', in R. Arp (ed.), *The X-Files and Philosophy: The Truth Is In Here*, Chicago: Open Court Publishing Company.

Voss, B. (2008), 'Big Gay Following: David Duchovny', Advocate, 19 June, Available online: https://www.advocate.com/news/2008/06/19/big-gay-following-david-duchovny?amp (accessed 29 July 2022).

Wilcox, R., and J. P. Williams (1996), '"What Do You Think?": *The X-Files*, Liminality, and Gender Pleasure', in D. Lavery, A. Hague and M. Cartwright (eds), *Deny All Knowledge: Reading* The X-Files, 99–120, New York: Syracuse University Press.

Wood, R. (2018), 'An Introduction to the American Horror Film', in B. K. Grant (ed.), *Robin Wood on the Horror Film: Collected Essays and Reviews*, 73–111, Detroit, MI: Wayne State University Press.

19

'A collection of human curiosities': Disability in *The X-Files*

Andrew Sydlik

The X-Files provoked television viewers and critics by its numerous innovative and controversial approaches to storytelling, such as its reversal of typical gender norms in FBI Special Agents Fox Mulder and Dana Scully, the postmodern style of many episodes, the exploration of government conspiracies and its series-spanning 'myth-arc' that gradually revealed the truth about extra-terrestrials' plans to colonize Earth and their collaboration with a global network of human authorities. *The X-Files* openly flaunts political and social commentary about how those in power manipulate the public to believe truths crafted during secret meetings in smoke-filled, dimly lit rooms. In short, *The X-Files* illuminates structures of power through entertaining paranormal crime thrillers.

In this chapter, I examine a currently overlooked aspect of *The X-Files*: the function of disability and ableism in a number of the stand-alone or 'monster-of-the-week' episodes. Through the lens of Disability Studies, the interdisciplinary field that analyses the cultural, political and social meanings of disability, I explore the ways in which *The X-Files* both reinforces and subverts ableist conceptions of disability (see Chapter 17 in this collection for a discussion of the representation of racialized disability in *The X-Files*). First, I analyse the episodes 'Roland' (S1: E23), 'The Walk' (S3: E: 07), 'Revelations' (S3: E11), 'Home' (S4: E02) and 'All Souls' (S5: E17), each of which incorporate ableist disability tropes. Second, I discuss three episodes that challenge ableist binaries: 'Humbug' (S2: E20), 'The Post-Modern Prometheus' (S5: E05) and 'Hungry' (S7: E03). I will focus in depth on 'Humbug' as an episode that levels the most effective critique of the ableist biases that shape our assumptions about others.

Ableism is the systematic oppression of people with disabilities that values some bodies and minds as 'normal' (able-bodied/able-minded) while devaluing other bodies and minds as 'abnormal' (disabled) (Berger 2013: 14; Siebers 2008: 4). Mulder and Scully constantly remind viewers of the series tagline, 'The Truth Is Out There', but the Truth is also 'in here', within our bodies and minds. Scully is trained as a medical doctor, conducting autopsies on victims as part of the X-Files investigations, and Mulder is a forensic psychologist who uses insights into behavioural science to understand the bizarre minds of disturbed killers. Both agents want to unlock the secrets of our physical and mental natures, and these secrets guide them through the structures of power they must navigate in their quest for Truth. Ableism is one of these structures of power.

Disability tropes in *The X-Files*: Victims and villains

Several disability tropes popular in media representation catalogued by scholars (Berger 2013; Dolmage 2013; Kriegel 1987; Mitchell and Snyder 2000; Norden 1994) recur throughout *The X-Files*. Rather than provide an exhaustive list of such examples, I will touch on two of the most prominent tropes: the *sweet innocent* and the *demonic cripple*. Disabled characters within these tropes tend to be limited to prescribed roles as victim (sweet innocent) and villain (demonic cripple) and draw on similar characters in literature, film and television. These tropes reinforce an ableist binary between disability and normalcy, reducing disabled bodies and minds to defects that signify innocence or evil. Despite the show's persistent attempts to counter conventional wisdom and value outsider perspectives, *The X-Files* also continually reflects dominant views of disability as 'other', abnormal and undesirable.

The sweet innocent is the tragic, pitiful disabled character whose innocence makes the 'affliction' of their disability even more terrible (Berger 2013; Norden 1994). Their limitations make them vulnerable to threats from antagonists or their own unwitting self-destructive behaviour. Sweet innocents are naïve and selfless, and their suffering elicits readers' or viewers' sympathies. Typically devoid of agency, any relief to their struggles comes from the charity or kindness of non-disabled characters. Tiny Tim in Charles Dickens's *A Christmas Carol* (1843) is the paradigmatic example of the sweet innocent: he is kind, uncomplaining and tragic, and he is 'saved' by the generosity of the reformed Ebenezer Scrooge. Many later examples are developmentally or intellectually disabled characters, including two of the most well-known sweet innocents: Lennie in John Steinbeck's novel *Of Mice and Men* (1937) and Raymond in the film *Rain Man* (1988). Three episodes of *The X-Files* exemplify the sweet innocent trope: 'Roland', 'Revelations' and 'All Souls'. In 'Roland' and 'All Souls', the sweet innocents are developmentally disabled and function as pawns manipulated by paranormal forces, while the sweet innocent of 'Revelations' possesses agency but sacrifices himself for the survival of the protagonist.

In 'Roland', the titular character is an autistic savant (much like Raymond in the 1988 film *Rain Man*) living in a group home whose innocence disguises his role in the brutal murders of aeronautics researchers. Under the psychic control of his dead twin brother, Dr Arthur Grable, Roland kills off the scientists who tried to steal Arthur's work. Roland's quiet, anxious demeanour elicits the compassion of other characters, including Scully and Mulder. His innocence affirms him as a tragic victim, an unwitting accomplice and mere tool for his brother's revenge. The episode concludes with poignant music as Roland prepares to leave the group home and face trial, implying that he will be held responsible for his dead brother's crimes – Arthur's disembodied consciousness being beyond the bounds of law. The episode functions as a paranormal twist on *Rain Man* without providing much depth to its titular autistic character.

'Revelations' and 'All Souls' feature sweet innocents who die for Scully's benefit by reinforcing her Catholicism, as her religious beliefs clash with her scientific approach to solving each case. The deaths of these sweet innocents link with another disability trope: *kill or cure*, referring to one of two fates relegated to disabled characters (Dolmage 2013: 39; Mitchell and Snyder 2000: 53–4). For example, Lennie is killed in *Of Mice and Men*, and Jake Sully is effectively 'cured' of his paralysis in the movie *Avatar* (2009) by transferring his consciousness into a genetically engineered alien body. By killing off or curing disabled characters, narratives fail to imagine the possibility of living with disability – a reflection of the *medical model*'s focus on 'fixing' disabled people and the eugenics movement's lingering cultural attitudes towards disability. Eugenics is the practice of preventing or minimizing the proliferation of the 'unfit', a loose category created by eugenicists of people with 'undesirable' traits that included people with disabilities and chronic illness, alcoholics, single mothers, criminals, poor rural whites, immigrants and people of colour (Bryan 2010: 52–9). Although eugenics culminated in the horrors of Nazi Germany's concentration camps during the Second World War, the eugenics movement began in the early-twentieth-century United States and United Kingdom. During its peak in the 1910s to the 1930s, eugenics led to the compulsory institutionalization and sterilization of tens of thousands of people in the United States.

In 'Revelations', the sweet innocent is a literal saint whose death and subsequent lack of decomposition assure Scully that the case involves supernatural forces. Scully vows to protect a young boy named Kevin exhibiting stigmata, wounds that echo the marks of Christ's crucifixion. Kevin is protected by Owen Jarvis, a deformed man played by Michael Berryman, whose unusual appearance helped make him one of the few working actors with disabilities in films such as *One Flew Over the Cuckoo's Nest* (1975) and *The Hills Have Eyes* (1977). Jarvis sacrifices himself to let Kevin escape from the Devil's disciple. During Jarvis's autopsy, Scully notes his body's lack of physical decay and a faint 'floral odour', leading her to think of him as an 'incorruptible' – according to Catholic belief, a saint whom God preserves after death. One moment in the episode does satirize ableist assumptions when Jarvis first enters to rescue Kevin, his face frightening other children – a misreading of his heroic purpose. Yet his role is reduced to dying for the innocent and a plot device to bolster Scully's faith.

In 'All Souls', Scully investigates the deaths of congenitally and developmentally disabled young girls, who are killed by an angel to save them from the Devil. With little character development, the girls function as a plot device to test Scully's conscience: she must decide whether to let the girls die so their souls can be saved or keep them alive but risk their corruption by evil. The sweet innocents of 'All Souls' teach Scully that belief requires hard-won faith, since she makes the decision after difficult deliberation given the loss of her own child Emily earlier in the season. But the episode carries the sinister subtext that severe disabilities make people unfit for earthly life and only at peace in Heaven (where their disabilities will ostensibly no longer affect their souls). Disability advocates contest the notion that people with significant disabilities cannot have a good quality of life, castigating movies such as *Million Dollar Baby* (2004) and *Me Before You* (2016) for promoting such a message (Dolmage 2013: 39). Organizations such as Not Dead Yet, who oppose the legalization of assisted suicide and promote informed consent in medical decision-making, strive to emphasize the extremely harmful consequences of such thinking. By presenting the elimination of disability as the only – or most 'humane' – choice for disabled people, the kill or cure trope reinforces the misconception that life with disability must be a life full of suffering.

Whereas the sweet innocent trope calls for us to pity disabled people, the demonic cripple trope reflects fears of disabled people. The demonic cripple is prevalent in media, especially in horror and science fiction. Leonard Kriegel (1987) coined the term to describe the disabled villain or anti-hero who lashes out in anger because of their disability. The demonic cripple links physical or mental impairment with moral degeneracy, harkening back to religious views of disability. Despite contemporary medical and political perspectives that pivot away from spiritual explanations to scientific and social ones, modern media continues to perpetuate associations between physical and mental differences with moral weakness. Paradigmatic examples in literature include William Shakespeare's *Richard III* (1597), Quasimodo in Victor Hugo's *The Hunchback of Notre-Dame* (1831) and Ahab in Herman Melville's *Moby-Dick* (1851). The killers in slasher films often exhibit deformities or some form of mental illness, from Norman Bates in *Psycho* (1960) to Jason Vorhees in *Friday the 13th Part 2* (1981).

Many of *The X-Files*' 'monster-of-the-week' episodes feature demonic cripples. For example, Mulder explains the killers in 'Squeeze' (S1: E03), '2Shy' (S3: E06) and 'Leonard Betts' (S4: E12) as 'genetic mutants', evolutionary deviants born with certain physiological deficiencies supplemented by feeding on others. Mentally disabled demonic cripples also appear in episodes such as 'Eve' (S1: E11), 'Duane Barry' (S2: E05) and 'Oubliette' (S3: E08). In 'Eve', women cloned from the DNA of Sally Kendrick inevitably present with violent psychosis. Although the episode warns against the dangers of attempting to maximize able-bodiedness via genetic engineering, it nevertheless perpetuates a link between mental illness and violence. The titular character in 'Duane Barry' is a disturbed alien abductee whose behaviour is partially caused by a traumatic brain injury. Scully explains that the paedophilic kidnapper in 'Oubliette', Carl Wade, is driven by bipolar disorder. Mental impairment in these last three examples serves only as a 'cause' of the villains' violent acts, with little to no exploration of mental disability as a lived experience.

Two episodes in particular, 'The Walk' and 'Home', serve as particularly troubling, if interesting, portrayals of the demonic cripple figure as outsiders cut off from an able-bodied society. 'The Walk' features a demonic cripple whose murderous rage dovetails with another trope: the *angry cripple*, the disabled person (often a veteran wounded during service) angry at the world because of their disability and their feelings of inferiority (Berger 2013: 192). A prominent example is Lieutenant Dan in *Forrest Gump* (1994). Mulder and Scully encounter the angry cripple when they investigate tragic deaths and reports of a 'phantom soldier' who torments officers at an army hospital. Mulder discovers that Rappo, a quadruple amputee, commits the murders via astral projection. Rappo is driven by anger and hate towards his commanding officers, whom he holds responsible for his suffering. Bitter towards everyone, Rappo does not elicit much empathy from viewers, though his story does point to the overlooked plight of veterans struggling with trauma and physical disabilities resulting from military service.

A different kind of demonic cripple, the *monstrous hillbilly*, appears in 'Home'. 'Hillbilly' refers to the stereotype of a stupid, culturally backwards rural person, typically appearing as white, poor and uneducated (Taylor 2020: 168). The monstrous hillbilly is marked by deformities, heightened strength, rural poverty and insatiable bloodlust. When the body of a severely deformed infant is found in the rural town of Home, Pennsylvania, Mulder and Scully face off against the Peacocks, a family of monstrous hillbillies extremely deformed due to generations of incest, who kill to protect their secret. Critics often overlook the eugenic roots of the monstrous hillbilly, as the trope populates several beloved horror and thriller films such as *Deliverance* (1972), *The Texas Chain Saw Massacre* (1974) and *The Hills Have Eyes*. Tosha Taylor notes that the monstrous hillbilly is itself a variant of the 'white trash' figure, a label that eugenicists used to describe genetically and morally inferior poor rural whites, who should be eliminated to create a purely white, abled society (2020: 168).

While praised for its shocking themes and imagery, 'Home' reinforces some of the most pernicious eugenic ideas of rural people as inbred, murderous and barely human (Taylor 2020: 169–70). Mulder even bases his strategies in his fight against the Peacock brothers on his previous night's viewing of a nature documentary about predatory animals, while the family name 'Peacock' ironically juxtaposes the brothers' grotesque bestiality with the colourful beauty of the bird of the same name. Mulder and Scully view the Peacocks as entirely monstrous, leaving viewers with little reason to empathize with them (as is usually the case for the monstrous hillbilly), completely ignoring the economic inequalities and lack of resources that disable those living in rural American spaces.

A collection of human curiosities

Despite the recurrence of disability tropes throughout *The X-Files*, the show also subverts ableist binaries in various episodes such as 'Humbug', 'The Post-Modern Prometheus' and 'Hungry'. These episodes challenge ableism not because they represent disability in a more accurate or 'progressive' way – they actually depict fantastical disabled bodies – but because their engagement with disability issues dovetails with critiques of narrative storytelling itself. Because 'Humbug' offers the most direct engagement with ableism as a concept, I will focus my analysis on that episode, but will offer a few brief thoughts on 'Post-Modern Prometheus' and 'Hungry' as well.

'Post-Modern Prometheus' is, as its title suggests, a Frankensteinian amalgam of old and new, updating the message of Mary Shelley's original 1818 novel *Frankenstein* (subtitled *The Modern Prometheus*) to warn against the dangers of genetic engineering. The episode is a pastiche of various incarnations of *Frankenstein*, from Shelley's novel to James Whale's *Frankenstein* (1931) and *Bride of Frankenstein* (1935), to forms of folklore, comic books and 1990s media icons such as Cher and Jerry Springer. Cary Jones (2007) points to the ways in which the episode's narrative also fractures into a Frankensteinian hodgepodge of conflicting accounts of events through written, verbal and televised forms. This postmodern approach questions the reliability of storytelling, and by extension, the reliability of the stories that we tell about certain kinds of bodies (such as disabled bodies). The stand-in for Victor Frankenstein is Dr Pollidori, who creates a deformed man (dubbed 'The Great Mutato' by one of the town's teen residents) through genetic experimentation. Pollidori views Mutato as a mistake and abandons him, only to be cared for by Pollidori's father, who tries to create a mate for him by drugging women and artificially inseminating them. The townspeople fear and try to kill Mutato until he gives an eloquent speech about his origins, which reveals Mutato to be kind and gentle, while Pollidori is clinical and cruel. The episode ultimately suggests that human connections matter more than genetics. Its message serves as valuable reminder about the pitfalls of scientific research into genetic engineering, which sometimes veers into eugenic attempts to erase disabilities such as deafness, Down syndrome and dwarfism from human experience. However, Pollidori's experiments create strange, new forms of life rather than select against genes that produce impairments. Also, a troubling aspect of the episode often overlooked is that Mutato and the elder Pollidori commit rape yet are made to look sympathetic. The experimentation on female bodies, which has been justified to enhance modern medicine, is no less horrific than Pollidori's callous treatment of Mutato.

'Hungry' is a unique episode in that it is told largely through the perspective of the killer rather than focusing on Mulder and Scully's investigation. The episode explores the psychological crisis faced by Rob Roberts, who consumes human brains for survival and parallels perceptions of disabled people as monstrous. 'Hungry' poses the question of whether one can live as a monster when everyone sees you (and your needs) as monstrous. Rob strives to resist his cravings for brains and to accept himself as he is but finds that the two desires seem irreconcilable. As a fast-food employee, Rob tries to sate his brain lust with leftover meat but finds it inadequate. He joins an Overeaters Anonymous group, hoping that their support can help him overcome his hunger, and befriends a therapist hired by his employer. Although the episode is a powerful reframing of the typical 'monster-of-the-week' story, making viewers wonder about the inner lives of those other genetic mutants, it still falls prey to the kill or cure trope. Rob is killed when he lunges at Mulder, who promptly shoots him. Rob's therapist asks him why, to which he answers, 'I can't be something I'm not.' Rob's answer implies that he could never live with his condition, because he would always be trying to be something other than a genetic mutant who feeds on brains. His hunger is too fundamental and basic to who he is, and it is too monstrous to live with.

Of the three episodes mentioned, 'Humbug' provides the most effective critique of ableism through its satire of attitudes based on physical appearance. The episode even parodies *The X-Files* itself as a kind of humbug about abnormal bodies. The narrative gradually makes Mulder, Scully and us as viewers aware that we are voyeurs of its 'collection of human curiosities'; we fetishize the very physical differences we stigmatize much like the audiences of so-called freak shows. Whether in the form of aliens, genetic mutants or people with disabilities, 'Humbug' reminds us that *The X-Files* parades unconventional bodies before viewers to horrify, repulse and fascinate us.

A pivotal episode, 'Humbug' embraces a comic tone that had only appeared sporadically in previous episodes. Its mix of horror and humour takes a playful and challenging approach to the series' themes of truth and extreme possibilities. The truth about our bodies and the diverse forms they take can be more shocking and empowering than the truth out there about government and interplanetary conspiracies. Mulder and Scully investigate the latest in a string of gruesome murders across the continental United States in Gibsonton, Florida, a town where sideshow performers live during the off-season. The agents encounter a motley crew of people with physical disabilities and eccentric self-made 'freaks'. Mulder speculates that one of P. T. Barnum's hoaxes, the Fiji Mermaid, is a real creature responsible for the deaths. Scully discovers that the real culprit has a more prosaic, if still rather unusual, origin: Leonard, an underdeveloped conjoined twin, detaches himself from his brother Lanny and kills people when he tries to attach himself to their bodies. Ironically, Sheriff Hamilton regards Scully's theory with the same scepticism that Scully often employs against Mulder's paranormal explanations. Through its mockery of knowledge and truth as mere humbug rooted in ableism, the episode destabilizes numerous binaries: normal/abnormal, truth/humbug, desirable/repulsive, fantasy/realism, outside(r)/inside(r) and believer/sceptic.

Ableism reifies these binaries through the belief that outward appearances signify an inner truth: conventionally beautiful abled bodies represent beautiful truths, while ugly disabled bodies represent ugly truths. Although disability is ostensibly conceptualized in terms of material bodily dysfunction (impairment), Disability Studies scholars such as Riva Lehrer (2014), Tobin Siebers (2010), Rosemarie Garland Thomson (1997) and Lennard Davis (1995) point out that attitudes towards disabled people depend on conventional visual standards of beauty (which also influence gender and racial norms, among others). As Davis puts it, 'Disability is a specular moment' (1995: 12). 'Humbug' continually challenges these norms, emphasizing that appearances deceive. Thus, when we base our treatment of others on appearances, we are falling victim to a humbug.

The opening sequence of 'Humbug' depicts the murder of Jerald Glazebrook (aka the 'Alligator Man') and foregrounds the untrustworthiness of appearances. The following scene establishes the investigation into Glazebrook's death and Mulder and Scully's roles in the episode as misguided voyeurs who must overcome their own biases. The episode begins with a view of two normal-looking boys playing in a pool while an unseen watcher looks on. Suspenseful music plays as the watcher enters the pool and swims towards the boys, all the visual and sonic cues anticipating a scare and the reveal of a hideous, murderous creature. At first, the watcher conforms with the expected appearance – a man covered with scales. But when one of the boys cries, 'Oh, Dad, cut it out!', the dynamic quickly changes as we realize that the man is merely the boys' father. Viewers breathe a sigh of relief as Glazebrook ushers the kids inside and relaxes in the pool, only to be unsettled once again by *another* seemingly grotesque watcher, who attacks Glazebrook. The fake-out plays upon viewers' assumptions that unconventional appearance signifies homicidal intent, juxtaposing an extraordinary body with ordinary domestic interactions – even though the actual killer is *not* ordinary.

In the next scene, Mulder introduces Scully to the case, serving a double purpose in setting up the mystery as well as the assumptions the agents will navigate in solving it. Mulder shows Scully a photo of Glazebrook and explains that his appearance is due to a condition called ichthyosis, which causes the skin to continually shed in a scale-like fashion, thus his stage name the 'Alligator Man'. (The evocation of animals in the stage names of freak show performers is linked to an ableist human/non-human binary, which dehumanizes disabled people by associating them with non-human animals.) Mulder explains that the unusual wounds found on Glazebrook match those on victims across the continental United States over the past twenty years from all different age groups, races and genders. The lack of a clear victim 'type' seems to rule out a serial killer or cult that would target a specific type of individual. This detail accords with the fact that Leonard kills wherever the circus takes him, but it also ties into the episode's theme that physical traits are not a reliable source of knowledge about someone's inner life.

However, Scully undermines this message when Mulder asks her initial thoughts on the case. She stares at Glazebrook's photo and opines, 'Imagine going through your whole life looking like this.' Apparently more disturbed by (her imagining of) Glazebrook's life than his death, Scully's words give voice to what many non-disabled viewers (and perhaps some disabled viewers as well) are thinking – the assumption that life with disability is a painful or pitiful experience (as embodied by the sweet innocent trope). Although the previous scene gave no indication that Glazebrook's life was pitiful, this sentimental idea of disability is so ingrained in our social consciousness that most viewers will probably resonate with Scully's thoughts.

Scully's sentimentalism suggests that she and Mulder will be able-bodied outsiders, which quickly becomes apparent as they meet various residents of Gibsonton. While meeting with Sheriff Hamilton, Scully evokes the notion of the demonic cripple to explain the murders, suggesting the killer could be motivated by being disabled, as 'their isolation from everyday society caused by their physical deformities could have built up pathological resentments so intense that murder might be—'. Hamilton interrupts her by noting that despite their unusual appearances, the residents of the town are as 'normal' as anyone else: 'Now, some of them may be different on the outside, but it's what's inside that counts. And on the inside, they're as normal as anybody.' Yet, the connection between disability and violence remains plausible for the agents, despite their awareness that such a belief lacks basis and plays upon prejudicial attitudes.

In another scene, Mulder and Scully become aware of this bias as a form of prejudice akin to racism. They discover that Sheriff Hamilton used to perform in a freak show himself as 'Jim-Jim the Dog-Faced Boy'; he lives with hypertrichosis, a condition that results in excessive hair growth, and quit the circus when he started to go bald. The agents spy on him and become suspicious when they find him burying something at night. After Hamilton walks away, Mulder stops to wonder if their suspicion is based on nothing more than bias: 'We're being highly discriminatory here. Just because a man was once afflicted with excessive hairiness, we've no reason to suspect him of aberrant behaviour.' Scully replies that their suspicion is indeed like racial profiling: 'It's like assuming guilt based solely on skin colour, isn't it?' They give each other a look of understanding, then commence to dig up the buried object only to find ... a potato. It is a comic moment loaded with social commentary, not only unearthing the ugly prejudices of both ableism and racism, but also revealing how people – including and especially law enforcement – will still act on such bigotry even when they are aware of it.

The mingling of social commentary and humour in the potato exhumation scene and throughout the episode confuses and disappoints viewers who find the episode's avowed message undercut by its comedic moments. Sheri Hoem (2001) analyses 'Humbug' through a Disability Studies lens, reading Mulder and Scully's roles in the story as analogous to 'freak show lecturers', Robert Bogdan's term for the professionals such as professors, doctors, scientists and clergy who defended freak shows as educational and morally uplifting (Hoem 2001: 52). However, as the above exchange with Hamilton indicates, Mulder and Scully are bumbling outsiders in this town of freaks, unable to understand the experiences of the people there, and are easily misled by their own biases.

Although Scully uses her medical knowledge to understand Leonard, she is no less prone to falling for humbug than Mulder (whose theory that the Fiji mermaid is the killer is perhaps one of his most preposterous yet). For example, Scully visits a museum that chronicles abnormalities, which the deformed curator tells her is a 'collection of human curiosities'. After priming her with an apocryphal story about the deaths of conjoined twins Chang and Eng, the curator tricks her into checking out a supposed P. T. Barnum exhibit called 'The Great Unknown'. He confides to her that he restricts this exhibit to 'those with the intellectual curiosity to appreciate it'. Interested enough to grant a five-dollar donation, Scully walks into a dark room with a single light illuminating a trunk. Seemingly tense with anticipation, Scully carefully opens the trunk to reveal ... nothing. Her 'intellectual curiosity', perhaps a bit too much like the freak show attendee, let her fall for the curator's humbug – a far cry from the authoritative aura of a freak show lecturer.

All the characters have comic moments, but the satire is squarely directed at Mulder and Scully as voyeuristic outsiders continually foiled by their own biases. In contrast, Hoem concludes that the episode's humour deflects its intended lampoon of ableism, its 'attempt at satire succumbs to mockery and ultimately reinforces the attitudes that it seems to be ridiculing' (2001: 51). As an example, when the agents check in at their 'hotel' (a trailer park), Mulder asks the little person manager Mr Nutt if he has done much circus work, a question that Nutt finds extremely offensive:

Nutt   And what makes you think I've ever spectated a circus, much less been enslaved by one?
Mulder   I know that many of the citizens here are former circus hands and I just thought that maybe you would have done—
Nutt   You thought that because I am a person of short stature that the only career I could procure for myself would be one confined to the so-called 'big top'. You took one quick look at me and decided that you could deduce my entire life. Never would it have occurred to you that a person of my height could have possibly obtained a degree in hotel management.
Mulder   I'm sorry, I meant no offense.
Nutt   Well, then why should I take offense? Just because it's human nature to make instantaneous judgments of others based solely upon their physical appearances? Why, I've done the same thing to you, for example. I've taken in your all-American features, your dour demeanour, your unimaginative necktie design ... and concluded that you work for the government. An FBI agent. But do you see the tragedy here? I have mistakenly reduced you to a stereotype. A caricature. Instead of regarding you as a specific, unique individual.
Mulder   But I am an FBI agent.

As with Scully and the curator, Mulder's intellectual curiosity here makes him have no qualms in asking Nutt about his past as a freak show performer, the sort of prying inquiry that non-disabled people direct towards disabled people. (I cannot count the number of times people have asked me why I am legally blind, for example.) Mulder's exchange with Mr Nutt is another instance in which one of the agents makes a mistaken assumption based solely on physical appearance, and although there is humour both in Nutt's exaggerated indignation and Mulder's embarrassment, Nutt's assessment of the situation proves completely valid. The fact that Nutt guesses at Mulder's occupation does not undermine his point; rather, it reinforces the notion that Nutt is an insider and Mulder is an outsider here – Nutt is part of the community (despite being a bit of curmudgeon), while Mulder is not.

The ultimate takeaway from 'Humbug' is a theme at the crux of the entire series: abnormal bodies provide greater insight into what it means to be human in a strange, deceptive world. While such thematic focus can easily slip into fetishization and stigmatization, as I have argued in my discussion of disability tropes, even the most 'problematic' representations of disability in *The X-Files* exist in tension with the series' relentless exploration of difference. In her fascinating Foucauldian/psychoanalytic reading of bodies in the series, Linda Badley (1996) asserts that the freaks in 'Humbug' serve as guides to knowledge. The freaks 'may be anomalous but are not abnormal. As mutations, they are maps or keys to biological past or future' (1996: 161). Throughout the series, Mulder and Scully's quest for 'the Truth' is (among other things) to discover those biological, anomalous pasts and futures, to discover what it means to live in a world populated by unconventional truths and unconventional bodies (aliens, monsters, mutants) purposely obscured from public view by those in power.

References

Avatar (2009), [Film] Dir. James Cameron, USA: 20th Century Fox.
Badley, L. (1996), 'The Rebirth of the Clinic: The Body as Alien in *The X-Files*', in D. Lavery, A. Hague and M. Cartwright (eds), *'Deny All Knowledge': Reading The X-Files*, 148–67, Syracuse, NY: Syracuse University Press.
Berger, R. J. (2013), *Introducing Disability Studies*, Boulder, CO: Lynne Rienner.
The Bride of Frankenstein (1935), [Film] Dir. James Whale, USA: Universal Pictures.
Bryan, W. V. (2010), *Sociopolitical Aspects of Disabilities: The Social Perspectives and Political History of Disabilities and Rehabilitation in the United States*, Springfield, IL: Charles C. Thomas.
Davis, L. J. (1995), *Enforcing Normalcy: Disability, Deafness, and the Body*, New York: Verso.
Deliverance (1972), [Film] Dir. John Boorman, USA: Warner Bros.
Dickens, C. (1843), *A Christmas Carol*, London: Chapman & Hall.
Dolmage, J. T. (2013), *Disability Rhetoric*, Syracuse, NY: Syracuse University Press.
Forrest Gump (1994), [Film] Dir. Robert Zemeckis, USA: Paramount Pictures.
Frankenstein (1931), [Film] Dir. James Whale, USA: Universal Pictures.
Friday the 13th Part 2 (1981), [Film] Dir. Steve Miner, USA: Paramount Pictures.
Garland Thomson, R. (1997), *Extraordinary Bodies: Figuring Physical Disability in American Culture and Literature*, New York: Columbia University Press.
The Hills Have Eyes (1977), [Film] Dir. Wes Craven, USA: Vanguard.
Hoem, S. (2001), 'The X-Files as Side Show', *Television Quarterly*, 32 (1): 51–3.
Hugo, V. (1831), *Notre-Dame de Paris (The Hunchback of Notre-Dame)*, Paris: Gosselin.

Jones, C. (2007), '"Post-Modern Prometheus", Postmodern Voices: *The X-Files* and Subjective Storytelling', in S. R. Yang (ed.), *The X-Files and Literature: Unweaving the Story, Unraveling the Lie to Find the Truth*, 174–93, Newcastle: Cambridge Scholars Publishing.
Kriegel, L. (1987), 'The Cripple in Literature', in A. Gartner and T. Joe (eds), *Images of the Disabled, Disabling Images*, 31–46, New York: Praeger.
Lehrer, R. (2014), 'Beauty in Exile', in C. Wood (ed.), *Criptiques*, 151–66, n.p.: May Day Publishing, PDF.
Me Before You (2016), [Film] Dir. Thea Sharrock, UK/USA: Warner Bros.
Melville, H. (1851), *Moby-Dick; or, The Whale*, New York: Harper & Brothers.
Million Dollar Baby (2004), [Film] Dir. Clint Eastwood, USA: Warner Bros.
Mitchell, D. T., and S. L. Snyder (2000), *Narrative Prosthesis: Disability and the Dependencies of Discourse*, Ann Arbor: University of Michigan Press.
Norden, M. F. (1994), *The Cinema of Isolation: A History of Physical Disability in the Movies*, New Brunswick, NJ: Rutgers University Press.
One Flew Over the Cuckoo's Nest (1975), [Film] Dir. Miloš Forman, USA: United Artists.
Psycho (1960), [Film] Dir. Alfred Hitchcock, USA: Paramount Pictures.
Rain Man (1988), [Film] Dir. Barry Levinson, USA: MGM/UA Communications.
Shelley, M. (1818), *Frankenstein; or, The Modern Prometheus*, London: Lackington, Hughes, Harding, Mavor and Jones.
Siebers, T. (2008), *Disability Theory*, Ann Arbor: University of Michigan Press.
Siebers, T. (2010), *Disability Aesthetics*, Ann Arbor: University of Michigan Press.
Steinbeck, J. (1937), *Of Mice and Men*, New York: Viking Press.
Taylor, T. R. (2020), 'Hillbilly Horror', in C. Bloom (ed.), *The Palgrave Handbook of Contemporary Gothic*, 163–80, Cham, Switzerland: Palgrave Macmillan.
The Texas Chain Saw Massacre (1974), [Film] Dir. Tobe Hooper, USA: Bryanston Distributing Company.

20

The Scully effect: *The X-Files* and women in STEM

Jolene Mendel

In 2018, the Geena Davis Institute on Gender in Media, 21st Century Fox and J. Walter Thompson Intelligence published a study titled 'The Scully Effect: I Want to Believe ... in STEM'. The study revealed that *The X-Files*, and the depiction of medical doctor turned FBI agent Dana Scully, had a profound impact on women and girls' attitudes towards STEM (Science, Technology, Engineering, Mathematics), specifically on their ability to enter into careers in these fields, which were long dominated by men. In the study, almost two-thirds of the American women respondents who participated in the study identified Scully as a role model. In addition, regular viewers were 50 per cent more likely to enter a STEM field than those who did not watch the programme as frequently.

This chapter closely examines the findings of the report to demonstrate the long-lasting effect *The X-Files* had on women viewers, many of whom viewed Dana Scully as a feminist role model, as well as their point of introduction to the sciences, not limited to medicine, laboratory analysis and forensic pathology, which were depicted throughout the series. The chapter will explore how the 'Scully Effect' is both supported and undermined by the series itself, as Scully is the rational, scientific mind in contrast to Fox Mulder's more mystical beliefs. However, many of the plots in which Scully is involved are stereotypical women's plots found in many previous television series, ranging from issues of pregnancy to motherhood. Likewise, the series rarely takes the side of science, with very few episodes resolving with a scientifically sound explanation, rather than a supernatural one. While the characterization of Dana Scully within the series has flaws, the character, and actress Gillian Anderson, inspired many women and girls to explore interests in STEM and to enter into these fields, undoubtedly making significant contributions to science and technology.

The Scully effect

In 2004, actress Geena Davis founded the Geena Davis Institute on Gender in Media, which 'is the only global research-based organization working collaboratively within the entertainment industry to create gender balance, foster inclusion and reduce negative stereotyping in family entertainment media' (2021). The institute has created numerous studies on the depiction of women in film and television with a stated goal of 'achieving gender parity for female lead characters in the top 100 largest grossing family films and the top Nielsen rated children's television programming' (2021). In 2018, Fox Television partnered with the Geena Davis Institute to study the Scully effect more formally, which had only been noted anecdotally in articles and discussions. The study of the Scully effect set out to understand why the gap between men and women entering STEM fields was still large even when college enrolments between genders has largely equalized. The study found that depictions in the media, or lack thereof, had significant impact on which academic fields students entered, as these depictions were often the first or only introduction to the field for many viewers. According to the study, most viewers held a specific image of scientists in their minds,

> that of a lone, 'nerdy' scientist in a lab coat, commonly portrayed as a 'mad scientist' or a socially awkward white man. This portrayal reinforces the belief that science is a male pursuit, one that is held by many children, adolescents, and adults. Children start implicitly pairing men and math as early as age seven, a bias that continues into adulthood. (2021: 2)[1]

According to the article 'Reducing Gender Bias in STEM', 'In film, men are depicted in STEM professions at five times the rate at which women are depicted. In family films, men are 14 times more likely to be depicted in STEM professions than women' (Kong et al. 2020: 56). From an early age, viewers have been receiving the message that science-based careers are primarily intended for men. Doctors on television were nearly almost male, especially amongst popular series such as *Dr Kildare* (1961–6), *Star Trek*

---

[1] Common depictions of the 'mad scientist' archetype were found in early horror films, such as *Dr Jekyll and Mr Hyde* (1931), *Frankenstein* (1931) and *The Invisible Man* (1933).

(1966–9) and *M*A*S*H* (1972–83). For many television viewers, their only knowledge of forensic science would have come from *Quincy ME* (1976–83), a crime serial whose main character was a coroner.

Characters like Dana Scully have long been discussed in changing attitudes towards sciences for women and girls, but much of this was relegated to anecdotal evidence. In her 1999 book *The Real Science behind The X-Files*, Anne Simon predicted the Scully effect, writing, 'Viewers, especially high school and college students, who make up the core of the fan base, are seeing scientists portrayed in a favorable light, perhaps for the first time' (1999:20). When asked about Scully's influence on women and girls in STEM at a 2013 Comicon, Gillian Anderson confirmed that she had been receiving letters from female viewers explaining that the fictional character inspired them to study science for years (Vineyard 2013:1). The 2018 study sought to empirically prove what many had believed for decades: the character of Dana Scully had a profound effect on women entering the STEM professions. The study queried 2,021 participants, American women of age twenty-five and older, and divided the respondents into two categories: non/light viewers and medium/heavy viewers.[2] While those in the latter category had more positive experiences with *The X-Files* than the former, respondents in all groups noted the importance of Dana Scully's character: 'Nearly two-thirds (63%) of women who are familiar with Dana Scully say she increased their belief in the importance of STEM' (2021: 3). Of the survey respondents, 56 per cent said that women should be encouraged to study STEM. Likewise, 'Among women who are familiar with Scully's character, half (50%) say Scully increased their interest in STEM' (2022: 3). Most importantly, however, is the fact that the survey respondents overwhelmingly viewed Scully as a positive, feminist role model:

- Among women who are familiar with Scully's character, 91 percent say she is a role model for girls and women.
- Nearly two-thirds (63 per cent) of women that work in STEM say Dana Scully served as their role model.
- Among women who are familiar with Scully's character, 63 per cent say Scully increased their confidence that they could excel in a male-dominated profession.
- Nine out of ten (91 per cent) women who are familiar with Scully's character say she stands out as being a strong female character on television.

---

[2]The age requirement was included to focus on those who saw the show as it originally aired, not those who learned about *The X-Files* after it had made a significant cultural impact.

- Women in the sample were asked about various attributes of Scully's character. The most frequently used words to describe her were 'smart', 'intelligent' and 'strong'. (2021: 4)

These findings demonstrate that the character of Scully was, and has been, both a positive role model for the women and girls watching *The X-Files* as well as their entry point into STEM careers, which were previously depicted mainly by men in television and movies.

Actress Gillian Anderson commented on the Scully effect in a 2013 interview with *Vulture* magazine. In the interview, Anderson talks about first learning about the phenomenon: 'We got a lot of letters all the time, and I was told quite frequently by girls who were going into the medical world or the science world or the FBI world or other worlds that I reigned, that they were pursuing those pursuits because of the character of Scully. And I said, "Yay!"' (Vineyard 2013).

Scully as feminist icon

Dana Scully's character was immediately seen as something different from other female characters, from the first episode of *The X-Files* in 1993. In the previous decade, most female characters on television were housewives or in other supporting roles such as secretaries or nurses. Soap operas like *Dallas* (1978–91) and *Dynasty* (1981–9) depicted women as glamorous and cunning. *Murphy Brown* (1988–97) depicted a strong career woman, but she worked in media, not science. In contrast, Scully is a medical doctor with a degree in physics who has been hired by the FBI to rein in her new partner Fox Mulder. In an inversion of traditional gender roles, it is Mulder who is interested in the supernatural and tends to lead with his emotions. Scully, in contrast, is the rational, science-minded sceptic who tends to keep her cool. She wears pant suits and lab coats, not tight-fitting dresses and stilettos, and she is often found doing difficult tasks that women had rarely been seen in the media doing before, such as difficult surgeries and autopsies. It is Mulder who is objectified, often seen doing physical feats without a shirt on and, in one memorable episode, swimming in a pair of speedos. In contrast, Scully looks for the answers to a problem to be found in rational science before accepting the possibility of a supernatural outcome. Author Dean Kowalski points out these notable differences between Mulder and Scully in the introduction to *The Philosophy of* The X-Files by describing a poignant scene in a season three episode:

> Also, recall the classic exchange about Robert Modell (Robert Wisden), aka 'Pusher', in which Mulder comments, 'Modell psyched the guy out. He put the whammy on him.' Scully immediately quips, 'Please explain

to me the scientific nature of the "whammy"'. A bit perturbed, Mulder asks for Scully's take on the Modell case. Scully admits that she believes Modell is guilty but adds, 'I'm just looking for an explanation a little more mundane than "the whammy"'. (2009: 26)

It is Dana Scully who is insistent on a rational, science-based explanation, not her male colleague who is open to explanations that involve the supernatural, aliens, spells, charms and more. Claire Elizabeth Knowles, scholar of English, argues that,

> Scully is, then, a capable, professional woman who not only remains professional at all times, but who also works as a powerful grounding force to her partner's more outlandish approaches and theories ... Scully and Mulder's relationship, a relationship that is at once personal and professional, is also grounded in genuine equality and respect. Mulder never undermines Scully, he (occasionally) knows when to bow to her superior scientific reasoning, and his eventual love for his partner is based in his understanding that Scully's skepticism offers the perfect counterpart to his openness to the paranormal. (2018: 1)

Scully demands respect from nearly everyone she encounters, and this is especially true in her relationship with Fox Mulder. He is unwavering in his respect of her opinions and knowledge, even if the two disagree. This in turn signals to the audience that she is a strong woman, workplace partner and scientist.

In the early seasons of *The X-Files*, Scully is often the only woman in the room and has to contend with male FBI agents, local police and officials. She has no problem defending herself to partner Mulder, assistant FBI Director Skinner or even the Cigarette Smoking Man. Her gender is rarely an issue for these men, who do seem to view her as an equal, or at least as the main person keeping Mulder and his wild ideas in check. In numerous episodes, the only women she encounters are those who are victims of crime, supernatural or otherwise. In all of these scenarios, she is able to effectively assert her position and ideas.

Scully's status as a feminist cannot be entirely separated from the actress Gillian Anderson, who has made a name for herself as a strong woman in Hollywood. For example, Anderson negotiated for a higher salary after learning she was earning half of what co-star David Duchovny was making (as also discussed in Chapter 18 of this volume).[3] Anderson was relatively

---

[3]Anderson received half of Duchovny's salary for the first three seasons. After renegotiating her salary, they were paid equally. When the series reboot occurred in 2016, Anderson had to again negotiate for equal salary.

unknown when initially cast in the role, although Duchovny's career was also limited at this point. In a 2016 interview, she recalls initially being told by directors to stand slightly behind Duchovny while filming, not at his side. 'I can only imagine that at the beginning, they wanted me to be the sidekick ... Or that, somehow, maybe it was enough of a change just to see a woman having this kind of intellectual repartee with a man on camera, and surely the audience couldn't deal with actually seeing them walk side by side!' (Leon 2017: 1). After receiving critical acclaim for the role and winning both a Golden Globe and an Emmy, she was able to negotiate a salary increase. She has also been a strong advocate for equal pay for women in Hollywood, and consistently calls herself a feminist in writings and in interviews. In 2017, she published the book *We: A Manifesto for Women Everywhere* with co-author Jennifer Nadel.

For viewers of the show, it can be difficult to separate the actress from the character, but it is clear that both are responsible for the view of Dana Scully as a role model for women. The character no doubt inspired many of the great women characters on television that came after, specifically those in serialized crime. There would be no Olivia Benson in *Law and Order: Special Victims Unit* (1999–) or Tempest Brennan in *Bones* (2005–17) without Scully. In these later series, we see strong women who are not intimidated by the men surrounding them and are quite focused on doing excellent work. While comparisons between Scully and Brennan are more apparent, as both are doing forensic science within a law enforcement community, Olivia Benson's level-headedness and work ethic routinely solve cases. Like Scully, Benson and Brennan often serve as the rational, calm voice in contract to their male partners' more outlandish ideas.

Problems with Scully's depiction in *The X-Files*

While Dana Scully is undoubtedly a feminist icon, many of the plots in which she found herself throughout the series are quite regressive in theme and subject. In season two, she is kidnapped by Duane Barry (Steve Railsback), a man who believes he has been abducted by aliens multiple times. In 'Ascension' (S2: E06) Barry takes Scully to a mountaintop ski resort, Skyland Mountain, with the aim of offering her up for abduction to the aliens in place of him. The plan works and Scully disappears, presumably abducted. Following her mysterious and sudden reappearance in 'One Breath' (S2: E08), Scully recalls having had procedures conducted on her not uncommon in alien abduction stories. However, her memories involve her stomach being inflated for laparoscopic surgery, which of course symbolizes pregnancy. Actress Gillian Anderson was indeed pregnant at the time this episode was filmed. The abduction trope is similar to rape, as the body is being used against the will of the individual; therefore, Scully's abduction can be viewed as a violation common to many female characters in film and television. Following her return, Scully finds an implant in her neck, a physical token of the violation. Subsequent tests reveal what the show calls 'branched DNA', meaning she has alien DNA alongside her human genes. Throughout seasons three and four, the government's plan to create a human–alien hybrid is uncovered, a plan that involves women like Scully being targeted as hosts for this DNA. In 'Scully Hits the Glass Ceiling', film and television scholar Linda Badley argues, 'The Alien abduction scenario central to *The X-Files* is a rape narrative; it echoes the countless stories in which women were abducted by sky gods with agendas' (2000: 66).

In 'Nisei' (S3: E09), Scully encounters a Mutual UFO network (MUFON) group who recognize her from the abduction. The group is made entirely of women, all of whom have similar implants to Scully's. In 'Memento Mori' (S4: E14), it is revealed that all the women in the group have died from an unspecified type of cancer. Mulder discovers that several of the women in the group had undergone infertility treatments, further reinforcing the idea that women were taken specifically to be used as hosts or had procedures that affected their fertility. Like the women in MUFON, Scully learns that she too is suffering from the same cancer (revealed at the end of 'Leonard Betts' (S4: E12) and diagnosed in 'Memento Mori'), although she does survive. The abduction/MUFON women's plot shows a close relationship between the female body, fertility and the lack of autonomy. The women had procedures done to them, specifically their female organs, without knowledge or consent.

Throughout *The X-Files*, there is subtle discussion about Scully's role as a caregiver and mother, and that the loss of her fertility from cancer is of great concern. While this is a sensitive subject for any woman, it is important to note that there is little thought given to Mulder's permanent bachelor status. Even as a high-ranking member of the FBI, there is still an expectation that Scully will take on a more traditional role as wife and mother. In the episode 'Home' (S4: E02) Scully demands that she and Mulder continue to work the case involving a dead baby, even though the case is not technically an X-file.[4] Mulder says to her, 'I never saw you as a mother before.' Indeed, she does eventually become pregnant, but is forced to give up the child due to the various forces coming for her and Mulder. In season seven, Scully discovers that she is pregnant after long believing previous cancer treatments had left her infertile. She undergoes in-vitro fertilization successfully, with Mulder serving as the donor father. In 'Per Manum' (S8: E13), she uncovers a plot to

---

[4] 'Home' was banned after its original airing and is the only episode of the entire series to receive an MA rating.

create human–alien hybrid children using women abductees like herself and is unsure whether her child is fully human or partially alien. In the episode 'William' (S9: E16), baby William begins exhibiting supernatural skills, and Scully decides to give him up for adoption in order to keep him safe from aliens, government agents and others looking to kidnap him. Throughout the series, Scully is often written into scenarios where she is 'less than' for either not being able to conceive or for not being able to raise her child. However, throughout these various experiences and difficulties, Scully remains focused on the importance of data-based analysis and science in her work. As Kowalski argues,

> Scully never deviates from this mission. In attempting to discover hidden truths about her cancer (in 'Redux' (S5: E01)), she tells us: If my work with Agent Mulder has tested the foundation of my beliefs, science has been and continues to be my guiding light. Now I'm again relying on its familiar and systematic methods to arrive at a truth, a fact that might explain the fate that has befallen me … If science serves me to these ends … it is not lost on me that the tool which I've come to depend on absolutely cannot save or protect me … but only bring into focus the darkness that lies ahead. (2009: 32)

Where's the science?

Another issue that Scully faces throughout the series is the fact that the supernatural almost always is the cause of the specific incident or crime she and Mulder are investigating. Biologist and atheist Richard Dawkins notably critiqued this aspect of the series in a 1996 lecture:

> This is fiction and therefore defensible as pure entertainment. A fair defence, you might think. But soap operas, cop series and the like are justly criticized if, week after week, they ram home the same prejudice or bias. Each week *The X-Files* poses a mystery and offers two rival kinds of explanation, the rational theory and the paranormal theory. And, week after week, the rational explanation loses. But it is only fiction, a bit of fun, why get so hot under the collar? Imagine a crime series in which, every week, there is a white suspect and a black suspect. And every week, lo and behold, the black one turns out to have done it. Unpardonable. You could not defend it by saying: 'But it's only fiction, only entertainment.' (1997: 10)

Throughout the series, the paranormal explanation is accepted, and the audience is shown that such phenomena as aliens, vampires, telekinetic mass murderers and all other manner of monster is real. In other cases, a lack of cogent explanation for strange phenomena is also considered acceptable. Chris Carter acknowledged this issue in the preface to the book *The Real Science behind* The X-Files, stating, 'The problem is, Agent Scully is rarely, if ever, right. Her science is unequal to the wonders of the universe, or at least to the wonders of Mulder's multitude of FBI case files' (1999:12). There are a few notable exceptions. In 'Never Again' (S4: E13) Scully meets recent divorcee Ed Jerse at a tattoo parlour. He begins to experience hallucinations, where the Bettie Page tattoo he recently acquired talks to him and encourages him to commit crimes against women.[5] Scully quickly determines that the hallucinations are caused by the rye added to the ink by the tattoo artist. In 'El Mundo Gira' (S4: E11), Scully reveals that the 'Chupacabra' ravaging the migrant work camp is actually a young man suffering from a severe fungal infection. Likewise, in 'Darkness Falls' (S1: E20) Scully determines that the deaths of Washington state loggers are being caused by larvae released from cutting down centuries-old trees. Scully uses science-based practices in nearly every episode, but throughout the series, it is the paranormal that wins out, not science.

Scully herself eventually begins to believe Mulder's theories, and with so much support for his beliefs, it is not a surprise. In 'All Things' (S7: E17) Scully comes in contact with a former lover who is dying. Mulder recommends she contact Colleen Azar, a woman who runs a Buddhist meditation centre. Azar uses alternative treatment on Daniel Waterston who recovers fully. Scully also has a vision at this time, which leads her to finally believe in the supernatural. The episode ends with the following conversation between the two agents:

Mulder I just find it hard to believe.
Scully What part?
Mulder The part where I go away for two days and your whole life changes.
Scully Mmm, I didn't say my whole life changed.
Mulder You speaking to God in a Buddhist temple. God speaking back.
Scully Mmm, and I didn't say that God spoke back. I said that I had some kind of a vision.

Scully witnesses many examples of the supernatural throughout the series, including her own alien abduction. She uses her rational mind to finally accept that not all the answers can be found in traditional science. While she still looks to science first, from the time of this vision on, she is accepting of paranormal solutions. Erin McKenna, professor of philosophy, argues that 'Over time Scully moves from being a scientific empiricist who seeks

---

[5] Jodie Foster served as the voice of Bettie Page in this episode.

materialist explanations that confirm a truth of the matter to being a pluralist and radical empiricist who seeks materialist explanations but is open to other input. She becomes more comfortable with uncertainty and develops an openness to multiple perspectives' (2009: 169).

In 'Daemonicus' (S9: E3), Scully tries to convince John Doggett that demonic possession may be the reason for the deaths he and his FBI partner Monica Reyes are investigating. He is not open to this possibility at first:

> Doggett I heard you say, Agent Scully, I heard you tell a classroom full of FBI cadets – most evil in the world comes from men.
> Scully But I also said that once science fails, we have to consider extreme possibilities.

By season nine, Dana Scully has grown to accept the supernatural, which undermines her position as the voice of science and scepticism in contrast to Fox Mulder's and eventually Monica Reyes's belief in things not quantifiable with science and medicine. While she will stay rooted primarily in forensic science throughout the remaining seasons and second film, *The X-Files: I Want to Believe* (2008), her change does undermine her original role in the early seasons as a foil for Mulder's theories. As McKenna notes, 'Scully offers her empiricist scientific explanation at the start of each case. She pursues her investigation along these lines until something she cannot explain clearly persists or something new arises. Then we are usually left to consider Mulder's more eccentric theory, with Scully's doubts ringing in our ears. She does not, however, usually rule out his ideas completely' (2009: 178).

Even with the prevalence of supernatural solutions to most of the cases, Dana Scully remains a symbol of the importance of science and logic. This is largely due to the fact that many cases, including those mentioned earlier, are rooted in real science. Anne Simon writes in *The Real Science behind The X-Files* that 'Scully in the quintessential scientist' (1999: 20).[6] Simon also notes that Scully's portrayal is rooted in realities of science and the work of real scientists: 'Rather, she uses her medical degree to perform autopsies and her knowledge of genetics and biochemistry to conduct experiments. As with any scientist, when the investigation leads to areas outside of her expertise, she consults with other experts' (1999: 21). Scully is respected by both the characters around her and the audience because she follows real-life scientific protocols so closely, providing a glimpse into the actual career

---

[6] Anne Simon served as the scientific adviser for the show and was responsible for many of the plots and scientific analysis found throughout. Her first contribution to the series was 'The Erlenmeyer Flask', the season one finale.

of a doctor or forensic pathologist, even within the setting of all manner of supernatural and other worldly cases.

Conclusion

Even with these problematic elements of the show, namely the traditional domestic roles for Scully and the fact that science rarely solves supernatural cases, it is clear that Dana Scully is an important feminist character that had a profound impact on the women and girls who watched the show, from when it first aired in the 1990s through until today. As the 2018 study 'The Scully Effect: I Want to Believe ... In Stem' demonstrated, the ground-breaking depiction of a woman in a scientific profession helped to introduce new career opportunities to women and girls viewing the show. The survey's data show a strong correlation between the positive portrayal of Dana Scully and an interest in STEM professions. The many obstacles Scully faced throughout the series, obstacles created by a largely male writing team that still relied on gender stereotypes, allowed the character to be seen week after week as someone dedicated to scientific inquiry and rational thought. Gillian Anderson's depiction of Scully, coupled with her own fight for equality, proved inspirational to viewers who rarely saw women in previously male-dominated roles. The Scully effect is proof that just one positive depiction of a woman in a laboratory or surgical suite is enough to inspire countless others to embark on careers that they thought were not open to them. Her adherence to scientific principles is unwavering throughout the series, even when she does come to believe in the supernatural. We can only hope going forward that we see more Scully effects from the many positive and non-traditional female characters in film and television today.

References

'All Things – 7x17' (n.d.), Available online: http://www.insidethex.co.uk/transcrp/scrp717.htm (accessed 8 December 2021).
Badley, L. (2000), 'Scully Hits the Glass Ceiling', in E. R. Helford (ed.), *Fantasy Girls: Gender in the New Universe of Science Fiction and Fantasy Television*, 61–90, Lanham, MD: Rowman and Littlefield.
Bones (2005–17), [TV programme] Fox.
Carter, C. (1999, 'Forward', in A. Simon, *The Real Science behind* The X-Files: *Microbes, Meteorites, and Mutants*, 12–15, New York: Touchstone.
'Daemonicus – 9x13' (n.d.), Available online: http://www.insidethex.co.uk/transcrp/scrp913.htm (accessed 8 December 2021).
Dallas (1978–91), [TV programme] CBS.

Dawkins, R. (1997), 'Science and *The X-Files* – Prospect Magazine'. Available online: https://www.prospectmagazine.co.uk/magazine/scienceandthexfiles (accessed 30 June 2022).
Dr. Jekyll and Mr. Hyde (1931), [Film] Dir. Rouben Mamoulian, USA: Paramount.
Dr. Kildare (1961–66), [TV programme] NBC.
Dynasty (1981–89), [TV programme] ABC.
Frankenstein (1931), [Film] Dir. James Whale, USA: Universal Pictures.
'Home – 4x03' (n.d.), Available online: http://www.insidethex.co.uk/transcrp/scrp 403.htm (accessed 8 December 2021).
The Invisible Man (1933), [Film] Dir. James Whale, USA: Universal Pictures.
Knowles, C. E. (2018), 'A Woman's Place Is in the Morgue: Understanding Scully in the Context of 1990s Feminism', *M/C Journal* 21 (5): https://doi.org/10.5204/mcj.1465.
Kong, S., K. Carroll, D. Lundberg, P. Omura and B. Lepe (2020), 'Reducing Gender Bias in STEM', *MIT Science Policy Review*, 1(8): 55–63.
Kowalski, D. A. (2009), 'Introduction', in D. Kowalski (ed.), *The Philosophy of* The X-Files, 21–36, Lexington: University Press of Kentucky.
Law and Order: Special Victims Unit (1999–), [TV programme] NBC.
Leon, M. (2017), 'Gillian Anderson: I Was Offered Half of Duchovny's Pay for *The X-Files* Revival', 12 July. Available online: https://www.thedailybeast.com/gillian-anderson-i-was-offered-half-duchovnys-pay-for-the-x-files-revival (accessed 10 July 2022).
M*A*S*H (1972–83), [TV programme] CBS.
McKenna, E. (2009), 'Scully as a Pragmatic Feminist', in D. Kowalski (ed.), *The Philosophy of* The X-Files, 165–82, Lexington: University Press of Kentucky.
Murphy Brown (1988–97), [TV programme] CBS.
Quincy M. E. (1976–83), [TV programme] NBC.
'The Scully Effect: I Want to Believe … In Stem' (2021), Available online: https://seejane.org/wp-content/uploads/x-files-scully-effect-report-geena-davis-institute.pdf (accessed 8 December 2021).
Simon, A. E. (1999, *The Real Science behind* The X-Files: *Microbes, Meteorites, and Mutants*, New York: Touchstone.
Star Trek (1966–9), [TV programme] CBS.
Vineyard, J. (2013), 'Nearly Everything *The X-Files*' David Duchovny and Gillian Anderson Said This Weekend', 14 October. Available online: https://www.vulture.com/2013/10/david-duchovny-gillian-anderson-nycc-paley-center-quotes.html (accessed 30 June 2022).
The X-Files: I Want to Believe (2008), [Film] Fox.

Appendix 1

List of series, episodes and films in chronological order

Below is a chronological guide to *The X-Files* episodes and films. The broadcast/release dates are based on the original transmission and release in the United States.

The X-Files Series 1 (1993–4), [TV series] Fox, 10 September 1993–13 May 1994.

1. Pilot
2. Deep Throat
3. Squeeze
4. Conduit
5. The Jersey Devil
6. Shadows
7. Ghost in the Machine
8. Ice
9. Space
10. Fallen Angel
11. Eve
12. Fire
13. Beyond the Sea
14. Gender Bender
15. Lazarus

16. Young at Heart
17. EBE
18. Miracle Man
19. Shapes
20. Darkness Falls
21. Tooms
22. Born Again
23. Roland
24. The Erlenmeyer Flask

The X-Files Series 2 (1994–5), [TV series] Fox, 16 September 1994–19 May 1995.

1. Little Green Men
2. The Host
3. Blood
4. Sleepless
5. Duane Barry
6. Ascension
7. 3
8. One Breath
9. Firewalker
10. Red Museum
11. Excelsis Dei
12. Aubrey
13. Irresistible
14. Die Hand Die Verletzt
15. Fresh Bones
16. Colony
17. End Game
18. Fearful Symmetry
19. Død Kalm
20. Humbug
21. The Calusari
22. F. Emasculata
23. Soft Light

24. Our Town
25. Anasazi

The X-Files Series 3 (1995–6), [TV series] Fox, 22 September 1995–17 May 1996.

1. The Blessing Way
2. Paper Clip
3. DPO
4. Clyde Bruckman's Final Repose
5. The List
6. 2Shy
7. The Walk
8. Oubliette
9. Nisei
10. 731
11. Revelations
12. War of the Coprophages
13. Syzygy
14. Grotesque
15. Piper Maru
16. Apocrypha
17. Pusher
18. Teso Dos Bichos
19. Hell Money
20. Jose Chung's *From Outer Space*
21. Avatar
22. Quagmire
23. Wetwired
24. Talitha Cumi

The X-Files Series 4 (1996–7), [TV series] Fox, 4 October 1996–18 May 1997.

1. Herrenvolk
2. Home
3. Teliko

4. Unruhe
5. The Field Where I Died
6. Sanguinarium
7. Musings of a Cigarette Smoking Man
8. Tunguska
9. Terma
10. Paper Hearts
11. El Mundo Gira
12. Leonard Betts
13. Never Again
14. Memento Mori
15. Kaddish
16. Unrequited
17. Tempus Fugit
18. Max
19. Synchrony
20. Small Potatoes
21. Zero Sum
22. Elegy
23. Demons
24. Gethesemane

The X-Files Series 5 (1997–8), [TV series] Fox, 2 November 1997–17 May 1998.

1. Redux
2. Redux II
3. Unusual Suspects
4. Detour
5. The Post-Modern Prometheus
6. Christmas Carol
7. Emily
8. Kitsunegari
9. Schizogeny
10. Chinga
11. Kill Switch

12. Bad Blood
13. Patient X
14. The Red and the Black
15. Travelers
16. Mind's Eye
17. All Souls
18. The Pine Bluff Variant
19. Folie à Deux
20. The End

The X-Files: Fight the Future (1998), [Film] Dir. Rob Bowman, USA: Ten Thirteen Productions (Released 19 June 1998).

The X-Files Series 6 (1998–9), [TV series] Fox, 8 November 1998–16 May 1998.

1. The Beginning
2. Drive
3. Triangle
4. Dreamland
5. Dreamland II
6. How the Ghosts Stole Christmas
7. Terms of Endearment
8. The Rain King
9. SR 819
10. Tithonus
11. Two Fathers
12. One Son
13. Agua Mala
14. Monday
15. Arcadia
16. Alpha
17. Trevor
18. Milagro
19. The Unnatural
20. Three of a Kind
21. Field Trip
22. Biogenesis

The X-Files Series 7 (1999–2000), [TV series] Fox, 7 November 1999–21 May 2000.

1. The Sixth Extinction
2. The Sixth Extinction II: Amor Fati
3. Hungry
4. Millennium
5. Rush
6. The Goldberg Variation
7. Orison
8. The Amazing Maleeni
9. Signs and Wonders
10. Sein und Zeit
11. Closure
12. X-Cops
13. First Person Shooter
14. Theef
15. En Ami
16. Chimera
17. All Things
18. Brand X
19. Hollywood AD
20. Fight Club
21. Je Souhaite
22. Requiem

The X-Files Series 8 (2000–1), [TV series] Fox, 5 November 2000–20 May 2001.

1. Within
2. Without
3. Patience
4. Roadrunners
5. Invocation
6. Redrum

7. Via Negativa
8. Surekill
9. Salvage
10. Badlaa
11. The Gift
12. Medusa
13. Per Manum
14. This Is Not Happening
15. Deadalive
16. Three Words
17. Empedocles
18. Vienen
19. Alone
20. Essence
21. Existence

The X-Files Series 9 (2001–2), [TV series] Fox, 11 November 2001–19 May 2002.

1. Nothing Important Happened Today
2. Nothing Important Happened Today II
3. Dæmonicus
4. 4-D
5. Lord of the Flies
6. Trust No 1
7. John Doe
8. Hellbound
9. Provenance
10. Providence
11. Audrey Pauley
12. Underneath
13. Improbable
14. Scary Monsters
15. Jump the Shark
16. William
17. Release

18. Sunshine Days
19. The Truth (part one)
20. The Truth (part two)

The X-Files: I Want to Believe (2008), [Film] Dir. Chris Carter, USA: Ten Thirteen Productions (Released 25 July 2008).

The X-Files Series 10 (2016), [TV series] Fox, 24 January–22 February 2016.

1. My Struggle
2. Founder's Mutation
3. Mulder and Scully Meet the Were-Monster
4. Home Again
5. Babylon
6. My Struggle II

The X-Files Series 11 (2018), [TV series] Fox, 3 January–21 March 2018.

1. My Struggle III
2. This
3. Plus One
4. The Lost Art of Forehead Sweat
5. Ghouli
6. Kitten
7. Rm9sbG93ZXJz
8. Familiar
9. Nothing Lasts Forever
10. My Struggle IV

Appendix 2

The X-Files main and recurring cast

Below is a list of the main and recurring characters in *The X-Files*, followed by the actor who portrayed them:

Fox Mulder (David Duchovny)
Dana Scully (Gillian Anderson)
Walter Skinner (Mitch Pileggi)
Cigarette Smoking Man (William B. Davies)
John Doggett (Robert Patrick)
Monica Reyes (Annabeth Gish)
Alex Krycek (Nicholas Lea)
Jeffrey Spender (Chris Owens)
Alvin Kersh (James Pickens, Jr)

INDEX

ableism 301–12
Adlard, Charles 196–7
All the President's Men 102, 135, 140, 142
Anderson, Gillian 8, 9, 47, 56, 152, 183, 210, 219, 271, 273–4, 281 n.11, 283–4, 320
  feminist icon 252, 271, 273, 316–19, 325
  relationship with David Duchovny 226, 273, 283, 319
  sex icon 1, 251
Anderson, Kevin J. 197
Anthropocene 81, 83
Area Fifty-One 96
Asimov, Isaac 61, 235
Avatar 303

Berryman, Michael 304
Black, Frank 201
black oil 20, 75–85, 173, 290, 295
Bride of Frankenstein 306
Buffy the Vampire Slayer 1, 88–9, 197–8, 200
Bush, George H. W. 12, 24, 151
Bush, George W. 41, 103

Califano, Silvia 203
Candyman 143
Carter, Chris 8–10, 87–8, 111–13, 142, 150, 152, 155–6, 159–60, 168, 183, 196, 200, 220, 225, 228–9, 281, 323
  biography 2–5, 116, 135, 151

and conspiracy culture 27, 105–6, 116, 135
Casagrande, Elena 203
Catatonia 1
Catholicism 303–4
CGI (computer generated imagery) 88–9
A Christmas Carol 302
Chu, Amy 203
Chung, Jose 184, 238, 289, 293, 296
Cigarette Smoking Man, The 9, 23, 31, 54, 81–2, 85, 96, 136, 156, 170, 199, 201–3, 274, 279, 280–1, 290–1, 294–5, 297, 319
  and Colquitt, Jack 202
  as Mulder's father 288, 294
  as Mr Hunt 202
Cioffi, Charles 28, 140
Clinton, Bill 11, 24, 27, 31, 136, 150–1
  and Monica Lewinsky 12, 41
Close Encounters of the Third Kind 29, 112, 168
conspiracy
  alien abduction 23, 102, 105–6, 108–13, 150, 321
  beliefs in the paranormal 10, 14, 97, 150, 160, 322–3
  fake news 89, 102, 156–9
  and the government 8, 10, 12–13, 26, 52, 75, 266, 284, 295
  and Kennedy assassination 137–41
  'post-truth' 9–12, 88, 156–7, 159
  QAnon 102, 156–8

Conversation, The 135, 140
cult
    religious 40, 102, 121–5, 127–30, 163, 176, 278, 309
    status of television series and audience 1, 5–7, 9, 163–4, 165, 207

Deep Throat 53, 106, 113, 116, 138, 140, 142, 151
Deliverance 306
Demon Seed 65
Denham, Brian 197
disability 301–12
    angry cripple (trope) 305
    deformity 305, 308–12
    demonic cripple (trope) 302, 304–6, 309
    developmental disability 303–4
    Disability Studies 301, 308, 310
    freak shows 308–12
    kill or cure (trope) 303–4, 307
    medical model 303
    mental disability/illness 305
    monstrous hillbilly (trope) 305
    sweet innocent (trope) 302–4, 309
disidentification 275, 283–4
Doggett, John 8, 79, 81, 83–4, 175, 201, 324
Don't Look Now 145
Duchovny, David 7–9, 47, 56, 89, 95, 182, 225, 273, 293, 320
    and *The Larry Sanders Show* 292
    leaving *The X-Files* 149
    relationship with Gillian Anderson 226, 283, 319
    sex icon 1, 251, 292
    and *South Park* 203
    and *Twin Peaks* 170

eugenics 303, 306

fandom 14, 164, 172, 174, 207–16, 219–24, 227–9, 234, 237, 272

FBI 10, 114, 136
    and FBI buildings (including J. Edgar Hoover Building) 23, 28–30, 52, 137, 222, 293
    representation of 14, 287–9, 296, 319
    uniform 48
Fleet, John van 197–9, 205
Ford, Gerald 136–7, 142
Forrest Gump 305
Fowley, Diana 171, 294
Fox Network 5, 9
    commissioning *The X-Files* 3–4
Frankenstein (Mary Shelley novel) 306
Frankenstein (1931 film) 306
Friday the 13th Part 2, 305
Frost, Mark 167, 172, 173–4

genetic engineering 305–7
Gibson, William 61, 66, 68, 89, 236
Gilligan, Vince 182
Godfather Part II, The 140
Gulka, Jeff 200

The Hills Have Eyes 304, 306
The Hunchback of Notre-Dame 305

Jean, Al 203
JFK 137–8, 140–1

Kennedy, John F. 27, 138
    and assassination (*see also* Conspiracy) 102, 113, 136–41, 145
Klute 135, 140
Kolchak: The Night Stalker 3, 5–6, 106, 168, 170, 183
Krycek, Alex 201, 266, 292
Kubrick, Stanley 61

legend 6, 101–3, 105–6, 108–9, 113–16, 204
Lone Gunmen, The (TV series) 8
The Lone Gunmen (characters) 103, 138, 201, 203, 236, 238–9, 244

Lynch, David 40, 167–8, 170, 173, 174–5

Mahlstedt, Larry 197
Mansfield, Jayne 201
The Matrix 62, 235, 237
Matthews, Menton J. (Menton3), III 201–2, 205
McCloud, Scott 199
Me Before You 304
Millennium 8, 164, 181–5, 187–8, 192–3
Million Dollar Baby 304
Minsky, Marvin 60–1, 68
Moby-Dick 305
Morgan, Darin 55, 153, 157, 175, 184, 276
Mulder, Fox
 and abduction 131, 280, 280 n.8
 apartment 30, 34, 140, 145, 298
 father's identity 139, 288, 295
 office 2, 29–30, 49, 117, 137, 203, 222, 239, 283, 293, 297
 relationship with Scully 24, 47, 49, 51–2, 56, 71, 82, 164, 219–20, 223–7, 229, 272, 280–1, 292, 298, 319, 321
 and sister's abduction 23, 49, 53, 111–12, 141–2, 149, 151, 173–4, 203, 226, 241, 274, 278, 290
 and 'Spooky' nickname 28, 293–4, 296, 298
Murdoch, Rupert 4–5
Musk, Elon 61, 68

new materialism 78, 80–2
Nixon, Richard 111, 116, 136–8, 140–2

Of Mice and Men 303
One Flew Over the Cuckoo's Nest 304

Panspermia 79
Parallax View, The 135, 140

Perry, Michael 184–5
petroculture 77, 81–2, 85
Petrucha, Stefan 196–7
Praise, Gibson 200
Psycho 305
Purcell, Gordon 197

queer
 identification and representation 240, 282–3, 287, 292–3, 296, 298
 theory 252, 287, 291–2

Raiders of the Lost Ark 23
Rain Man 303
Reagan, Ronald 12, 103, 136, 145
Reiss, Mike 203
Reyes, Monica 8, 201, 324
Richard III 305
Roth, Peter 4–5

Saviuk, Alexander 197
Scully, Dana
 abduction 49, 65, 228, 274, 279, 320–1, 323
 cancer 65, 140, 279, 280 n.7, 321–2
 and Emily 182, 188, 190, 279, 281, 304
 as final girl 277–8
 mortuary chamber 30
 myth-arc 272, 274–5, 277–9, 282, 285
 pregnancy 200, 228, 279–81, 321–2
 rape-by-deception trope 271, 274, 277
 relationship with Mulder 24, 47, 49, 51–2, 55–6, 71, 82, 164, 219–20, 223–7, 229, 272, 280–1, 292, 298, 319, 321
 and religion 122–4, 131, 188, 303–4
 reproductive violence 279, 281
 the 'Scully effect' 253, 273, 315–18, 325
 sister (Melissa) 182, 190
Simpsons, The 1, 4, 203

Skinner, Walter 28, 30–1, 33, 40, 52, 54, 143–5, 156, 170, 201, 224, 276, 279–81, 319
Snow, Mark 169, 175, 185–6
Spender, Jeffrey 171
Spotnitz, Frank 37, 182–3, 197
Star Trek 3, 26–7, 43, 171, 179, 219, 316, 326
Stranger Things 13
surveillance studies 62–3
The Syndicate 8, 75–7, 136, 142, 170, 173, 208, 252, 255, 274, 278–80, 282, 284, 291, 294

The Texas Chain Saw Massacre 306
Thomas, Roy 197
Thompson, Jill 197
Three Days of the Condor 135, 141
Tipton, Denton J. 201–2, 205
Todd, Tony 143, 255
Trump, Donald 11, 89, 103, 150, 153, 155–60
Tunguska event 79
Turing, Alan 60–1
Twilight Zone, The 3, 13, 38, 88–9, 106, 171, 213
Twin Peaks 1, 3, 7, 164, 167–77
2001: A Space Odyssey 61, 65

UFOs (*see also* 'conspiracy')
belief in and sightings 5, 102, 105–13, 115–16, 150, 153, 197
UFO conventions 7
Wreckage 77, 114–16

Vietnam War 26, 102, 113, 136–8, 141–5, 255, 257, 262–7

Watergate 11, 25, 27, 53, 102, 111, 113–14, 116, 135–8, 140–2, 145, 150–1, 272
Whedon, Joss 200
William (character) 82, 160, 200–1, 274, 280–1, 281 n.11, 322

X-Files, The
cancellation 8, 81
critical awards 7
cult television series 1–2, 5–7, 163–4, 207
cynicism (*see also* Conspiracy) 5, 9, 11–13
fan memories 207–8, 210, 212–14, 216
fandom 6, 13–14, 172–4, 207–16, 219–24, 227–9, 237, 272, 292
filming in Canada 4, 7–8, 23, 31, 169
filming in Los Angeles 7–8, 169
influence on science fiction television 1, 13
influences on *The X-Files* 3, 5, 135, 140, 168, 183
and the Internet 5, 7, 9, 13–14, 109, 154, 172, 237
merchandise 1, 7, 9, 48, 196–7
music (*see also* Snow, Mark) 69, 175, 185–6, 275, 303, 308
nostalgia 207–8, 210–11, 213, 215
opening credits 236
origins 2–5
parodies 14, 203
participatory culture 207, 209
premiere 5, 45–6, 111, 137, 252
revival series 9, 13, 47, 56, 89, 150–60, 177, 195, 272, 280
September 11th, 2001, terrorist attacks (*see also* Conspiracy) 9, 12–13, 25, 149, 151–4, 282
Shippers 164–5, 219–27, 229, 272 n.3
tie-in novels and comics 7, 9, 196–205
X-Philes 6, 14, 116, 163–5, 174, 196, 202, 207–8, 210, 212–13, 215–16, 222
The X-Files: Fight the Future 7–8, 48, 75–7, 106, 177, 182, 215, 279
The X-Files: I Want to Believe 8–9, 89, 150, 152, 177, 197, 199, 324

www.ingramcontent.com/pod-product-compliance
Lightning Source LLC
Chambersburg PA
CBHW070012010526
44117CB00011B/1524